# Surviving Transphobia

*of related interest*

**Written on the Body**
Letters from Trans and Non-Binary Survivors of
Sexual Assault and Domestic Violence
*Edited by Lexie Bean*
*Foreword and additional pieces by Dean Spade, Nyala Moon,*
*Alex Valdes, Sawyer DeVuyst and Ieshai Bailey*
ISBN 978 1 78592 797 3
eISBN 978 1 78450 803 6

**Supporting Transgender Autistic Youth and Adults**
A Guide for Professionals and Families
*Finn V. Gratton, LMFT, LPCC*
*Illustrated by Harper Cheaney*
ISBN 978 1 78592 803 1
eISBN 978 1 78450 830 2

**Yes, You Are Trans Enough**
My Transition from Self-Loathing to Self-Love
*Mia Violet*
ISBN 978 1 78592 315 9
eISBN 978 1 78450 628 5

**To My Trans Sisters**
*Charlie Craggs*
ISBN 978 1 78592 343 2
eISBN 978 1 78450 668 1

**All the Things They Said We Couldn't Have**
Stories of Trans Joy
*T. C. Oakes-Monger*
*Illustrated by Flatboy*
ISBN 978 1 83997 149 5
eISBN 978 1 83997 150 1

**Trans Power**
Own Your Gender
*Juno Roche*
ISBN 978 1 78775 019 7
eISBN 978 1 78775 020 3

**In Their Shoes**
Navigating Non-Binary Life
*Jamie Windust*
ISBN 978 1 78775 242 9
eISBN 978 1 78775 243 6

# SURVIVING TRANS PHOBIA

## LAURA A. JACOBS, LCSW-R, EDITOR

**Jessica Kingsley Publishers**
London and Philadelphia

First published in Great Britain in 2024 by Jessica Kingsley Publishers
An imprint of John Murray Press

1

Content warning: This book mentions suicide, physical, emotional and sexual abuse,
drug use and abuse, homophobia and transphobia, sex, BDSM, and sex work.

A CIP catalogue record for this title is available from the
British Library and the Library of Congress.

ISBN 978 1 78775 965 7
eISBN 978 1 78775 966 4

Printed and bound in the United States by Integrated Books International

Jessica Kingsley Publishers' policy is to use papers that are natural,
renewable and recyclable products and made from wood grown in
sustainable forests. The logging and manufacturing processes are expected
to conform to the environmental regulations of the country of origin.

Jessica Kingsley Publishers
Carmelite House
50 Victoria Embankment
London EC4Y 0DZ

www.jkp.com

John Murray Press
Part of Hodder & Stoughton Limited
An Hachette UK Company

*I studied history...and what I know is that queer
and trans people don't write down our shit enough.*

—Jacob Tobia

Note: The contributors, editors, ghostwriters, web designers for the book's promotional page, public relations consultants, commissioning editor at Jessica Kingsley Publishers, and more all identify as members of the transgender and gender nonbinary community, though other cisgender staff at JKP have aided the book as well. Cis friends and allies have chimed in too.

# Contents

# Acknowledgements

I am flattered by the support I've received from chosen family and other treasured people in my life. My warmest gratitude and love extend to:

Noelle Penelope "Don't Call Me Shirley" Vandertuin

Alex Pitagora, Cyndi Darnell, and Jillien Kahn

Layth for being endearing, Leila for being considerate, and Rob for being eternally unsuccessful at sororicide

Michele, Delano, Laura, Karen, Midori, Leah, Eli, Garth, Phoebe, Sarah, et al.

Jim Henson

The Lizzes, both Margolies and Komar

Adrian Shanker, for invaluable guidance

Justus Eisfeld and Johnny Capozuca

Jordan Spivack, lifelong queer inspiration

My wonderful and nameless ghosts

The remaining members of the Coterie

Lexie Bean and Ariel Churchill

MJ Barker, profuse thanks

Ray Bradbury

Mahshad Aryafar

Tarah Cohen

Jes Bedwinek

Courtney Padjen

Jude Roth

Anne Erzebet Ferenczy

Christie Block

Andres, best masseuse anywhere

Vicki and Bart: you know why

Franca Piperni, for attempting to keep me..."straightened"

Richard Kennedy

Cindi Creager

Gene Roddenberry

Timothy Westbrook

The genderqueer/nonbinary bartender at Henrietta Hudson whose name I don't know

David Valentine, professor who facilitated the most profound clarification of my thinking

Alex DiFrancesco, Andrew James, Claire Robinson, Laura Dignum-Smith, Katelynn Bartleson, and the rest of the staff at Jessica Kingsley Publishers

Wendy Stark and the entire staff and Board at Callen-Lorde

Each and every contributor—some of whom are my own role models—for their willingness to expose vulnerabilities

...and The Frances and Peter Jacobs Foundation for the Wayward Children of Frances and Peter Jacobs.

This book is for my clients and for those under the broadest possible umbrella of the transgender and gender nonbinary community, and for Susan. With much love.

Finally, a most heartfelt *fuck you!* to those who do not vote or who do for right-wing candidates that would use transgender and gender nonbinary people—especially our youth, those most at risk—as scapegoats to gain political power. You are complicit in the actions of the xenophobes, misogynists, and bigots attempting to deny me and those in my community from our very existence.

# Preface

Genocide. "They" seem intent on nothing less.

The horrors we expected are now: "they" enact new and more severe bans on healthcare for transgender and gender nonbinary youth and adults, with harsher punishments and threats of removing children from supportive parents. Meanwhile, additional states ban trans participation in sports and politicians make plainly false claims in the media, discrimination based on the disinformation spread by shadowy organizations and intolerant public figures. And all this despite yet more confirmation of what was already unambiguous: disaffirming environments cause harm.

"They" are adults bullying the vulnerable, rejecting science in favor of transparent bigotry, and their strategy is so very plain: incite hate, violence, fear, and despair. Silence our voices, minimize our access to services, limit our ability to exist in the public sphere...to generate votes and to establish precedent to later restrict any form of "otherhood" they choose as part of their extremist coup to create a white supremacist, Christian nationalist, fascist America.[1] Our community is increasingly traumatized.

To "them" I say: Not happening. You forget that we are fierce. We reject your attempts to eliminate us. We refuse to vanish just to make it easier for you to ignore your un-Christlike intolerance. We have confronted the gender binary and transphobia since the earliest moment of recorded history and we will still exist ages after your attempts to exterminate us ultimately fail. Get over it.

Fuck the fascists.

—*Laura A. Jacobs*
*May, 2023*

# Introduction

## Surviving Transphobia

The transgender and gender nonbinary community is under siege.

Each day we endure assaults from verbal abuse to murder; meanwhile, institutional transphobia is proposed, debated, and enacted by those who would transform this world into a 1950s-esque white, heteronormative, patriarchal fantasy that never genuinely existed. They would make a humanity devoid of trans folk, queer and LGBTQIA+* folk, people of color, immigrants, and so many other marginalized populations by intimidating or legislating us all into nonexistence.[1, 2] This is even more challenging for those with multiple intersecting and stigmatized identities. Merely living can be an ordeal[3, 4] as we simply hope to survive and, with luck, find joy.

*Surviving Transphobia* is an anthology by transgender women, transgender men, and people nonbinary or genderqueer who are activists, actors, athletes, authors, lawyers, doctors, nurses, psychotherapists, sex workers, clergy, diplomats, and military veterans with visibility either in mainstream culture or in specific areas of the transgender and gender nonbinary (TGNB)** community. We are Black, Latine, white, African, Middle Eastern, Asian/Pacific Islander, Indigenous, and of other descents; we vary socioeconomically, educationally, and geographically within the U.S. Some are neurotypical and others neurodivergent, and several are disabled or have serious, chronic, or acute

---

*   Lesbian, gay, bisexual, trans, queer/questioning, intersex, asexual, and other marginalized sexualities and genders.
**  Trans and "TGNB" are both used throughout the book to reference the broadest definition of "transgender and gender nonbinary."

illnesses. A few are HIV+. A small number were born elsewhere. We range in age from 30 to our 70s.

You may see the contributors as role models, pursuing our lives with dignity, but you have not witnessed the moments when we ourselves were victims of bullying, had our needs dismissed, or were discriminated against for pursuing our own trans identities. I suspect these chapters will resonate—they recount universal trans and nonbinary experiences—and we hope to provide guidance to all who have endured through similar agony. In these chapters we offer the message: "We have survived, here's how. And if we can survive...so can you."

Those of us in leadership positions combat rising civil and governmental discrimination yet are often equally as traumatized as those we serve: after each new transphobic event we too curl in blankets and clutch stuffed animals in dread, sob to our therapists about feelings of powerlessness, or turn to social media for comfort then become overwhelmed by the horrifying stories posted by others. We too are afraid, yet still we demand a voice within the public sphere. You'll read of this duality and of how our efforts have led to both exhaustion and pride.

Transphobia did not begin with the 2016 U.S. presidential election, nor will it end any time soon. It is not limited to this country. The narratives here will be relevant far beyond their initial publication. We also aim to chronicle our experiences for current and future generations of our community (which *will* exist) here and elsewhere, and to provide insight for academics and researchers on how we live today.

Ultimately, *Surviving Transphobia* demonstrates that, despite the vehemence of those who would see us returned to the shadows, the closets, or worse, we are still here, we are still trans and nonbinary and genderqueer, and anyone opposed had better get used to it. *Surviving Transphobia* is unapologetically political.

This is my community and that of all the contributors of this book. Perhaps it is yours as well. If so, these pages were lovingly written for you.

*Surviving Transphobia* is also for our allies and all those who provide empathetic support. It is even for people uncertain about transgender rights.

And this book is for our predecessors; only due to you can I be me.

Please read with compassion. Also, language and concepts evolve; the authors here are using what is best and available at the time of writing.

Care for yourself while reading. Many chapters feature unbearable dysphoria, graphic violence, self-harm, and discussions of suicide alongside moments of beautifully passionate euphoria. Be sure to allow yourself pauses, sips of water, trips to the bathroom, and whatever other care practices help you soothe.

Also please do not worry about being "not good enough." This plagues us all and only keeps us limited. As Jack Thompson, one of the contributors, says, "If you are enough for you, you are enough."

Thank you for your interest.

I began mulling this book in 2016.

I am a psychotherapist working primarily with trans and nonbinary, LGBTQIA+, kinky, nonmonogamous, and sex worker clients. My first client after the election was a 14-year-old trans girl who had come out only a year before. We sat in midtown Manhattan, an imperfect LGBTQIA+ oasis, as she struggled to articulate words between sobs, her panic so visceral. Only a week earlier she'd worn a flowery cotton dress and tights for the first time; to her these represented the true embodiment of her femininity. With help from her father, she had scheduled an endocrinology intake to discuss puberty blockers. And though her parents initially doubted her trans identity, they witnessed her increasing confidence and cautiously began backing their daughter's transition.

What did she most need from me? She had just begun to present as her authentic self, but the election suggested her identity would soon be abolished by a malevolent autocracy. Was it best to disclose my fear so she might feel less alone, or was that my own distress seeking companionship? Aware that over 40 percent of the trans community have attempted suicide, I was cautious about any intervention that might provoke despair. Was she instead best served by a demonstration of defiance? It could suggest that her anxiety was unfounded, or that I was taking the situation too lightly. My judgment was confused.

She knew so little of how we have survived in the past.

She didn't realize that, in 1969, grassroots organizations like the St. Marks Clinic and the Gay Men's Health Project began in backrooms with supplies donated by doctors and allies or "scavenged" from their everyday employers or overprescribed so medications could be shared or collected from those who had died, then redistributed to those in need. These and other projects developed client-centered philosophies of care and gradually evolved into Callen-Lorde and other LGBTQIA+ healthcare centers. Ronald Reagan never uttered "AIDS" though it devastated us throughout his presidency, yet our elders cared for thousands rejected by the mainstream. We found ways.

She was also unaware of how we built community through "secret handshake" words like "queer" in the 1920s (only in the 1950s–60s did it become a term of hate) and hidden social clubs, or how we assembled support systems of peers and allies. Reclaiming "queer" in the 1990s was a deliberate act of rebellion when we refused to go on accepting the scorn of outsiders. Today's joyous Pride parades began as hostile protest marches against police brutality, and past generations began gay militancy at Stonewall in NYC in 1969 and Compton's Cafeteria in San Francisco in 1966 and Dewey's lunch counter in Philadelphia in 1965 and Cooper Do-nuts in Los Angeles in 1959 and in countless other acts of (sometimes violent) disobedience. Lawyers, doctors, mental health clinicians, teachers, politicians, and others risked careers and safety. Dr. Anonymous* confronted the American Psychiatric Association. Harvey Milk and Marsha P. Johnson were assassinated.[5]

How could this 14-year-old know? She had believed that advances in trans rights would steadily continue. What was I to say? Secretly, I was uncertain myself that we could overcome. I paused for deep breaths and decided to be more candid than usual. I revealed a glimpse into my own emotions, tearing up beside her. I said that our movement was too powerful for "them" to extinguish, that progress is rarely linear,

---

* Dr. John Fryer.

that I was stunned as well but that I and others would redouble our activism. I spoke to myself as much as to her.

From there, *Surviving Transphobia* seemed obvious.

* * *

Transphobes often occupy positions of power. Fanatics, those with egoistic needs for control, and others would impose their ideologies on us all.

Legislative and physical transphobia have spiked since the 2016 election and the subsequent attempts to undo all pro-LGBTQIA+ regulation, transgender and gender nonbinary protections first.[6, 7] The *New York Times* article "'Transgender' Could be Defined Out of Existence Under Trump Administration" documented that regime's strategy to classify gender by chromosomes alone, denying gender identity altogether,[8, 9] and the Department of Housing and Urban Development's so-called "How to Spot a Trans Woman" memo[10] was disturbingly reminiscent of Nazi propaganda. Texas, Georgia, Idaho, South Dakota, Missouri, Tennessee, Florida, Colorado, Illinois, Oklahoma, South Carolina, Kentucky, and more all followed gleefully along.[11, 12, 13]

Since President Biden's inauguration, those states plus others have continued this brutal campaign through a similar pattern: define mental health and medical care to transgender and gender nonbinary youth as child abuse, then criminalize supportive doctors, nurses, psychotherapists, teachers, clergy, and school coaches. Threaten severe fines, loss of professional licenses, incarceration. Demand all mandated reporters inform on anyone who provides assistance or face the same punishments themselves. List parents as sex offenders. Have 36 states draft laws in 2021 alone to limit trans participation in sports, despite clear research documenting that we have no special advantage and that participation in team sports provides exercise, yields better grades, and leads to improved self-esteem.[14, 15]

They have also renewed calls for anti-trans "bathroom bills" citing "the need to protect women and children,"[16] though these manufactured arguments are just thinly veiled bigotry.[17] The opposite is more accurate; trans people are regularly victims of violence in public bathrooms,[18] and there have been more accounts of cisgender male conservative lawmakers committing misconduct in bathrooms than of trans people.[19, 20] But still they would limit our access, knowing that if we cannot *pee* in public, we cannot *be* in public.

Individual states each follow a similar pattern and even use similar or identical language in their legislation; it's almost as though they all received the same manual.[21, 22]

Meanwhile, some within the medical establishment continue promoting flawed notions like "Rapid Onset Gender Dysphoria," allegations that " 80 percent desist," or that trans women who undergo surgery show "no objective improvement" compared to those rejected for care, all of which have been cited as being methodologically atrocious and having conclusions unsupported by data and potential author bias.[23, 24, 25] Or these people suggest "wait and see," something known to cause harm by prolonging suffering.[26] And public figures like J.K. Rowling, a once-beloved author who centered stigmatized identities and transformation, defend ideologies hostile to our very existence.[27]

Transphobes also misconstrue the stories of "de/retransitioners" to further their cause.* It's been reported that only around 1 percent choose to undo their decisions to transition,[28, 29] meaning that affirmative medical care around social and medical transition has an approximately 99 percent success rate. Any other medical intervention with such a statistic would be acclaimed as a miracle cure. Only a few who have medically and/or socially transitioned do return to their genders assigned at birth,[30] and the vast majority of those report no regret but say that exploring other genders was necessary for greater self-understanding. Or that social pressures, not a change in identities, forced them back.[31] The voices alleging that "de/retransitioners" demonstrate a need for caution or to prevent transition altogether are but the loudest of a tiny subset of a subset of a diverse community.

---

* Personally, I welcome de/retransitioners to the community of people exploring gender.

And the June 2022 Supreme Court decision overturning Roe v. Wade was not only troubling for cisgender women and transmasculine people of childbearing age; in signaling their intent to impose a Christian fascist agenda, the justices gave control of all "uterine bearing" reproductive systems to the government and made plain that queer bodies, most especially those of transgender and gender nonbinary youth and adults, would be next.[32, *]

Their position that people do not have the fundamental right to body autonomy contradicts the internationally accepted Yogyakarta Principles, a document by global human rights experts released in 2007 and updated in 2017 calling on governments to "[a]dopt appropriate legislative and other measures to prohibit and eliminate discrimination in the public and private spheres on the basis of sexual orientation and gender identity."[33]

The transphobes fear what we represent: possibility, limitlessness. A world of nuance, a world beyond their influence, a world that transcends their narrow imaginations about the potentials for human existence. They fear the truth that gender, sexuality, and identity, like life, are infinite.

Study after study after study and countless studies more all document the same thing: transgender and gender nonbinary youth and adults in supportive, empathetic, and safe environments do well, and those disaffirmed do poorly. The data are clear and consistent. To cite just a few of the many:

In 1993: "Among female-to-male transsexuals[**] after SRS,[***] i.e., in men, no regrets were reported in the author's sample, and in the

---

[*] Supreme Court assaults on the LGBTQIA+ community may have happened even before publication.

[**] "Transsexual" was the term widely used at the time. Later it fell out of common use; it is currently considered to be pejorative by most in the transgender and gender nonbinary community. However, many people do still identify with it and object to having their identities policed from within their own communities.

[***] Sexual reassignment surgery (SRS), an earlier term for procedures to align one's body with the stereotypical primary and secondary sex characteristics of their self-identified gender.

literature they amount to less than 1%. Among male-to-female trans-sexuals after SRS, i.e., in women, regrets are reported in 1–1.5%."[34]

2011: "Results of the study indicate that female-to-male transsexuals [sic] who receive testosterone have lower levels of depression, anxiety, and stress, and higher levels of social support and health related to quality of life. Testosterone use was not related to problems with drugs, alcohol, or suicidality. Overall findings provide clear evidence that HRT [hormone replacement therapy] is associated with improved mental health outcomes in female-to-male transsexuals."[35]

2011: "The results of this study support the development of affirmative approaches in supporting gender-variant children and their parents. This is particularly evidenced by the parents' own approaches to supporting their children where parents experimented with different ways of responding to various scenarios and realized that acceptance of their child was the only option as they learned that their child's need for expression was not changed by their attitude or management of the behavior."[36]

2012: "The results suggest that most transsexual patients attending a gender identity unit reported subclinical levels of social distress, anxiety, and depression. Moreover, patients under cross-sex hormonal treatment displayed a lower prevalence of these symptoms than patients who had not initiated hormonal therapy."[37]

2012: "...the needs of children that emerged were most notably, for parents, school staff and other authority figures to be educated so that children do not need to hide themselves and their gender expression for fear of adversity."[38]

2013: "Children not allowed [to explore their genders]...are at later risk for developing a downward cascade of psychosocial adversities including depressive symptoms, low life satisfaction, self-harm, iso-lation, homelessness, incarceration, posttraumatic stress, and suicide ideation and attempts."[39]

2014: "[A] treatment protocol including puberty suppression leads to improved psychological functioning of transgender adolescents. While enabling them to make important age-appropriate developmental transitions, it contributes to a satisfactory objective and subjective well-being in young adulthood."[40]

2015: "The findings indicated that...family of origin may have the most influence in protecting against psychological distress."[41]

2016: "Socially transitioned transgender children who are supported in their gender identity have developmentally normative levels of depression and only minimal elevations in anxiety, suggesting that psychopathology is not inevitable within this group...socially transitioned transgender children have notably lower rates of internalizing psychopathology than previously reported among children with GID [gender identity disorder] living as their natal sex."[42]

2017: "We found remarkably good mental health outcomes in socially transitioned transgender children." "Our findings of normative levels of depression, slightly higher rates of anxiety, and high self-worth in socially transitioned transgender children stand in marked contrast with previous work with gender-nonconforming children who had not socially transitioned..."[43]

2018: "Supportive involvement of parents and family is associated with better mental and physical health outcomes. Gender affirmation among adolescents with gender dysphoria often reduces the emphasis on gender in their lives, allowing them to attend to other developmental tasks, such as academic success, relationship building, and future-oriented planning."[44]

2018: "Of 56 peer-reviewed studies, 52 (93 percent) found that gender transition improves the overall well-being of transgender people. The other 7 percent reported mixed or null findings. None of the reviewed studies showed that gender transition harms well-being." "Regrets following gender transition are extremely rare and have become increasingly rarer."[45]

2019: "[T]ransgender children strongly...show gender-typed preferences and behaviors that are strongly associated with their current gender, not the gender typically associated with their sex assigned at birth."[46]

2020: "Most people who have regrets do so because of a lack of support or acceptance from their family, social groups, work, or other organizations. Conversely, the benefits that these medically necessary interventions have for the overwhelming majority of youth whose identities are incongruent with their sex assigned at birth are well-documented."[47]

2021: "There is increasing evidence that gender-affirming interventions improve mental health outcomes for TGD [transgender and gender diverse] youth. TGD youth report worse mental health outcomes in invalidating school and family environments and improved outcomes in affirming climates."[48]

2022: "These results suggest that retransitions are infrequent. More commonly, transgender youth who socially transitioned at early ages continued to identify that way." And, "Five years after an initial binary social transition...[m]ost youth (94%) were [still] living as binary transgender youth."[49]

2022: "This study found that transgender people who accessed GAH [gender-affirming hormones] during early or late adolescence had lower odds of past-month suicidal ideation and past-month severe psychological distress in adulthood, when compared to those who desired but did not access GAH..." "The results also provide additional evidence to suggest that legislation restricting transgender adolescents' access to gender-affirming medical care would result in adverse mental health outcomes."[50]

We can thrive. Affirming approaches are safe and lead to optimal outcomes. Research makes clear that transgender and gender nonbinary people overwhelmingly do better after transition than before. We have diverse, vibrant communities and we witness increasing acceptance from the broader culture.[51] We have the support of countless major medical and mental health organizations, including:

The American Academy of Child and Adolescent Psychiatry[52]

The American Academy of Family Physicians[53]

The American Academy of Pediatrics[54]

The American College of Nurse-Midwives[55]

The American College of Physicians[56]

The American Counseling Association[57]

The American Heart Association[58]

The American Medical Association[59, 60]

The American Mental Health Counselors Association[61]

The American Nurses Association[62]

The American Osteopathic Association[63]

The American Psychiatric Association[64]

The American Psychological Association[65]

The American Public Health Association[66]

The Endocrine Society[67]

The National Association of Social Workers[68]

The Pediatric Endocrine Society[69]

The Society for Adolescent Health and Medicine[70]

The World Professional Association for Transgender Health[71]

and many more.

In November 2016, my peers and I—transgender and gender non-binary providers, LGBTQIA+ professionals, and even our cisgender, heterosexual allies—knew exactly what was to come. Hostility toward the "transgender movement" has been easy to incite through mis- and dis-information; trans children and adolescents are easy targets, with many critics alleging that therapists, doctors, and the trans community overall have coerced these youth into hormones and surgeries to further our own political agendas. I am undoubtedly one of the "radical trans activists" they refer to.

It is too late to return us to a box hidden from sight. We have learned from history. We are determined not to see past atrocities repeated. I remain optimistic that this bigotry, incited by a minority that do not represent the nation or the world, will ultimately end.

And after seeing articles like the March 2022 "Texas Students Heckle Anti-Trans GOP Candidate With 'F**k These Fascists' Chant After He Comes to Their School,"[72] I'm slightly less concerned about the future.

We of this book pledge to continue the fight.

Join us.

—*Laura A. Jacobs*
*June, 2022*

# Jamison Green

# Recognizing the Existential

**Jamison Green** (he/him) is a white trans man and
professional writer who began medical transition
in 1988, when resources and awareness were limited. He started his activism soon after, leading
FTM\* International from 1991 to 1999, the first
community-based organization for transmasculine
people, and authoring the classic *Becoming a
Visible Man*. He contributes to many academic
anthologies and journals and holds BA and MFA degrees from
the University of Oregon (1970, 1972), and a PhD in Law from
Manchester Metropolitan University (2011); he has been featured
regularly in the media and at innumerable conferences and has
consulted globally on trans rights. He served 15 years on the board
of directors of the World Professional Association for Transgender
Health, including six as the second trans-identified president.

I first encountered Jamison in Loren Cameron's 1996 book, *Body
Alchemy: Transsexual Portraits*, an early, rare example of nonsensa-
tionalist literature published in the first years of my own transition.
He has remained a role model ever since, and later became a warm
friend. Here he writes about how prevalent transphobia is in our
society, and how insidious it can be. www.jamisongreen.com

---

\*    Female to male.

24

My first conscious encounter with transphobia was when I heard it coming out of my own mouth.

Shortly before Christmas 1978, I told my parents that my partner—a woman who they knew as my roommate—was my lover and that we wanted to spend the holidays with both our families. I would be attending her family's festivities and she would be joining ours, I said. My mother often bought *Redbook* and *Family Circle* from the grocery store checkout line, and she knew the signs from articles like *"How to Tell if Your Daughter is a Lesbian."* She knew I had refused to wear women's clothing since graduating high school in 1966; I'd tried not to wear any since I was about two years old, but I often lost those battles. She knew I had mostly played with the boys in the neighborhood and that my college friends were largely girls. And she knew that the few young men I trusted enough to bring home were buddies and not romantic interests.

So I came out as a lesbian. I insisted that they honor the four-year, committed relationship we'd had. I'd introduced her to my parents during the first six months of our becoming partners and they had always treated her well, but now my mother's reaction was so thoroughly, vehemently antagonistic that my father was stunned. "She's using you," she spat. "She's going to ruin you." How could she say such things about a such a kind, gentle woman as my partner? I was so frightened that I blurted out, "Well, at least I'm not changing my sex!"

It was then that I realized that I had been exposed to a great deal of transphobia, so much so that I was now spouting it back.

Every time I was "mistaken" for a boy was a psychic triumph that I held inside and never discussed with anyone, especially not my parents. By the time I was a sophomore in college, I knew I was "crossgendered," that somehow the "wires were tangled" or maybe "shorted" between my brain and my body. I didn't know any other words. No one among my family or friends talked about transsexual** people. In 1968, I hid in a bookstore for hours to read as much as I could of Gore

---

** I know many people now consider this word an insult, and some are even triggered by it, but it was the word in use at the time. Other words like "transgender" did not emerge until later.

Vidal's sex-change satire *Myra Breckinridge*, but I was uninterested in seeing the 1970 film; nothing in this comedic romp seemed relevant to my experience of gender.

In 1974, Jan Morris's *Conundrum* introduced the public to the "born in the wrong body" trope, though that seemed like another kind of fantasy, a simple, childlike explanation for feeling different that never sat well with me. I had been born into the body I had, and there was nothing wrong except that it told people to think of me as a girl. My masculinity was not invisible, and it was that dichotomy—the dissonance between my body and my gender expression—that made other people uncomfortable with me, that made people tell me I was not behaving properly for a girl. But I wasn't behaving improperly; I was being myself. This is the existential predicament in which some of us find ourselves: other people refuse to see us, and when we try to express ourselves, they think we are lying, or trying to deceive.

People like Jan Morris and Christine Jorgensen solved their existential predicaments by transitioning—through hormones and surgeries—to outwardly express the women they knew themselves to be inside, and people generally seemed to accept them, so why couldn't others treat me as the young man I was? I'd never heard of anyone transitioning from female to male. The possibility simply had never crossed my mind. I felt that I was different, not that I was broken or that someone else (someone's God?) had made a mistake.

In 1977, I had read an article in the feminist journal *Chrysalis*, subtitled "a magazine of women's culture," in which Janice Raymond proposed that transsexualism be "morally mandated out of existence."[1] She challenged transsexual people to resist the sex role stereotypes that everyone struggled with by confronting them rather than "going under the knife" to be made to conform, "thus reinforcing the fabric by which a sexist society is held together."[2] I was all about resisting stereotypes. I was all about demonstrating that people with female-coded bodies had more potential than society credited us with. But I thought Raymond was far off base with her idea that "a society that generates such rigid stereotypes of masculinity and femininity is itself the primary cause of transsexualism."[3] That's like saying we are all incapable of differentiating ourselves from our peers, that all women are Stepford Wives and all men G.I. Joes. I felt her statements were insulting to everyone! I later realized that this article was the blueprint, the trial balloon, the first reveal for Raymond's 1979 *The Transsexual Empire*,[4] which was more accurately a manual for transphobia than a beacon of feminist thought. And we still struggle against her followers' identical diatribes today.

*Myra Breckinridge* seemed the kind of "icky" you could look at but wouldn't want to touch, while Janice Raymond accused doctors of creating fem-bots to control and replace women with manufactured caricatures as retaliation for the rise of feminist consciousness. Both were so far from my experience that I didn't realize how much transphobia I'd internalized; it had seeped in so deeply that I felt compelled to distance myself in a defensive "I'm-not-as-bad-as-THOSE-people" diversion to sidetrack my mother's wrath somewhere, anywhere else. I was immediately filled with shame, which they probably interpreted as a shame of being homosexual. No. I discovered I was ashamed of being transsexual, and that I was ashamed of being ashamed.

This self-imposed humiliation went completely against my personal code of honor, the sense of myself that buoyed my entire existence. Since childhood I'd been the outsider, the freak, the one who nobody could tell whether they were a boy or a girl. I was determined not to let people make fun of me or to allow them to think they had power over me, as though they were elevated by putting me down. Nobody was permitted to score points on me. If they couldn't determine my sex, that was their problem and not mine. If they needed to know, I'd share, but damn if they were going to *coerce* me to reveal myself. In women's restrooms, when challenged, I'd reply, "Do you need to see my chest? I know which restroom is mine." And still women would sometimes make their boyfriends threaten to beat me up for being a man in the women's room, though I was only 5'3" and 120 pounds.

I forgive them. They had been conditioned by stereotypes to which I could not and would not conform. I wore jeans, leather boots, and denim shirts with the sleeves rolled up, and I had a scruffy boy haircut: not short, not long, and always messy. I had broad shoulders and muscular hands and forearms from being the first female-bodied construction cable splicer for Pacific Northwest Bell Telephone Company in 1973. I left that work in 1976 and began doing odd jobs, interior painting, teaching legal writing, performing with rock and folk bands. In 1976, I published a book of short stories in which I concealed myself behind genderless narrators; still, a reviewer from a women's journal noted the stories were "informed by a refined feminist consciousness." I was proud, of the ambiguity, the strength, the ruggedness, the tenderness, the mussed hair and the dirty jeans and the scuffed boots. I was me. I existed, therefore, I was.

I didn't lack for friends or would-be lovers, but I was selective, reserving intimacy for only those I thought would respect my difference. I was wrong sometimes, like when I found partners who only wanted to transform me into something more like themselves. But I learned from those experiences, just like I tried to learn from everything and everyone that I encountered and to whom I tried to give something of myself. I learned how to recognize the existential self that is beneath any façade, that will remain when I am all alone.

Transphobia is opportunistic and aggressive.

It's a powerful, insidious force, especially for those of us trans ourselves. It creeps into our psyches through tiny crevices. It lurks in the questions we ask about who or what we are and why we might feel different from other people. It grows stronger when we feel the tiniest shame; even when that shame is about something else, it can release a landslide of doubt that crumbles our self-confidences from every direction. Any toehold it can find inside our spirits has to be confronted, stared down, deconstructed, disintegrated, and swept away. There are no shortcuts. We must understand it first, learn to recognize it for what it is, and learn how and when to challenge it, which situations require what level of response, and to keep ourselves strong and on an even footing when we do confront it, especially when other people are involved. Through this introspection and wise, not desperate, engagement, we will prevail; otherwise, by ignoring it we've merely thrown a tarp over it. Transphobia will regroup in hiding until it's strong enough to assault us again.

Fighting my own internalized transphobia, for me, was easier than opposing the external bigots. I spent many years—three decades of considering what transition might mean for my family, friends, and myself, of questioning, wondering, turning things over in my mind, getting in touch with what was core to my existence, what could never be shaken or taken from me—before making steps to change my body. It was during that pre-medical exploration that I learned what transphobia was and how to resist it within me, in part by talking to many different trans people and by gaining compassion for our community. I didn't just fantasize about what I might become. I didn't think much at all about what other people would see because I had no fucking idea what I would look like if I transitioned. I peered inside, I pondered being alone, how embodying myself fully would enable me to be more present and engaged with whatever I chose to do in the world. Wherever I found myself, there I would be. All this made it easier for me to accept the difficulties and limitations of social and medical transition.

Cis* people are often startled when learning about someone's transness, and for those who are susceptible or who are already infected by transphobia, the notion that someone they've known is in some fundamental way not who they believed us to be can be alarming. It can overwhelm them with anger. Some feel as though reality has suddenly been disrupted, like everything they've understood about the world has been spun incessantly awhirl.

The people who are hostile, often uncontrollably so, are the most dangerous. They are cornered animals who lash out, committing violence or even murder. Some believe the aggressive, callous responses are the transphobia itself, but I think they're a manifestation of it; transphobia is the deep-seated fear and hatred of "the other" that arises in people because we destabilize their beliefs about identity and society in ways

---

\*  "Cisgender," i.e., nontrans: people comfortable in the sex they were assigned at birth.

they do not understand. They refuse to adapt and so can only resolve their fear by attempting to eliminate the source. As if they could.

That aggression is so terrifying that we may be pressured to decide whether to stand our ground or to flee. I avoid physical trouble. I'm an old man now. But even when I was younger, I would carefully take the measure of any assailant and make every effort to diffuse tension with words, sometimes humor, sometimes dismissal and graceful retreat. I reject violence as a solution to problems.

Not all manifestations of transphobia appear or are acted out in the same way. Some are far more subtle ignorance or insensitivity. Others are bumbling expressions of curiosity or even well-meaning but ineffective attempts at support. Often it is difficult to respond to these with a forgiving spirit, but I've realized it's better to answer as helpfully as possible, to further the growth of a potential ally rather than to create an enemy by instilling shame or embarrassment.

Of course, many cis people who are surprised are capable of welcoming our transness. These more secure cis people can become intrigued, interested, even excited to learn more. Some may be "chasers" who objectify us for their own gratification, but most will live as friends, family, or partners of various types, people who can appreciate us and the social conditions of our lives, allies who can rise up beside us in our fight against oppression and injustice.

I thought long and hard about how I would explain my transition—explain myself—to family and friends. When I was young, I was more afraid of losing things than I am now. I imagined dialogue with various important people in my life, so I practiced anticipating their reactions and rehearsed how I might respond. Sometimes I'd force myself to cry over their possible replies but then I compelled myself to stay composed, to attempt to aid them past their transphobia and to make sense of who I was and would always be.

I also tried to foresee the obstacles I might encounter in my workplace, which, before my transition, was a very small, publicly held software development and publishing company in the San Francisco Bay Area where I was vice president of operations. I had a great deal of privilege due to that position, but just one week after I submitted my application to the Sex Reassignment Program at Stanford University I was fired, along with all the other vice presidents, due to corporate reorganization. I hadn't done anything wrong, and no one knew that I'd committed to social and medical transition.

But losing my job upset my plans. I didn't know how I would pay for my transition without an income, and in 1988 almost no companies offered health insurance that would cover "transsexualism" ("gender identity disorder" and "gender dysphoria" hadn't been established as diagnoses yet).

High-tech companies had access to the internet before most others, but there was little on the World Wide Web that would help. Every trans person was alone and only able to establish loose connections through a few, inaccessible-to-most support groups. Some of these published newsletters found their way to isolated trans folks through friends, queer bars, bookstores, and porn shops, but they had very limited reach. Occasionally, trans people would be featured on television and an organization's address or phone number might appear for a few moments; we would frantically search for pen and paper before it vanished. It was such a different world. Even with the many forms of connection we have today, often members of our community still feel alone and that they are the only person who feels as they do.

A few months after I was fired, I was offered a position at a very large, rapidly growing computer design and manufacturing company as a mid-level manager with a staff of 12 and a need to interact with several other divisions for my department to be successful. I still hadn't been accepted by the sex reassignment program but would need to come out to a lot of strangers, so I attempted to keep a low profile, hoping that I'd soon get permission to begin taking testosterone and to use male pronouns. I informed my supervisor and my staff first, and most of them were very understanding. But one of my peers laughed uncontrollably. Any respect he'd held for me clearly had vanished, and probably any hope for his cooperation with me or my staff as well. I had to regain his esteem. I saw a photo of a woman and two young children on his desk, so I interrupted his laughter by stating, "You know, I have a wife and a daughter, and another child on the way." He sobered up immediately and said, "Well, you're doing the right thing, then." Clearly, he was a homophobe and I just accepted that without comment, thanked him for listening, and avoided interaction with him until he quit the company one year later. I left after three years, after my medical transition was complete, looking for work with more integrity.

I started doing contract writing and public speaking. In 1994, after several years of advocacy from myself and others, the San Francisco Board of Supervisors passed an ordinance preventing discrimination on the basis of gender identity or expression in employment, housing, and public accommodations. A few years of our prodding later, and the Board of Supervisors removed the exclusion allowing the city's employee health insurance to refuse medical coverage for transgender employees; a trans-inclusive plan would become available in 2001. I spoke on the local news/talk radio station with the city's Human Rights Commission staff to answer questions, and some callers spewed opinions like "You're sick!" and "I'd rather pay for the bullet for you to kill yourself with than to have my taxes pay for your fucking sex change, wacko!" But we persisted with our message about trans people deserving access to medically necessary treatment and steadfastly refused to rise to the bait. I've found that staying calm and sticking to one's message is much more effective than engaging in a shouting match.

The transphobia hasn't changed, either. We are more visible so transphobia is more apparent, but it's more than that. I'm very uneasy about the steady rise in antagonism being fueled by religious and right-wing extremism in the United States and elsewhere. Even before 2016, trans people had disproportionately suffered from violence, unemployment, poverty, lack of access to healthcare, racial and socioeconomic disparities, the transphobic policies of biased institutions, and the legislative assaults from governmental entities. Now it's worse. I'm also deeply concerned that *anyone* suffers from these bigotries in a world as sophisticated, complex, and wealthy as ours. Too many state and national governments around the world cannot—or more accurately *will not*—serve all the people. Transphobia thriving is an indication of how alienated we are from each other as humans, of how selfish and insensitive are many of the individuals who seek power. Transphobia makes me profoundly sad as well. This is not the kind of society in which I want to live. But I will stay and fight back.

I believe in nonviolent protest and fundamental rights for all. Maybe because I lived through the civil rights movement of the 1960s and the social upheavals of the 1970s, I still believe in fighting injustice with dignity and grace. I believe we can overcome transphobia through unwavering love for ourselves and for all human beings. The qualities that I admire in both gender diverse and cis people throughout history are integrity, kindness, compassion, creativity, competence, honesty, authenticity, and respect for others. My desire to embody these qualities was the foundation for my own decision to transition, yet a transition is not necessary to cultivate such traits; it was recognizing the existential core of who I was as a living being within this universe that led me to transition, and nothing can shake my identity.

If we cultivate those traits, we can vanquish our fears; if we listen to one another, we can eradicate bigotry in all its manifestations. I am determined to use my sadness to further my commitments to our community and to channel my anger to energize my compassion. I choose to always be alert to ways I can empower others to overcome their own misery, dread, and resentment, to work constructively for our many trans communities and for our interconnected world. Our individual spheres may be large or small, but if we each manage to live our best lives while consciously supporting the common good, good can prevail.

# Dana Delgardo

# A Trans Man in the Military

**Dana Delgardo** (he/him) is a mixed-race trans man who served 30 years in the U.S. Air Force, retiring as a Major in Flight Medicine Operations in 2018 due to the hateful Trump edicts against transgender people in the military. He is a member and was medical co-chair of SPART*A (Servicemembers, Partners, and Allies for Respect and Tolerance for All), still serving as wellness co-chair.
He is a family nurse practitioner, has a Master's in Nursing Science, an Advanced Practice Nurse Care certification, and a certification from the American Academy of HIV Medicine. For many years he was a medical practitioner at Callen-Lorde, the not-for-profit health center in NYC, providing high-quality, compassionate healthcare to LGBTQIA+ communities in all their diversity, regardless of ability to pay. Additionally, he led the medical delegation sent by Callen-Lorde to Puerto Rico following the devastation of Hurricane Maria in September 2017, when the federal government did little.

I don't recall where we met; we've crossed paths many times at conferences, through friends, and at Callen-Lorde. He is a gentle man, perhaps a bit shy, warm-hearted, and devoted to whatever task is before him. It's not clear how many serve, but not often enough do we see the complicated lives of transgender and gender nonbinary people in the military.

On June 30, 2016, late in the Obama administration, the Secretary of Defense announced the allowance of open transgender service in the military. It was life-changing for those of us who had fallen under the "T" of invisibility. We could be ourselves within an organization that we loved and had served with unwavering dedication! We were ecstatic. And relieved. I remember a group call for Servicemembers, Partners, and Allies for Respect and Tolerance for All (SPART*A) to watch the announcement live, all of us with bated breath. When Secretary Ash Carter said, "We can't allow barriers unrelated to a person's qualifications to prevent us from recruiting and retaining those who can best accomplish the mission,"[1] we all cried tears of joy. Finally, the official transphobic policy was gone. We were free!

Once we could serve openly, with guidance from myself and SPART*A, we scrambled to get our gender markers updated through an Exception to Policy (ETP). This process was done with one's commander and medical group. It was a way to update all your records within the military, equivalent to changing your driver's license and social security card.

After the announcement in June, I scrambled to get my ETP and assisted other military personnel to do the same. I processed mine by October 1, 2016. Hell, with the permission of the base psychologist and my commander, I even invited my psychologist fiancé, a gender specialist, to do an in-service training on gender affirmation. We scheduled it on a drill weekend so we could do Gender 101 to a large group of cisgender pilots. Through my own transition I was able to help other members of the trans military community, and to teach outsiders the importance of acceptance for basic respect and unit cohesion. Trans rights in the Air Force was moving forward, and I was part of it…I was overjoyed.

Then Trump happened.

\* \* \*

I am a mixed-race heterosexual transgender man who had little choice about where my life began. I did not choose my religion, national origin, ethnicity, sex, or socioeconomic status. It was only later that I realized I did have control over my own life, though some of the decisions I made were complex and had limitations. Still, I endured.

I was born into a low-income Catholic family in Boston. My father was a second-generation Irishman and my mother a multi-race laborer; they never married, and I was branded the bastard child. My mom did what any good Catholic girl would: She gave me my stepfather's last name. Not my preference. Also, I was assigned female at birth, and my birth certificate defined how I was viewed by the world, again without my input. Maybe this is why advocacy is my life's work—having had little choice early on set the stage for my future.

I didn't join the military to fight for my country, I was more desperate: I enlisted to save myself. My dad had died six months before, and I was spiraling into a destructive abyss. What could I do? My brother joined the Army infantry, but I hoped I was Air Force officer material.

I found camaraderie, dedication, belonging, and self-worth. The recruiting posters were right! We were stripped down and rebuilt to become a team, a unit more concerned with the group than with individual needs. Success depended on everyone opting in to the whole as greater than the sum of the parts, and self-worth derived from being part of the whole.

I coasted early on, keeping my gender ambiguous. I was accepted as a masculine female, so I was content to live as a lesbian. I had no awareness of anything else. Transgender, what the hell was that? I had no mentors nor any access to the language. This was as close as I could get to what I sensed about me, but in the recesses of my mind, I always knew it wasn't quite right.

I spent most of my career at McGuire Air Force Base in New Jersey as a technical sergeant, then as a nurse practitioner. I went to Officer Training School (OTS) in Alabama and graduated as a First Lieutenant in 2012. I was the shit! For the first time! I was fearless and felt I could accomplish anything.

My next challenge was to be my true self, and I had no clue how but I was determined to figure it out. I had repressed who I was for 51 years to appease my mom and to save my military career. I hid internally, choking on the world's view of me as a female, straining in vain to see a man in the mirror. But in 2013, my mother's death freed my soul, and I felt that it was time to live life as my true, authentic self. That year I began gender-affirming hormone therapy.

Somewhere along the way, I discovered my superpower: resilience.

It took many different events and connections. Before Obama's decree, the military was inherently transphobic; trans people were not allowed to serve openly, though a few managed to exist as their self-identified genders with the tacit permission of their commanders. More were in the closet.

Finding peers can be essential, and only a few years into my transition I came across SPART*A. I saw this organization as a parachute to help me keep my secret safe. Alongside LGBTQIA+ others, I could be Captain Delgardo and male identified. I'd found community and another team. I felt whole. But I was twenty years into the military and a newly appointed officer, terrified I'd somehow jeopardize my pension and benefits, my family's wellbeing, and the years invested. The fear paralyzed me, and so I declined to become a chapter leader. I felt ashamed for not being more of a trailblazer. I was in "fight or flight," and frozen to inaction.

We called our LGBTQIA+ community "The Q Force," and these friends helped me survive as a young airman. We protected one another during war and peace. The group we developed kept us all fearless, cohesive, and mission-ready: coveted qualities in the military. We were chosen family and still have an unbroken bond to this day.

I loved my position as a flight nurse but transferred to air mobility operations because no one knew me there. This felt like the safest way of affirming my gender identity. I thought I could transition gradually and no one would notice, but testosterone-induced changes were visible, so next I shifted to active reserve.

As I tried to hide my true gender in the military, I was out in civilian life. My tenure as a family nurse practitioner with Callen-Lorde, a gender-affirming healthcare organization in NYC, saved my career and even pushed me to grow as an officer. It made me aware that I had outgrown passive conformity. Applying for the job was so thrilling; I was ecstatic to interview with one of the best LGBTQIA+ medical clinics on the East Coast! Like at SPART*A, I would fit in somewhere with no need to pretend.

I interviewed twice. The first time I was offered a position but had to decline because of a deployment: service first, civilian life second. So what do you do when you miss the opportunity to do your dream job? You try again, of course!

I interviewed once more and was hired. I was so proud. I felt accepted and safe, a member of an organization that respected and accepted my true self, something I had never experienced in twenty-plus years in the Air Force. I was again part of a team. Being there gave me courage. How was I to combine being an out, proud transgender medical provider and a closeted but active Air Force officer? With this newfound confidence, I was resolute.

I lived a double life that wasn't the same as being an out lesbian. I felt like an impostor. To protect my military career, I had to keep my gender identity a secret. I remember the intense anxiety and depression that hit every time I drove through the base gate. It ripped my heart out, and to survive I placed it in the glove compartment for safekeeping. Sometimes we have to make harsh compromises, and I developed PTSD so strong that I considered resigning. As I became more myself at Callen-Lorde, the "female" Air Force officer I pretended to be struggled to continue the charade.

I'd been deployed before, but this deployment made me anxious because I'd been on testosterone for over two years. This was February 2016, and I was on active reserve, already physically male though there was still no open transgender service, so my military ID listed me as female. On my second night in Germany, I was assigned a male roommate. When the reality of sharing a bathroom hit, I panicked.

I was terrified of transphobic violence, so I disclosed to him that I was female. He was quickly moved elsewhere.

Who would be next? The thought made me furious. I went for a walk to cool down and left it to fate. Upon my return, the room was empty! Hallelujah! A one-night reprieve.

The next day, there was a knock on the door from a female officer. Had I seen her luggage? I replied, "Yes, it's here." She was perplexed, looked at me, then looked at the hotel manager. She said, "I obviously can't room here with a male." The housekeeper gave me the evil eye, probably suspecting that I hoped for shenanigans. Not wanting another male roommate, I panicked and shouted, "It's all right! You can stay!" The hotel manager was the only one who understood. He examined me, nodded, said, "It's okay," then left. There was an awkward pause when my potential roomie looked me up and down, and then I could tell a light bulb clicked and she realized my assigned gender was female. She stayed. This seemed the safest.

I worked in the Air Operations Center (AOC) during the deployment. My work days were a constant warfare of mixed emotions. Some military personnel who did not know my history just saw me as male and gendered me correctly as "sir," which made me feel alive. But I was not out to my command, so I had to remind others to use "ma'am" around superiors. I was validated and humiliated together.

Like so many trans people everywhere, I was overcome with anxiety about the simplest things. Because of my male appearance, I could not use the female restrooms. Using the male toilet was not an option either for fear of running into certain others and being outed. I developed a routine: Report to work at 7 a.m., update the commanding officer, take a break at 10:15 until 10:45 a.m., walk approximately two Manhattan blocks to the officers' club, pee, return and take lunch at noon, making a fast trek back to my room to pee again and eat, return, and finish my work by 4 p.m. The transphobia existed every moment. In my off hours, I mostly hung in my room or played basketball with a group from my base.

I could have seen it as traumatizing, but I chose not to be a victim of circumstances. I pressed on and chalked it up to experience. During that tour, I experienced uncomfortable situations and gender euphoria as well. My resilience had gotten me this far, but I decided never to deploy again as a female, and this was my last tour abroad.

How did I cope with all those years of adversity? Like many others, I needed to help and give back. Somewhere between 2012 and 2013, I was asked by SPART*A to be the medical co-chair, which I accepted, and I used my expertise as a provider to advocate behind the scenes. I had guided my own affirmation, so why not help others? I mentored and advised many servicepeople about trans military policy, gender-affirming hormones and resources, and did plain old peer counseling.

I became a surrogate father figure to a few, and I watched them navigate through the unsafe bureaucracy. Civilian gender affirmation was decades ahead of the military. Most servicepeople I knew were obtaining mental health and gender-affirming hormone treatment outside the military. Callen-Lorde and the other LGBTQIA+ health centers nationwide provide care to many service members. Callen-Lorde is a true pioneer of inclusion and advocacy and has created a safe and private place; I am proud to have been a part.

My experience prior to being out helped me aid the survival of others. They asked the same questions I did, like, "Would I be promoted based solely on merit as an open transgender soldier, or denied because of it?" "How can I access hormones safely?" "How can I deploy safely?" "Will I be allowed to retire with full benefits like my nontrans coworkers?" And, "How will I support my family if I am discharged without benefits?" Aiding them gave my service additional meaning and helped my own sometimes-waning confidence.

One day, everything changed. In 2017, just a few months after the Obama rewrite of policy and following the shift in federal administration, I was asked to reprocess my ETP. I could not make sense of it because my gender marker, the Defense Enrollment Eligibility Reporting System (DEERS) database listing, and my military ID all reflected my gender as male. The only explanation I received was that the process now had to be done through Air Force headquarters, where previously the Medical Multidisciplinary Team (MMDT) head-quarters in San Antonio, Texas, validated one's gender dysphoria and facilitated the in-service transition. I was first told I was grandfathered in and that all I needed was a letter to that effect. I tried multiple avenues at the Pentagon to get one but was then informed by the person in charge, the same person who had asked me a year before to help them understand and implement the process, that I had to repeat everything through regular channels like everyone else. I didn't know if this was a paperwork snafu or my fear of a return to military transphobia coming true.

My entire medical and psychological history was questioned. It felt like I was being harassed and discriminated against because of who I was yet again. It felt like reopening an old wound. The process reflected ignorance, stigma, bias, lack of training, and how transphobia persists. The senior master sergeant's first question was, "Did you have *all* the surgeries?" I was mortified.

It wasn't this noncommissioned officer's (NCO's) place to question a senior officer about their surgical history unless they had a "need to know." I again had no control over my identity, or what information about my body was spread to who. The second discussion focused on my random urine drug screenings and what gender of person would escort me. How was that relevant to readiness? If anything, this process was what impeded it.

I questioned whether that NCO had read the policy, to which she replied, "Some of it." I was a subject matter expert. I recited verbatim the *Air Force Policy Memorandum on In-Service Transition of Airmen Identifying as Transgender, Guideline 2h:* "When a military medical provider [which she was not] in coordination with the Medical Multidisciplinary Team determines that a transgender Airman's gender transition is complete and approved by the commander, the service member's gender marker will be changed in their record. The service member will be recognized in the preferred gender."[2] She did not know the process and made inferences based on personal biases and cultural incompetence. The most frustrating thing was that I was affirmed in my gender as a civilian. Everything including my birth certificate listed my gender as male, and yet here it was all of a sudden rejected for no valid reason.

I was threatened with "comply, or else." I gave them all my mental health notes, and still they asked for more. They wanted my health history prior to my affirmation. I felt they were on a witch hunt, digging for something they could use against me. I had seen it before when people were kicked out for being gay. At one point I told the doc, "Do you want me to make things up? I do not have anything else to give!"

Even with the help of my commander, a lieutenant colonel and strong ally, the resubmission process was hell. I desperately contacted legal advocates and wrote a letter to my congressman. It seemed like the military was targeting me and was intent on reversing my gender marker to female. I felt hopeless. I even tried to get help from civilian agencies, including GLAAD,* but to no avail. They didn't seem to give a shit, either. I had made a conscious decision to save my life and my military career by changing my records to male.

Then on July 26, 2017, the Trump administration announced a ban on trans military service.[3] I was enraged, offended, hurt, and confused about the sudden turn of policy. So many servicepeople had come out and now were exposed. We felt betrayed by an institution we trusted and had dedicated our entire lives to. The POTUS reversed Secretary Carter's accession and retention of trans military personnel, stating across three tweets:

> After consultation with my Generals and military experts, please be advised that the United States Government will not accept or allow... Transgender individuals to serve in any capacity in the U.S. Military. Our military must be focused on decisive and overwhelming...victory and cannot be burdened with the tremendous medical costs and disruption that transgender in the military would entail. Thank you.[4]

* www.glaad.org

Never mind that:

> [A 2016] analysis by the Rand Corporation...found that the costs of allowing transgender people to serve in the military would have a "minimal impact" on the budget, amounting to $2.4 million to $8.4 million each year, or 0.04 percent to 0.13 percent of the military healthcare budget. That's little more than a rounding error when compared to the total U.S. military budget of roughly $700 billion.[5]

This announcement set off a gut-wrenching fear and nausea that I had experienced many times before.

Secretary of Defense Colonel James Mattis was reportedly "caught off guard" and "appalled." "[Mattis] was infuriated by the tweets, and saw them as an insult to transgender Americans currently serving in the military."[6] Republican Senator John McCain said, "There is no reason to force service members who are able to fight, train and deploy to leave the military—regardless of their gender identity."[7]

However, on February 22, 2018, Mattis seemingly reversed his position, signing the *Memorandum for the President, Subject: Military Service by Transgender Individuals*, which states:

> The Department of Defense concludes that there are substantial risks associated with allowing the accession and retention of individuals with a history or diagnosis of gender dysphoria and require, or have already undertaken, a course of treatment to change their gender. Furthermore, the Department also finds that exempting such persons from well-established mental health, physical health, and sex-based standards, which apply to all Service members, including transgender Service members without gender dysphoria, could undermine readiness, disrupt unit cohesion, and impose an unreasonable burden on the military that is not conducive to military effectiveness and lethality...I firmly believe that compelling behavioral health reasons require the Department to proceed with caution...[8]

You can imagine our horror and disgust. Before Trump's 2017 tweet we briefly felt safe, but once again, that safety was replaced by fear. Fear of discrimination, fear of nonprogression of careers, and fear of retaliation all based on our gender identities. It also brought about a series of lawsuits by military members and others asserting that the ban was unconstitutional. The environment was uncertain and there was poor communication to leadership, providers, and members. And without direction on how this policy would be implemented, we lived in limbo.

During that same period, the officer in charge of my Air Force duty section approached me and said, "You know, we are going in the bucket, and it may be time to look at your options." She did not explain, but implicit in her message was that my unit was being deployed soon, probably without me, and that she was concerned for my safety. It was the worst-case scenario for reservists: "no points, no pay." I was coded as undeployable for almost two years. I sat in this limbo and felt useless to my squadron, the team I had bonded with for years, knowing they relied on me as I relied on them. "Readiness" is crucial to being in the military, and I was being judged on it solely because I was trans. I was ready physically, scored 99 percent on my fit-to-fight ratings based on male (not female) standards, and had no mental health issues, yet I was nondeployable? Then came the big announcement.

After several delays and legal challenges, the ban was to be implemented. "The Mattis Transgender Policy Will Go into Effect Next Friday"[9] an April 1, 2019 article was titled. "[C]urrent service-members may no longer be 'grandfathered' into the previous 'Carter policy' unless they received a diagnosis of gender dysphoria before last Tuesday, March 26."

Trans troops no longer had protection from harassment, investigation, and medical/mental healthcare delay. Our choices were terrible: remain in the closet, return to it if that was even possible, or separate. The landscape was no longer safe.

* * *

You may ask, "Why did you remain so long in an organization that didn't recognize you as a human being and that believed you were a deviant misfit?" We stay because we belong. This is all we have known since we were young. I think of the Air Force as the dad I lost when I was at the early, vulnerable age of 23. It filled the chasm left by his absence, he who had supported me emotionally, physically, and financially. The Air Force met my needs as identified by Maslow's hierarchy of physiological safety, love, belonging, self-esteem, respect, and self-actualization. It provided me with an education, skills, opportunities to travel, and the profession that I still hold today.

For every military person, the answers are different. But when considering remaining in the Air Force, my reasons were twofold.

First, I'd earned it. I had served 30 years during numerous deployments in which I had helped protect and save lives. I'd demonstrated that I was fit and successful in my positions. It was my right. I was proud of my accomplishments as an active member of the military and a veteran. I started out as an Airman First Class and worked my way up to Major, a feat that no one should be ashamed of. I labored hard to merit that rank and the rights and benefits that came with it. I'd be damned if I'd let anyone take that away from me.

Also, military service was my identity and my legacy, and to deny those parts of me would have been to deny my past and who I had become. I thought leaving the military would be like suddenly missing an appendage and that its absence would be a daily reminder of physical and emotional loss. I had stayed in the military because there was hope. And there is hope, even now, that one day I can serve openly without fear of being discharged, dishonorably or administratively, or of losing my benefits or pension, based on the whims of politicians.

But ultimately, I cut my losses and retired. Why? There were a few reasons. I had more than the necessary 20 years and was due a full pension. My children were older and needed me to be present, and I'd also met a human that I wanted to build a life with, and my devotions would have been split if I had still been within the military. And given the 2018 changes in policy, being an out trans man made it impossible to meet the requirements for me to do my job and to feel safe myself. I could not take the chance of yet again being humiliated, discriminated against, or hurt.

Being transgender and open in an organization that thrives on assimilation was not difficult for me; the ignorance was. I did not retire because I was transgender; I retired because I was concerned about the hostile environment perpetuated by the medical group at my base. I observed the adverse mental health effects on other service members and didn't want them for myself. And I knew I'd be forever "on alert" to not be outed.

My gender identity was only visible to me. But as I completed the Exception to Policy to change my gender marker the second time, I realized nothing was private. Not even my private health information, although we were told it was. I worked in flight medicine; I knew others had access to records and could easily gossip. I was forced to share the one intimate thing that took me a lifetime to come to accept. The Air Force lacked guidance, training, good communication for leadership, and qualified healthcare providers for their transgender members. Staying felt hopeless.

I concluded that my experience as a trans-identified healthcare provider would be more impactful if I worked directly with the community. So I reluctantly retired in September 2018 as a Major with full benefits.

Looking back now, I wonder if my sense of loss is what folks feel like when they leave the physical world and experience death. I still feel sad for all my transgender military friends and colleagues who could not endure seeing open trans service ended. It came suddenly and left just as fast but fortunately has returned since. So many retired before it arrived, and many others, me included, left during the assaults on us from 2017 to 2021. We were forced to end our careers prematurely.

This chapter talks about why I joined the Air Force, stayed, retired, and everything in between. I hope it will help transgender and gender nonbinary people facing similar obstacles understand that it is possible to overcome, despite transphobia.

Sometimes as transgender people, we have to walk away for safety despite our wishes to continue in a setting we love. I hope everyone else was as lucky as me to find another path they enjoyed as much.

People have called me resilient. I think resilience is choosing peace over pain. I believe the obstacles in my path may have created pauses, but they were temporary, and I found healthy ways around them. "I did not survive. I had to learn to thrive." My growth as a provider, military officer, and trans man have all contributed to my existence as a human being. My path was always forward. I wanted more for myself, and failure was never an option. I am here.

# Pooya Mohseni

## Them, Me, You

**Pooya Mohseni** (she/her) is an Iranian-born trans woman and actress who starred in the award winning film *See You Then* (2021), about which RogerEbert.com said, "Mohseni and Chen [Pooya's co-star] are an excellent on-screen pair throughout...Mohseni's genuine warmth makes [her character's] defensiveness all the more layered, showing the tragedy in a meaningful connection

that was nearly lost forever."[1] She was also featured in the play *English* (2022), to rave reviews and award nominations. Her film and television credits include *Law & Order: SVU, Big Dogs, Falling Water, Madam Secretary, Lucky,* and *Terrifier. See You Then* is now available to stream.

We first met in 2015 on the set of *What Goes Unsaid*, a short intended to educate medical and mental health professionals on how to provide affirming care to transgender and gender nonbinary patients; she was in a lead role while I was the creative consultant and co-scriptwriter. And she is every bit as fabulous in adulthood as her adolescent dreams hoped she would be. www.pooyaland.com

I divide my life's evolution into three eras: "Them," when I concerned myself with what *they* thought or wanted me to be and do; "Me," where all my actions were to please *me* and to strive toward what *I* wanted for my life; and "You," which concerns what I want *you*, the readers, the audiences, the world, to see, to learn and be inspired by, to carry forth as my legacy. These three don't have neat edges and they morph together, affecting one another and becoming visible or disappearing as they're needed.

So, here goes a condensed tale of my existence:

*Them*: the earlier part of my life from 1978 until 2003 revolved mainly around myself as a child then a tween and what "they" had to say, when most aspects of my life were beyond my control.

I was born in Iran in 1978, one year before the Islamic Revolution that changed so many things about my country, its direction, its relationship to the world, and the livelihood of every Iranian.* I won't sugarcoat the tyranny of the Shah's regime, but by all accounts, the unrest, arrests, executions, political assassinations, and war that came after made the Pahlavi era seem benign by comparison. I wasn't born into a particularly political family, but being in Iran inevitably makes one political, because unlike in the U.S., everyone there talks politics.

When I was three, the Iran/Iraq war began, lasting eight years. I became familiar with the concept of refugees, waking up at 3 a.m. to hide in the basement with my parents from the bombers overhead, waiting to see if we would be hit or if it was some other unfortunate family that got bombed. Power outages for hours, every day, the sounds of sirens and explosions, the food rations, and the general panic that came with war were just everyday parts of my childhood. Living through active combat is like wading through frigid water in the dark: you are constantly shivering, but as long as nothing bites you and you don't drown, you stay grateful. I learned early on that how I behaved, meaning the clothes I wore or how I played, were also things I needed to be careful about, because otherwise I might get scolded, ridiculed, laughed at, or worse, yelled at or beaten.

Children don't have sophisticated language to describe what is going on inside, but there is a lot they see, hear, and feel about their

---

* Iran had been a bold example of progressivity in the Middle East until the overthrow of their monarchy in the 1979 Iranian Revolution, or Islamic Revolution. Afterward, it became a conservative Shia theocracy where women and other minorities now face very restrictive conditions.

environments. I knew that while my mom was somewhat okay with me wearing her clothes when I was three or four, she definitely was unhappy with it by the time I was six. I became a seasoned illusionist, playing with a Barbie that some friend had probably left behind, or with my mini clay tea kettle and cups set from Hamedan that featured beautiful hand-painted drawings giving some reality to me pretending to be a mother, but none of this in front of my parents, most especially my dad. I would try on mom's makeup, my favorite being the lipstick, maybe a bit of blush, but would make sure that it was cleaned up before my parents came home. I now know that I was definitely not impervious to my mother's detail-oriented gaze, but if my dad noticed he said nothing, because "If you don't acknowledge it, then it's not real."

This charade continued outside of the home, including with family, school, and neighbors. It's not a surprise to me that I feel like I've been an actor all my life...because I have been. I offered people a reasonably seamless portrayal of a boy, or at least thought I did. I dressed like a well-groomed preppy kid with neatly combed hair, a washed face, and tidy clothes. I don't know how convincing my mannerisms were for a boy, but still I gave the performance of a lifetime and most people, *I think*, accepted it. A less feisty soul or maybe a smarter one would have simply learned to conform, but not I. My skull is too thick, and I couldn't be someone else because, in my heart, I simply could not betray my truth. I hid it, or tried to, but deny it? NO! What also helped me survive was that I was an A student liked by teachers and school admins, and so my parents had something "positive" to focus on. It made ignoring the less appealing parts of me, in their eyes, simpler.

Life at school was not easy, because the moment I opened my mouth or strode into a room, everyone knew I wasn't like the other kids. I was truly too fabulous to be an ordinary child: I talked passionately about Beethoven by eight. I hoped to strut like Marilyn Monroe and bat my eyelashes like Elizabeth Taylor. I wanted to learn to tango at six, I had a crush on Roger Moore as James Bond at nine, and I hoped to marry Luke Perry at twelve. I was a smoldering, sassy, 1950s diva stuck in the body of a little boy in a Muslim country, and no one, not even I, knew what the hell to do about it. If you heard what I said and how I said it, or if you were a member of the very small circle of friends with whom I shared my inner thoughts and desires, you knew that inside me beat a very unusual drummer.

Although I grew up in a Muslim country that had no space for anyone who violated the status quo, my personality made it impossible to be anything but me. I paid the price by being bullied, propositioned, threatened, and assaulted throughout school, but none of it made me stop being myself. Even if they took away everything else, I would still retain my soul, my thoughts, and my desires; I'd let NO ONE rob me of those. I was isolated and depressed, sure. I even attempted suicide multiple times, but it wasn't meant to be, and now I'm glad. It all made me recognize that my purpose was to do my part in making this a better place for me, for you, and yes, even for them. The world includes everyone. We all deserve equal rights, because as human beings we are all of value and consequence, and the greatest gifts a person can give themself are love, respect, and accountability.

Now the "me" section, but remember: These parts, the *them/me/you*, are each always present, just in different proportions.

*Me*: If I were to guess when this "me" started flourishing, I'd say around age 19–20, but it probably began long before I was aware of it. My mom and I moved to the New York area from Iran in 1997 so I could start college and a new life where I could be safer and where I had a greater chance for a future as my true self. Keep in mind that this was before the internet connected people across the globe. Also New York was just recovering from the dark days of the HIV/AIDS epidemic, and while being here gave me more opportunities, my life was far from perfect.

I was still young and feisty, but bitter, hurt, depressed, and pretty lost. Two years before coming to the U.S. I had been assaulted by three men while others watched, but it was me who got arrested. Throughout my time in Iran, I had been denied the right to live as who I was, and that suffering wasn't erased just because I crossed an ocean and spoke a different language.

What saved me? Therapy and community. I owe so much to my counselors at The Hetrick-Martin Institute, a not-for-profit organization that provides social services to LGBTQIA+ youth, and to Safe Space, another not-for-profit delivering mental health services; I went there when I first moved to NYC in 1997. Also to those at my own university, FIT, the Fashion Institute of Technology. The staff and others at all three places allowed me to open myself, gradually, and to slowly exorcise my demons. They let me show myself to me through hours of talking about what had happened, hours of crying "Why?" and "Why me?," and still more hours acknowledging that, deep inside, I believed it when people said that I was to blame and had brought those things on myself. Not society. Not antiquated ideas about gender and sexuality, but that my own difference was the thing that needed to be hidden and left abandoned.

But that's garbage. I was *not* at fault for the shortcomings of others, and neither are you. Don't forget self-discipline and accountability, but don't confuse them with a society coercing you to be someone other than who you are.

I started medical and social transition about three months after I arrived in New York, and college at the same time. It was difficult, and what made it more challenging was that I knew no one else going through the same journey. I learned things as they happened. This is the best thing about the internet: It allows you to locate others who can guide you and let you know that you are a member of a broader community. But I didn't have access yet.

At FIT, even though it was a fashion school, there still existed prejudice and ignorance. I was still pointed at. I heard the chuckles and the unkind murmurs. I was told that I was not allowed to join the model forum, because I was "going to make the other girls uncomfortable."

I was outed when I was a background actor on the set of a famous TV show. Someone I didn't know, and who didn't know me, loudly asked in front of everyone, "So, you taking hormones, or what?" Everyone looked puzzled and I was overwhelmed with fear. I denied even knowing what he was talking about...a total lie! I'll never know why he did that, but harassment comes in many forms. Not long after, the agency that helped me get background jobs dropped me, with no specific reason cited. It was 2001 and I was just out of FIT. I was forced to completely abandon acting and to become invisible, stealth, just so I could work, study, or walk down the street and not be hassled. This is why I dislike the word "passing" for the horrible things it implies. We should not have to hide. Never!!

After school, I founded a design company and did not tell anyone I was trans. A few discovered and it was serious to some, funny to others. I looked the part of the Upper East Side New Yorker that I was, an elegant designer in understated black and a dash of pearls who others might want to emulate. Still, I focused on assimilation for financial independence and to have control of my environment. I interacted only with those I worked closely with and we became friends, but otherwise I was uninterested in connections beyond those that were necessary. I didn't say it was easy; realizing that people view you as an exotic anomaly can be amusing for a short, very short period, but the excitement is quickly replaced by exhaustion and resentment. "I AM NOT A FREAK!" I so often wanted to scream. Still, my focus was on finding my place in this world. I searched everywhere, romantic relationships, friendships, work, style. What did I learn? Don't seek your purpose anywhere but in your own heart. If you listen, you will hear. If you ask the question, truly ask, you will get the answer. From within.

I got into a relationship that left me bruised and traumatized. I was in it because I didn't believe I was worth more. I didn't think anyone better would love me because I didn't love myself. When you begin a relationship "to find your other half" you end up with someone else also incomplete, and in my opinion, two "halves" do not make a good "whole." We were each lost in our own ways. As time passed, I realized that he was not my savior. Yet through that relationship, and through the tears, sleepless nights, and violent confrontations, I found me: I recognized my strength and resilience, and I realized that I didn't need someone else to lean on because I was enough. I learned that being trans didn't mean I was worth less than anyone else or that I should settle for bad treatment. The "me" inside had suffered one too many pushes, and the camel's back had been broken. Hallelujah! Not all people are able to leave abusive relationships, but I was.

That evolution didn't happen in one night or one month or even one year, and I'm still not sure it has ended. Life is an unending path of evolution, some of which is in our control and some of which isn't, so the decisions we make do shape what our lives become. I have sympathy for people in abusive relationships. I was one of them and didn't know what to do or where to go until I did; only then could I take one step after another, and I never stopped.

Now, 17 years after ending it, I still look at that relationship as one of the most educational periods of my life because the "me" that was hiding got up, was able to brush off the dust, and walk on. I rented my first apartment when I was 26. I worked full time and put myself through school at night. I dated, with some success, but my best decision was to look inward for guidance instead of outward, which gave me confidence that I previously lacked, and I started becoming more certain that whatever the world threw at me, I would somehow find my way. That is a gift that you can only appreciate when you receive it. What do I mean? You know how negative or overwhelming experiences make you think that they will be your end and that you will never move past them or do better? Now you'll *know* that you can rise up and keep going. That's the lesson you learn from earned resilience and faith in yourself.

We have casually slid into the "you" part of the journey. Welcome: You are a winner! You are alive, you are willing to change and to learn how. This places you ahead of so many others, trust me!

After the relationship ended, my journey to find my purpose intensified. Then when I left my last design job, the question kept popping up, "What now?" I worked for myself, owned my own studio in NYC, but with no one to guide me I needed to decide what to do with my life. Earning money and being my own boss weren't enough. Acting filled some of the void as I hadn't been able to pursue it fully until I had the money and time, but even that felt awkward because I wasn't living fully "out." The world had no idea who I was and what I had endured. More importantly, I was trying to find a way to transform my trauma, pain, and darkness into something of significance. Otherwise, what was the point?

In 2015, I felt like I was receiving signs from the universe that it was time to come out of the closet. In many ways I was living the dream as an attractive, stylish, sophisticated woman, and most people didn't know I was trans, and while that may not seem like a problem, I had grown weary of carrying the fear of "What if they find out?" So, on June 26, 2015, the day that marriage equality was passed as the new law of the land, I decided it was time. I logged in to Facebook and, through much fear and trepidation, came out to the world. I was willing to face whatever consequences might come and move on from there. I was not going to come out to individuals, slowly, one at a time; instead, I came out to every one of my followers in a single post!

Living my complete truth seems more important than continuing a career as stealth for two reasons: First, because I have survived everything yet I am still standing, and the child inside me needs to appreciate that they are seen and validated. Second, because it is important that others witness transgender and gender nonbinary people willing to rise up and reveal to the world who we are, even in our fear of rejection and marginalization. It is important to me that the broader world, and young members of our community particularly, know that we exist and that we are a diverse group with grit, guts, and resilience. I want LGBTQIA+ kids and young adults, just now finding themselves and their places, to appreciate that there are transgender and gender nonbinary mothers, fathers, sisters, brothers, and otherwise-gendered family members who are open to receive them as our own, to acknowledge them, to affirm them, and to love them. It isn't a noble thought but a human one, and I believe it is our strength. And living my truth was one of the best decisions of my life.

Now, years after coming out, my life may appear identical from the outside, but from the inside it's lighter and brighter as I am no longer cowering in the shadows. Nor am I weighed down by fear. If someone rejects me for who I am, that's their loss. I strive to be my best, most authentic self, every day. I can't respond to everyone's ignorance and bigotry. My energy has value and is limited so should be spent where it is the most useful, aiding those who need support in being themselves and cherishing who they are, fully. I accomplish that as an actor, as an activist, as a writer, and as a storyteller. I have also begun collaborating with others to create theatrical performances where queer characters can occupy the world at large together with others who may identify differently.

This entire chapter is to make clear that my life has had downs and ups, both in Iran and NYC, and that you can command your way through them if you believe in yourself. You have the ability to overcome situations that seem larger than you or beyond your understanding. Yes, senseless things can happen even here in the U.S., like presidents and state legislatures intent on eliminating our ability to exist, but these will pass. I stayed up that election night, like so many people, until three or four in the morning; then I woke early, eyes red, and recorded an Instagram post revealing to everyone that it had made me feel just how hated I am by so many, but that only makes me work harder for our rights.

We can also control how we view the world and how we choose to act on it; I take my lemons and make lemon jelly. It is only after years of distress that I can accept that I am not sick, damaged, or somehow cursed. I am a human, in my glorious complexity and nuance, as are you. When you find how to be your most authentic self, then you'll discover your path and shine your light on the world. You will assume your rightful place at the table, and I can't wait to cheer you on. Our entire community is rooting for you, because the world needs your truth.

As for the haters...well, they'll always exist. They can't help it. They're stuck in their limited perspectives, but don't allow them to make it your problem. The voices of narrowmindedness and exclusion have always existed and have tried to shout over everything else. We can make sure the voices of love and inclusion are just as loud, and even louder. That's the fight I'm in. If you want to join, I'd be eager to have you by my side. Until then: *Seek* yourself. *Find* yourself. *Love* yourself. *Be* yourself.

# Dee Dee Watters

## Trans Rights Are Human Rights!

**Dee Dee Watters** (she/her) is a Black trans woman who until recently lived in Texas. She is a prominent activist, performer, public speaker, and awardee, having been featured on TLC, HBO's *Vice*, The Travel Channel, AJ Media, and *Ripley's Believe It or Not*. She hosts the show *TransGriot Weekly* on Facebook.

I first recognized how exceptional she is during the town hall at a trans health conference in 2018 when she confronted someone in authority about an unexamined racist comment; I was impressed by her patience and willingness to constructively intercede between an upset audience of many hundreds and a resistant white trans woman of privilege. Her chapter demonstrates how her fierce spirit, even when in an environment of hate and violence, has led to self-esteem and political change. We know that trans women of color are at the highest risk of violence in the world at large and in interactions with police; this chapter highlights some of the amazing work being done to address this crisis. Be sure to exercise care of self when reading. www.transgriot.com; www. deedeewatters.com

I was a kid in middle school when a Black man was beaten and tied to the back of a pickup truck, then dragged to his death by three white men in East Texas. This was 1998 and we were in the same area at the time visiting my father's family, to enjoy country living and red clay dirt roads. I remember my family talking about the event and saying that it was wrong but that "Them white boys will get away with it."

My father and uncle pulled me and my cousins together and told us about being Black in the South and our need to be involved in change, that as we grew to become men (this was prior to transitioning) we held the responsibility to fight for our rights. They went on and on about civil rights, slavery, safety, and even the dangers of being Black when interacting with the police. They mentioned Martin Luther King Jr. and Malcolm X, but also told us we must never forget what was done to Black boys and Black men like Emmett Till and James Byrd Jr. There were many others whose names neither me nor my cousins had heard of, but as my uncle said, they were the ones you didn't learn about in school. I was frightened that it could happen to me or to any of my cousins.

A few years after that talk, the Texas James Byrd Jr. Hate Crimes Act was signed into law by Governor Rick Perry in 2001. It strengthened penalties for crimes motivated by a victim's race, religion, color, sex, disability, sexual preference, age, or national origin, but omitted gender identity and perceived gender.

Although the murder occurred in 1998, it was like it had happened all over again because the law was the talk of the school. Many of the teachers were glad that finally there were additional protections for Blacks on a state level, while others believed it wasn't enough and that it wouldn't change much of anything. It seemed as if many of the students didn't have the same talk as my cousins and I did with their dads or parents.

During transition I found myself homeless, a victim of unreported hate crimes, and definitely a victim of discrimination. One incident took place in 2007 while on the Houston METRO. Back then, a trans woman riding public transportation was almost guaranteed to have somebody say something smart if they "figured you out." On this specific day, right after I paid my fare, I went to find a seat and heard loudly, "That's a man!" Always quick to say something back, I responded with "Your mama!" The man immediately got up and said "What you said, faggot?" as I sat down. We exchanged words, the driver stopped the bus and kept telling him to go back to his seat or she'd call the police. He started to poke at me and I said "Get your finger out of my face, bitch!" He said "When I see a faggot slap a faggot, bitch" and then slapped me so hard my ears started to ring. I fought back as if I was fighting for my life.

We were pulled apart by the police and interviewed. Witnesses told the officers that he called me a man, faggot numerous times, and that he assaulted me first. The officers eventually told me that there was nothing they could do and that they didn't think it was a hate crime because he said I called him a bitch, and all I had were broken nails and some scratches while the guy may have had a broken nose and a couple of broken ribs. The officer went on and said, "I guess you showed him, huh? Under all that you're still a man."

I remember wanting to curse the cop out too, but I knew it would only make things worse. I said, "No! He needs to be arrested. He attacked me because I'm trans! That's a hate crime!"

He then said he'd need to get a supervisor because he didn't know what to do about that.

Within five minutes a supervisor arrived with an attitude. The first thing he asked was, "Why is this bus still here? Did you get witness statements?"

The officer said yes.

"Well, the bus can go," said the supervisor.

The officer then told the supervisor, "'He' [speaking about me] says this was a hate crime." Long story short, the supervisor told me, "Listen, you are still on the scene and the person you're saying committed a hate crime is at the hospital, so this doesn't look good for you."

I answered, "He assaulted me, and I defended myself! There were witnesses!"

He cut me off with, "So was it a hate crime or self-defense?"

I responded, "Both!"

He said, "I'll be straight with you, if you pursue this, we will have to arrest you both and METRO may press charges since you interrupted the trip and fought on a bus."

Stunned and pissed, I decided to drop it. I felt so unprotected because I knew the police should have done more. After that I went home and I cried.

Often we can't stop people from saying or doing things to hurt us, but we can do things to lift up ourselves and others. I decided to start writing and performing spoken word and poetry, telling my stories and those of the people I've met. It wouldn't change what happened on the bus, but I realized I could use my voice and talent as a tool to engage, to spread thought-provoking performances, and to help others understand the hurt I already felt. It gave me purpose. Being in front of a crowd means that maybe I'll change a life, and hopefully at minimum one person will be convinced that my Black trans life matters! I realized this was one way I could fight for myself that didn't involve breaking my nails.

Then I had the pleasure of meeting the remarkable Monica Roberts,[*] who became my sister and one of my best friends.

Monica was big on politics and lit a fire under me about advocacy work. She truly assisted me in understanding the importance of things being on paper and the reasons why my being seen and heard was necessary in politics. She told me that when we don't use our voices, we allow the bigots to say we don't exist! If we're not telling our stories, then who would? Some cis white person? Monica reminded me that if I spoke up for myself, I was doing it for all of us!

Thinking of all the assaults on trans people and trans people of color, I asked her, "Why the hell are they not using the national hate crimes language and winning these cases? Why are they dropping the hate crimes and pursuing other charges? The bigots will get more time for the hate crime." Monica then blew my mind when she explained how complicated it was to get a hate crime investigation started, let alone to get a conviction. She even informed me that there were no

---

[*] Sadly, Monica died on October 5, 2020, as the result of a blood clot in her lung.

protections in Houston like there were in Austin, Dallas, and San Antonio. Each city had enacted local nondiscrimination laws, but Houston hadn't.

All I could think about was the time I was attacked on the bus, and how the police did nothing. Now I understood better.

I really wanted to fix things. We heard that Mayor Annise Parker was looking to pass an equal rights ordinance. This was my chance to assist in creating change that could possibly save lives. Many of the local trans leaders came together to be sure that trans folks weren't being left out. Nothing about us without us! We went each week, and soon elected officials were calling me by name, not just while at city hall, but even out in the community. I was beginning to feel seen. Monica even noticed it and said, "See! I told you that your voice was needed!"

A few weeks went by and Mayor Parker introduced HERO, the Houston Equal Rights Ordinance. It was very similar to the national hate crimes legislation but it made clear that trans Houstonians had equal rights just like trans people in the other big cities.

You'd think that, since other places already had similar regulations, this one would have passed with no issues. Ohhh, we were fooled!

The Houston City Council votes on all ordinances, and testimony is welcomed for or against any issue. Both Monica and I were asked to speak, and of course we were on board. It was an opportunity to be pivotal in getting protection for everyone who looked like me, who had similar experiences to me, and who deserved to feel safe in Houston without discrimination. But hundreds of people gathered on the steps of City Hall protesting HERO, many of them chanting over bullhorns, "No men in women's restrooms!" Even though it wasn't about that.

As frustrating as it was to hear them shout out this foolishness, what happened next nearly broke my heart. A group of older men known as the Black Baptist Pastor Association attempted to use scripture to chastise trans and LGB folks by saying that God didn't love us because we were different. And they repeated that line that is still so popular, "God created Adam and Eve, not Adam and Steve!" Luckily, I learned at a young age that the bigotry they spewed was false and had nothing to do with me, but as a Black woman of trans experience who grew up in church, to see those Black Baptist pastors spewing hate not love upset me in a way I never imagined.

It reminded me of how cruel it felt when I was put out by my mother and went to the church where the pastors had said the door was always open, only for it to have been slammed in my face. During the HERO protests I felt so much hurt and disappointment seeing the Black "men of God" doing the exact opposite of what Jesus preached. My heart was torn all over again, but this time I wasn't alone, and I knew better!

Monica and I saw them surround a group of white trans folks, screaming scripture and backing them against a wall. I'd never seen Monica move so fast! Luckily both of us knew the Bible well, and we'd be damned if these fools thought they could bully trans folks and get away with it! We ran them off, just the two of us, by arguing in response with scripture that affirmed us and by standing our ground, making clear that that we weren't going to concede. But the highlight was seeing those trans youngsters lift their heads with pride knowing that Aunty Moni and Aunty Dee Dee had their backs! We fought the pastors on their own turf, and won.

The protests went on for a couple of weeks but eventually we did it...HERO was passed!

In May 2014, with Mayor Annise Parker's backing, the Houston City Council enacted the order in an 11–6 vote. We celebrated! I cried like a baby because now we had a HERO! We did it!

Monica blogged about it, saying:

Many of us on Team HERO had planned to go to City Council, thank Mayor Parker and the 10 council members who voted in favor of expanding rights for all Houstonians. But it looks like our haters also targeted this June 3 council meeting to express their HERO hatred. They were frustrated that Team HERO dominated the chambers and the speaker counts 447-98. Pro-HERO ministers outnumbered the anti-HERO hater ministers by a 2-1 margin and most importantly, we dominated the media optics during the HERO passage fight.

Note to the HERO haters. The city is still standing. The Houston skies did not see fire and brimstone descend upon it. The mayor and the ten council members who voted for passage didn't turn into pillars of salt. The sun has continued to rise in the east and set in the west. No Houston baker has been forced to bake a swastika cake against their will. Transpeople are using the bathrooms according to their outward gender presentation without incident.

None of your parade of horribles has happened short of y'all showing your nekulturny* asses and issuing death threats to Mayor Parker.

And you faith based bigots are STILL on the wrong side of history. You lied, you lost 11-6 and you need to get over it. Houston is a much better city because that ordinance is on the books. Your reprehensible behavior is our best evidence why the HERO needed to pass.[1]

She said everything I wanted to say, too.

For a few months Houston started to feel really safe, like if someone committed a hate crime, justice would be served. Most importantly to me, discrimination aimed at this Black body was not allowed.

Walking in stores, restaurants, or clubs that I never would've gone into prior to HERO passing and not seeing the sign "We Reserve the Right to Refuse Service!" made me feel like I was finally being recognized as a full person!

But it wasn't over, and though we'd fought hard, the bigots fought dirty. Over the next year they scared voters into thinking that trans women would rape little girls in restrooms, and on November 3, 2015, Harris County voters decided that Houston would again be a city where discrimination was allowed. I was so hurt seeing people change their minds just because of the lies these conservatives made up. Still, I was glad to see community leaders, elected officials, and business owners continue their support by implementing policies where they could, similar to the ordinance, so that trans people and others would feel safe while patronizing their stores.

We tried to find other ways. This time we joined with other trans

---

\* Urbandictionary.com defines "nekulturny" as: "Russian pejorative term. Literally means uncultured, but has connotations of white trash, chav, or naco."

and LGB Texans and decided that our focus would be to add gender identity and expression to the state's James Byrd Jr. Hate Crimes Act. We worked with Senator Royce West, but the proposed changes never made it off the floor. Still, allies are important, and he vowed to never stop the fight. He would always say that trans Texans were important and valued.

\* \* \*

On April 12, 2019, a large crowd gathered outside an apartment complex in the Oak Cliff neighborhood just south of downtown Dallas. The crowd anticipated a fight in the wake of a minor traffic accident.

During a verbal argument, a man began assaulting a Black trans woman, and several more joined in. The horrific video showed her trying to shield her face as they took turns kicking, stomping, and punching her unconscious. The crowd cheered and called her a man, a faggot, and many other transphobic and homophobic slurs. Dallas Mayor Mike Rawlings said the brutal beating looked like mob violence, and it most certainly was.

The victim was 23-year-old Muhlaysia Booker, who sustained serious injuries. They eventually arrested Edward Thomas for aggravated assault, not for a hate crime. To make matters worse, he was released from jail and the other men involved in the assault weren't even arrested or charged.

So what *is* a hate crime? According to justice.gov, hate crimes are "crimes committed on the basis of the victim's perceived or actual race, color, religion, national origin, sexual orientation, gender, gender identity, or disability."[2]

Although perceived gender and gender identity are included in the national Matthew Shepard and James Byrd Jr. Hate Crimes Act signed by President Obama, at the time we were living under Trump, who attacked us by using executive orders to overturn the progress we'd made over the past fifty years. The mayor requested the support of the FBI, but the FBI answers to the president, so that support never happened. Trump's racism didn't help, either.

Muhlaysia's LGBTQIA+ chosen family in Dallas had its share of community leaders, including my sister Poca (a Black trans woman) who was the founder of TransFusion, a trans-themed internet radio station. Muhlaysia was one of their first guests. On the show she reclaimed her voice to fight back, talking about the attack and the importance of advocating for the safety of Black trans women.

Soon after, Muhlaysia Booker was killed in Dallas. Monica wrote a blog post, which really explained how we felt:

This latest report of a trans murder in 2019 is not only coming from my home state of Texas, it is shocking and mindnumbingly sad for me.

23 year old Muhlaysia Booker survived a brutal April 12 assault by a mob in an apartment complex in Dallas' Oak Cliff neighborhood. Today it is my sad duty to report that Ms Booker was found shot to death Saturday morning by responding Dallas police officers at 6:40 AM CDT in the 7200 block of Valley Glen Dr. near the Tenison Park golf course in east Dallas.

Booker was pronounced dead at the scene due to "homicidal violence." There are also no suspects as of yet in her murder. I know where y'all can start looking, DPD. How about every transphobic fool that was videotaped throwing blows at her on April 12?

Rest in power and peace Muhlaysia.

This one's personal to me, her loved ones, BTAC [Black Trans Advocacy Coalition] and every trans Texan. As BTMI [Black Transwomen Inc] president Trenton Johnson said on my FB page, "They attack her in one month and then take her life the next!! This has to stop!"

I agree. It needs to stop. I want the waste of DNA who killed Muhlaysia to be expeditiously captured and brought to justice...

What is really pissing me off is that we are still sorting out the fallout from the transphobic April 12 mob assault on her in Oak Cliff and were engaged in getting justice for her in that case.

Now she's dead and her family is now planning her funeral.[3]

It was now imperative that trans folks be added to the Texas James Byrd Jr. Hate Crimes Act immediately!

Monica and I spoke with multiple state senators but spent the most time with Senators Royce West and John Whitmire. Senator West asked if anything was needed for Muhlaysia's funeral. Senator Whitmire extended his condolences and gave us his cell number, saying, "Know that I see you both as well as the trans community as humans. And I agree with something I've heard Monica Roberts say herself, and that is 'Trans rights are human rights!'" I remember Monica looking at me shortly after and saying that we made the right decision to come to the capitol when we did.*

Just days after Muhlaysia Booker's funeral, the two senators both said her name and followed it with statements to honor her on the Senate floor. "She was beaten, just because. She was murdered, just because," Senator West said during a speech that Thursday evening. "When will we move past 'just because'? Transgender rights are human rights." West concluded by saying, "I'd ask that when we adjourn that we remember the name Muhlaysia Booker. M-U-H-L-A-Y-S-I-A. Because I'll never forget it."

Senator Whitmire pointed out that gender identity is not a protected category in the state's hate crimes law and urged lawmakers, who were about to close out their biennial session, to change this when they next met in 2021. It didn't happen.

Although we didn't get gender identity, perceived gender, or gender expression added to the James Byrd Jr. Hate Crimes Act of Texas, we did put a face and name to the incident and publicly expressed the urgent need for these changes. State officials were now aware of the Muhlaysia Booker mob attack, and the video went viral with people learning that only one person was taken in custody and that he was later released.

Following the murder, Poca and many others saw how the system failed Muhlaysia, and we could only imagine how many others had similar stories.

Another way Poca and others helped was by opening the House of Rebirth, a temporary shelter for Black trans women of Dallas and

---

* Our trip was sponsored and supported by Transgender Education Network of Texas (TENT); an organization that has my support and my love as they continue this push for trans equality every day.

surrounding areas, which has assisted so many in turning their lives around. Many earned their GED, became gainfully employed, broke habits of addiction. This project shows how safe and affirming housing can dramatically impact the lives of Black trans women.

Muhlaysia's mother started an organization in Muhlaysia's honor and became a strong ally for the trans community. She told both her story and that of Muhlaysia herself, talking passionately about the importance of supporting your Black trans child as a Black mother. This message was so important to me because I have always wondered what it would have been like if my own Black mother had supported me. Would my life have been different if I'd experienced that closeness? To the parents of trans kids: Please simply love and support your child.

I've given myself the right to live authentically. Although it's been a hell of a journey with lots of lows and some amazing highs, transitioning and living in my truth as an unapologetic Black woman of trans experience has been the greatest gift of all! So be the best you that you can be! There will always be haters attacking our trans bodies and our equal rights, so we must fight back, because only that way can we stop this nonsense. Tell your story and contact your elected officials via phone, email, written letter, or in person! Find an Auntie Monica or Auntie Dee Dee to help you along the way! Continue to live!

And most importantly, let them know you exist and that you demand your equal rights!

# Mashuq Mushtaq Deen

## Liminal Spaces

**Mashuq Mushtaq Deen** (he/they) is a trans man and child of Indian American, Muslim immigrant parents. He is a 2018 Lambda Literary Award winner, a 2020 Silver Medalist for India's international Sultan Padamsee Playwriting Prize, and the first runner up for the Woodward International Playwriting Prize. His publications include two plays, *Draw the Circle* (Dramatists Play Service)  and *The Betterment Society* (Methuen Books), as well as short stories and essays, which have been published in the *Journal of Asian American Studies*, *In the Margins* (an online publication of the Asian American Writers Workshop), and elsewhere. In the chapter below he shares a touching story of intersections: of race, sex, gender, faith, crosscultural and intergenerational expectations, transphobia, compassion, and love. Please note this chapter includes explicit discussion of suicide.

We came to know each other through this book, though I'd read some of his pieces in the past. His works, bringing trans and other marginalized identities to the page and the stage, have never failed to inspire me. www.mashuqmushtaqdeen.com

### i. complicated gifts

Being transgender is not the most important part of who I am. It feels like a very small thing, actually. However, my journey to manhood has been...*scenic*. First I had to fight myself, and then I had to fight the culture around me. There were no directions on how to get there, and nowhere near the amount of information that is now available online—and so a lot of bushwhacking was required. It was a hard path. And yet, on the other side of the struggle, there were complicated gifts to be found.

As an Indian-American child of Muslim immigrant parents, I feel that I am expected to see myself (and all South Asians) as oppressed by the white dominant culture—the culture of white supremacy—and to rally with my Brown siblings. But this is complicated for me, since my family was where I faced the most rejection, where I experienced exile, and it was friends and mentors, many of whom were white, who gave me safe harbor. This was true in my small Connecticut hometown, and also when I went to college in the 1990s. Even at my diverse New York City college, the South Asian student group spaces were overwhelmingly heteronormative and Hindu-centric, and I did not feel welcome there. And yet, of course I know that my Muslim American family faces danger too in the world we live in. Increasingly so. Racial discrimination and bias are real, and my family has experienced them both during their five decades in this country. But I am not like my Asian American friends who felt racial tensions at their high schools, who felt they were treated as outsiders by those around them, the danger coming from outside of their family unit. For me, as I became increasingly more masculine, increasingly more independent, the danger came from within my family, from gendered cultural expectations that girls behave and look a certain way, from an increasing anger (and very real confusion) that I was not meeting this expectation. And so, in the mostly white, two-stoplight town where I grew up, it was to mostly white friends and teachers who I turned. And I was fortunate. They were good to me.

But how to reconcile this dilemma? How to reconcile that the people who hurt me most were also the people who loved me most, and whom I loved more than all others? How to reconcile the many white people who were there for me when they didn't have to be with what feels like a call to choose the "oppressed Brown side" over the "supremacist white side"? How to navigate a world without an easy bad guy to hate, without someone to *other*? For me, there is only complication and nuance. There is only love and hurt. I believe there is a great and painful gift wrapped up in this experience: We do not choose our families and we do not always agree with them, but we love them, and for the most part, we cannot really choose that either. It happens before we are rational beings, before children know they are separate from their parents; before parents fathom that their children will leave them. Maybe some of us will hate our families, but really, that's just another facet of our love.

And so, what a place to practice love! (Love being a verb, and not a noun.) However my family treated me, however much their silence and their exile hurt me, I was close enough to see other things: that they were good people, if not always to me, then to others. That they came from a different culture and time. That they sacrificed their own comfort to help their family in India, to quietly donate their money to charity. That they were shy people, still uncertain, uncomfortable to take up space in this country that had been their home for decades. That they were sometimes treated unfairly because they were Brown, and that they sometimes talked about other people in unfair ways because of race or economics. That they were capable of changing these ways of being, that they were capable of shifting their views on politics, on inequality, and eventually, on me.

What distance had they to cover to change those views? They were not poor by Indian standards, but they grew up in a different time, a different place, and with a different set of expectations. "My father walked uphill to school, both ways, in 100-degree weather, in the snow, in India." I'm being facetious, but I am also not. Perhaps growing up in India in the mid-1900s and then having a child who is transgender *and* an artist *is* a little like climbing uphill to school both ways in the snow in sweltering weather.

And this is not to excuse poor behavior. The point of this narrative isn't about excuses, because life isn't about excuses. It's about limitations. About flaws. And sometimes, about transcendence.

It is a child's naïveté that causes us to see our parents as gods, as infallible, as doing the right thing or wrong thing on purpose, rather than because parents are faulty humans lost in the dark of a new time and a new and evolving culture. Parents do not help matters, they do not admit their flaws and limitations readily. They are fearful of losing their authority and respect, and maybe also the adoration and love of a child. And so, as we get older, we children both judge harshly our fallen-God parents, and also cannot stop our desire for their approval.

And so it can take us a very long time to grow up.

We think the infallible parent is possible, even if our parent failed to live up to their promise, and we then undertake the self-defeating journey ourselves.

And so it takes even longer to grow up.

## ii. the first moment

There are two moments in my life when I grew up. The first was the day I tried to end my life. I was 21 years old.

At 17, I was a high school valedictorian headed to an ivy-league college. By the age of 20, I had dropped out because I could no longer function: I couldn't understand what was happening in my classes, I couldn't meet deadlines, my personality was fragmenting, and I was increasingly more self-destructive—and though I tried to hide all this, people noticed. I was put on a medical leave and sent back home to Connecticut, where my depression got predictably worse. I was hospitalized twice, in short-term facilities, before beginning treatment at a long-term hospital in western Massachusetts. (I owe them a debt of gratitude.) I had been there about ten months when my parents, dissatisfied with how my treatment was going, put a date on when they would pull the plug on funding it. As medical doctors, they did not understand psychoanalysis; in their minds, doctors were supposed to tell the patient what to do and the patient was supposed to do it and get better. I, however, still had a shaved head and I hadn't stopped being queer, nor had the hospital made any attempt to stop me from being queer, and so from my parents' point of view, I had not gotten any better.

With the date of my departure fast approaching, I felt trapped. I did not believe I could keep the suicidal feelings at bay outside of the hospital, and in a little over a month, there would be no more hospital for me. I was wearied by the struggle to stay alive. I felt I had lost the battle.

One morning, I packed my laundry into my car and drove myself north, with no particular destination in mind. I checked myself in at a Motel 8 in a nothing stretch between Northampton and Brattleboro. I did my laundry. I wrote a goodbye letter. I had dinner. I looked at all the people going about their lives as I ticked off the hours left in mine. After dinner, I went back to the motel, put a warning note on the bathroom door for housekeeping, and then, standing in front of the sink and looking at myself in the mirror, I tried to find an artery in my left wrist with a hefty shard of glass from the ashtray I had just broken.

It's hard for me to describe this moment so you can understand it. It is a moment when I was compelled to let everyone go, all of the people I loved and had disappointed and would disappoint again by ending my life. I also let their expectations of me go: I was not and would not ever be the child my parents wanted; and I was not strong enough to stay alive, to keep fighting this fight for my therapists. It was a moment when I gave up the struggle, the fight against myself, when I admitted my inability to meet my own expectations, my own demands. I admitted my limitations and flaws. I accepted them. I could not be greater than I was. As I was bleeding into the sink, I surrendered to my human fallibility, to my ordinariness.

I forgave myself.

How did I do it? This is also difficult to explain in words. When I let go, finally, of everything. When all of the encumbrances of other people's expectations fell off of my shoulders, there was a small voice that remained, a quiet voice that I could finally hear now that the room had gone still. And this voice was, to me, God, or the part of God that is my soul, or an echo of me from the future, or the vast well of the universe showing me something—I can't define it for you. All I can say is that from this voice I felt kindness. I felt a love that was unconditional, that required nothing of me. And this allowed me to forgive myself for being the flawed, imperfect person that I was, and, at the same time, there was nothing to forgive, no need for forgiveness.

That moment changed everything about my life afterward.

I would have to forgive myself again and again, of course, over the next many decades. But whereas before the well-worn path led to failure, now I was beginning, one step at a time, to wear a new path—to forgiveness. Maybe that sounds trite. But let me just say that warriors fall at the gates of forgiveness. Because the hardest person to forgive is yourself.

It was not magically all over. My depression would be a struggle for years, every year better, but still a challenge. My relationship with my parents would be hard for two decades. But I should have died that day. Every day afterward has been extra time. My desire is only to live it well. Not successfully, not ambitiously, but *well*. Worthy of the kindness that came to me that night.

### iii. the second moment

Things with my family were rough into my late 30s. During that time, I was exiled twice. The first was after I physically transitioned: my voice changed, my beard grew, and my family wouldn't see me for almost two years. But the second moment in my life when I grew up came after the second period of exile. Things had been going passably well for a few years, but then a cousin in India had invited me to her wedding...and things stopped going well. However much my parents tried to keep me a secret, social media was the great secret-breaker; all the cousins were connected online, we were adults, we were making our own decisions. So it was that I (and my partner) were invited to my cousin's wedding, and we found ourselves planning a trip to India. That is, until we were *uninvited*. My mother and her sister had interceded and our invitation was revoked.

By this point, at 38, I was used to being invited, then uninvited, and very occasionally *re*-invited to family gatherings. But used to it or not, it had taken its toll. And this meddling, outside of our immediate family, finally crossed a line inside of me. No formal declaration was made—and my cousin's wedding was her own, I wouldn't interfere—but there was a phone call where I said, "You have no right to interfere," and they responded with, "You don't understand how it is." After that, I did not call and they did not call, and so no one called. For two more years.

And again, like many times before, I was angry, hurt, confused. I couldn't wrap my mind around it. I knew they were not bad people; they had even come to accept my gender—perhaps with caveats—but they had traversed cultural distances for me. And yet the way they excluded me from the family—and the way the family allowed it to happen—I could not fathom treating someone I cared about this way. And so, in some very deep place, I was trying to figure out what I had done that was so wrong that I deserved this. Wasn't I a good person? I certainly tried very hard to be one. Then why else would they do it? Around and around in my head it went. Even if my head understood that they were afraid of something, my heart could not reconcile it.

Sometime during this period, I was involved with various Asian American queer advocacy organizations. I remember going to an event where parents, who looked a lot like my parents, talked about supporting their queer and transgender children, but instead of feeling hopeful about the culture shift that was happening, I felt despair. Their parents could love them; why could my parents not love me? I knew there was nothing wrong with being transgender or queer, nothing wrong with me...and yet, there must be *something* wrong with me, otherwise why would my entire family have agreed to cast me out?

It would take a long time for me to really understand the ways in which children (and all of us) would rather blame ourselves for the poor treatment we receive, because if we have done something *wrong*, then there is a chance we could next time do something *right*. By blaming myself, I was holding out hope that this world was still one in which I could exert some control. The truth of the world—that suffering comes and we cannot stop it, that it is out of our control, that the world is unpredictable—is the more unbearable option. The mind would prefer to blame itself.

During my two years of exile, my partner and I weren't invited to any weddings, but we *did* go to India and we *did* manage to see a few rogue relatives who were willing to see us. My mother would secretly call whoever we happened to be visiting, this uncle or that one, and give them instructions not to take us out in public, not to let anyone see us. She never asked to speak to me. At one point, I even got to see my grandmother, who was very old, and her hands were just as soft as I remembered, and she was just as tiny and round. But when we left, she pulled me aside and in her broken English she warned me not to go to the family's hometown, not to be seen by anyone there. I pretended not to understand.

That was the last time I saw her alive. She was a remarkable woman, a loving mother who raised eight children, whose husband died young, who did not receive more than a sixth-grade education, yet taught herself to read basic English, who traveled from her small village in India to the biggest city in America to be with her daughter when I was born. And she was also limited by her times and her ideas.

After that trip to India, there was one last phone call with my parents, which ended with us yelling at each other: They shouted that I was ungrateful and disrespectful, and I shouted that when they were ready to see a family therapist, they could have her call me. And then I hung up.

You do not hang up on your family in my culture. You do not even speak to your elders in the wrong tone of voice. These things are simply not allowed.

When I hung up, something felt broken. Irreparably broken. Something I had tried and tried to hold and save and protect, and even if it wasn't great, I tried to make do with it—this thing that was now broken. I had been so afraid to lose them that I had put up with too much, and that had confused me and made me resentful, and I had felt somehow that it was all my fault. And even though this "too much" was a poor substitute for the relationship I wanted with them, it was *something*, and something was better than nothing. That's what I thought.

What a cage we were stuck in with each other! They constantly disappointed me. I constantly disappointed them. Or maybe it was more than disappointment, maybe I threatened them, confused them, scared them. As a transgender man, I was going places they did not understand and they could not keep me safe. And something that I would not understand until later is that almost more than love, parents feel a great fear that they will not be able to keep their children safe. I wonder if sometimes it might seem preferable to hurt a child in a known way than to allow the child to be at the mercy of unknown hurts from unknown sectors.

Because I am me, because I had almost died once and for the rest of my life would feel that life is something uncertain and fragile, I did not want my last words to my parents to have been said in anger. They are only getting older. I am only getting older. We are only running out of time with each other. And so I wrote them a goodbye letter. It was not unlike my suicide letter in that I had to admit things. *I cannot be who you want me to be, even if I wanted to, I don't know how to do it. And I can see that you cannot be the people I want you to be, either.* I forgave myself and I forgave them.

So I grew up again. My parents shifted from God-parents to people-parents. They became flawed humans doing the best they could, which sometimes wasn't good enough for me. I didn't know how to want less and they didn't know how to give more. I allowed them their humanity. I stopped needing their approval. I let them go.

How did I do this? Is forgiveness a choice? Could I choose to forgive them? Could I choose to let them go? I don't think so. In much the same way, we didn't get to choose whether we would love each other or not. We are, most of us, woven into the people who raise us, and they are woven into us, well before we have any choice in the matter.

Something in the heart had to let go. And because I was holding on so hard, so desperately, something had to break in order for me to let go.

I believe something in our hearts must be willing to forgive ourselves—for the irrational belief that if only we were special enough, lovable enough, *something*-enough, we would be loved. For the irrational belief that it is our fault. Children will blame themselves even for the worst abuses because, deeper than rational reasoning, it is preferable to think that they did something wrong, *and therefore next time they can do something right*; and thus might have some control over the hurt they experience. It is too hard to reconcile a world where hurt is unexpected and undeserved.

The complicated gift that I was afforded was to know the *other* as also the *loved one*. To come to know their fallibility and limitations, and to come to know my own capacity for forgiveness, both of myself and of them. Hating another keeps us tethered to them and keeps them in control of what we want or need. Forgiveness is not about excusing poor behavior, but about seeing what is human and limited. Some people can transcend their limitations, and some people cannot (yet). To the degree that we don't forgive people, or cannot forgive them, to that degree we are tethered to them and to the past.

And since forgiveness is not really a choice, not a rational thing the brain can decide to do, we must also learn to forgive ourselves for not being able to forgive.

This complicated gift of loving the people who hurt me most (and probably vice versa) makes me look at the world differently. Is not each person I encounter a similarly flawed, limited human being? If I knew as much about them as I know about my own family, might I love them in spite of themselves? Might I know where they feel vulnerable, where they feel scared, where they overcompensate with bravado?

I have made my career being a storyteller. I write stories for the stage. My job is to look at characters and to see what they try to accomplish in spite of themselves. How they attempt to transcend their limitations. Sometimes they succeed, sometimes they fail. But it is the struggle that is the most human, the most inspiring. Not the succeeding.

Sometime after that goodbye letter to my parents, they came back on their own. We have a different relationship now. Perhaps I finally learned how to grow up. Perhaps the irreparable break made space for something new to be born.

## iv. liminal spaces

At the beginning of this essay, I said there were two gifts to come from my journey. If the first gift is the complicated nature of loving people who hurt me and hurting people I loved, the second gift is a transposition of the first: To be transgender, for me, is to stand on a bridge between the Isle of Woman and the Isle of Man. These worlds, histories, categories, boxes, encampments, are horizons in the distance. And I am both of these, historically, physically, emotionally. I have spent 30 years in the body of a woman, and 16 years in the body of a man. (The man is catching up, but the woman had a head start.) This bridge, this liminal space, is something I feel in my body. When we go to war with each other in the world, I feel it inside of my body. "Us and them." I can find no easy "us" and "them" divisions within my body. Everything is woven together. There is no division without ripping the threads that bind us together, that bind me together.

I am the child of immigrants, and so India is the place where my parents are from, but it will never be the place where I am from. And while America is my home, some Americans will never see me as American.

I am neither straight nor gay, but somewhere in the middle.

I have known poverty and government assistance, and I have known wealth.

These bridges, these liminal spaces, they are not just my home, they *are me*.

When people say "Men are..." or "White people are..." I feel these things in my body. These rips of the fabric. I feel that we are tearing away part of ourselves in order to save another part, but the fabric is weakened by the tearing. We see people as *others*. We *other* people the way we have been othered.

It is very human to do this.

But the complicated gift of being a bridge is that the ease of the binary is not afforded to me. Blindness to the other is not afforded to me. I am both/and.* I am me and I am you. I am all of it.

Every day I try to give others the kindness I would like to receive. Every so often, I remember that I deserve the same kindness that I give to others and forget to give to myself.

---

* Read more about the concept of "both/and" in the chapter by Colt St. Amand.

*Liminal Spaces* was written at the MacDowell artists' residency program.

# Chris Mosier

## Running, Away and To

**Chris Mosier** (he/him) is a white trans man who was called "The Man who Changed the Olympics." In 2015 he became the first openly trans man to make Team U.S.A. and was the catalyst for change of the International Olympic Committee's policy on transgender athletes. He is sponsored by Nike and was the first transgender athlete to land a contract with a major sporting company.

He still competes, trains others, and advocates for inclusive sports policies at all levels, especially during this time of unprecedented hostility. And perhaps he is most importantly a visible role model to countless other gender diverse people who want nothing more than to participate in sports like anyone else. When not fighting the good fight, he mentors transgender and nonbinary athletes around the world in hopes that he can live by his motto of "Be who you needed when you were younger."

We first met when he was an awardee at a Callen-Lorde gala while I was chair of the board of directors. We were seated at the same table, as were my mother and father, who were awestruck. Sometimes even chairs of LGBTQIA+ healthcare organizations want to impress their parents. His website is the go-to source for information about transgender athletes in sport. www.thechrismosier.com

When I was a child, I didn't know I was possible. But I was determined to find out if there was a space for me—in life, in family, in sport, and in the world.

I was confident and independent until others told me I shouldn't be. I kept the illusion of confidence through high school and college, but in fact, I was running from family and close relationships, and mostly from figuring out how to articulate my identity to myself and to others.

It's fitting that running became how I express my identity, share myself with the world, and create change for others.

I've always had a very strong sense of who I am. I've just forever been...me, and it was never a problem until it was. Some people, mostly adults, would tell me, "Hey, little girls don't act like that" or "Little girls don't wear their hats backward" or that I shouldn't like certain things. I hated it.

When I was about seven, I became infatuated with skateboarding. Long before skaters were considered athletes or skateboarding was in the Olympics, I read issues of *Thrasher* magazine and watched Tony Hawk break new ground, dreaming of my own deck. I loved the freedom and self-expression, and while I wasn't seeing any girls skating in my neighborhood or in print, I didn't feel like skating wasn't for me. It may have been the lack of girls that made it more attractive.

The next summer, my mom caved when we saw a very used skateboard—a Tony Hawk model, at that—at a garage sale. I rode it outside our apartment for hours, and soon other boys joined me. Adults told me, "Little girls don't skateboard." I thought, "You're telling me that I'm a little girl, and I like to skateboard, so little girls skateboard." But again, I got messages that I should perform gender differently, or at the very least not draw so much attention to myself.

I internalized these lessons in ways that still impact me. In writing this chapter, I recognized that I still carry shame and fear about "getting it wrong." As a young person, I didn't understand the idea of gender constructs and heteronormativity, but I felt them heavily applied to how I dressed, how I moved, and what I liked.

From the time I could dress myself, some people called me a boy and used "he/him," and others had trouble assigning me a pronoun or a gender. I loved it. I lit up when called "he," though I had no words to put to the experience. I remember a time around age ten when I was shopping with my mom and opened a door for a stranger, who later was behind us at the checkout. I wore a black-and-neon-yellow shirt with a black hat on backwards and black shorts, an outfit that felt made for me. The person said, "Your son is so kind. Such a well-mannered young man," but my mom was quick to correct them, loudly declaring so everyone could hear, "That's a little girl!" I didn't understand why it upset her so much, but I got the message that being seen as male was wrong and something I should be ashamed of. Any secret joy I'd felt dissipated immediately. Throughout those years, I struggled to balance the elation with the messages that I should be embarrassed and work to correct my behavior.

As a child, I loved being an athlete because sports was a place where I was allowed to explore my gender. Maybe it was the protection of being on a girls' team that eliminated some of the superficial questioning, but on the court or the field, I felt freer than anywhere else. I was always active and thrived in having a goal. I found excitement in being able to practice and in seeing myself improve. But most alluring was that sports gave me an opportunity to excel. I longed to feel the acceptance that I assumed other kids felt, so I poured myself into athletics, where I was valued because of my performance and contribution. Sports was a level-setter for me.

At my small high school, most girls who played sports ended up playing two or three each year, including volleyball in the fall, basketball in the winter, and softball in the spring. I was around many of the same people year-round, and sports became what we could bond over, which was particularly important as we shared very few interests otherwise.

Sports allowed me to improve my communication skills, to exist with and to learn from people who were different. It forced me to better allocate my time between schoolwork and extracurricular activities. Most of all, it gave me the confidence to be myself, which was critically important as I navigated puberty.

I knew opposing competitors, fans, and sometimes even teammates would heckle players who are good. I felt proud when I was singled out for my skills, but I was still harassed because of my gender expression. Before the senior night basketball game, a celebration of those graduating, some fans yelled at me, "That's a guy! Number 32 is a dude!"

I was ecstatic! And terrified. There was nothing to warrant their comments, at least not in my mind: I had the same uniform as the other girls, the same ponytail, did the same warm-up exercises. But it was more than my outfit or hair: they were seeing *me*. Who I *really was*. I knew they were right, but those early moments of trans joy came through strangers' accidents and quickly turned to embarrassment when I realized that other people had heard too. This was another experience of the deep shame I'd internalized.

Still, I learned so much through playing girls' sports. Those lessons of communication, leadership, goal setting, patience, hard work, and dedication were important, yet the most impactful were persistence and resilience. Both of these skills I absorbed in sports and they continue to be integral to my existence as a trans person. In basketball practice, my coach would push us to our limits of fatigue and decision-making, then run one more drill to make sure we were prepared to execute our game plan while tired. This training also created a pattern where I would prepare for every potential outcome, a valuable ability for me as I thought through the possibilities for social and later medical transition. Being able to control all that I could was a learned skill that I still apply often.

In 2008, as I considered options for what my future may look like, I felt isolated and alone, despite being in New York City where I assumed it would be easier to find people like me. The opposite was true: I saw no one who looked like me, no role models or examples of the life I wanted to live. It seemed impossible. But though it felt lonely and uncertain, I realized there was no blueprint to match. In my own transition, I could become exactly who I wanted to be and knew I was, without having to follow in anyone's footsteps. It was both freeing and terrifying.

When I finally had the words, I was hesitant to come out publicly because I didn't see other trans men in the media or in men's sports. At the same time, I knew that I could only come out once because the internet is forever, so I thought a lot about how I wanted to do it, why I wanted to do it, and what the possible repercussions might be.

I was anxious about rejection, ridicule, being seen as less than a man, so I hid who I was, at times even from myself. I still lived in fear of "doing it wrong," something I share in common with many of the trans people I meet and mentor. It was difficult to see a future where I was not rejected by everyone in my life. I would have been the first trans person most (if not all) of my family and friends had ever met, and all I could imagine was losing them. I assumed I'd be fired from work.

I lived in daily fear of someone finding out and of not being in control of my own narrative, but I also lived in the fear of existing as someone androgynous and masculine. I was reprimanded for my gender expression after a security guard at work physically removed me from the women's restroom because another woman thought I didn't belong. Passing coworkers watched, exponentially adding to my embarrassment and distress. For years after, I only used the one single-occupancy restroom, and if it was occupied or closed, I just held it. Eventually I stopped drinking so much water and risked dehydration, in another attempt to avoid using the restroom at work altogether. Neither was healthy. Again, my experience was like so many in the trans community, especially trans kids in disaffirming schools.

I was concerned about all these things, but I was even more terrified I'd lose my ability to exist in the sports world I loved. Back then, there were no policies to follow. I had no idea how to be who I knew myself to be and to still fit in to the very binary athletic system. I wasn't sure if I could, or wanted to, compromise my passion to be more fully myself. Even when I knew I was trans and wanted to tell others,

I still delayed social transition for over a year and a half because I was terrified to lose my ability to compete.

After many discussions with those closest to me and many therapy sessions considering what I could and could not control, I decided to move forward. I couldn't see a space for me that already existed, so instead I'd make one.

Transgender and gender nonbinary people have existed across cultures and throughout history, but it took over two decades of my own lived experience to realize it was possible to transition and live as my true self. As I educated myself about the experiences of other transgender people, I realized that there was nothing wrong with me. And slowly but surely, I began to accept myself.

After I did come out, I felt a huge sense of relief, but also a heightened awareness of the challenges I would face. To control my narrative, in 2010 I wrote an article in *The Advocate* magazine discussing the first time I raced in an Ironman triathlon as my authentic self. Sharing my experience in my own words gave me the sense of control that I longed for: I could manage how others saw me, referred to me, and positioned me in this world.

I didn't know it was being published until the morning it was released, so I didn't have time to overthink it in advance. But when I got the link, I felt both exhilaration and dread; I reloaded the article every work break to look at the responses. There were many negative comments, from dismissive ones like "Who cares?" and "Why is this a story?" to more hateful ones misgendering and harassing me, like "You'll always be a woman" and "You can chop your tits off all you want but you'll never be a real man." I wondered why people I'd never met would wish me harm, but I also realized that my life had always been that way, from the days of strangers interjecting their thoughts about my clothes or mannerisms long before the internet. I clung to the affirming reactions instead. I felt prepared, or as prepared as I could be, for whatever would come next.

Coming out online is a one-time thing. The internet has a long memory, and I knew that doing it in an article would forever make me "The Transgender Athlete." It would also open me to criticism from those who had harsh opinions about the trans community. It was difficult; part of me wanted to quit my job, move to another state, and start over as the person I was meant to be. I wanted to be just an ordinary guy on the men's team. I wanted to run. But I also saw a huge opportunity to find some closure by being the person I wish I could have been when I was younger. I saw an opportunity to be who I had needed, the role model I wanted to have. I thought maybe it might also inspire others. And I knew that this decision would come at a cost—those bigoted comments were the price I would have to pay.

Those messages I'd received in my childhood, the ones telling me that my authentic self was not acceptable, were no different from the comments I still receive online. They are the same as the persistent rhetoric we hear in today's media and political landscapes: that trans people are monsters, that we are deceptive, that we don't belong. This is what I and other trans and nonbinary people hear each day. They are meant to intimidate, and they are exhausting.

How we are discussed in public influences how cis people think about and treat us. These overt and subtle messages of hate traumatize, most especially our already vulnerable youth.

During the year or so before I began my social and medical transition through the first few years into it, I experienced near daily harassment and criticism and a severe increase in anxiety. Beyond a growing fear of using any public restroom after the incident at work, I also developed a low-level fear of groups and, oddly enough, of children, who have no filters on what they say. Kids would ask their parents about my gender in supermarkets and restaurants. Again, it felt like a win, but it also felt extremely unsafe when kids called attention to the fact that I clearly didn't fit in. Sport was again my refuge, a place where I was loved and supported because I was a great teammate, coach, and leader. Outside that bubble, I moved through the world hypervigilant about what I might be doing to prompt the ridicule from passers-by and other strangers. Leaving the house at times took a Herculean effort. Pretending like the "jokes" didn't hurt took even greater resilience, and sometimes acting.

At the gym, I felt too nervous to use the men's locker room but was already experiencing harassment in the women's. I tried to arrive already in workout clothes, but it wasn't always possible. While playing in a just-for-fun dodgeball league in New York City, I asked the clerk if there was a private area where I could change. They told me there were only two options, the men's and the women's, and that I "just needed to choose one." Both felt unsafe, and I weighed my options as my teammates and friends passed me by in the lobby. I was ultimately told that I could change at the McDonalds down the street. They asked me to leave, and I was utterly humiliated and vulnerable at having to explain to my team why there was no safe place for me. I was overcome with sadness and rage.

This wasn't unique to me. Transgender and nonbinary people in the United States and elsewhere experience discrimination and violence on a daily basis. Transgender people broadly are twice as likely as cisgender people to experience poverty; for transgender women of color it is nearly four times as likely.[1] Trans people are at a higher risk for homelessness, unemployment, and mental health issues.[2] Even though transgender adults make up only 0.5% of the U.S. population and 1.4% of youth are estimated to be trans,[3] 72% of reported hate murders against LGBTQ people and people living with HIV in 2013 were committed against transgender women,[4] and assaults against our community in the recent past have continued to escalate.[5]

In many states, there are no legal protections against discrimination based on gender identity or expression, meaning that transgender people can be fired from their jobs, denied housing, or refused service simply because of who we are.[6] Moreover, lawmakers across the country have introduced "bathroom bills" that would force us to use facilities that don't match our genders, putting us at risk yet again for verbal harassment and physical violence.

We also see legislation to bar transgender people from sports.[7] I have been a very intentional advocate for more inclusive spaces, so these bills have really hit me hard. A young trans girl in Kentucky helped create a girls' field hockey team since one did not exist; after Kentucky banned trans athletes, she could no longer participate on the team she helped create.[8] Worse yet, she was the only known transgender athlete in the entire state, so the ban impacted her alone.[9] There was no large group of trans people with an already discredited "competitive advantage" against cis opponents, nor a single instance of a trans athlete assaulting a cisgender boy or girl in locker rooms. Her story makes me wonder what my childhood might have been like had sports been taken away from me. The idea is devastating, and it's even more painful to watch a youth experience this in real time.

In 2013, I started www.transathlete.com, a compilation of trans-inclusive policies. For many years, I saw more and more inclusive guidelines created around the world. My goal was to give other transgender athletes a resource to know their options and to feel connected to a larger community, also to help cis people learn how to meaningfully balance fairness and inclusion. But in 2019 I began noticing a backslide, with a spike of anti-trans lawmakers and hate groups seeking to keep transgender people, specifically trans women, out of sports.

The first state in the United States to ban trans youth from school sports was Idaho in 2020.[10] Following that, a wave of bills was introduced in over two-thirds of the country.[11] In most states, lawmakers could not name a single trans youth in sports in their state nor an instance where there was any reason to bar them.[12] In other states, the bills targeted just a handful of youth.[13] Sports quite literally saved my life as an adolescent, and the thought of another young person not being allowed to have the same experiences is absolutely heartbreaking.

Following the sports bans came attacks on young people's ability to access gender-affirming care and attempts to prevent trans people from being able to get identification papers that matched their identities.[14] Sports was an issue to test the waters. Given the well documented lack of problems with trans participation in school sports, this is not about sports, just as it is also not about medical care or IDs—it's about creating barriers to prevent transgender kids from becoming transgender adults. And barriers to the trans community existing at all.

Politicians have weaponized trans identity as a political and partisan issue. Many people forget that trans people are real, living, breathing people; as a society, we need to remember the humanity of all transgender people especially now, as our community faces ongoing assaults.

As a transgender adult, I've made it my mission to fight for my community and to share my joy. These bills send a cruel message that transgender people are not welcome. They call into question who we are. They reflect outsiders' desperation and the belief that they have the authority to control our identities. They influence those who haven't met or don't know someone trans. The media covers us as an "issue" or a topic of debate, which further divides "us" from "them" and results in even more threat and harm. The challenges facing transgender people in the United States are significant, and we must continue to fight for our rights and dignities every day. I will not stand for it. I share my moments of happiness to provide hope for others.

I've struggled these last few years. I've woken up exhausted and angry. I've gone to bed numb. I've wondered why I should fight for youth sports when trans women of color are being murdered. But I also believe that sports can be a vehicle for social change, and that change can happen when sports are where the dialogue begins. As an athlete, if I don't rest to properly recover, I'm likely to burn out, experience injury, and lose my love of what I do. Days off and self-care are just as critical to my activism. Because this is my daily job, it can be challenging to separate the horrible news from my personal life, so time away from the awful world affairs, the transphobic media, and social media altogether are essential. Taking care of yourself makes you better able to withstand the challenges of being transgender or gender nonbinary in a world that tells you that you shouldn't be.

Whether it's being misgendered or being excluded from spaces, I've had to be resilient in the face of adversity. One of the most important things I've learned is to build a support network. These are the people who understand what I'm going through and who can offer advice and nurturing; having them to call on has given me strength in times when I haven't been sure I'd make it alone. In many ways, this personal safety net is my life team, similar to my teammates in sports: they have my back, they want me to succeed, and they root for me always.

It's also important to find allies who may not be transgender themselves but who are willing to stand up for you. These people can amplify your voice and create allies within their own communities.

Today, I am many years into life as my authentic self. I confidently navigate locker rooms and restrooms, I show up at starting lines knowing that I've created a place for myself, and I proudly wear my Team U.S.A. uniform like every other man on the squad. While I didn't see a future for myself when I was younger, I now know without question that it is possible to have the future I dreamed of—the confidence of knowing I do belong and of feeling secure in who I am. I believe that if you can see it, you can be it. We need real examples of success, which is why I think it's so important for me to be out and proud and visible as a transgender athlete so that other people know that they can do it too.

I want trans youth and adults to know there are others like them. And that there is a future for them in this world.

While there are challenges and obstacles that trans people still face, I am hopeful. Because we are determined. Every day is an opportunity to step into our truths, to be seen and heard as our authentic selves, to be resilient, powerful, and whole.

By being visible and by speaking out against discrimination, transgender and gender nonbinary people are helping to create a more inclusive world for everyone. I love being transgender. While I know my life would have been very different if I had been assigned male at birth, I am so grateful for the experiences I've had because they've made me who I am and have given me the perspectives I have today. I've learned and grown as a human. Being trans is a magical way of existing in the world that allows me to tap into a force that is beyond what most people can even imagine. My strength and confidence come from knowing that I am living my truth. Owning my identity has given my life meaning and purpose. And it's something that I wouldn't trade for anything in the world.

# Laura A. Jacobs

# ❶ Train, Downtown

This is my chapter, and I am a white trans and genderqueer kinky lesbian transfemme spectrum person who does female masculinity from an educated, middle class, suburban Jewish upbringing, whatever that may mean. My pronouns are she/he/they/none. To me, "genderqueer" refers to an active "queering" of gender, a deliberate and often political confrontation of gender norms to  raise awareness of the artificial nature of categories so often considered to be "natural." It is also a secret delight to watch others struggle to parse my identity. I am a licensed clinical social worker with the psychotherapy privilege in New York and a licensed clinical social worker in New Jersey. I work as a psychotherapist with transgender and gender nonbinary people, LGBTQIA+ people more broadly, and those involved in BDSM, consensual nonmonogamy, and sex work. Additionally, I do extensive public speaking, writing, and activism, was on the nonbinary chapter working group for the World Professional Association for Transgender Health (WPATH) Standards of Care, Version 8, and am a member of the Kink Clinical Guidelines Workgroup, which developed the first best practices for the care of those involved in kink, BDSM, and/or fetish eroticism.

I served as the first trans-identified chair of the board of directors for the Callen-Lorde Community Health Center from

2016 to 2020.* I have received numerous awards, including the 2019 Standard of Excellence Award by AASECT (the American Association of Sexuality Educators, Counselors, and Therapists). As Lawrence Jacobs, I worked in the arts as a musician, composer, photographer, and in rather boring corporate middle management. www.LauraAJacobs.com

Riding the subway through Manhattan, the day after the 2016 U.S. presidential election, I saw a gay male couple embracing one another in tears. We made eye contact, sharing a deep sorrow I felt as viscerally as they did. Even that first morning, I feared for my safety and my very ability to live given the possible loss of access to healthcare and the likely increase in persecution of trans and nonbinary people to come; throughout that administration and beyond I have been in continual fear about being put to death in a concentration camp as were my German Jewish great-grandparents and the great aunt Lore for whom I was named.** All I could offer those two men was a glance of solidarity, but the mental snapshot still fuels both rage and activism.

I was born when being openly trans was unthinkable. The 1970s, 80s, and 90s were decades where the old, tired tropes were all that was visible; the rare depictions I saw were of unfortunate, rejected, transsexuals-as-freaks, often desperate sex workers*** on the margins of society. I realized that coming out would only subject me to psychotherapy intended to "correct" my desires, and that medical care

---

\* I was on the board of directors from January 2011 through June 2021, serving as secretary from 2013 to 2016 and as chair from June 2016 to June 2020. Callen-Lorde's annual budget for FY2019 was ~$100M U.S.D.

\*\* Pronounced as English speakers would say "Laura." We have documentation that she boarded a train, perhaps to Auschwitz, in 1942. She was not heard from again.

\*\*\* I reject any stigmatization of sex work, but at the time, demeaning representations were all I saw.

would demand I pretend to be the "ideal" trans woman: fully femme presenting with no hobbies or interests implying a connection to masculinity, avowing a heterosexuality as female that I did not feel, abandoning everyone I knew to move to a new city where I could restart afresh. My inner, deeply repressed understanding of myself was that I was born in the wrong body, the victim of a genetic mistake I was otherwise powerless to fix, that I desperately needed hormones, surgery, or magical transformation to wake some morning as a girl. But the reality would have become a life of despair.

I have countless examples of internal and external transphobia.

It is 1974 or 1975, and my childhood self lies on his back beneath a children's playset chair as carpeting prickles my skin. The matching table stands to one side, overflowing with LEGO blocks, as the chair legs tower from my shoulders to my thighs.

I imagine *Star Trek: The Original Series*, where injured crewmembers are depicted prone with torsos covered by an angular operating structure as the physician performs within. Light and sound imply mysteries happening inside; with luck and post-post-postmodern medical science, the crewmember survives.

I'm also thinking of *The Six Million Dollar Man* featuring Lee Majors as an astronaut disfigured during a training mishap. "We can rebuild him. We have the technology. We can make him better...stronger... faster," says the introduction.[1] Experimental surgery transforms his body; he is no longer who he was. He is different. He is improved.

To my very young imagination, the chair is an approximate operating chamber and I have internalized the idea of an individual remade through surgery. In the two, characters metamorphose, butterflies from larvae, and my childhood uncertainty of the difference between "television reality" and "real reality" means I both can and cannot distinguish the objective world from fantasy. Maybe these are possible? I have the very clear thought, "If they can fix those people and make them better than they were before, why can't they make me into the girl I'm supposed to be?" But I know to keep silent.

At summer camp, eating soup when I am eleven, the boy across the table says, "You eat with your tongue like a girl." He doesn't mean any harm, but I'm so afraid my secret will be revealed that I immediately question everything about my posture, how I hold the utensils, and the movements I use to bring the food to my mouth.

One afternoon on the school bus I huddle against the window, staring idly out and hoping to go unnoticed by the bullies in the rear. It is sixth or seventh grade. I hear them talking, "If you're a guy, you make a fist and look at your fingernails with the palm up. But if you do it with your hand flat and your palm down, you're gay." They ask all the boys to look, row by row. When it's my turn, frightened they'll see me in any way associated with femininity, I do it the "manly" way and they move on. I panic alongside the relief. Sometimes my hyperawareness kept me safe, back then.

These memories still make me a bit uneasy, though I try to forgive my younger self, forty or more years later. I was so very young, still a child really, frightened of the world and with no self-assurance to speak up, no language, not a single role model to have provided distant, imagined support. How could I have been openly trans and lived an everyday teen life if "trans teen" didn't exist at the time? As a youth I am shy and ostracize myself, knowing that to reveal my secret, intentionally or accidentally, will only subject me to yet more ridicule than I already experience as someone Jewish and nerdy in a school almost entirely Irish Catholic that does not value intelligence or creativity. One Saturday while sitting in the passenger seat of my mother's station wagon, three girls from another town express interest in hanging out and I so desperately want to say yes but am completely flustered and give a noncommittal and vague response, so we never meet. I'm ashamed for weeks. Not very often but occasionally I look back and ponder what I might have become had I just said yes. Happier? Or would it have made me even more vulnerable? Even now, I recall the experience so vividly that I dissociate slightly in sadness. I desperately want to return in time and "fix" those few seconds, but the compulsion to undo my past trans-related regrets is a powerlessness I can never fully resolve. Now at my desk I pause and take several long breaths, and letting the emotions wash me like an ocean tide, I allow myself to briefly drown, submerged in the seemingly endless sorrow. I pause and remember. Then, while looking around the room to identify items and to remember that I'm an adult with agency and self-assurance, I intentionally relax my chest and breathe slowly out to sense my body flush with warmth as the emotions recede. And I remember to have compassion for my younger self who was so entirely consumed by fear. I sip at water, use the bathroom, and only return to writing this chapter an hour later.

As a teen I am confused, with no access to trans community or information. I "steal" my father's *Playboys*, knowing where he hides them and mindful to return them exactly as they were. I make certain to note whether they are face up or face down, between the third and fourth towels on the second shelf of the bathroom closet or underneath his notepad in the nightstand or between the mattress and the bedframe, spine facing in or out, about an inch back and a little left of center or sticking out a quarter to the right. I lust after the women, both craving them and desperate to be them. I know some women do have sex with women and I imagine myself to be one, but I've never heard the term "lesbian" and have no framework to understand experiencing both the "yearning for" and the "longing to be" at the same time.

When I begin medical and social transition it is my late twenties and early thirties and the external becomes more threatening. I obsess about passing, and I walk the streets presenting femme but on high alert and looking over my shoulder in trepidation, always unsure about how people view me. Is it safe? Am I passing? Or am I not, but people either don't look closely or don't care? I've heard so many stories of transbashing, I'm scared each time I leave my house.

I exit Callen-Lorde and turn south on 9th Avenue. It's early afternoon. Immediately I spot four or five larger, late-adolescent boys on a bench outside a pizzeria. I try to walk past and not make eye contact. I hear "It's a DUDE!!" and every muscle from my jaw to my anus clenches, trembling and panicked that I'm about to be the next trans statistic. The boys follow, only ten feet behind, shouting, jeering, throwing whatever they have. Something hits my shoulder as a glass Snapple bottle shatters by my left foot. I walk faster, they walk faster. I head toward a nearby school, hoping the teachers and security will dissuade them. At some point the teens vanish and I return to my car, lock the doors, and sob for an hour before being able to drive off. I don't sleep for two days. Other incidents happened as well.

Internal and external transphobia still arise in me even now.

Not many years ago I gave a lecture at a trans mental health conference, dressed in a navy-blue button-down shirt, purple tie, and a black vest with slacks and masculine leather boots. During the talk I briefly mention my identity as trans and genderqueer.

Afterward I'm approached by someone I read as a queer cis woman. "I got a lot from your presentation!" she says enthusiastically. I thank her. She continues, unprompted, "I have to say, I was really attracted to you until you said you were male assigned. Then I realized I couldn't date you. It was weird for me."

I haven't flirted nor asked her to coffee. Why does she feel a need to disclose this? Why to my face? And what about it being a trans mental health conference makes her conclude she has permission to question my sexuality, or to utter such a blatantly insensitive comment? *What the fuck?*

Sadly, I'd encountered this before and have again numerous times since, as have most transfeminine-spectrum people, whoever our desired partners are. For me, it is an agony each time a queer/lesbian-identified cis woman has announced that trans women are somehow "undateable," especially as transmasculine people with gender expressions similar to my female masculinity are so often seen as desirable. The dissimilarity is especially stinging. Many times it's been said openly, sometimes it's a slightly less overt "seeking a cis woman" or "women born women only thx" on a dating profile, and other times the sentiment seems present but remains unspoken. My strongly boundaried youth, social awkwardness, and fear of abandonment haven't helped, either. I experience visceral connection to my sexuality, but have too often lacked partners to express it with. I feel out of balance, hailed professionally but unwanted and unsupported around relationships, devoid of the touch I so desperately crave in the body I've struggled so determinedly to get.

I've labored hard to develop confidence through psychotherapy, experience, risk, and age. I also refuse to take on a narrative in which I am a victim, or "damaged and in need of repair," or that transition was a race to a predetermined finish line; instead, I am secure in my identity and body autonomy, even emboldened. I gradually proceeded through transition as an open-ended, nonjudgmental exploration where at each moment I questioned the alternatives and decided how best to proceed. Only through that process did I arrive at the gender I live today. It was *slow.* And arduous. And fraught with pain. And existential. And... imperfect. My gender is the result of grueling, conscious, intentional choice. I'm proud of who I am and I firmly reject the notion that any of us trans or nonbinary should be at all ashamed, but I'm not ignorant and I fully realize we are still so vulnerable, especially now.

Being in leadership has been trying. In June 2016, only a few months before the federal elections, I was appointed chair of the board of directors for the Callen-Lorde Community Health Center, one of the largest LGBTQIA+ health organizations in the world with the social justice-oriented mission of providing "Sensitive, quality health care and related services targeted to New York's lesbian, gay, bisexual, and transgender communities—in all their diversity—regardless of ability to pay."[2] I had no private practice clients that post-election Wednesday, but being in shock I was thoroughly unable to focus on writing for a previous book, so I walked through our multiple sites to provide a demonstration of strength. I had no idea what else to do. I reminded staff that our communities have survived adversity in the past and would do so again. We were too numerous, had too many allies, and had too much momentum to be swept aside, I said, only half believing it myself. I surrounded myself with community to feel less powerless and to keep from wallowing alone in my disbelief.

I was terrified. Even given my privilege as someone white, middle class, educated, and accomplished in an urban and progressive environment, if the administration removed all protections for transgender and gender nonbinary people, or legislatively redefined us into non-existence, how would I get hormones? Insurance companies would likely refuse medical and pharmaceutical coverage for a community disavowed by the government, so would I have to shop overseas for medications, if that were even possible? Would those packages be intercepted by customs? Or would I be merely one of countless desperate refugees to somewhere across the Atlantic, fleeing persecution as did my grandparents to a new land, frantic for healthcare, housing, and jobs?

I meet the executive director for lunch a few days later. We both acknowledge the countless ways the government might shutter such organizations overnight, through revising how gender and sexual orientation are understood by the federal government, or by recognizing gender only as chromosomal sex and by eliminating sexual orientation as a protected class...by them removing funding streams that are the financial backbone of all Federally Qualified Health Centers (FQHCs), which enable organizations like Callen-Lorde to serve marginalized populations with Medicaid, Medicare, and HIV, for sexual health, transgender health, women's health, healthcare for the undocumented, the homeless, those without insurance, and for so many other issues central to the needs of LGBTQIA+ people...by terminating FQHC status for all such LGBTQIA+ organizations...* I stare numbly at my salmon and she at her eggs, yet we promise together that Callen-Lorde will not be shuttered during our watch. It is a solidity I cling to through the rest of my term.

In my private practice, those first weeks after the election, clients and I bond in our shared agony as I am now even more clearly both their support and their peer, a therapist tasked with providing strength, reassurance, and teaching resilience while also an equally traumatized member of the community myself. They cry and I cry with them. At times, even in talk therapy, we lack words. I return home only to

---

* Many of these fears actually proved true; the Trump years saw attempts to redefine the nature of gender to biological sex, the removal of countless healthcare, housing, asylum, and other protections for LGBTQIA+ individuals, bans on the participation of trans youth in sports, a ban on transgender people in the military, and so much more. See the introduction chapter, and visit: https://transequality. org/the-discrimination-administration

scream incessantly and curl fetal in bed after hearing identical stories of disbelief, dread, and fear, session after session.

About a third of my clients are trans or nonbinary youth and adolescents who had only witnessed the advancements of the 2000s–2010s. They believed progress would be linear and ongoing, and how were they to know otherwise? To them, the results of November 8, 2016, suggested their lives would be unlivable; most had only recently come out and were still addressing acne, dating, and the beginnings of independence while simultaneously questioning their genders and already anxious about decisions that would have lifelong impact. Almost all were now panicked that they would need to flee due to increasing violence and the incoming administration's transparent intent to assault transgender and gender nonbinary people in all ways possible. They could only interpret increased oppression as an inevitable turn toward fascism and compulsory heteronormativity. Many expected to be dead.

I had the same fears, and was shaken by the intergenerational post-traumatic stress that I'd be herded to a camp and murdered by my own government as were so many of my grandparents' and great-grandparents' generations. I reminded clients that I faced the same situation they did, and revealed more of my internal life than I might have otherwise. Likely I needed them, too. Simultaneously, I attempted to portray a determination I didn't always feel in session and when speaking at conferences and in the media, again both "traumatized community member" and "confident expert." Occasionally I dissociated with clients, and twice I asked that they restrain their outrage at current events when I was already overwhelmed. Some moments I've had less to give.

Certain clients have challenged my very ability to provide care, like ideological conservatives who seek my help as a gender specialist. There have been several. They report voting for extremist candidates and rejecting that LGBTQIA+ people, people of color, and those from other marginalized groups are vulnerable. They argue that these communities have no need for protected rights, even when within these communities themselves. Some have praised politicians for supporting legislation to ban affirming care to trans youth. A few have been tormented by the conflict between identity and values, but most seem to think themselves immune, believing that their socioeconomic status, race, religion, or current/prior male privilege will protect them from consequences.

It's awkward. I get torn between my obligation to safeguard a non-judgmental environment even when their beliefs are an affront to mine and my hope that they might realize that their attitudes contradict their needs, at least as I see it. I so often want to apply a firm dope slap to the backs of their heads.

Would confronting these clients be a concern for their safety, an attempt to challenge their cognitive dissonance, or a plea from my inner activist for them to "wake the fuck up!!"? How can I reconcile my clinical judgment with my personal feelings? Fanatical right-wing trans people are a terrifying contradiction. How am I to sit with them, aware they support legislation to imprison me for providing help to others just as I have provided it to them? How am I to feel safe? These clients also represent a breakdown of the "us/them" wall: I can no longer depersonalize "them" since some of "them" are now in "my" private space and are also "us." The threat is now inside my world; with certain clients, I have been petrified every moment.

These issues have been a constant emotional drain, compelling me to question my philosophies of care, my boundaries, my decision-making, my professionalism, and my own reactions. Every new instance of political transphobia and interpersonal violence I spot on Facebook, Instagram, in the *New York Times*, or in the glimpses I have of TV news is another jolt out of whatever equilibrium I can sometimes find. I write this two days after Texas instituted policy legally defining trans youth healthcare as child abuse, investigating and criminalizing supportive parents, teachers, neighbors, and providers, and as Florida implements the so-called "don't say gay" bill, threatening teachers for references to LGBTQIA+ content in school. Other states are enacting similar laws and opposing trans participation in sports, all this despite the overwhelming scientific evidence documenting that trans youth in hostile environments have devastatingly high rates of depression, anxiety, smoking, substance use and abuse, obesity, self-harm, suicidal ideation, and even suicide itself. Or because of that evidence. It is not ignorance, but hate and the deliberate weaponization of trans youth in a larger culture war. I'm furious that a national women's health organization that invited me to speak just two years ago is now in 2022 holding its annual conference in Texas, despite protest from many about the state's aggression toward the poor, women, people of color, LGBTQIA+ people, and trans people ourselves. I feel livid and betrayed. Adding to this, COVID has only heightened my own distress, with me starving for in-person time alongside friends over pizza, and yesterday Russia invaded Ukraine, threatening world stability.

I've adopted the same coping strategies as everyone else. I regulate news intake, schedule online and in person experiences with friends (coffee hours, dinner hours, and boozy happy hours via Zoom), I (attempt to) eat and sleep consistently. I exit the apartment for walks (perhaps less frequently than I should), steer my convertible through tree-lined curves, and devour countless Oreos. I see a therapist of my own. I took a trapeze class with friends despite my glaring lack of agility. (My shoulders hurt for weeks.) I stream *The Muppet Show* while swathed in my Muppet quilt. I continue to confront bigotry. And I embrace two mottos for emotional survival: "Work less, fun more," and "Don't postpone joy."

In acting "as if" to staff at Callen-Lorde, with clients, when speaking, and for the broader community, I adopt some of that strength myself. Addressing my own needs while creating moments of pleasure sets boundaries and ensures my ability to be of service to others. My time with friends allows me to feel loved. And even from that initial Wednesday, I've drawn upon my rage to fuel my activism, speaking, and writing; that couple and I on the subway shared the most fleeting of moments, a few seconds of wordless exchange, yet so important was it as an experience of LGBTQIA+ unity that the sorrow, connection, and my attempt to provide support remain with me, over five years later. In that instant, it was enough.

All of these strategies I highlight when counseling my clients. Even occasionally revealing my own vulnerability to them is a lesson:

I demonstrate that while role models may sometimes feel fragile, we persevere, and therefore so can they.

My chapter encapsulates the overall theme of *Surviving Transphobia*: During the past administration and into these years after, I have been proud, despondent, livid, exhausted, defiant. As someone transgender and genderqueer who provides services to marginalized people and is visible to the public eye, my ire gnaws and yet I persist because the alternative would mean being complicit in my own destruction. My transition, my career, and even this book are personal acts of resistance, allowing me to fuck compulsory heteronormativity and to channel my indignation into empowerment. Because only through these strategies can I—and can we as a community—survive.

# Finn Gratton

## A Trans Autistic Vision

**Finn Gratton** (they/them) is a leading expert on the intersection of autism and trans identities, providing supportive, nonjudgmental psychotherapy to children, teens, and adults who find themselves "out of the box." Finn describes themself as "A momentary organization of waveforms, perceptually distinct, yet permeated by life that cannot be called Finn. To the trees they are carbon dioxide and a small hum. To their ancestors they are the next step. To the hologram of life that is perceived as early 21st-century human reality, they are white, autistic, nonbinary, parent, somatic therapist, writer, teacher, partner, friend, another animal that needs to eat and wants to play. In the future, they will be effects they can't imagine now." They have written and spoken extensively for providers and organizations and are a licensed marriage and family therapist.

They are someone I've known personally only for a year or so, but I've benefitted from their work for ages. And I've found Finn to be a warm, loving human being. Finn's book, *Supporting Transgender Autistic Youth and Adults*, is also available from Jessica Kingsley Publishers. As a neurotypical ally myself, our discussions have been an invaluable help for my own work with autistic trans clients, and Finn's language and cadence here has provided me valuable insight into the headspace of autistic people. www.grattonpsychotherapy.com

I'm going to sing my vision here. I'm going to sing what is possible, what is potent and pleasurable. I'm going to sing the spinning, rocking, flapping, humming play that is human, that is all of us, that is the universe playing with us, playing through us. I am going to sing the freedom (oh, the price we pay) of trans autistic people. I am going to lift up the saving power—the power I say!—of trans autistic people and their knowing, against all signs indicating otherwise, that the self, that life itself, can't be compromised.

Oh, we compromise or are compromised, just like everyone else, and, like everyone else, lose the thrumming pulse of here and now, get lost from ourselves, from life moving through us. Yet at the same time, we can't help it, we keep sticking out, we keep not doing it "right." A hand jumps, an eye twitches, a hum erupts. Life keeps moving through us. From our infancies we have been unintentional rebels against the colonization of our bodies, and we have paid for that rebellion since before we knew we were doing anything wrong. Some of us learned, through stick and carrot, to withhold, to draw away from life, while always knowing that the guard would slip, and with that slip, a piece of our personal wilderness would break over the bow. It would break and we would pay. We would pay in the coinage of rejection, of punishment and of shame. And that wild holy water of life that betrayed us would bless us too, bless us with remembrance of who we are, and what life truly is.

Some of us can't hold it back well at all, can't restrain the innate urges, the reactions to pain and pleasure, the irritation at the abrasions incurred at the interface with the domesticated world—not with the birds and the trees, not with the water that dances with us, but with the walls, the rules, the abrupt changes in rhythm. Those who pathologize want to divide us, spread us out along a spectrum. Those who can't contain their aliveness and their pain, who can't bridge the neurotypical interface with a neutral face or a nod, are labeled "low functioning" and "classically autistic," a conceit aimed to divide us from our kin and from ourselves. Transpose this to the socially accepted trans narrative, the one that places those trans men and women who most nearly represent cisgender (and white) people at the top of the ladder. "Low functioning" trans people?—they are the ones judged to be "doing it wrong," to not be "trans enough" to be real—the nonbinary, the agender, the gender fluid, the ones who can't or won't "pass" as cisgender. Everyone is lined up against the measuring lines on the wall, except the ones who can't make sense of all this measuring, the ones who keep wandering around balancing the stick on the palm of their hands, tapping out a rhythm on the floor with it, turning it into a sword and drawing it up then slicing through the air, the ones whose relating has nothing to do with acknowledging or creating a power differential, but instead are all about playing with life. I won't be divided from them. I'm going to balance my measuring stick in the palm of my hand and follow it until it falls.

If you say everyone is a little bit autistic, I say everyone is a little, more than a little alive, and that aliveness is splashed out in the world by the dancing hands, the rhythmic sounds, the wondering wandering of autistic people. It's an aliveness that disrupts, butts up against convention, bangs against the compromises made by those more easily socialized, those more easily domesticated. If the domesticated world could quit making trans people and autistic people wrong, diminished, pitiful, dangerous, and illegible, then oh, what life would come streaming through! It'd be the breaking of a great logjam, a logjam that traps not only the neuro and gender minorities but also everyone who has relegated the wilderness in themselves to some subjugated minority status in their own being. Does this sound crazy? Like some kind of gender fluid neurodivergent crazed vision? I say it is no crazier than the magma welling up under the crust. Life trapped finds a way out. We can open the doors or see what happens if we don't. It's happening anyway—all over the world the doors open and life rolls forth, and all over the world doors remain nailed shut and destruction ensues. Life moves, one way or another. If Pandora's box wasn't opened, it would have exploded.

In fourth grade I was slapped by Sister Marion for smiling. I was smiling at the wrong time, smiling at someone who had gotten into trouble for doing too much homework—a mistake Sister Marion had just discovered in *my* catechism workbook too. I was looking at the co-overachiever and relating!—which I didn't do very well then, so maybe it was a weird smile. And Sister Marion thought she knew what I was thinking. Of course, she thought I was making fun of her with that smile. She wasn't very good at relating either, but she had power. I was having what is called a paradoxical reaction, which means I was freaking out because I couldn't figure out this unpredictable situation, and instead of crying or collapsing, I was smiling. I was probably trying not to laugh, which back then and still just happens for me at most inappropriate times. Energy has to move. I guess the same was true for Sister Marion. She was having some kind of weird freak-out, perhaps triggering some trauma that probably first overtook her way before she became a nun.

Late-recognized autistic people play a mental game (or a parlor game, if the parlor is full of autistic people) of "that could have been a sign." That I was slapped in fourth grade for a weird smile and none of the other kids talked with me about it and I didn't have a way to talk about it—that was a sign.

We do the same thing when we don't recognize that we are nonbinary or trans until we are teens or adults. We go back and collect the signs. Always wearing shorts under my Catholic school plaid skirt? Sign. Being the only assumed female student in first grade not talking about dolls? Sign. Wanting to be a Boy Scout because they got to do the cool things for their badges? Sign.

Parents of my clients sometimes tell me they didn't see the signs. Sometimes their children didn't either...until they did. Then they look back and say, "Oh, now that makes sense." It's all more obvious in retrospect.

The thing is, for me those signs were nearly invisible back then because the assumption that I was cisgender and neurotypical was a brick-wall assumption. All the signs I could see were of a different kind—signs that were rules, rules that kept me from seeing the signs that I was nonbinary or neurodivergent. These signs said: "Stop," "Yield," "This way," "Do not enter." Some of them were clear to me and some were written in invisible ink, and a whole lot of them didn't make any sense at all. This isn't just a trans issue. This isn't just an autistic issue. This is an issue of colonization. Those signs are meant to separate—especially the invisible ones.

The Catholic school smile-slap story is an old story. It probably took place long before you were born. Our world is full of stories like this. Trans stories. Nonbinary stories. Autistic stories. Neurodivergent stories. Immigrant stories. Indigenous stories. Incarcerated stories. Pick your oppressed group. Maybe you've got thousands of these stories yourself. There are rules. You know them but can't follow them. Or you don't know them even though others magically do. On account of your incapacity and ignorance, you get slapped, shunned, shamed, thrown in jail. It would be less traumatizing to be in willful defiance: "Ha, I'm going to look you in the eye and give you my evil smile and you will slap me for it, and I will know I got to you for a moment." That would be less traumatic than my stunned silence, my "What the fuck?? Where did that come from?" It would be even less traumatic if we all simultaneously looked the Sister Marions of the world in the eye and made weird smiles. That would be fun. It might even shift the balance of power for a moment, and shifting the balance for a moment inevitably shifts the balance for the next moment. Maybe there would be retribution, but we'd all be smiling together for a while.

Sometimes we find we aren't alone after all. We see a TikTok, read a post, watch a comedian talk about prepositions and a box,* and pull ourselves up out of a globally orchestrated gaslight festival called Life as We Know It and announce our startling recognition that It Is All Made Up, all of it—gender, race, what is okay and what is not—All Made Up. If we get enough of us together, maybe we can pull down some signs, topple a few statues of famous rule makers, and begin to ask ourselves and others, "How did all this get started?" and "How are we going to change things?"

Before I leave the whole sign-maker, rule-breaker metaphor, I want you to grab your internet access device and find the fifth verse of Woody Guthrie's "This Land Is Your Land." Read it if you want,

---

* Hannah Gadsby's comedy performance, *Douglas*, reflected many autistic people's experiences.

but I really want you to listen to it if you can. Let your body rock, like mine. Like yours. We all rock. Rocking is normal. No, rocking is human. "Normal" just means it was made acceptable by the dominant group. So let's be human together. Let's rock and sway and hum. It's the verse we weren't taught in school—unless you went to a way cool school. It's the verse about the sign that says "No Trespassing" and what it says on the other side, and who that side of the sign was made for. (It may not be the first version your search engine brings up.)

That verse was made for trans autistic people. That verse was made for everyone who never saw the sign, couldn't make sense of the sign, or knew down deep that if they did what was expected it would just kill something in them. (I don't think "this land" was "made" for anyone. It just *is*, and isn't anyone's to have, but I don't think that's what Woody Guthrie meant.)

You may wonder how autistic people, who quite often are rule and routine bound, can also be such rule breakers. I, too, get really anxious about breaking rules. That's why I bought a T-shirt that says, "Non-compliance is a social skill." I'm trying to break that anxiety-driven tendency, the way the dominant society slipped past my cell membranes. The truth is, trans autistic people are natural-born scofflaws of unreasonable rules, especially unspoken, unreasonable rules. Many of us get really anxious breaking rules that shouldn't even be there in the first place, anxious because we're going to have to stand out again, anxious because we'll be subject to more abuse or rejection. Some of us get so anxious we glue ourselves to the rules. Often, a deeper ethic forces us to break societal rules, and then we are called a threat, or odd, or naïve, depending on the rules we break and the color of our skin.

I want to praise the power of that resolution, that strength of character burnished by being an outlier who is committed to the greater good, the quality seen clearly in Greta Thunberg. There are so many Greta Thunbergs. A lot of them are both autistic and trans, nonbinary, or somehow gender nonconforming. I know them: They are my clients, my colleagues, my community, my family, my teachers. They are people whose altruism doesn't feel exceptional, but feels simply what they should do, what everyone in their place should do. When trans people come together to meet the waves of attacks against trans bodies, trans life, please hold on to and care for the trans autistic. There are so many of us, of every race and gender and class, and we can be quite good at knowing what must be done, even when it's the hard thing to do. What must be done, first of all, is to hold all of us.

Researchers keep trying to ascertain how many there are of us trans autistic, trans nonbinary, trans-what-the-fuck people. And bless them, because those numbers send providers to trainings to learn the part they don't know. But oh, curses too, for all the people who took the higher correlation of autism and trans identities as some kind of evidence that all those "extra" trans autistic people were not really trans, couldn't really be trans, because the prevalence was so much higher than for allistic (non-autistic) people. They said, "It must not be trans, but 'autistic obsessive thinking'"; "It must not be trans, but (I kid you not) a love of shiny things and soft textures."

They are asking the wrong question. They see deviance and in deviance can only find improper deviance. The real question, as reframed by Reubs Walsh and David Jackson-Perry,[1] after analyzing past efforts to explain the high coincidence, is: *Why are so many allistic people also cisgender?* As soon as the question is turned, the whole device of pathologizing autism begins to reveal itself for what it is.

There can be no deviance without the creation of the norms. You and I know every time we cross a norm—though maybe not before we cross it. We find out soon enough. We have since we were babies. We shook our heads, threw our cups to the floor, stomped and said, "No, I won't." We cried in utter frustration and confusion: "Why are you angry at me?" Then the norms slid inside of us—because rejection, because punishment, because fear. For some of us, the norms didn't slide far in, but continued to abrade. We couldn't get comfortable. The fight between "I am" and "You mustn't" became constant. We became *other*. We became distressed, deviant, disordered, diseased, delinquent in the eyes of the ones who had swallowed the norms whole and mistook them for truth, accepting only the deviances allowed for "individual-ity," these small concessions divvied inequitably depending on race, gender, class, and ability. Go beyond the allowance and an example will be made of you. If you're a white, wealthy, cisgender male, someone might laugh or laud you for your eccentricity. If you're a Black, poor, trans woman, they will punish you, fire you, arrest you for disturbing the peace.

Now is time for a lament. Before I affirm again the hope that shines, the beauty and joy that is trans and autistic, nonbinary and neurodivergent, I call time-out for a lament. Light a candle, cue the keeners, resume the rocking, sing with me. Are you with me? We need to do this together—even if together is asynchronous.

We pay with our whole and truest selves for the imposition of white supremacy, for the colonization of body and mind. We all pay. Those who are directly targeted by these systems pay with their lives and freedom. Those who are dealt racial and other privilege pay with their integrity and clarity, and those who swallowed the norms whole push their undigested pain onto others, onto Black others, Indigenous others, immigrant others, disabled others, queer others. Any other will do. And in all this, for all of us, we pay with our joy, with our connectedness, with the ability to inhabit our bodies and minds outside the confines that colonization demands.

Here and now, let us lament the pain, the trodden beauty and joy of trans and nonbinary people, of autistic and otherwise neurodivergent people. Sing for us and with us.

Let us sing for those whose joints ache, bodies drag, minds fog after years of struggle and fear. Let us add our voices to their fury at every healthcare provider, family member, teacher, or boss who has told them they are fine, that it is just their depression, their bad sleep or eating or exercising habits, their failure at mindfulness or gratitude or gumption. We will moan for the many years, full of the accusations of malingering and "making excuses for your behavior," that it took to get the diagnosis, or the five diagnoses. Let us make a great echolalic wail of pain with those so disabled they did not have the ability to access healthcare that would result in autism diagnoses or medical support for transition, for the pain at the indecipherable healthcare system, the patient portal, the list of recommendations, the misgendering, mis-attuned office staff, and the refusal to consider needs without a diagnosis that could not be attained, or, if the diagnosis existed, the refusal to honor one's self-knowledge due to the delegitimizing of neurodivergent bodies, trans bodies, nonmale bodies, BIPOC bodies. Let us slam the door on the medicalization of difference that requires a diagnosis for difference to be acknowledged and honored. Let us roar the frustration of those who have given up on medical providers, who will not go back, who refuse to call or go to urgent care when sick because of the many times they went and came home with hopelessness and shame at their "not real" disease, plus a bill to pay for it.

Let us chant those missed diagnoses until everyone knows them, until we make them so real they can't be ignored: Ehlers-Danlos syndrome, joint hypermobility syndrome, postural orthostatic tachycardia syndrome, fibromyalgia, migraines, mast cell activation syndrome, multiple chemical sensitivity syndrome, myalgic encephalomyelitis. I've missed the ones I don't know yet. I've missed the ones they don't have names for yet. They are not rare. Not with trans autistic people. I've come to expect it. I say, tell me everything that aches.

While we're at it, let us cry for the doctors who have 15 minutes, who have 2500 patients, who didn't learn this in med school, who want there to be a list of recommendations that will make things better, a short list. It *is* a short list. Here it is: End white supremacy, and with it, sexism, ableism, colonialism, and capitalism. Let us cry for everyone who is trying to help, who needs to be held, who is burning out as fast as their trans and autistic patients.

Let us cry for everyone whose spoken and unspoken communication about their gender was made illegible, inaudible, inadmissible by the fact of the gulf between their communication and their providers' and caregivers' ears, eyes, and minds. Rage is a kind of grief, a grief fueled by the knowledge that it could have been, should have been, different. We rage with those who were turned away from medical treatment, from affirming clothing and language and love as their beautiful selves because a professional declared them intellectually or emotionally stunted, unable to truly sense their gender, leaving them to live in a body and presentation that makes them ache. We sing along with the pain and confusion of those caregivers strung between their child, their providers, family, and community, everyone warning them of dark and terrible futures whichever way they move.

We are singing with all the teens and adults at home, unable to leave, unable to work or go to school because they hurt all the time, because they are so tired, because there is no safe place, because no one is hiring someone like them, because they were fired, because they were molested or bullied, because they failed, because they were burnt out at 16, rallied and burnt out again at 20, rallied and burnt out again at 26 and they just can't get up again. We sing for those trans neurodivergent people whose home is a tent, a car, a sofa for the night, those without hormones, without assistance, without knowledge that there are others like them, without a way to find those others. We sing their lonely pain and hear the songs drift up from a million curled-up bodies.

We sing a requiem for those who did not make it.

Let us cry for the neurodivergent children whose caregivers don't believe their child is really trans because if their child *was* trans, then they would know that they had done their beloved child a decade or two of wrong, which they cannot bear to acknowledge. Let us cry for the parents who don't believe their child is really neurodivergent because their child is so much like themselves and *they* are not autistic, not trans, no that can't be. Let us cry for all the intergenerational pain packed behind that fear, so many generations, so many unmet trans and autistic ancestors.

And now we are at the center of this loss, the tragedy of the relationship that could have been, that everyone wants but can't make real, the sad reality that family and child must settle for something so much less. Let us cry for that child who depends on that relationship for a roof and food and somebody who cares imperfectly. Let us cry for how we know, no matter how good that home is, it will not last, that caregivers will get old, funds will become scarce. Let us cry for the parents who are afraid and for everything and everyone that made them afraid. Let us cry for the children who were able to leave and will not go back home, cry for the doors that have closed, and sing out for those trying to raise the heart and the will to knock, or to open the door.

Another chorus rises from concrete institutions, from the

incarcerated trans/nonbinary neurodivergent. Someday we may know how many neurodivergent trans people are incarcerated. There must be so many—you cross enough lines and a number gets painted on your back. If you're Black or Brown. If you're Indigenous, if you're poor, if they called it conduct disorder in school instead of autism or ADHD, there's a good chance you're going to end up imprisoned, and when you are also trans or nonbinary, that number on your back just gets bolder and brighter. Do you know we're singing with you now? Crying with you? Tears are rolling down.

Tears. Let there be tears. If you don't cry anymore because it's been too much, or it will be too much, or because testosterone dried up the tears but you have the same feeling, just not much salt water, never mind. Let there be a moaning, a growling. You've been carrying that visceral ache and didn't know how much was in there. I just threw more into the pot. Are you still rocking? You need to rock or sway or shake. It's colonization that holds our bodies stuck, stuck in the seat, in the line, in the form, in the norm. Grief doesn't hold form. They teach you that at hospice. Everyone grieves in their own way, in their own time.

Now is a good time. We are here with you. All the people reading these lines. And the person writing them. I've got clients. I've got family. I've got caregivers, all in my heart, making me rock side to side, front to back, making me cry. You know people too. We're all together now in this sorrow, in this fury, in compassion, because we're part of it too. We thought we knew something because someone taught us so. Once we thought there was a way trans looked and acted, thought we knew how autistic looked and acted. We were afraid. We let the norms into ourselves. We couldn't help it. We made others wrong. We made ourselves wrong. We still do it. It will take generations. It has taken generations. There are ancestors behind us holding our backs—trans ancestors, neurodivergent ancestors.

Can you feel them? Can you feel us together? Time isn't straight. Distance is as short as the space between your eyes and the page or the screen, between your ears and the person reading to you. *We're this close.* We need to feel us. I need to feel us to keep doing this work I do, to keep being me.

I need to feel us, and I believe I do. Do I make myself believe this because I need to? If I do, I don't care. It's the better option. I don't feel alone and confused the way I did in fourth grade. I don't feel alone in my grief. I know you are there with yours, with ours. It is a gift curse of neurodivergent people to feel things very sensitively, and so grief, pain, and rejection are felt acutely, as is sound, light, energy. The worst for me is the experience of dissonance when someone's words say one thing and the body is crying out another thing. In the world today, the near absence of stomping, howling, grieving is the most dissonant thing, followed closely by the rarity of sweet cries of pleasure and joy in the aliveness of us all. We are told to not be "so sensitive," to save our effusions of joy and pain for the theater or the bedroom, to code and hold our exquisite responsivity, our grief, rage, and tenderness.

Trans autistic people can't or won't code it or hold it as we are taught. We are made wrong for this, and we suffer for our inability or refusal. And yet I truly believe noncompliance is a social skill, and one of the deepest ways trans autistic people are healers and leaders. It is a social skill that requires calculation of the costs that will be paid in loss, pain, or some version of incarceration versus the cost of the pain, loss, and incarceration of not being our authentic, beautiful wildness. We stretch the unnatural limits of gender identity, of gender expression, of relationship and of being human, making room for everyone to breathe a little bit wider. In our dancing, flapping, humming, rocking humanity we open the accordions of our beings, and, by so doing, remind other bodies of what it was, and what it still is, to be free—to be moved by life.

In an in-person, three-day event, "Techniques for Neurodiversity," facilitated by Erin Manning and Brian Massumi in 2019,[2] there were two nonspeaking autistic people who stimmed a lot. By the end of the three days, everyone in the largely neurotypical room was moving and stimming, playing with the environment. Why are so many neurotypical people preternaturally still? Are you still rocking and swaying? Did it stop? What made it stop?

Why are so many allistic people also cisgender? Why don't they wonder about this? What would happen if everyone could spin free and wander? Wander with me. Spin with me. I think what would happen is what needs to happen. It will be disruptive. We will cross lines. We will fall down. We will fall down laughing and crying. We will all be falling down, and getting up, laughing and crying, humming and moaning, spinning free. Come spin free with us.

# Jack Thompson

## Enough

**Jack Thompson** (he/him) is a proud biracial HIV+ transgender man who was awarded the title International Mr. Leather (IML) in 2019. The second trans-identified person to win, he describes himself as a "Leather craftsman, performer, and wolf. Naturally inclined to serve, Jack has been an active member of the leather community for over 15 years." In his role as IML, he traveled worldwide to promote the leather community values of respect, love, tradition, community, and dirty sex. He has earned numerous other titles and awards as well. He is a founding father of ONYX Northwest and a current member of ONYX Mid-Atlantic. In 2018, Jack represented Mr. May on the Bare Chest Calendar (San Francisco) and is Mr. January for the same calendar's 2022 Alumni Edition. He became Leatherman of Color in 2019, was also awarded The Pantheon of Leather's Man of the Year award, ONYX's Mufasa's Lion Strength Award, and the Imperial Court's Marcus Hernandez International Leather Leadership Award.

He lives at home with two dogs, a very needy and dog-like cat, and his husbear/Daddy who was first runner up for both International Mr. Bootblack 2019 and International Mr. Leather 2017. Jack flags black and navy on the right, light pink and kelly green on the left, and houndstooth down the middle.

I have spoken, danced, flexed, and shaken my butt on stage; I have appeared clad in leather, a jockstrap, with a tail, and once, in nothing at all. In fact, the first time I came out as *all the things* (which is to say: biracial, transgender, HIV+) and fully revealed every square inch of my hairy-assed body was when competing for International Mr. Leather in 2019. There is very little that I have not laid bare. Yet the one thing I refuse to carry with me on stage, or anywhere else, is shame.

As a visible Black trans man in the gay male leather world,*,1 I've faced stigma and condemnation. Many would love to see me disappear. But I have found that the greatest weapon against shame is acceptance, and the first step toward acceptance involves making yourself vulnerable.

For years we abided by a "touch first" policy. A tap on the shoulder, the pinch of a chapped ass—cops didn't touch you that way, and for a community long subjected to arbitrary police raids, the need for this kind of immediate affection seemed obvious. An undercover officer might flirt across a bar, offer a drink, ask you to dance, but he wouldn't *initiate* anything physical.

As the need to defend against this harassment subsided, "touch first" became less common. With good reason. Now we are more concerned with consent issues, thanks in part to #MeToo. Still, our need to quickly establish trust remains, not only to preserve our community, but to preserve our lives. So we have found other ways, and it is through this kind of intimacy, through the thrilling and scary and uniquely safe form of vulnerability we experience together as a subculture or individually when bared, bound to a wooden frame, and delightfully

---

\* "Leather culture" is defined as a series of "practices and styles of dress organized around sexual activities that involve leather garments, such as leather jackets, vests, boots, chaps, harnesses, or other items. Wearing leather garments is one way that participants in this culture self-consciously distinguish themselves from mainstream sexual cultures." It is sometimes synonymous with or incorporates BDSM, "a combination of the abbreviations B/D (Bondage and Discipline), D/s (Dominance and submission), and S/M (Sadism and Masochism, sometimes also abbreviated SM or called sadomasochism). To practice BDSM means to engage in consensual bondage, discipline, dominance, submission, sadism, and/or masochism."
Leather culture. (n.d.). Leatherpedia. Retrieved from: www.leatherpedia.org/leather-culture
BDSM. (n.d.). Leatherpedia. Retrieved from: www.leatherpedia.org/bdsm

tormented by a sadist with a leather flogger, that I have survived and thrived despite intense transphobia.

Hi. I'm Jack, and I'm a volunteer-a-holic.

This may come as a surprise if you've seen me compete, but I'm actually pretty awkward. When I'm on stage, I have a job to do, a role to play. Knowing my place provides me a structured freedom to be myself without fear, but when that harness comes off, I'm just like anyone else—unsure, clumsy, and even a little shy. I can't so much as flirt unless someone else has already broken the ice. I need to know it's safe before jumping in, and even then I hear a little voice saying, "They can't possibly be interested in me."

All my life I've dealt with low self-esteem, partly from being trans, partly for other reasons. Ironically, that's how I ended up on stage in the first place, trying to ditch this ever-present sense that to be included I needed to do everything, and that to be of value, I had to serve everyone.

Like many others, I came out via the lesbian-to-trans-man pipeline in middle and high school and got pretty involved with youth activism. Afterward I became a sex educator. I did drag, then burlesque. That's how I eventually found my way into leather: Though I knew from a young age that I was kinky, for a while I lacked the language and experience (not to mention the shockingly expensive gear!) to join in. I've always identified pretty heavily with dogs and wolves—as a kid, I was constantly growling and biting and howling at the moon—so at first I pretty naturally gravitated toward the furry community.* My first foray

---

\* Furries are "People with an interest in anthropomorphized animals, like Sonic the Hedgehog or Pokémon, [and] have come in for a lot of ridicule over the years from posters on sites like Something Awful and 4chan. Mainstream press accounts tend to portray furries as sexual fetishists united by a common interest in sex in animal costumes. But survey evidence suggests a lot of these stereotypes are wrong (very few furries think sex in animal costumes is a good idea, for instance)."
Matthews, D. (2015) 9 Questions About Furries You Were Too Embarrassed to Ask. *Vox.* Retrieved from: www.vox.com/2014/12/10/7362321/9-questions-about-furries-you-were-too-embarrassed-to-ask

into anything kinky was coming out as one on LiveJournal. Then later my mom dropped me off at a convention, exclaiming, "Oh, look at all these cute costumes! Have fun volunteering at this...*thing*...this weekend!" She didn't get it, and thankfully she didn't ask many questions.

As an adult, I have dipped my toes into one area of the community then another and continued volunteering, which gradually eased my social awkwardness. As a trans person—hell, as a person of any gender—I'd spent far, far too much energy trying to fit into societal boxes. But in the leather scene, I could unleash my desires...or I could hand my leash to someone else! In play space,** we uncage the lustful, animalistic natures we pretend not to have. Puppy play, bondage, dominance, submission, whips and chains and leather and latex and lace, all these free us to experience the full potential of gender and sex. Fucking this way is a primal, controlled chaos. It's messy, sticky, sweaty, and sweet. It's exhilarating, it's terrifying. It's fun. BDSM and kink offer opportunities to embrace our vulnerabilities and to create our own boxes in which to explore, to want and be wanted, and to have pleasure without shame.

Many outsiders imagine leathermen to be like the Tom of Finland*** illustrations from the 1960s and 70s featuring square-jawed, mustachioed, hypermasculine, motorcycle-riding hunks with perfect asses and comically large, permanently erect, and ready-for-blowjobs cocks. Or sometimes people reference the leather-clad, bearish daddies they may have seen at Pride events. But these don't represent the full diversity of our communities, and my first connections in leather were with women and trans folks, who are far more plentiful than we are sometimes led to believe.

I fucked in a dungeon for the first time in my mid-twenties. All dressed up in a collar and tail, my then-girlfriend led me around and I stared, mouth going dry and "junk" getting wet, as I watched other couples, triads, and more bite and writhe and fight in every direction.

---

** Play spaces are social events or private settings where BDSM and sexual activities are allowed and encouraged without judgment.

*** "Tom of Finland" was the penname of Finnish artist Touko Laaksonen, who signed his iconic erotic illustrations "Tom."

People were tangled in dim corners and spot lit while bound on St. Andrew's crosses. There was no "type" in that room; all kinds of bodies were on display.

My girlfriend locked me inside a large metal dog cage. Poking and prodding with fiendish devices, she teased me into that primal, wolfy headspace and I snarled and thrashed against the bars. I hungered and I ached. When she opened the door I was so exhausted from the frenzy that all I could do was lie there as she went down on me. That cage had actually been freeing: It was as if I had simply forgotten to feel humiliated or embarrassed. I hadn't even noticed the gawkers. In the bright afterglow of orgasm, I started to blush before realizing I had spent all night doing the same—watching, gaping at the unabashed people around me—and all that anxiety, all that bubbling shame I'd felt, transformed into exhilaration.

Auntie Midori, revered BDSM elder, performance artist, and educator, says, "BDSM is childhood joyous play with adult sexual privilege and cool toys."[2] That night I cracked open the grown-up toy box. Now leather is my favorite toy.

The material itself is sexy; it's soft and pliable, yet tough. It can be a kiss or a punch. It can accentuate certain body features and draw attention away from others, leading the eye from heavy hips toward a surgically sculpted chest (speaking of expensive gear!). It is literally a second skin. Leather culture, and BDSM more broadly, also provide venues to experiment with masculinity, femininity, other genders, and the spaces between coyness and strength, toughness and submission, dominance and vulnerability—to experience both gender *and* sexual euphoria in safe and controlled environments where *we* get to write the rules about our bodies.

About ten years after that initial dungeon scene I experienced another "loss of virginity"—my first time dominating someone else. I rarely attempt to direct or control the situation, but I am occasionally the Dominant when a playmate asks me to be. It's just not my comfort zone. I like instructions, but this time was different.

I'd hooked up with "Tony" months before. He was early in transition and suddenly faced an unexpected, testosterone-induced *"Oh shit!"* spike in sex drive and openness to new sexual possibilities.

We met after the IML uniform party; he rolled up with a friend and I could smell Tony's restless arousal and excitement. Another person met us there, us all in zippered flight suits. An open spot on wrestling mats was the perfect area for a locker room hazing scene starring Tony as the hot, young, new recruit.

We pushed him around, a little, at first, snapping towels on his ass, calling him names. "You new little shit. Rookie, think you're hot stuff?" We jostled him more firmly. "Think you can play with the big dogs?" He smiled in glee. We wrestled him, shoved him down, pinned his wrists and ankles to the floor. We followed the cliché script. "You're just another newbie who needs to be taught who's in charge." I ripped his flight suit to his ankles and relentlessly, brutally, sadistically fucked him in the ass. He squealed and squirmed. I thrust harder. His cheeks clapped for all to see. I plunged into him once more. Once more again. As he reached a breaking point, I whispered in his ear, "Fine. Go ahead and orgasm if you want, pig," and at that very moment we launched into song.

All at once, in a spectacular, coordinated, mindfuck of hilarity, the three of us domming Tony joined together in an off-key chorus of "You've Lost That Lovin' Feeling." Tony was humiliated and elated. He was red in his face and in his butt. He cackled "I fucking hate you guys," as he came all over the mat.

We forget, whether we're having missionary sex in a tidy bedroom or gangbanging in a grubby dungeon: Sex is supposed to be exciting. It doesn't always have to be solemn and sensitive. We have elbows and knees and awkward angles and we bump heads. We fart and make silly noises. And still it's fun, because our bodies are just bodies; we should enjoy them in ways that make us feel good, safe, and whole. I have had many steamy encounters and a lot of hot sex, but that scene remains one of my favorite memories because it taught him that, yes, we trans and nonbinary people are allowed to *enjoy* our bodies. We, too, are allowed to *play.*

✳ ✳ ✳

It was my husband who first got involved in competition, going on to become Mr. San Francisco. Meanwhile, I appeared in the Bare Chest Calendar, a nearly 40-year-old charity raising funds for HIV/AIDS organizations, and I was a founding member of the Northwest chapter of ONYX, a national leather organization exclusively for men of color. When my husband's tenure as Mr. San Francisco came to a close, we settled in Baltimore where I knew I could count on a nearby ONYX chapter for community support. It seemed the perfect time for me to wade into the world of titles and sashes myself.

I won Leatherman of Color in 2019! A national title based in Washington, D.C., it had previously been affiliated with ONYX, so it felt like a natural entry point. Most of the winners had been Black, but even within ONYX, there weren't a lot of guys who looked like me—trans, biracial, ginger, and covered in freckles. I wanted to represent another side of POC masculinity.

The Leatherman of Color (LOC) competition has suffered the same marginalization as other spaces made for people of color. Outside non-white competitors, most of the male leather world hadn't even heard of it until recently. When I moved across the country and told my friends that I was going to run, *none* except a few of the ONYX guys knew what it was. Color me surprised. Even within a community that prides itself on inclusivity and openness, we were still reproducing the same marginalization we'd been subject to in broader society. Frustrated with the lack of representation, I decided to run for International Mr. Leather largely with the intention of raising the profile of Leatherman of Color broadly. I had the support of my community back home on the West Coast, and also my new community in the East, and I was about as well poised as I could be—and figured I ever would be—to rep the LOC title on the international stage.

Competing with 67 other leather-clad hunks from all over the world, and especially being so new to the scene and a trans man at that, I really hadn't even hoped I would win. I figured I'd make friends, have fun, maybe get a cutesy medal for participation. At best I thought I might make the top 20 and be allowed to give my speech, which I'd worked hard on. But I certainly didn't expect to win the damn thing.

In fact, for a while, I wasn't even sure if I would make it *to* the competition. Though IML allows transgender contestants to enter, they require that all supporting documents list the contestant's sex as male. Mine did not. Any trans person who has tried to navigate the bureaucratic nightmare of getting legal documents changed will know the scramble I faced and the fear that the changes wouldn't go through soon enough. Even in the best of times, those basic, compulsory tasks of citizenship are a game of wait-and-see for trans folks, and in the back of my mind there was always the possibility that my application would get stopped by the next Kim Davis[3] or would become the central issue of a Supreme Court case. Many days, it was my first thought when I woke up, and it kept me awake at night. I made back-up plans and tried not to work up too much hope in case things didn't work out. When the notification finally came that I was registered, I let out a sigh like I'd been holding my breath for a month. I had been living and moving through the world as a man for more years than not, and yet there I was, once again fighting for scraps of respect and recognition—even within my own community. That year, there was one other trans man running for IML, and I know they faced those same stressors.

Eventually I did make it to Chicago, and then came a whole other kind of anxiety. Here's the thing: For all the money and awareness we'd each raised, IML is still, when you get down to it, a beauty pageant. IML and other leather contests have helped to raise millions for HIV/AIDS organizations and other civil rights-focused causes, but the competitions themselves still revolve around a bunch of men looking pretty. Christmas hams in strappy leather jocks, oiled skin, and rippling muscles aglow under glaring spotlights. We tried to remember to smile.

I was in the best shape of my life. I'd also spent years overcoming any kind of stage fright by participating in drag and burlesque. For an all-spectrum male event a few years before, I had gone full nude as a challenge to myself. Once you've been on stage in your birthday suit, most other things come pretty easy. Still, as a five-foot-nothing trans guy in a space dominated by towering cis men with bulging pecs and packages barely restrained by a few square inches of leather, I felt totally intimidated. For me, baring my trans ass in nothing but a jock strap, just to have my masculinity scrutinized by thousands of people and *literal judges*, was unimaginable. I had rehearsed my speech until it was as automatic as breathing, and I relied on muscle memory for the movements.

My presence as a trans man was also still fairly controversial. Before 2019, only one trans person had ever won IML—Tyler McCormick in 2010—and despite him cutting a path for future trans contestants, he had gone through a pretty shitty year as the titleholder, complete with transphobic jeers, blog posts and other media saying he was invalid, and being excluded from some clubs. Even a community founded on openness and the exploration of sexual possibility has its share of bigots, and as in any other group, they tend to be loud and tenacious. So yeah, I was nervous, maybe even a little insecure, but I also knew I had a job to do. I was there to rep my people, and I was going to do my damnedest to do it well.

What I ultimately found in that field of 67 contestants was not bigotry. It was hardly even competition, at least not beyond a friendly sort. What I found was brotherhood. I was aware that some people in the crowd, in the organizing committees, and among the sponsors opposed my presence, thinking I wasn't "man enough" to claim a place on that stage, but a lot of that melted away once we were up there, in it, together.

And the crowd wasn't looking for our flaws or our weaknesses; they were admiring our strengths. We were all raised above the audience in our shined-within-a-hair-of-their-life boots and harnesses, all exposed before the crowd, all stylized and idealized representations of masculinity revealing our scars and our hearts, our body hair (or lack thereof) and our blemishes, each of us the embodiment of the grit and power that has sustained our community. Tough exteriors of a people hardened by decades of mistreatment and misunderstanding. And I was one of them. For one brief moment, I felt a sense of pure gender euphoria, free from the weight of the "trans narrative."

This community has always been about survival in the face of oppression and embracing love in spite of the hate we receive. That day, this community lifted me up. When I won, people in San Francisco won, people in my new hometown of Baltimore won, people of color won, people of diverse gender experiences and expressions won. The intersecting threads of my marginalized identities tangled into knots of insecurity and a sense of obligation to the communities that I came from, but they also produced an unbreakable chain of love and support, a safety net to catch me when the wider world tried to cast me out—as it continues to try to cast me, and people like me, out of society.

Thanks to that safety net, I know that I can be dropped almost anywhere in the world and still find community, and as a Black trans man living in America, that is a rare privilege. One of my major motivations had been simply to meet others like me and to feel a little less alone. I'd tried to be of service, yes, to be a force for good, raising money and visibility, but it was always at least in part because it also helped me feel comfortable and find my place in the world. It wasn't an exchange, exactly, and I never thought of it that way, but it did turn out that all of those small investments I had made by volunteering, getting involved, and giving of myself would not only be repaid but returned beyond my wildest dreams.

My time as a leader helped my community, and helped me as well.

I was sashed International Mr. Leather in May of 2019, and my title "year" was an absolute whirlwind; due to COVID, IML canceled their competitions in 2020 and 2021, and I remained the *de facto* title holder for two additional years.

Even before the outbreak, my time had already been wild. The winner of International Mr. Leather is expected to travel, give guest appearances at fundraisers and parties, speak on panels, and serve as a judge for various regional competitions. Between May of 2019 and March of 2020 (when COVID restrictions were implemented), I was home a grand total of four weekends. I was exhausted and also feeling the weight of my "historic" win. As the first trans person of color to hold the title, I felt a unique responsibility to represent Black and trans people—as if we had something to prove. My husband/Daddy really kept me alive, taking care of the house and making endless bowls of soup to help me recover from the "con crud" that came with so much travel.

However, this is also when I started to truly appreciate the ways that my community was reshaping itself to better hold space for people of trans identities. As the titleholder of International Mr. Leather, I was no longer simply one unusual contestant in a crowded field—I became a leader by default, and my community responded to that leadership by embracing and supporting me as well.

"Does this person deserve IML? They're not even really a man," one person wrote on social media. I thought we were a community of inclusion? But people rallied around me! He was the leader of an organization in Florida, and others had tried to engage him in hard conversations before, with little success. Now his biases were so clearly on display that the community had to decide if he was really the person they wanted representing them. They pushed him out, and it was one of the first times I actually saw consequences for this kind of blatant transphobia.

The leather community has always been very tactile, very touch oriented. Our origins were in grimy bathrooms and shadowy hallways, sucking and fucking and groping our way toward liberation. In the 1980s, our community was forced to evolve to protect one another from the AIDS crisis; it was a revolutionary time where we re-formed our collective notions of intimacy and community safety.

Now we were once again stripped away of much of what we understood as integral to our culture by COVID, and it left us trying, once more, to find our way. Suddenly we were all spending a lot *more* time online. Without those in person interactions, the formerly anonymous bigotry became a lot *less* anonymous. A curtain had been drawn back, or the lights had been flicked on, exposing the racist, transphobic, and hateful cockroaches lurking in the shadows. This bar owner or that event organizer would reveal themselves to be a Trump supporter or worse, and we could no longer just look the other way. We were no longer as reliant on them for physical space, and we were finally able, or were finally forced, to be more intentional about the people we accepted or worked with. It turns out that the people who spew hate speech about trans people, women, people of color, or other noncis nonwhite guys in leather tend not to give a shit about other people's safety in general. COVID made it clearer than ever that we needed to act for the survival of all of us.

And doing so made our world safer. The polarization of the last several years did a lot to expose the cracks of racism and transphobia in our foundations. At the same time, I have seen my community embrace me and, I hope I will see it embrace others both *like* and *unlike* me in the future. This year, we reconvened in Chicago and Gael Leung Chong was sashed IML 2022; he is the first man of Asian descent to hold the title of International Mr. Leather and I could not be more proud.

As transgender and gender nonconforming people, we are constantly making and re-making ourselves, and through that process, we are also shaping the world in which we want and need to live. By defining our bodies and our identities, we expand definitions and lift the limitations for all. Nine years before me, the trans man Tyler McCormick took that stage in Chicago and won, and though I won't presume to speak for him, I have to imagine that he shared at least a few of my reasons for doing so. No matter how messed up it is, or how much we want to believe it isn't true, it still seems like we have something to prove. The act of stepping out on that stage and baring it all was a loud *fuck you!* to the haters and transphobes who would have preferred to keep us locked away. But. It was also a leap of faith—an act of absolute vulnerability in hopes that the community will catch you gently. Whatever Tyler's motivations were for entering IML, he acted in a way that was authentic to him. In making himself visible and vulnerable, he helped move the needle and make a way for me, and now that I am on the other side of my own term, I hope that I do the same for others.

I think this is what it means to say that our very survival as trans people is an act of resistance. The things we do to survive, to make life more beautiful, more loving, more interesting, even more sexy, not only help us make it through the day to day but really do make the world a better, safer place for all of us. When I gave my speech at

IML, I talked about being *enough*. It's kind of become my catchphrase; I said, "If you are enough for you, you are enough." This idea was born out of my own insecurities and my lifelong struggle with self-esteem. For years I had been told I wasn't strong enough, wasn't Black enough, wasn't smart enough. Looking out at the crowd in Chicago, I knew there were people out there who thought I wasn't man enough to be on that stage. But it didn't matter. I was enough *for me*. That moment was the culmination of years of work to believe it was true. And it was, more than I think I realized at the time. Because I wasn't just enough for me. In that moment, I was enough for *us*.

# Cecilia Gentili

# Tango Between Two Worlds

**Cecilia Gentili** (she/her) is a trans Latina and a
fierce activist, a dedicated advocate, a striking
actress on the hit TV program *Pose*, and a sex
worker. She has done direct service through The
Lesbian, Gay, Bisexual, and Transgender Community Center and the APICHA* Community Health
Center in NYC, and later was managing director
of policy for the world-renowned GMHC.**
Several years ago she founded Trans Equity Consulting and has
collaborated with many major organizations on transgender and
gender nonbinary rights. Cecilia is also a founding member of
Decrim NY, a coalition working toward decriminalization, decarcer-
ation, and destigmatization of people in the sex trade. Cecilia's
memoir, *Faltas*, was published in late 2022 by Little Puss Press, Inc.

She is at all times delightfully and unapologetically herself,
keenly aware of the horrors of the world yet someone who still
maintains a spark of innocence, and it shines. We first met ages
ago, and she is rarely without a tender smile. Here she compares
and contrasts her experiences of transphobia in Argentina and the
U.S. www.transequityconsulting.com

---

\*   Originally the Asian and Pacific Islander Coalition on HIV/AIDS.
\*\*  Originally the Gay Men's Health Crisis.

Every morning I wake up between six and seven. I have my coffee, maybe a walk, and I always read the *New York Times*. I need to know what's happening here in the U.S., and as a Latina, I always check on my people in South America. It's necessary because I have to know what we fight against. If the news is terrible, you can start your day in a really bad way. And even though I live in New York, what they call a liberal city, what I learn can still be hard to accept. This sort of morning ritual I never imagined for myself growing up under the dictatorship in Argentina, when family members were *disappearing** and when information didn't come so easily.

Now I'm an adult, and well past the age that trans women of color like me are expected to live. My life is good; I have a successful career, a life partner, I help people who struggle just like I did, I'm on TV and have a book of my own! People see me everywhere! Yet sometimes I can't help but wonder if I made a mistake coming to the United States.

On one page of the paper, of course not the front page, I read about the rise of anti-trans legislation in Alabama, Texas, and across the United States. It's so disturbing how many people in this country hate trans people! These governments won't protect trans girls in sports or even provide basic healthcare to at-risk trans youth. So many people want to make it impossible for us to be called by a name we chose for ourselves. They say they are going to put parents and doctors in jail; they make it a police state! And they take away all the protections. It's written in black and white—our rights are in decline in the United States.

Then I turn deeper into the paper to read about my home country, the one I was so eager to leave for safety, for economic freedom, and for some idea of equality. Instead I find that Argentina is paying financial reparations to trans people who were sex workers during the dictatorship! Yes, the state is offering pensions to trans people! They're also talking about compensation for trans people who came out later on—people like me!

I felt the same way—a sort of betrayal—when I read about Trump's

---

* Referring to "The Disappeared," the 30,000 people who were abducted by the state during Argentina's "Dirty War" throughout the 1970s. A majority of those missing were tortured and killed.

coup in the United States, having survived Argentina's dictatorship, which also started with a coup. I did not plan on coming to this country to relive my childhood.

What would have happened had I stayed and fought with my sisters, my friends, my comrades in Argentina? Would I get reparations too? Trans rights are happening in Argentina in ways that I can't even fantasize about in this country. Will the United States ever get there? Argentina is considered a "third world" country, and the U.S. "first world," so you'd expect the opposite. Of course, my life now is here and I'm okay, but it's hard not to consider the differences.

But, trust me, both countries do have something important in common. The governments and their police do not reflect the wants and needs of the people. As I always say: As long as we fight, we are still winning.

* * *

As a child living under state oppression, my family in South America was in constant fear for their lives. Nobody really cared about queer or trans liberation because there wasn't time and there certainly weren't resources. I grew up watching American movies showing many types of people thriving, living with big backyards, and I truly did not understand what they meant when they showed lives where people could be themselves and be safe.

Adults who lived through the dictatorship adapted to that life, the opposite of people being themselves. I still have uncles who say, "I wish I still had the dictatorship," if only for the comfort of understanding what was going on and who was in charge. Now people like me, who were born during the regime, want continued change toward freedom and democracy and to move away from the terrors we saw as children. And now we've got kids born post-dictatorship; young people who have no idea about the tyranny and what it meant. Now we have all these different kinds of people living at the same time, and together creating the reality of Argentina today.

The dictatorship ended in 1983, when I was only twelve years old.

Before then, all the "rainbow" identities were hidden. I was shocked with what felt like new discoveries, like "Oh, there's gay people out there!" or "Wow! You can write about oppression?! I never knew!!" I am the product of that shift from full dictatorship to freedom. I am grateful to know the difference between both extremes when I am reading the paper or working for trans and trans sex worker justice. It shaped me to say, "I don't want this shit! Never again! I don't want to live in war! I don't want my family members to disappear! I don't want to experience any more loss!" This is easy to scream and shout now, it's obvious, but back then, I needed to hide.

My mother, before she died, told me how sorry she was for being so harsh toward me and my fluidity when I was a child. She said, "I want you to know that I was trying to protect you. I knew that if I had just let you be, you would get taken away." That's a hard reality to live with because I had so much resentment toward her during my transition and as I became who I am today. At the same time, I have to be grateful to her for *not* letting me be. She only wanted us to live under the radar and to be safe. I was flamboyant and hard to keep closeted, and the challenge for her only grew after I was exposed to new information and ways of being as a teen.

The experiences with my mother and my mother country have shaped my voice as an activist. In the U.S. LGBTQIA+ world, people say, "Be yourself. Be authentic. Come out and experience freedom," right? There's a lot of pressure on me and on our leaders to always be positive and empowering in such a specific way. Well, I respect that narrative, but mine is a little bit different. Reader, whoever you are, maybe because I was born where and when I was, I believe that being yourself is very important. But I prefer you to be alive and in the closet than to be out and dead. This way, you can still fight and enjoy some of life. I say this to trans people, trans women of color, and to trans women of color who are undocumented or sex workers or both, people like me: *Do what you can to achieve whatever level of empowerment you can get, but also be safe.*

Negotiating has been one of my primary ways of seeking safety. I have spent most of my life as a negotiator, perhaps because of the scarcity of my growing up; lack of safety makes you either a militant or a mediator. I know some people feel differently, but for me, as a trans woman with so many intersections, I'd take a piece of something rather than nothing. I always strive to meet people in the middle, even when they want to set fire to the entire establishment. As I always say, "Let's not try to burn it down and maybe instead we can make it more adaptable for everybody, okay?" We must do what we can to survive, whatever that means for you.

For example: I worked in social services and cared for more than six hundred people. I had clients on hormones who were still going to work as the sex they were assigned at birth because to be their true gender wasn't safe for them. My role was to say, "Let's see what we can do. We can help you be yourself in many ways. Maybe you can be on hormones or have surgeries, but not come out at work if you're going to lose your job." I helped them make those types of decisions. A person shouldn't have to starve or die to be themselves, and this transphobic society is to blame, not the person trying to find a way to eat. We must remember that not everybody has the privilege to medically and/or socially transition. Sometimes compromises are just necessary.

*So, what makes you feel empowered? What makes you feel safe? How can we get you there?*

I actually have this conversation a lot with my friends. All my idols are more extreme, like Miss Major. My sisters were the ones throwing bricks, disrupting government meetings, and spitting in politicians' faces. When I'm with my chosen family, they tell me, "Oh, Cecilia, you're so fucking radical like them!" But I always answer, "No, no! That's not me! I'm a diplomat!" It's not sexy, but it's my truth.

I know that maybe I am scared of being seen as radical and that is why I don't think of myself that way. My uncle in Argentina disappeared; he was really fortunate and came back when not a lot of people did. He confronted the oppressive state and had an aggressive mind. I'll probably never call myself radical, especially in two countries with such high rates of trans femicide and histories of coups. I'm okay with it. I never want to judge my work by how "radical" I am. But I do judge it on what I'm doing for my people and for myself.

* * *

Before I came to the U.S., I wanted ease and access to "the American dream." I was tired of being poor in a country struggling with its comeback. If you go to poor people around the world and you ask about the United States, they say "luxury" and expect to find it for themselves. They think everybody lives the "Kardashian" life because that is what they are exposed to on TV. I simply did not know that poverty existed in this country! I was here for the house and the swimming pool! No, this was not a fantasy. I thought it was the truth! It wouldn't matter if I was trans or an immigrant; I expected people would be waiting at the airport with signs about jobs and fighting to employ me!

I am not ashamed of what happened next, but it was so different from my assumptions.

The same night I arrived in the United States, I walked the streets looking for johns because I was hungry. A month later, I was still doing sex work. I couldn't get a job as someone transgender and undocumented, and I didn't speak English. At least in Argentina, I was legal, I spoke Spanish, and I could understand what clients wanted. And I thought the U.S. was a place that celebrated diversity. I questioned it all, and asked myself, "What am I doing? Am I better off going back to where I came from?"

And I decided my answer was yes. I'd go back to my family in Argentina and could do sex work with less taboo than in the United States, but the night before my flight home, I got arrested for what they call "prostitution." Quickly, they also realized I was an immigrant. They confiscated my Argentinian passport and sent me to a diversion program, but my visa expired before I got released. It wasn't what I wanted, but I decided to stay. I continued sex work to survive and even to reclaim my agency.

So...it wasn't exactly the welcome to North America I had painted in my mind.

I'm not ashamed. My narrative might be shocking or even radical to some, but it is simply my story. I saw democracy rise from dictatorship, and I now see fascism in a place that championed equality. So I have long understood that there are different forms of "normal." And letting go of the tendency to judge myself for my own complicated story or for what other people call "risky behavior" is an important survival strategy. I always say, "We all have different ideas of risk." What risk means for me is different than for you; it is different for a transgender Black female sex worker than for a cisgender white businessman. And that's okay. Our identities shape our beliefs about risk, which shape our ideas about normality.

For example, most of my white trans friends have never even considered injecting silicone to shape their bodies, though this is done by many trans Latinas. "It's risky, right?" But to think about the danger first means someone has privilege. I, as a sex worker and immigrant of color, knew that every day could be my last day. That's how I faced everything. So, one of my sisters might use silicone if she needs it to pass for safety or work. The calculation is different. Or, back when I was using drugs and working the block, I'd think, "I *should* have ten bags of heroin. Who cares?" Or "I've already been arrested for that. So what if I get arrested again?" I knew that someone might attack or kill me at any time for not being their idea of human. Or, maybe, that a doctor would just let me die after an attack, which still seems like a problem in the Americas.

So I am not scared of these risks because my life involves risk in so many other ways too. As trans people, immigrants, or sex workers, we are so often assaulted for the decisions we make. But how could I have been expected to thrive when so many other trans people who look like me were living the same way? Only after I met a counselor who was also trans did I realize that we could have mainstream jobs or access community spaces that weren't street corners or jails.

I have also learned that working at LGBTQIA+ organizations doesn't always save trans people, especially trans women of color, from exploitation. Working in human services and doing more visible activism in the not-for-profit/industrial complex can help us develop careers and help us build confidence, and it is a huge benefit for our communities. Because of our intersections, people want to hire us, and we need to be represented in the organizations giving us care! But even well-meaning not-for-profits are businesses with the desire to grow; they are the pimps, and the rest of us produce that growth. I sometimes feel objectified because they want someone with my identities so they look more diverse, and also I feel the pressure because I can tell people don't always think I am capable. I have to repeatedly prove my worth, that I'm not there just for affirmative action, and it can be exhausting. Sex work or office job, you can get empowered and you can get played.

However, my experiences of risk have changed since coming to the United States. I'm not walking the streets looking for ten people to hire me for sex anymore, any of whom might also be my killer. No cop can tap on my bench or sexually harass me. I'm not endangering my health just to make money for food. I even have a stable place to live where I can't easily get kicked out. Now I do different work through the virtual world, where a person can be nasty but they can't physically hurt me. Because my experiences have changed, partly from COVID, my understanding of normal has changed and my mental health has shifted to a better space. My wellbeing and self-confidence too. Just the other day, somebody I really liked in a sexual way invited me to share meth with him, which would probably have led to sex. Ten years ago, I would have said, "Yes, let's do it. Let's talk. Make it *hot*." Nowadays, I'm like, "You're really hot, and I really fantasize about this, but I don't want to be around meth today, so I pass."

It's all negotiating.

But, let me make this clear—my changing exposure or thoughts about risk as an immigrant trans woman of color do not make me any better as a person. It doesn't make me more or less human than my sisters in the U.S., or my comrades in Argentina, or my more radical idols. We all need each other.

And with all of this labor, I happily take the moments in life where I am not negotiating and I am simply human.

I feel most human in situations that seem opposite. I feel fully myself when I am in the immensity of nature, in the middle of a lake kayaking and all I see is water, trees, birds, and animals. Or when I have simple moments with my sister Lala, as we prepare food, talk about tomatoes, and gossip on the couch. But I also feel most human when I am shouting for sex workers' rights, fighting for the dignity of others, demanding to be heard as I shout in English or Spanish, "Your rainbow isn't doing shit if it's not doing anything for sex workers!" This is *not* negotiating.

Many areas of my life seem to contain opposites, but they do not conflict. Both sides show me purpose. Both show me future. Both show me who I am: fluid, trans, Latina, immigrant, sex worker, activist, and so much more. I dance between them. They show me I am someone who can dance through two opposite worlds and live to tell the tale.

# M. Dru Levasseur

## Your Authenticity Is Your Power—Tales from a Trans Lawyer

**M. Dru Levasseur** (he/him) is a white trans first-generation lawyer who began his legal advocacy well before completing law school. His resume includes being a Harvard Law Wasserstein Fellow; the director of diversity, equity, and inclusion for the National LGBTQ+ Bar Association; the director of Lambda Legal's Transgender Rights Project; and the first staff attorney for the
Transgender Legal Defense & Education Fund, Inc. Dru was senior attorney and transgender rights project director for Lambda Legal, the oldest and largest national legal organization committed to achieving full recognition of the civil rights of LGBTQ+ people and people living with HIV. For a decade, Dru led Lambda Legal's transgender rights work through strategy development, impact litigation, policy, advocacy, and public education and served as counsel in landmark impact litigation cases and amicus briefs in federal courts, including the U.S. Supreme Court.

Currently, Dru is the director of diversity, equity, and inclusion for the National LGBTQ+ Bar Association, and leads Lavender Law 365®, an LGBTQ+ inclusion coaching and consulting initiative perfect for law firms, law schools, and workplaces. As a prominent figure in the LGBTQ+ equality movement for 25 years, 15 from within the legal profession, Dru has extensive experience in law, advocacy, philanthropy, and community organizing. We have known each other many years, and I deeply respect his work. www. drulevasseur.com

I want you to know that if I can do it, you can do it. You deserve to be on this earth even if you struggle to find a sense of belonging. You have a place. You are a human being who has every right to be treated with dignity and respect under the eyes of the law and by society.

Your identity, most especially your gender identity, is the most sacred part of you. It is your birthright to bring all parts of yourself to light, to grow and to uncover your authentic self. You are worthy.

This chapter is a love letter to other queer and trans people, and a window for our allies.

* * *

I have faced resistance from individuals, from organizations, and from our cultural and political systems, all of which have caused me great anguish. So many forces have worked against me. And yet, even during my most extreme suffering, I endured, and it was in becoming a lawyer and legal advocate for transgender rights when I came into my own and found myself the most powerful to make change.

Through school I felt like an outsider, a girl who acted like a boy, and I began to see myself as others labeled me: tomboy, shy, smart, athletic, vulnerable. I was the younger sibling in a Catholic family with an ex-nun mother. We attended Mass and Catholic school, where emotional abuse and shame were everyday experiences for anyone different. Binary stereotypes were consistently enforced. Boys here, girls there. Rocking the boat was a sin. I believed that if I acted perfectly, God would love me and I would be safe.

It backfired. I drew unwanted attention from nuns and peers, and the stress manifested as anxiety attacks beginning in junior high. Kids like me frequently self-harm or bury our differences deep where shame hardens into stone. We may lack the language to express what we know inside. We hide because being different is dangerous.

To cope, I ran home each day to shed my pleated jumper and blouse and to change into pants. I envied the boys as they were given the benefit of the doubt by adults, worshipped even, provided the freedom to be their full selves. My first experience crossdressing was wearing men's boxer shorts underneath my skirt; it was a rebellion against the rigid systems in which I found myself. It felt protective.

I started therapy, bought a book on agoraphobia and panic attacks, and started meditation and saying affirmations at age eleven with my Shakti Gawain *Creative Visualization* cassette tape. I was determined to survive.

Looking back at pictures, I chuckle at how clear it was that I was queer and trans.

I grew up believing there was something wrong with me. It would have made a world of difference to meet someone trans when I was young and to know that I could make it, that my life was possible. Perhaps with visible role models I could have formed an image of myself as an adult; this is why I am so passionate about mentorship and choose daily to be openly trans. It makes a difference.

\* \* \*

I came out as gay in the early 1990s, pre-internet and pre-Ellen. I was eighteen. I called home across the country from college to say I thought I liked a cool rollerblade chick; but that did *not* go over well.

I anticipated that life would be difficult and that I would likely experience discrimination, harassment, perhaps violence. At least there were gay bars, gay clubs, gay bookstores, and even travel books to help me locate friendly places to visit, and a thriving subculture with underground scenes where I could find a sense of belonging. The power of community helped save me, but my parents reacted differently. They needed time to process their own baggage, which sadly took years, and in the interim they had little knowledge or energy to provide the support I needed. My coming out was the height of my vulnerability, but this was when my family was at the height of theirs as well, lacking in information and resources. And unfortunately, I even faced hostility from within the queer community, as I have always been bisexual but felt I had to publicly identify as a lesbian in response to pervasive biphobia, including an attempted physical assault by a drunk, lesbian-identified stranger after she learned that I was bi.

My entire self-identity formed around these struggles. I was white, poor, visibly queer, and perceived as female but was not feminine enough to avoid gender-policing or gender-based violence. My gender nonconformity drew the most negative attention, harassment, and physical threats, such as a bottle thrown from a car full of cisgender men that nearly missed my head and was accompanied with the hostile shout, "Dyke!" Cisgender straight women let me know how disgusting and wrong I was, and cisgender straight men threatened corrective rape to "fix" me. I didn't feel safe in the world because I wasn't. My life in my twenties revolved around working minimum wage jobs to pay for food and rent and participating in any available gay event or gathering, from lesbian softball leagues to the LGBT Millennium March on Washington in 2000. These spaces made me feel normal, safe, and wanted, feelings I couldn't get anywhere else in the world. And it meant I was fighting back.

Another way I challenged the mainstream was in my same-sex interracial wedding in 2001, long before it was even legal. I had been in a long-term relationship with a Black woman, and we were each other's family. We celebrated our six-year anniversary by marrying. Not having our relationship acknowledged by families and friends was deeply painful and invisibilizing, and I was tired of people delegitimizing it by referring to her as my "friend" or "roommate." Even though, at the time, we could not receive legal recognition, our wedding gave many an opportunity to acknowledge our relationship and to be a part of our life. Not everyone chose to attend, but it was unbelievably healing to witness those who did, especially older relatives and ones who brought their young children. We did it to be seen and validated for who we were in the world. Years later, I was in the ironic position of having to argue against prioritizing gay marriage; it sucked so much energy and funding from our community that other urgent problems were going unaddressed. I'd experienced the harm of not having my queer relationships recognized socially or legally, but as a trans person, I knew we needed to focus on survival issues first.

My coming out as trans was a contrast. I knew I would again face significant hardship, but this time I felt very alone. I did not know other trans people or where to find community. Beyond the fear and shame that I learned from movies or song references, my exposure to transgender issues taught me that it is a very isolating experience where the world considers you mentally ill, that medical care is not covered by insurance, and that you are likely to die of suicide or murder. I did not want to be trans; I pushed it away and hoped it wasn't true. I told very few people, but I started with a therapist.

Not all therapists are created equal. In the early 2000s there were few with experience in trans issues. One told me she knew nothing and to find someone else. Another claimed to be knowledgeable, so I trusted her, but after three years of work she denied my request for a letter to access hormone therapy based on her recent reading of a trans person's photography book where he discussed his personal experience of testosterone. Had she been better experienced in trans healthcare, she would have known that such gatekeeping is not only dangerous because it denied me the medical care I needed but also it risked derailing my self-trust. I searched to find a new therapist, who immediately reassured me that I was in the driver's seat and that she would be a passenger to support me. It was life-changing, and life-saving.

Trust us. We are the experts on our own lives. The medical community has come a long way, in large part because openly trans providers and activists have chipped away at the uneven power dynamics, but so much more needs to be done.

Although I was resistant at first, I gathered the courage to attend a local FTM* group, where I met people with different identities and experiences, including older trans men who had transitioned decades earlier under previous guidelines that demanded people change their name, start a new life in a new town, and never tell anyone they were trans. Although there were a handful of positive role models in our group, the peer setting had its limits. Posturing happened with an unspoken hierarchy of masculinity: who was on testosterone, who had facial hair and how much, who was tall or muscular, who'd had top surgery or genital surgery, and, of course, how big was their dick. Each had its level of status. We all struggled to navigate a world that pathologized our identities and judged us as not real or "not man enough," and we also discussed how few legal rights we had and how few of us could change our identity documents or access basic healthcare. I started law school at the same time as transition. I didn't time it that way on purpose, but that's how it happened. I didn't anticipate building my career out of working for the rights of the larger trans community, but this is where I found my voice.

My first experience in public presenting as male was exactly one month before starting law school. I had just lost my 29-year-old childhood best friend to a totally unexpected brain aneurysm. I was grief-stricken so I went to the only nearby gay bar for community support. Channeling my best friend, I found the courage to use the men's room for the first time, but a large, muscular, white, cisgender man in a black security shirt followed me and told me that I was in the wrong bathroom. I looked him in the eye and said that I wasn't. He looked at my chest, then with a look of disdain insisted, "Yes, you are." He demanded my ID. I stood my ground and he called the police, but feeling intimidated I grabbed my license and left, passing the cops on the stairs outside. They asked me if there was a problem and I replied, "No." I was devastated and betrayed.

But I mark this as the beginning of my trans advocacy: When I started law school, I filed a complaint against the bar with the local human rights commission. I testified at a hearing where the lesbian

---

*   Female to male.

owners stated, "We don't have to do anything for *those* people." It was shocking and hurtful to see what I considered to be my community turn on me, but legally they were correct. There was no local legislation protecting trans people, so even gay people could feel safe discriminating against us. Though I lost at the hearing, I felt pride at speaking out.

My identity as a lawyer formed alongside my trans identity. Sometimes your advocacy starts from your own experiences of injustice. Stand up. Learn the skills to do it for yourself and for the others who will benefit from your work.

This was my wake-up call. Like mainstream culture, the 1990s to 2000s LGBT community was (and often still is) a caste system based on race, class, gender, ability/disability, socioeconomics, and many other factors based on an assimilationist goal of hetero/cisnormativity and of fitting in with conventional society. Many gay leaders openly questioned why trans people were included in the movement, and some were unabashedly transphobic. Cisgender leadership prioritized the issues of white, wealthy gay and lesbian people in positions of power with the (unfulfilled) promise to come back for the rest later. This tension caught the public eye in 2007 when the community divided over a gay-only version of the Employment Nondiscrimination Act (ENDA) introduced by openly gay Congressman Barney Frank and supported by the Human Rights Campaign, the most influential LGBT organization of the time. The trans community's response was a campaign of four hundred organizations supporting a trans-inclusive United ENDA, politicizing many of us in the community, spurring us into action.

I was also deeply moved while marching in the first Trans Day of Action in 2005. It was pivotal for me to feel the safety and power of numbers. We marched to call attention to the violence, discrimination, and institutionalization enacted on trans and gender-nonconforming people, and we connected this to the broader struggle for justice for all oppressed people. Led by trans leaders of color and protected by legal observers, we roared, "Whose streets? Our streets!" I was emboldened by the community building and action.

In 2007, I was invited to be the sole "trans political speaker" at

Northampton Pride. The tokenization felt insufficient, particularly given the background of the United ENDA momentum. It was time for trans people to move into political action like what I experienced with the march for Trans Day of Action in 2005. I had recently graduated law school and was completing my second year of a clerkship in western Massachusetts, and a group of us were raring for action. I used my credit card to rent a room at the local community center, we printed fliers inviting people to attend the first ever New England Trans Pride March organizing meeting, and we hoped people would come. Sometimes you need to take a risk, even if you fail. But if there is a community need, somehow it will be met.

And it was. Nearly 50 people attended from multiple support groups that were all in the local area but who had never been in the same room. Allies showed up. There was dialogue and tension. A long-time Black trans leader questioned if trans people of color really needed a march over a safe space to connect. Others expressed fear that only a few people would march and that we would be ridiculed. It was eight solid months of tense, messy community organizing. We held meetings at organizers' homes and used consensus decision-making. We approached fundraising as an opportunity for engagement and raised enough money, dollar by dollar, to fly trans leaders in for the march itself, including the Stonewall veteran Miss Major Griffin-Gracy. We experienced barriers in obtaining permits and blowback in op-eds by cisgender gay people accusing us of dividing the community. But we proved our point when over a thousand people strode down the street on June 7, 2008 for trans justice. Trans musicians and political organizers filled six hours on the stage under a blazing hot sun. Our slogan was: "Remember Stonewall? That was us." The GLBTQ Legal Advocates & Defenders (GLAD) used the day to launch its Transgender Rights Project, and, after they apologized to me, the gay bar that had kicked me out of the men's room even hosted the afterparty.

The organizing was challenging and imperfect, but we created a community and the only family some people had, as well as a powerful sense of purpose, which translated into political progress. Sadly, our work did not protect everyone from the harsh realities trans people face; we lost two trans community members to suicide during the eight months of organizing. A decade afterward, steering committee member Christa Leigh Steele-Knudslien, who later transformed the event into the Miss Trans America Pageant, was murdered by her husband in 2018.

The connections helped fuel trust in myself and in my community that I used to do even more. Shortly after the march, fellow trans activist Tony Ferraiolo and I collaborated on a trans-led not-for-profit. We both knew how critical it was for trans people to access affirming surgeries, and that they were out of reach for most of the trans community due to discrimination and poverty. In 2008, we launched the Jim Collins Foundation, a national not-for-profit with a mission to fund surgeries for trans people in need. We learned from mentors that others had tried to start similar organizations but none had yet succeeded. We were challenged by long-time community activists publicly to not "get people's hopes up." It was disappointing that so many didn't believe. We also faced systemic transphobia, as the IRS originally denied not-for-profit recognition, asking us to show how these surgeries "are truly medically necessary." This was no surprise given their position in a case brought by GLAD on behalf of Rhiannon O'Donnabhain in *O'Donnabhain v. Commissioner*, which was happening at the same time. In the O'Donnabhain case, the brave plaintiff, Rhiannon O'Donnabhain, challenged the refusal of the IRS to deem her transition-related medical care as medically necessary under the tax code. In 2010, Rhiannon won her case, which provided an important building block to the future of trans healthcare. The IRS lost and we celebrated. When they were compelled to recognize the medical necessity of gender-affirming surgeries in that case, they had no choice but to recognize the same for us. We received our not-for-profit recognition.

When Tony and I stepped down after a decade of volunteer work on the board, leaving the foundation in the hands of new trans leadership, we had successfully funded twenty surgery grants to trans people in need and raised awareness of the need for trans healthcare. The organization continues to flourish.

✷ ✷ ✷

My decision to attend law school took my activism even further. After experiencing blatant discrimination when interviewing with firms, I quickly realized that I would need to leverage all my expertise and identity not just to survive as a first-generation lawyer, to pay my law school debt, and to make it in the legal profession, but to make change. I can attest that it matters who is at the table, and sometimes you have to make waves. I've heard advice given to people in underrepresented communities to "Keep your head down, do your job well, and then you will be in a position of power to make a difference." But that didn't work for me. Disruption might be your most important legacy.

I moved to New York City terrifyingly without a job, but thankfully I landed a position as the first staff attorney for the Transgender Legal Defense & Education Fund, Inc., although I wasn't making enough to eat and pay rent in NYC. A little over a year later, I was hired as the transgender rights attorney for Lambda Legal, the nation's oldest and largest LGBT legal organization.

For several years, I was the only transgender attorney at the table. Over the course of the decade I spent at Lambda Legal, I advocated to expand from my one tokenized position to the creation of a formal Transgender Rights Project. I was appointed director and hired a diverse staff, increasing power within the organization for trans people and those from other marginalized groups. Externally we focused on visibility through the creation of the Transgender Rights Toolkit, which included actual photos and stories of trans people. We created videos of our plaintiffs, the most famous being of Robina Asti, at the time a 92-year-old trans woman and World War II veteran who was denied survivor benefits after the death of her husband when the social security administration claimed she was not a woman at the time of her marriage. We were victorious! And in doing so we secured a win not only for Robina but for all trans people in similar positions. And most importantly, we introduced Robina's story to the world. She launched her legacy organization, the Cloud Dancers Foundation, to bring visibility to trans seniors, and when she died at age 99, the *New York Times* covered her obituary.

My voice was amplified when I was a spokesperson in the media and on the evening news, but be warned: Do media work on your terms. There is risk in putting your personal story out there as an openly trans person, and I was targeted with hate, including by allegedly progressive "trans-exclusionary radical feminist" groups that claim the label of feminism but who also—in a seeming contradiction to the notion that we all have the right to body and identity autonomy—reject the validity of trans people. Be sure that your work, especially if on behalf of an organization, is rightly valued. Be authentic and be careful to not be misused by others. Make the opportunity a space for more stories than your own, particularly for those most marginalized in our society.

I've also had the opportunity to do some international work, forming connections with trans leaders around the world. It has been powerful to have these connections and to support each other in the work we do, and we each see the common threads of colonialism, imperialism, and racism in varying degrees. Here again, it is imperative to persevere and to step forward; we are the experts in our own lives and need to lead the work, not just be the subjects of the work.

I hope I've played a role, in some small way, in the gains made by our community.

* * *

Politically, there has been progress and then devastation. We were lifted high by President Obama, but then fell hard when the Trump machine rolled back so many of the advances I and others had made. For me, this time caused the most severe anxiety and despair I've ever experienced.

Doors opened during the Obama Administration. I was invited to join the first Trans White House Convening in 2011. We made tremendous progress in trans-inclusive legislation across the country, and the Department of Justice was aggressive in shutting down laws harmful to our community like the North Carolina bill to exclude trans people from appropriate restrooms. They even released positive guidance on how to interpret trans inclusion in Title IX. Attorney General Loretta Lynch made a famous speech in 2016, telling trans people:

> Let me also speak directly to the transgender community itself. Some of you have lived freely for decades. Others of you are still wondering how you can possibly live the lives you were born to lead. But no matter how isolated or scared you may feel today, the Department of Justice and the entire Obama Administration wants you to know that we see you; we stand with you; and we will do everything we can to protect you going forward. Please know that history is on your side. This country was founded on a promise of equal rights for all, and we have always managed to move closer to that promise, little by little, one day at a time. It may not be easy—but we'll get there together.[1]

The outlook seemed promising.

But once same-sex marriage was secured, the right wing needed another scapegoat, and trans people were the easy target. We have very little political power, are deeply misunderstood by the general public, and are still marginalized even within the larger LGBTQIA+ movement. According to LGBTQ Funder, trans communities receive only three cents to every hundred dollars spent on overall LGBTQ issues.[2] Meanwhile, anti-trans groups are well-organized, well-funded, and fueled by hate and public ignorance.[3]

The blowback from our success was worse than many of us could imagine. It is an uphill battle once again.

The right wing seeks to capitalize on a fundamental lack of understanding of who trans people are, and whether gender identity is even real. Their choice of the term "biological sex" in anti-trans propaganda, state laws, and anti-trans litigation is a direct challenge to the validity of trans people: If chromosomes or genital characteristics are ruled as the only definers of gender, then trans people's identities will suddenly be "unreal." In other words, trans people won't exist. Thus, the social and political movement made popular in 2018 of #WontBeErased.

One of my most important contributions as a lawyer was to address the validity of gender identity head-on in a way that even my cisgender allied colleagues could grasp. In 2015, I wrote a law review article aimed at my fellow litigators arguing that we must first understand what gender identity is and why it matters to be successful advocates. I knew that the battle being waged in the courts would be about whether gender identity is real. When I and others represent trans people, we cite medical science to explain how sex determinations involve multiple factors, such as hormone levels, chromosomes, genital characteristics, secondary sex characteristics, and so on. There is natural human variation, and intersex traits are more common than people think. But for all people—cisgender, transgender, intersex—the most important factor in determining gender is one's deeply held internal understanding of themselves. It is core to one's self. It is impossible to change one's gender identity and unethical to try. It is also why, for some, treatment is to adjust the body to match the mind.

The victories we have had in the courts, even during the Trump era, have been incremental and heartening. The rule seems to be that when we can put a face on our trans clients as the vulnerable and dignified human beings that they are, we win. Courts cannot deny our humanity and have no option but to acknowledge us as full persons under the law, deserving basic dignities like the right to use a restroom in public, the right to access housing and healthcare, to be free from violence and cruel and unusual punishment in prisons. Conversely, we continue to lose in the courts and in the court of public opinion when our opponents put forward pretend hypotheticals about the *idea* of us and how we allegedly threaten cisgender people's comfort or safety. Fearmongering continues to be their powerful and effective strategy, forcing trans people to risk life and limb when being out and proud, which is necessary but much to ask when violence against our community has increased and when murders of trans women of color has been named an epidemic by the American Medical Association.[4,5]

It has been terrifying to be a visible trans leader in the face of such targeted, organized anti-trans animus by the Trump Administration, appropriately labeled the "Discrimination Administration."[6] When Trump was elected, we anticipated our lives would become more difficult, but couldn't fathom the reality of enduring the daily onslaught of attempts to dehumanize our already deeply marginalized population. The volume and frequency were too much. The pain and burnout were real. It impacted me. I had fought for decades to increase the visibility and legal recognition of trans people, and then we were in the crosshairs of a calculated political attack like the easy targets of a playground bully. Those of us on the front lines existed in continuous fight or flight, seemingly outnumbered and outmaneuvered. We needed our allies in greater numbers and needed new perspectives on our own experiences and our value as leaders. We could no longer allow cisgender gay people to speak for or over us. We had to speak for ourselves. We had to trust ourselves.

Surviving transphobia means that we must take things into our own hands, mobilize, create community, and build support for each other even in the hardest of times. I have been so inspired to see the numbers of cisgender allies who have stepped forward in solidarity. I wish it didn't take such blatant and extreme injustice to spur people to action, but I am grateful nonetheless. I am also glad to see our numbers growing, and the movement including nonbinary visibility. We are no longer deeply in the shadows. We are living authentically, and we have a right to be here.

# Colt St. Amand

## Both/And

Colt St. Amand (he/they) is a transgenderqueer Two Spirit queer lesbimandyke of white and Indigenous heritage, both binary and nonbinary at once. He is now the medical director of the Gender Wellness Center at the Bassett Healthcare Network in upstate New York. He holds an MD from the University of Texas Medical Branch and a PhD from the University of Houston, and has  recently completed his Family Medicine residency at the Mayo Clinic. Like most contributors to this book, he is an extraordinarily devoted activist, appearing regularly in journals, in books, and in the media. He is an assistant professor teaching gender and sexual health at Baylor College of Medicine and the University of Houston. He has published dozens of peer-reviewed manuscripts in the field of gender health. He has given presentations at universities, medical schools, residency programs, mental health conferences, trans and queer community events, public and private schools, nonprofit groups, agencies, youth groups, places of worship, and corporations. Where he finds the energy, I have no idea.

A pet person, he lives with his partner Sean (they) and a sharpei mix Phoenix. Colt and I have known each other through the unofficial trans healthcare activist community for a decade or more. www.thegenderdoctor.com

A bell rang, and the names of the dead were read aloud alongside the gruesome details of the transphobic violence that took their lives. It was Trans Day of Remembrance (TDOR) in 2007, and I was a newly out trans person. This was the first community event I'd ever attended. I looked around the vigil between the trauma stories and it was then that I thought, "Whoa...this is my first time surrounded by other transgender siblings." It scared me and I spun in my head thinking about the future, about everyone's safety. At the same time, I embraced that I truly wasn't alone in feeling the presences around me. Trans Day of Remembrance—a necessary day of honoring our dead, especially the Black and Brown trans femmes no longer among us—was the only holiday our community had at the time.

Two truths existed at once: the "both/and," as I call it. We held the knowledge that our community was, and still is, at very high risk of being murdered or of dying by suicide. *And* I felt a deep pride in being a trans person and in connection with the others, honoring our presence on Earth. *Both* were true. I felt an internal "yikes" and a peace at the same time. Looking around at the TDOR's elders and yelders (young people who have identified as trans for longer than us, a term taught to me by my chosen sister Dee Dee Watters*) allowed me to embrace how wondrous our gender diverse community, or as I like to call us, our gender family, was. So, as you graze these pages, know that you are in good company.

I've always been clear that I wasn't a girl, but understanding my gender beyond that has been a lifelong journey. I'm clearer about what I am not than what I am. One of the biggest lessons I've learned since that first TDOR is to respect the "both/ands" in my own being. If I meet someone at a staff meeting for a quick hello, I will introduce myself simply as a transgender man, as I do not owe a thorough explanation of my identity to anybody, plus it's tiring to have to explain my identities over and over. On the other hand, when talking to someone who speaks fluent "gender," I'll say something more descriptive, like

---

* You can read Dee Dee's chapter earlier in this book.

"I'm a transgenderqueer lesbimandyke, both binary and nonbinary at once," and even Two Spirit if there's time.

I didn't realize that this label fit until I met a Two Spirit person, Kelley Blair (they). They listened to me speak about my "both/and" identities—the ongoing feeling of having one foot over here and another over there. They replied, "That is a very Two Spirit way of thinking. Do you have any Native heritage?" I hesitated, but then let out, "Well, my parents have always said so, but it's really remote and I don't think of myself as Indigenous because I am so white..." They stopped me before I could continue, and said, "Nope. Nope. You're Two Spirit and I am going to mentor you."

So much of being trans involves holding multiple things that may not obviously go together, but each can be true. There's a humanization here. I am both Catholic and trans. I am both a psychologist and a physician. I am both binary and nonbinary. I can have a Two Spirit guide even when outsiders may not understand. None of these cancels another out. I sometimes intuitively tell myself, "You can't be this because you're that." But where did I get that notion? These limiting ideas come from colonization and the politics of fear and run contrary to many Indigenous teachings that trans, nonbinary, and Two Spirit people are sacred. We do not owe anyone an explanation of our truth, and our truth does not have to make sense to anyone except ourselves.

After all these years of learning and unlearning, I insist on saying I am who I am: "both/and." Dualities offer honesty and connection. I encourage you, reader, to honor your own contrasts, because not everybody will. I found this to be especially true in care settings.

My early encounters with doctors included a lot of misinformation that did not create room for nuance. In 2007, when I first considered the possibilities of hormone therapy, any care that respected transgender people as human beings with unique identities was considered radical. I went to a clinic in the island city of Galveston, Texas, known for having offered revolutionary care to transgender people since the 1970s. However, the research to support my nontraditional gender simply did not exist yet. I sat in the office with décor that had not been updated since the 1970s, and they asked me about my sexuality.

They reiterated the stereotype that it was rare for trans men to be attracted to men; according to them, trans people were uniformly heterosexual. Perhaps this was a conscious or unconscious attempt to police gender and sexuality, and to position trans people neatly within a binary, cishet society. Perhaps they thought they were doing what was best for me.

But I knew I was queer, so instead of believing the doctors and questioning my own identity, which I had done before, I held my chin up and thought, "No." It simply was not my lived experience nor what I saw in my own community. Sometimes they only see the surface, but you don't always need to accept what they say. It was another reminder that we each contain deep truths that outsider "experts" may never understand. I told them that most of the trans men I knew in the community were not heterosexual; they were surprised but did not argue with my experience.

A few weeks later, I walked back in through the revolving doors, resolved to pursue hormone therapy regardless. This time, I asked the providers about what changes to anticipate if I were to use testosterone, and here again the information was limited or objectively incorrect. I'd grow more hair, build muscle more easily, my voice would drop—they knew this and so did I. However, the doctors couldn't provide much data about how hormones might impact my mental health and relationships. Instead, they told me, "Maybe these hormones will make you angrier, and you might be more likely to go to jail." Their only thought was that I would become a changed and unrecognizable person. I did not know how to express my emotions in that moment without being scrutinized. All I could do was listen; I played along so I would be deemed an "appropriate candidate" for transition. I had no other choice. According to them, the testosterone I knew I needed might make me a risk to myself and to society.

But absolutely none of this was the case.

As I began testosterone, my cat Haley remained my companion and I didn't become hostile. In fact, I became more level in my emotions and thoughts. Sometimes, it's simply the unknown that other people fear. Which is to say that the most important "both/and" they forgot here is that I am *both* trans *and* human.

Growing up in rural Texas and attending Catholic schools didn't make matters easier. There are so many expectations invented by others just to limit people who are different. Governments and individuals within the state, and administrations in religious schools, have long pointed at queer and trans people and said that "Those people are just messed up." They believe we are sick, perverted, delusional, sinful, eager to enact our depravities upon innocents and to convert them to our immoral ways. Others who also claim to have "good intentions" assume that we are all sad, depressed, and suicidal—while ignoring the impact of the hostile environments in which we exist. They attempt to manipulate us into believing we are better off alive and miserable, or dead. They discounted my vision of becoming a happy, healthy transgenderqueer adult.

Honoring our divinity stands in the face of the false and shallow narratives. When I was subject to many, many religious messages that I was sinful and that the way I love could never be sanctified, I had to unlearn those messages and embrace my own sacredness. I survived by holding to my own truth and with the support of my blood and chosen family. I think of my many lineages often. I recommend it to anyone feeling alone or trapped in a corner. The transcestors and Two Spirit Indigenous relatives who came before us paved a way for us to exist and to thrive. I am forever grateful to them.

I've framed my career around pushing back against restrictions. I felt obligated to get the best education I could to take care of us, using my privilege, access, and parents' encouragement to get my PhD in clinical psychology, because I believe it's essential that we are centered as experts on our own experiences. When I began seeing clients, I refused to replicate the oppression I experienced as a patient. I noticed patterns in the trans people across from me. The majority had no immediate need for psychotherapy but simply required access to hormones, surgery, or an affirming medical provider who could give a pelvic exam without it being traumatizing. To this day, I try to keep my waitlist for surgery letters as short as possible, and I avoid direct questions that would stigmatize my patients in the way I was not long ago. Here again I am *both* a provider subject to medical ethics and laws *and* a trans person attempting to minimize the harm these rules cause. It's essential that we learn from our pasts and build a better future.

In another "both/and," I completed my thesis on transmasculine sexuality to document that we are *not* nearly all heterosexual as my former doctors believed. I was *both* a researcher *and* member of the community being researched. This descriptive study examined romantic relationships in a large-scale, international sample, and the data revealed what I knew to be true: We are not at all uniform in our sexual orientations. Rather, about a third of the participants were attracted to men only, another third were exclusively interested in women, and the final third were romantically open to all genders. Most commonly, the transmasculine people in my research identified their sexual orientation as queer and not straight, as previously assumed by professionals.[1]

Seeing the results, I felt proud of myself for challenging the mainstream false and restrictive narratives about who we are. Additionally, I achieved my goal of generating an early resource; now many other trans researchers have conducted important work of their own. Through trans-led studies and other writing, we create a body of literature based on our own understandings of ourselves that we can use to get our genuine needs met, not our "needs" as defined by outsiders.[2] If you're research-minded, we can use your help!

Later, I pursued another project in response to my doctors' incorrect ideas. Starting well before my first transition-related medical appointment, I had seen LiveJournal and other forums where community members taking testosterone shared statements like "My life has changed for the better" and "It's been so amazing," so I already knew testosterone and social transition could have positive emotional effects. I was not seeing anyone saying that they became an aggressive monster. Why weren't doctors telling me this? Why were they so focused on the physical effects? This is why we must tell our own stories. My papers showed that neither anger nor inappropriate behavior were represented in the data. Just the opposite: I found that most experienced mental health benefits, including decreased levels of stress, depression, and anxiety. In fact, the trans patients sampled reported that taking testosterone helped their emotional wellbeing more than daily psychotherapy, starting psychiatric medication, or electroshock therapy.[3] The results were plain to see. Now there was even more data with more accurate information for doctors to cite, if only they'd read it. They forget that you and I are not just physical beings. We, as a gender family, are multidimensional, emotional, spiritual beings with vibrant lives and who take interest in things far beyond our appearances.

These past few years have been difficult for those of us who are healthcare workers, therapists, and researchers who are also gender family. We hear right-wing myths targeting our communities, especially our youth, while we aim to provide accurate and comprehensive healthcare. Many of us have experienced the very human desire to hide away or to numb ourselves out of reality. Sometimes I just want to stay home and hug my dog; if you've felt that too, that urge is completely understandable and okay. I am both a professional and an advocate serving trans communities, expressing strength and resilience, and a vulnerable, anxious trans person myself. As we help our patients, we must also care for ourselves and each other.

On any given day I am at a baby's delivery, setting an appointment for a trans person who needs a letter for surgery, presenting at a conference, seeing patients in the clinic; it's challenging to take a breather. I am a true "tranpa," though I am only in my late thirties, sharing my experience and advising others. I often feel myself running close to empty. I try to address my basic needs first, like "Am I hydrated? When was the last time I ate?" I am grateful to have a partner who is so emotionally aware and my colleagues, a community of professionals with whom I feel a kinship. One more "both/and"—I am *both* exhausted *and* grateful. My peers and I have all become better about asking, "Hey, how are ya? Should we chat? What would help you?" In a time of chaos, it's about keeping tabs on our own self-care while also checking in with others for mutual support. These are things you can try as well.

At the same time, many of us in the trans and nonbinary family, whether we're intersex, agender, demi, Two Spirit, genderqueer, trans men or trans women, or anything else, experience isolation. For those of us in medical school, residency, or other clinical settings, there are often no other trans medical folk around us or even who we know. There can be a loneliness.

To address this isolation, I created a multidirectional mentoring group for trans providers and graduate students where we could come together for mutual support and education. We mentor each other. It's beautiful to experience settings of mostly other trans professionals. Very few of us were or are supervised by people who knew or know how to appropriately support transgender providers or patients, so we assist each other through peer support and wisdom sharing. For instance, simply gathering with other trans people in the profession has done a lot of necessary normalizing for me, in stark contrast to the solitude of working or studying. With intentional coalition building, we can be better able to survive and even thrive in our own lives. We build power to continue making a way for our community to exist in our full beauty. Maybe think about ways you can create networks within your own circles. What does it mean to receive appropriate training?

I've had to find ways to do advocacy and, at the same time, to not burn out. Because there's a lack of infrastructure for training mental health and medical providers on working with trans clients, there are countless individual talks, panels, and media interviews where outsiders want to learn. But these are also situations where they can take advantage of us. For community endeavors, such as PFLAG or trans-led coalitions, I'll gladly contribute without being paid. But I regularly get asked by large institutions to provide education, and often they expect this to be free or "for exposure." I offer this advice to anyone in our gender fam: Be very intentional in establishing boundaries around working pro bono. Who will honor your own "both/ands"? I've created a standardized email: "Dr. Colt no longer provides labor without compensation." Excitement is not enough when well-funded, endocisgender-led organizations ask to learn about trans people in a transnegative society. I remind them that they are asking for work, work that has value, and offer to negotiate a fee. We all deserve more than temporary validation. We deserve to be paid.

The Trans Day of Visibility is an effort to celebrate us while we are alive and exuberant, but the irony is that this was created only to have a more joyous version of a day where we demand to be seen than the Trans Day of Remembrance. And my own public presence is complicated, as a white-passing person navigating a binary presentation in professional spaces when my identity is so much more complex. I sometimes mourn not being more obviously readable as a trans person, and the ongoing pressure of needing to look more like a "queer butch person" or an endocis man. We must ask ourselves: What does being visible look like, and when is it necessary?

To me, "both/and" involves waking up in the morning, recognizing the ongoing struggle *and* leaning in to my queer ancestors and transcestors in times of doubt and celebration. I honor the value of being visible to myself and to my puppy when she jumps into my lap with a wagging tail. I look for the gifts of being trans, like choosing my own name, or the delight I experience when a young person asks questions with their eyes lit up. The hostile laws trying to limit our visibility will insist again and again on minimizing our ability to live. *And* I never forget what was said by educator, artist, and community advocate Johnny Boucher, "Queer ancestors are the people who took [pieces of] broken glass and turned them into stained glass." Be that yourself, too. So, I refocus the light back here: We can *both* honor our suffering *and* we can be so much more...a source of sacred beauty and wisdom.

# Lexie Bean

# When I Didn't Have the Words

**Lexie Bean** (they/he) is a white, nonbinary, trans, and neurodivergent artist whose work for the past 15 years has involved aiding fellow trans survivors of domestic violence and sexual assault. They began their activism at a rape crisis hotline in rural Ohio, and have since published *Written on the Body*, an anthology of letters authored by survivors to their body parts of choice, and *The Ship We Built*, noted as the first middle-grade novel released by a major U.S. publisher centering a trans boy to be penned by one. Additionally, they have been interviewed by and written for *Teen Vogue*, *Them*, *Kirkus Reviews*, *Autostraddle*, and more, and serve on the leadership council for RAINN, the nation's largest anti-sexual violence organization. They are "passionate about creating honest and complex trans narratives through writing, performance, and film." Currently Lexie is co-directing their first feature-length documentary, *What Will I Become?*

We met through friends of friends of friends as I was outlining this book and had numerous discussions on their own chapter and the overall themes of *Surviving Transphobia*, which I've found valuable. Here they share the nuances of being a trans survivor of sexual abuse; please read with care. www.lexiebean.com

I stopped speaking at the age of nine.

As a child, I was not out as someone transgender because I didn't know that the term existed. I was not out as a survivor of sexual violence because I didn't know those words were an option for me or for anyone else, either.

I can say it now: I am a trans survivor of childhood sexual abuse with cycles repeated well into my adulthood.

My transness was treated as an emergency long before my abuse. I was sent, with good intention, to a therapist to "know my true identity," but it only made me feel further from myself and from wanting to live. I was consumed with grief because of other people's flawed understandings of how to protect a vulnerable child in a transphobic world.

The fact that I'm speaking to this now is hopeful. It's all I can offer you, reader, that time and distance have allowed me to find the words "survivor" and "trans." To have language can add to the suffering by making it more real, but it also allows me to name my identities and provides an understanding that I'm not the only one.

Writing my debut novel, *The Ship We Built*, offered a rare opportunity to revisit my own story for personal healing and growth. The book follows a ten-year-old trans child who never found the words I did, but who did discover many ways to build a world that he wanted to live in. *The Ship We Built* was published in 2020 and is banned in much of Texas as part of their ridiculous attempt to take allegedly "dangerous" terms out of young minds.[1] This should be no surprise given that Texas is officially unwilling to tell the difference between abuse and affirming transness through harmful policymaking.[2]

I call for change: We need to recognize that transgender survivors of childhood sexual abuse exist. Those of us at this intersection have the same challenges as anyone trans, and we have ones unique to us.

So let me tell you about *Ship*'s protagonist, Rowan, someone I created to help me feel less lonely as I navigated my own survival. Like me, he gave up on speaking. Like me, he was afraid of exploring a masculinity that reminded him of the people who'd hurt him most. Like me, he thought what happened at home was normal.

If Rowan resonates with you, know that the people who make the rules, often transphobic at their core, fear our words because words give us power and the bigots can then no longer pretend that we're invisible. We have bodies. They're ours. They take up space. We take up space. I learned the term "childhood sexual abuse" because I was passing time in Barnes and Noble and picked up a book much like the one you are holding now. One that also named both harm and resilience, loudly and clearly. I sat in the carpeted aisle and thought, "That's me." I found the word "trans" while scrolling on Facebook, seeing a friend's coming-out post, and immediately realizing I had the same feelings too. The former gave me a deep dread, the latter a euphoria. Both discoveries made clear that there would be a long journey ahead without guaranteed support.

Through *The Ship We Built* and other advocacy with fellow trans survivors, including an anthology I edited called *Written on the Body* and well over a hundred workshops and panels, I've studied the harm of equating transness to abuse and that of sexual abuse victims being ignored.

There are many reasons why transgender and gender nonbinary people of all ages, but namely youth, are more vulnerable to domestic violence and sexual abuse. Pairing Rowan's stories of harm and coping with my own, here are nine problems with how we address this in our culture and how they perpetuate transphobia.

**One**, many trans people face social isolation. In *Ship*, Rowan countered his loneliness by attaching letters to balloons. The reader became the sole witness to what he found impossible to describe to anyone else. Like so many of us, he yearned for a friend.

I too had a lonely coming out and didn't trust those around me to hold my story either. My partner at the time, not yet aware of their own transness, feared being in their first gay relationship—not what they signed up for. Some of my dearest friends, cisgender bisexuals and lesbians, accused me of diluting dyke culture. *Why not just let women be masculine?* It was just another manifestation of transphobia, and my desire to disappear grew. Like Rowan, others told me how I should live based on their expectations, not my own.

I claim my agency by scheduling a top surgery consultation in NYC, but I feel anxious as soon as I enter the glass doors. Faceless before and after photos of cis women and a cluster of cis sisters gossiping about Botox fill the lobby. The forms have no field for pronouns. I'm glad to have left my caterpillar backpack at home, afraid the doctor might think I am too feminine, and therefore "a confused woman" in a binary world. Just another way we, trans people, lose autonomy.

The surgeon says big words while plastic models of perfectly shaped boobs stare at me. I wish I'm not alone but I put on the gown and open my arms while he pushes away the thin floral fabric and *feels*. He continues talking, his hands still there, cold and firmly cupping me.

With a stray of his gaze, I think he has the information he needs. But his hands are still there and he gives another squeeze. He never tells me it is okay to close my gown.

He probably took the training where he was told how grateful I, as a trans patient, would be for this experience; how lonely, yet eager, I'd feel.

I swallow hard, trying to thwart PTSD and dissociation, glad that my previous consultation somewhere else was virtual. I feel a strange relief knowing that it isn't always this way. I have to convince myself it isn't that bad: Hardly anybody knows I'm here. So I just call this normal—a doctor's appointment where I get felt up.

I need you to know that this was misogyny and transphobia, as he looked for the woman that I was not. But alone and intimidated, I said nothing but "Thank you" and gave the receptionist my insurance information.

That night I see my then-partner for dinner. I promise myself not to tell them what happened because behind closed doors they do the same—focus on my womanhood and fondle me, even when I say no. It's a particular loneliness to not fit in to the traditional narrative of male perpetrator and female victim. My partner yells at me outside the subway to announce to passersby that they are straight, that they resent me for letting go of a femininity that they were initially drawn to. Trans-on-trans violence. Again I lose my voice. I walk to the apartment embarrassed and wait for them to come home. Later, with no one to tell in person, I write my feelings to the anonymous readers of *Ship*.

Have I told you that you're not alone? This is true no matter how small your support system. What happened was much bigger than me and the traditional survivor story, and more than just the people who'd harmed me. It's systemic. Realizing this gave me the courage to write it all down.

**Two**, trans people, especially youth, experience pressure to be "heroes" and to be brave enough to not need protection. But we are human, and we do.

Shortly after that visit with the surgeon I began compiling my next anthology, *Written on the Body*, a collection of letters by trans survivors to their body parts. Over 40 people contributed, many struggling to feel "trans enough" or "survivor enough." There's an expectation that we only speak as "cured" and as having "finished" transition, that we frame our narratives as beautifully conclusive. But this is a mistake.

I held space for the writers to say whatever they needed so they could rebuild their relationships with otherwise-disconnected parts of themselves. I participated too. I wrote to my back, to the stray hair on my cheek; I wrote to my voice, which arguably isn't a body part, but I say, yes, it's something body related that can be broken and that can heal.

Yet I couldn't find the strength to write my own sections until everybody else's were complete. I was praised as the survivor advocate, starting as a rape crisis hotline volunteer in college, leading workshops and performance tours throughout my twenties. But the deeper irony was that I kept my ongoing abusive relationship a secret. I told myself I could handle it, and even tricked myself into believing it was inevitable. I knew the statistics of trans sexual and domestic abuse but remained with my partner regardless. I was supposed to be strong.

It's (allegedly) the trans way. We have to be so confident in our need to change so we can convince outsiders we're real, and we sometimes apply that pressure to other aspects of life too.

This is when I took Rowan's story more seriously and he started filling up my notebook. I gave him the softness and doubt I felt but could not have in my daily life. He was ten and saved no one but me. Through him I had these qualities and experienced the vulnerability

I couldn't show, especially while trying to build my relationship with masculinity. This is what made storytelling a pathway to survival.

**Three,** as trans people, we often lack vocabulary for our own bodies, so we don't always have the ability to describe the violations we've undergone.

Rowan refers to bodies as shadows and he explains his fear to readers through Beanie Babies. He never names what happens; he's too lost inside himself and simultaneously too far away. As a kid, I referred to the sites of harm as my ribs, as close as I could get to the truth. Whether trans or cis, children are not usually taught accurate language, so I protected my ribs with my hands and starved myself to find them with ease.

In my twenties I referred to a rape as someone "going inside without asking." That vagueness was enough to stay in denial, but it also kept me separate from myself. I didn't want to name my abuser's trans body or my own. Now 30 years old, I offer this suggestion to advocates and counselors when I lead trainings: Allow trans clients to define their own body parts, as we often use nonstandard or even playful terms, such as tranny-clit, cockpit, chest, man-boobs, popsicle, and more. An outsider applying traditional words to a trans person's body without asking is not only an act of transphobia, but it keeps people like me disempowered. And you, reader, can name yours too. Do it slowly, but it might just help.

**Four,** we have few public examples of healthy trans people in couples or polycules, leaving us to believe that relationships involving trans people should only happen in private.

All my early relationships were unspoken, and I was taught to keep my sexuality secret, healthy or otherwise. The only places it was allowed to be named were in letters, like for Rowan, or on Instant Messenger, another secret communication with a distant audience. My first examples of trans love were of sex workers with blurred faces on the show *Cops*, where it was something to be laughed at and criminal. I intentionally wrote a scene of Rowan watching his dad, his taboo lover, enjoying the show. It was clear that nobody should ever know. *Why can't we see Laverne Cox as a healthy, career-driven trans woman and spouse in an ongoing TV drama?*

My anxiety about being open around sex continued in college as I asked nearly every person I hooked up with if they planned to share it on Facebook. I'm sure this was a turn off for them, but I really didn't know what was safe to reveal openly. Whether it was sex with another queer person or someone reminding me of past abuse, I had no idea who would be watching or if the "TV police" would come for me too.

Even in my most public relationship, I struggled with the prospect of being discovered as a survivor and advocate in active abuse. I denied it even during my partner's repeated verbal and nonverbal misgendering; "Oh, I forgot," they'd say to me on the train home. Maybe they were only trying to protect me from the opinions of nearby families. Or perhaps they did forget because they too were learning about existing in public as someone trans themselves. Either way, because I never saw a healthy trans relationship, I never challenged the problems in my own. Until I did.

**Five**, societal transphobia keeps many trans survivors from coming forward in fear of reinforcing the negative stereotypes about our community.

The title, *The Ship We Built*, refers to the boxes Rowan and I were given at birth containing all the conditions and stereotypes foisted upon us—our genders, our home lives, what we are supposed to desire—and how we turned those boxes into ships to sail us away from harm. Through society's assumptions, we were fed the myth that we would never have a future if we were trans and abused.

I tried to free myself by dating as an out trans adult. After my former partner's internalized homophobia and transphobia, I was glad to meet bisexual and pansexual folks who I believed would be less likely to make assumptions. *Other people out of the box would know better, right?* But then I got so very hurt by a cis bisexual person who likely meant no harm. I accidentally said yes to something I didn't realize I'd said yes to, and he believed that I, a trans queer person, might enjoy it without appropriately communicating.

This assault was more challenging than any previous boundary crossing because I was afraid of being a queer or transgender stereotype. What happened is something I've only ever heard of in jokes.

I was afraid of being laughed at. I was afraid of getting my words wrong, or even worse, that this harm was inherent to who I am. *I know deep down that's not true.* And how was I to tell this story without worrying that cis people would twist my experience and make it even harder for trans community members to safely come out?

As an important reminder: The trans community will not be harmed by us speaking up. For much of my life I believed, as Rowan did, as many trans people and abuse survivors do, that we have little choice around what happens when we are intimate with others. Love outside of society's mold is possible and can be beautifully rewarding, but not when you don't think you can say no. I'm still learning what I want, and it's so hard to be sure when people have been choosing for me since childhood. I'm telling you this: it's okay to say no or to come up with your own safety words, and to say them aloud.

**Six**, trans people and sexual assault survivors already have difficulty being believed by ourselves and by others. Both are truths we hold inside, but both are identities where outsiders so often reject or demand proof of before accepting.

There was a time when I didn't want to walk in public because of the invisibility of my transness, but as a survivor I didn't want to stay home with certain people or memories either. In neither place did I feel believed. Rowan tries so hard to trust in himself. He tries to honor his gender fluidity by visiting a local river, or to address his abuse by drawing maps of what he knows and futures of what he wants.

The first #MeToo post I encounter is on Facebook. It's a night of final edits for *Written on the Body* and I am already drained by the emotional labor of the project. The post says "Copy and paste if you're a woman," presumably one cisgender, "who has been assaulted." The usual story is that all survivors are hyperfeminine, cis, straight women who have experienced abuse by men and for the first time in college, but I am none of those things. I've spent months on a book about survivors who were also none of those things, or who once did have those identities and have since come out as trans. I can only cry.

I think it might be a moment for nuance. Maybe organizations supporting #MeToo will be more willing to include trans people.

Instead, I receive responses that "We unfortunately do not have the time" to do a workshop about trans people. And in trainings, attendees frequently question, "How can we make space for trans survivors when abuse in women happens so often?" That they again mean cisgender women goes unsaid. A very smart trans social worker I interview says, "Just getting to say #MeToo is a luxury."

In an often-transphobic world, we have far too often been forced to give extra details about our private lives and to educate just to be acknowledged. We should not have to convince a professional that our transness is not the result of abuse or to overly explain to them what language is affirming.

While transgender people are less likely to be accepted in the survivor community, it's more likely for people to assume we are perpetrators. Rowan and I have each dealt with times where people have interpreted direct eye contact, an invitation for a hug, or even being asked on a date as an attack because of their unexamined transphobia. So many in our community suffer such loneliness for this as well. This has sometimes been labeled "walking while trans" and many trans women, especially less financially privileged trans women of color, have been charged as sex workers simply for existing outdoors.[3] Meanwhile, among community members using testosterone, a patch of facial hair, shortness, or a newly dropping voice is frequently labeled as "creepy" by strangers, close friends, and the cis men who once loved us.

All we ask is that they believe we are human and not monsters, and that they accept us at our word.

**Seven**, asking for help often isn't simple for trans people.

Trans boys and transmasculine-spectrum nonbinary people usually have trouble being accepted as victims because so many services are just for women. Trans girls and nonbinary femmes can be similarly rejected by organizations who still see them as men. These factors often exclude trans people from getting to participate in national conversations about intimate partner violence and from accessing life-saving resources like shelters—even though our community suffers very high rates of assault.[4]

We see this with Rowan in *The Ship We Built* and in my own story:

failure to pretend he's female often leads to harmful labels and violent care, like the conversion therapy I suffered when I came out.

While having the courage and space to write this down is important, feeling my anger is also hopeful. As are the moments I notice tides of forgiveness and try to continue my life.

Inappropriate medical interventions happen outside of emergencies too, like the time I meet a new primary doctor in New York. Outsiders often assume this city is safe for us, and it is when compared to most other places. But when I disclose, he assumes I am a trans woman because he hasn't heard of anything else. I try to be calm while teaching him trans 101.

After too long, he says, "So, you're trapped in the wrong body?"

"It's more like society doesn't see me," I explain, not even having had my temperature checked yet.

He scans me up and down and announces, "Seems like you care too much what people think. You should see a psychiatrist."

I could have ignored him, but this showed me that the person responsible for my care believed I was unstable. And I had to let him put the stethoscope on me anyhow.

By this time I finally had words including "trans" and "survivor," but there were consequences. I promised to lie to my doctors in the future when I needed, and five years later I am still seeking a primary care doctor or gyn I feel comfortable coming out to. As other authors in this book suggest, I need to offer myself grace when it's not safe to share all of me. We shouldn't have to, but it's okay to do what's necessary to get the basic care we need.

**Eight,** social services, especially in states pushing for transphobic laws, do not provide adequate resources to support trans people. Or the services we need simply don't exist. This leads many trans people and trans survivors of abuse to believe that help isn't for us.

The first time I write about my experience with abuse, gender, and sexuality, I am in high school. After turning in a written piece for a scholarship, which I hope will help me go off to college, I get pulled from class. I'm taken to a white room lined with banners for Midwest universities. The counselor says, "If what you wrote is true, I'm going to have to call the police." I'm seventeen. I want to go back to journalism class. I'm desperate to graduate so I can get far away from my abuser. All I can think about are the transphobic episodes of *Cops* or what foster care does to queer youth. I might even lose my scholarship and the opportunity to escape my own childhood sexual assault.

I guard my facial expression as I mull the options. First, I imagine myself telling the truth. Public schools are designed to identify people in need of help, but in my case, I knew the "help" they wanted to give would have caused an uproar of law enforcement, telling my story over and over to strangers, leaving my friends and our Gay-Straight Alliance, and maybe not even being believed in the end. Ultimately this would have just caused additional trauma.

Realizing I can't trust the system, I say to the brunette 40-something across from me, "It's not true. None of it."

She leaves it there. I return to my sixth-period class and watch the clock for the final bell, just hoping they've accepted my lie. Rowan also knows that involving the police usually leads to more harm than good, especially for trans people and people of color. He and his companion, Sofie, dream about going to the moon; they create maps and fetch a ladder from the garage, but they agree not to go if the moon has jails as well. Because if it does, it's not a different place.

It's terrible that the existing systems so poorly meet the needs of our most vulnerable people. *What does it mean for you to ask for help? What systems do you need to usher you and your loved ones to a safer world, maybe even to the moon?* I ask because I wish that counselor had asked me.

**And finally, nine**, trans people are coming out younger than ever.[5] This leaves trans youth at heightened risk of rejection from families as well as for houselessness, poverty, survival sex work, smoking, dropping out of school, substance abuse, saying yes to risky situations because they need to flee even more dangerous people and situations, self-harm, and even suicide.[6] Like everything else, this is because of society's transphobia and not anything about being trans itself.

Shortly after my incident at school I plan to run away, but when I drive, I can only think about steering off the highway's bridge. So, I don't go anywhere, not externally at least. I spend college trying to find an escape inside myself. I go in and out of the hospital in rural Ohio, searching for a cure for something I think nobody understands, only one state away from where I was raised.

I came out as a survivor at 22 through a self-published anthology. This is when I finally tried to escape everything I knew. I lived in over 40 homes in eight different countries, which my whiteness and fresh Bachelor's degree disguised as wanderlust. In reality, it was done in hope that neither my feelings nor specific people could catch up. Of course, this ended with another hospital visit, so I resolved that staying in one place was easier. This is a reminder that you don't owe anyone your story until you're ready.

*The Ship We Built* ends before Rowan meets the consequences of overtly coming out as trans or as a survivor. People ask how I chose the ending. I wanted readers to know that it finishes when he decides what he does and doesn't want to be normal. He hopes his normal, in the future, may not include his father. Maybe his normal will involve a phone call to someone who can help him get through the day, or a house with its own moon bounce. You too can dream of this, the big things and the little things. Whatever is within your reach. Building a new normal feels harder and harder right now under the loudmouth xenophobic politicians and their hateful policies, but new normals will still be possible as long as trans people build our own resources, like this book, and look out for each other.

The transphobia faced by survivors is profound. These nine barriers are the direct result of a culture that belittles childhood abuse survivors into savior acts and adult survivors as people who have simply made "the wrong decisions," and are some of the consequences of a transphobic society that ignores our voices even in progressive movements.

Some people are trans; some people are abused. Sometimes they're both. We deserve books and resources where our experiences are reflected and addressed. We deserve homes where we can be safe and doctors we can speak to openly. And we deserve genuine care, not further abuse in the guise of help from people in power. Not a government questioning whether a young reader's book about a transgender survivor of sexual abuse is young reader-appropriate.

One way to heal is to honor the trans sexual abuse survivors of all ages in our own lives, including ourselves. None of us deserved what happened. Another way to heal is to know that I lived this too, as did Rowan and so many others. We need community for reflection, for the mess, and for the reminders of words still unknown. And whenever you do find your words, whatever they may be, you will always be more than them. You are vibrant, alive, and always changing.

# Asa Radix

# A Call for Trans Providers and Researchers

**Asa Radix** (he/him) is a Black transgender man of Caribbean descent, the most brilliant and dedicated activist I know. He is also the most prolific and has authored or co-authored various standards and guidelines, including serving as a primary editor for the World Professional Association for Transgender Health (WPATH) Standards of Care, Version 8. He has published  countless peer-reviewed journal articles, his writing has appeared in textbooks and elsewhere, and he is a well-known lecturer at conferences worldwide. Asa currently works as the senior director of research and education at the Callen-Lorde Community Health Center and as a clinical associate professor of medicine at New York University. Asa trained in internal medicine and infectious disease at the University of Connecticut and later received an MPhil in epidemiology from Cambridge University and a PhD from Columbia University. His research focuses on STI/HIV risk, HIV prevention, and LGBTQIA+ health.

Another person I've known for many years, Asa is a shy man with an endearing smile, and who you want nothing more than to hug.

An extensive body of literature confirms that skilled and affirming healthcare is essential to the wellbeing of transgender and gender nonbinary people.[1,2] Over the last 50 years and with much effort, activists and medical providers have developed a broad network of community-led organizations, and I am honored to call many of these people colleagues, collaborators, and friends. Personally, I have also long been mentoring TGNB* medical school students, residents, and early career doctors and researchers, many of whom share the same passion for change. Sadly, countless in our communities still lack access.

Through my work as a physician and researcher, seeing clients, co-developing guidelines, establishing policy, and serving on boards, I see that one of the biggest systemic issues is that there are many providers without knowledge or cultural humility. Often, they enact their own biases. Sometimes it's less explicit.

One solution would be to increase the number of trans professionals in medicine and research. Less than 1 percent of U.S. medical students and physicians self-identify as transgender or gender nonbinary,[3] not because we're incapable, but because barriers prevent us from thriving in the field. I see my mentees, my professional peers, and those within research encounter these difficulties often.

I was the principal investigator on a 2019 study called "Experiences of Transgender and Gender Nonbinary Medical Students and Physicians."[4] Key results included: only 67 percent of current TGNB medical students and 57 percent of residents disclosed their trans identities to peers and supervisors, and 78 percent censored themselves to avoid accidental disclosure. And 69 percent had witnessed colleagues disparaging transgender and gender nonbinary patients, deducing from this that the environment was not safe for them to come out themselves. One does not need to be "out" to be discriminated against. Many trans physicians-to-be resign from their programs due to the lack of support and the loneliness that are common results of transphobia in the medical systems. As a trans physician and researcher, but also as a human, it's heartbreaking. This is in part what motivates me to keep doing my work.

---

\* Transgender and gender nonbinary.

We found that a high majority of participants experienced anxiety or depression. One reported, "I witnessed a lot of jokes about trans patients. Misgendering, misnaming, speculating about sex, gender, and judging a person's identity and the successfulness of their transition based on how they looked." This was an assault on both the patient and the student. Another student witnessed a resident perform a genital exam on a transgender woman against her will, not for any medical reason but specifically because the patient was trans and the doctor was curious. Other participants reported that their schools offered no protections and no advocates for them, even when facing overt verbal abuse and discrimination.

I've had mentees in medical schools around the country relate these same stories each time we speak. I had one doing a pediatrics rotation. The office had toys for the children, including blue bears and pink bears. When one toddler chose a bear that did not align with the "pink-girl/blue-boy" stereotype, they were reprimanded by the nurse, leading the child to be upset. My mentee reported that they witnessed this repeatedly, along with countless similar examples of providers again reinforcing the gender binary.

The options for advocacy are limited. A trans or nonbinary medical student, or even a junior-level provider, may find themselves around a superior making derogatory comments and then feel trapped between the alternatives of speaking up and risking being labeled a troublemaker or remaining silent so as not to provoke a retaliatory poor evaluation. I could suggest something like, "Get out, get a passing grade, and move on. You have to graduate medical school or you can't practice to benefit our community." But there is no safe space to report such discrimination. I always tell my mentees to "be super, *super* careful." Some will take it upon themselves to provide training to their institutions on trans issues, but why should they have to? Trans people deserve appropriate educational settings. Trans people deserve advocates who understand the needs of such vulnerable students.

Trans providers in these settings may find their options difficult, yet they simply want to do their jobs with dignity. I often ask my mentees, "Do you think you'll be supported if you approach someone with your concerns?" Some are already hesitant to be out, let alone to voice their worries. I see the same in students of color who experience racial discrimination, and even more so as the number of intersections increase: Black and trans...Black and trans and woman...Black and trans and woman and lesbian...Black and trans and woman and lesbian and from poverty...or Black and nonbinary/nonpassing and anything else...and so on. It shouldn't be that way. This pattern becomes a self-reinforcing cycle, but I hope for a future with more trans people and people of color in human resources as well.

Being labeled as "difficult" means upcoming trans doctors risk losing a residency placement. In another recent study, nearly 30 percent felt that they were poorly ranked as a result of their gender identity.[5] This research also uncovered that nearly half of trans medical students were misnamed or misgendered during placement interviews. This is blatant discrimination, creating a hierarchy of safety and opportunity in which trans medical students are inherently disempowered and viewed with skepticism whatever the setting, and where trans patients are the modern "Hottentot Venuses," objects to be examined and subject to the will of the providers.

The system needs to evolve.

* * *

I wake each morning wondering what might happen next, especially for those in states proposing or enacting legislation to prohibit care to trans youth and banning discussion of gender identity in schools. These vile laws seem intended to scapegoat trans people, primarily trans youth, and to incite fear and bigotry so as to drive conservative voters to the polls.

The politicians cite physicians long accused of being transphobic as well as biased but legitimate sounding "advocacy groups" such as the American College of Pediatricians, an organization with somewhere between 200 and 500 members and listed as a fringe anti-LGBTQ hate group by the Southern Poverty Law Center.[6] Their logo features an overtly heteronormative family holding hands, making clear their philosophical perspective. This group releases public statements and "studies" that have been criticized as methodologically lacking and ideologically prejudiced;[7, 8, 9, 10] the organization has also associated homosexuality with pedophilia,[11] endorsed conversion therapy,[12, 13] opposed civil rights for LGBTQIA+ communities,[14] opposed LGBTQIA+ marriage and adoption,[15, 16, 17, 18] called for the election of candidates opposed to trans and LGBTQIA+ support,[19] and has forwarded the narrative that affirmative healthcare for transgender and gender nonbinary youth is child abuse.[20, 21, 22]

Those quoting this "research" allege that transgender youth care includes mandatory sterilization and forced surgeries, also that medical providers "make" kids trans so as to further our own radical political agenda. *These simply do not happen.*

Such hostile organizations get significant airtime in conservative media like Fox News, and when young people and anxious caregivers are exposed to this messaging, it often leads to doubt, reluctance, and prolonged suffering. Uncertain parents may encounter this messaging and become confused into inaction or into being unwilling to support their transgender child, which we know only causes further distress.[23] These providers and organizations seem unwilling to listen to anything outside their predetermined narrative, and while they are vocal, it is important to realize that these people are a very small minority.

The name is likely intended to mirror the more genuine American Academy of Pediatrics (AAP), which has over 67,000 members committed to the physical, mental, and social health of infants and youth, and which has released many public statements in support of gender-affirming care. They have published numerous pro-trans studies and policy statements, including "Ensuring Comprehensive Care and Support to Transgender and Gender-Diverse Children and Adolescents"[24] and others.

Ask the American Academy of Pediatrics, the true leader in the field: Affirming care leads to optimal outcomes. It includes providing children and adolescents a safe environment in which they can freely explore their genders through use of alternate names, pronouns, and clothing, case management, and mental healthcare intended to help the youth gradually determine for themselves how they might want to live. This position is also supported by the vast majority of healthcare organizations* and a far more significant body of rigorously conducted studies.** The genuine science is clear.

Regardless, this legislation puts medical providers in an awkward position between the law and well-established, evidence-based best practice, whether they are trans-identified or an ally. Many fear for their physical safety as well. I wish I could say that I would have provided care in Alabama had legislation proposing the criminalization of gender-affirming care to trans youth not been blocked by a court injunction,[25] but I'm not certain. Would it have been worth a felony conviction, jail time, and the loss of my medical license? We cannot sacrifice providers willing to advocate for the transgender community. I care for myself by sometimes unplugging from the news. Some mentees contact me before even going to medical school, and I must hope they are resilient enough to endure, and their willingness to reach out for support certainly helps.

What propels my TGNB mentees and peers is that they are determined to aid their community. There exist far more trans healthcare professionals than there were just five years ago, and I hope all find mentors and friends. I am rarely their only mentor, but I can listen, offer advice, and facilitate connections. And there are also Facebook groups to provide support. I maintain close relationships with my mostly trans and LGBQIA+ colleagues. It is not a large community, but it helps me survive.

Of course, alongside improved justice for transgender workers in healthcare, service delivery to trans people of all ages and identities must evolve. I've had a patient arrive unexpectedly and reporting chest pain, unsure if they are having a heart attack but refusing to go to an emergency room because they are worried about institutional transphobia in hospital systems. This even happens in the LGBTQIA+ metropolis of New York. I have yet to meet a transgender person who

---

\*　See the introduction chapter for just a few.
\*\*　Again, please see the introduction chapter.

hasn't considered postponing necessary care at least once, and this is not an irrational fear, as nearly half of TGNB people surveyed report having been mistreated by medical providers,[26] ranging from misgendering to a provider using a client's birth name or deadname to sexual and physical assault. This can lead to mental health concerns and post-traumatic stress disorder, and such mistreatment is so endemic that the community has normalized the experience.

Accompaniment programs help. If a transgender person requires medical care, they can request an escort to advocate, to provide oversight, and to offer emotional support in moments when the patient in crisis may feel especially vulnerable. When a trans patient enters an urgent care facility with a broken wrist, they often question what to share with staff. They should be able to say, "Treat my wrist." Medical providers generally ask about medications and the reasons a person is on them, a discussion that often leads to queries about surgeries and identity, the body, and sexuality. All while their hand is still throbbing. Well-meaning or not, this is intrusive and alienating. If you are the provider: Treat the limb and recognize that the body is otherwise not yours to interrogate.

To trans patients: *You generally do not need to disclose in a setting where you don't feel safe.*

When is it necessary to provide more information? When are questions truly relevant? I tell clients that it is vital they specify when and where they are experiencing symptoms. Assume a trans man with abdominal pain requires an evaluation: Sharing about reproductive systems and hormone use are necessary, but other questions may not be. Those about a hysterectomy and menstruation are, but chest and voice masculinization are not. It is crucial that providers and staff ask *only* what they need. Other inquiries are fetishizing and a waste of critical time in emergency settings.

Overall, improvements have been made that are largely the result of our newfound visibility and passionate activism. Obamacare's non-discrimination policy also led to sensitivity trainings, though seminars are only one facet of the necessary education. Healthcare settings have generally understood the need to change, superficially if not wholeheartedly, and they may or may not do it well. If I have a negative experience, I complete a feedback form and I encourage others to do the same when they undergo discrimination themselves. Sometimes institutions will issue a response. But not even LGBTQIA+-focused health centers can guarantee ideal treatment at every interaction. Clients encounter too many people. It might be a security guard who says something inappropriate; the nurses might be experienced and empathetic, but a pharmacist could misgender you. Or a new young staff member, queer but unfamiliar yet with the nuances of nonbinary identity, may express confusion. And legitimate mistakes do happen. We sometimes need patience.

Even the most progressive health institutions still have difficulty obtaining or developing inclusive record-keeping systems, impacting care whether the individual is out or stealth. A trans man updating his legal gender to male might not receive a critical screening because the software doesn't recognize that he has a cervix, or it may assume that women do not have prostates, and systems are rarely equipped to appropriately document nonbinary people. Some health record software manufacturers are only now recognizing the need to be more comprehensive.

If a patient instead decides to leave their gender assigned at birth on their identity documents, one of two things often happens:

- If that person has medically transitioned, they may be subject to stares and endless questions, as there is a mismatch between their body/identity and their insurance card. This can deter them from seeking care.

- If the trans patient has not medically transitioned, their avowed gender may not be respected. Well-intentioned institutions will offer patients a more comprehensive list of pronouns on intake forms, but someone who doesn't pass will still be misgendered often.

My advice to providers and staff: Don't ask such questions if you're unwilling to review the forms at every interaction. Trans patients can be especially guarded, having learned to distrust institutions after decades of mistreatment. They might be outed when asked to respond verbally. They realize health record systems can be accessed by many other staff and not trust the mechanisms in place to ensure confidentiality. Or consider the impact on a patient who specifies their gender on a form only to have it disregarded. In response, some organizations mandate staff wear pronoun buttons on lanyards, and many health centers offer pronoun stickers a patient can adhere to their shirt to make their gender more obvious. Or a trans person can take it upon themselves to purchase and wear a visible indicator.

Insurance companies also create barriers. The American health-care system requires that almost everyone use insurance, but these are for-profit companies that benefit from limiting care or intimidating clients into paying out of pocket. They may deny care altogether if the client's legal gender does not align with the needs of their body, like a transmasculine nonbinary person seeking gynecology. Often official guidelines require two mental health references for certain surgeries; our clinic offers separate providers to each write one. But occasionally an insurance company will still resist, next demanding three letters or that the letters be from providers at different organizations, or something else. These criteria are rarely published in their explanation of benefits documentation nor are they recommendations by the World Professional Association for Transgender Health (WPATH). There is no apparent rationale or valid medical justification, nor are they consistent about imposing such rules, suggesting they have quotas and only seek a pretext not to pay. A client then must pursue a lengthy appeal or take time from work and incur added costs to meet with an additional provider elsewhere, all causing anxiety and delay.

Insurance companies also at times rely on outdated science and older Standards of Care, or requirements not aligned with the current needs of the trans community. For instance, criteria may include 12 months on hormones before approving a client for vaginoplasty, demanding every trans person follow an identical path from living full time to hormones to surgery to a fully passing binary gender, though not everyone desires hormones or heteronormativity and this prerequisite is unnecessary according to WPATH. Or insurers follow independent guidelines rather than the current Standards of Care written by medical professionals. It's infuriating to witness medically necessary care pointlessly delayed, apparently just for profits.

I see the future as community-based initiatives. Trans leadership is vital for patient-driven healthcare, also for necessary research and appropriate guidelines reflecting our genuine needs. Far too often academic institutions engage in unimportant fact-finding and analyses of issues irrelevant to our daily lives. Instead, they pursue imaging studies along with examination of etiology and brain difference, research we fear will lead to some form of anti-trans eugenics and gatekeeping, all for clout, to add a publication to their resume, or to obtain an invitation to lecture. We have no need for a test to determine if someone is "genuinely" trans, nor for a scale to document "how trans" someone is. *Someone's word is enough.* Thankfully, many of these proposals fail because they lack willing participants. Often, I will be asked to refer people; however, *we need not contribute to research so divorced from our realities.*

We would prefer they study the impact of societal transphobia and how we can live happier lives. Other concerns far more relevant than "why": "I'm aging. Should I change my hormone regimen?" Or, "How long must I stop testosterone before I can safely carry a child?" "What are the rates of cancer for someone like me?" The best questions are from trans patients, and answers would be vital.

This could be remedied by trans-led participatory research and shifts in funding priorities, but it would also require some cisgender researchers to acknowledge that time has come for them to step back.

Frustratingly, potentially harmful studies riddled with cis biases expressed in pseudo-academic language continue to be done, and institutional review boards, groups designated to assess and monitor biomedical research to ensure it is conducted ethically, continue to endorse them. These publications headline at the largest medical conferences while community-based proposals are marginalized; cis academics rarely attend trans-led lectures at such events. Meanwhile cis academics simultaneously claim that trans researchers are "too close to the problem," making it more challenging for trans-led research to be approved.[27] This is yet another expression of colonialism using the language of "objectivity." Everyone seems eager to learn about transgender people, but only from the cisgender imagination.

While these barriers exist, they also propel me in my work as a clinician and researcher. Before there was trans-led medical activism, every transgender person received identical treatment aimed at an outcome of binary heteronormativity, and any variance meant that the patient would be dismissed from the program. I and those I collaborate with provide what is called "patient-centered care," which involves identifying an individual's goals and adjusting treatment accordingly. This is the future of service delivery.

And our community is not a monolith; we have undocumented trans people, trans people of color, disabled trans people, trans people who vary socioeconomically, also nonbinary, genderqueer, agender, and an extensive list of otherwise-gendered trans people as well. We have wonderfully different bodies and countless intersections.

Cis people must be the leaders in undoing transphobia in the medical system and beyond.

But it is trans people who must be the leaders in the research done about trans people and in our own community's care, and we need more of us.

# Robyn Alice McCutcheon

# The Highs and Lows of Trans at State

**Robyn Alice McCutcheon** (she/her) is a transgender woman and retired foreign service officer who served in Washington, DC; Moscow, Russia; Astana, Kazakhstan; Bucharest, Romania; and Tashkent, Uzbekistan. Prior to joining the U.S. Department of State, Robyn worked for over 25 years as an engineer and programmer on NASA missions, primarily the Hubble Space Tele-scope, and was the recipient of numerous NASA awards. Although Ms. McCutcheon was employed by the U.S. Department of State, the views expressed in this chapter are strictly her own and do not represent the views of the Department of State, NASA, or the U.S. Government.

An early memory of mine is of the *Star Trek* Enterprise (TOS version, of course) in orbit around a red planet; as a lifelong dreamer, I'm envious of her career as a rocket scientist. We were introduced by a mutual friend; Robyn is devoted to her bicycle and cycling, having completed dozens of tours through Europe and the U.S. Rarely are we privy to the experiences of trans people inside the workings of diplomatic organizations and the government itself.

For so much of my life I have faced transphobia, first internally, a wall I built surrounding my heart that may have first been for protection, and later externally, from doctors, society, and even the government I was trying to serve. But there are so many ways to create safe space when we are excluded. Some people march in the streets, hold signs, or write politicians, hoping for broad legal change, though when I became both a representative of our nation and an out trans woman at the same time, I had to fight alongside my peers from within an inherently transphobic structure. Together we made an environment in which we could help others and live as we are.

I contribute this as a transgender American who served her country as a commissioned foreign service officer (FSO) at the U.S. Department of State. For over 15 years I lived and worked in Washington, DC; Moscow; Bucharest; and throughout Central Asia. At the time I retired as an FS-02 mid-level FSO in 2019, I held the diplomatic title of first secretary, roughly the equivalent of a lieutenant colonel in the military.

"Foreign Service?" you ask.

The Foreign Service staffs our embassies, consulates, and other diplomatic missions, and is sometimes referred to as "America's other army."[1] Foreign Service Officers are America's diplomats.

To the transgender Americans who want to serve our country I say: Military service is not the only option, and as ambassador Bill Burns notoriously wrote, "Diplomacy is America's foreign policy tool of first resort."[2] Interests in languages, cultures, and international relations are prerequisites, but being transgender is no obstacle, and the Foreign Service may be one of the most welcoming branches of the U.S. government.

Was it always that way? No. The Foreign Service was a cisgender, heterosexual male bastion from its inception. Women were largely excluded, and women who married were required to resign as recently as 1971.

In the 1950s, the Department rooted out anyone they could in the so-called "Lavender Scare,"[3] a witch hunt to purge the government of anyone gay or lesbian. Careers were destroyed. A few outed FSOs committed suicide. The persecution lessened after the 1950s, but it was still official policy into the 1990s to revoke security clearances from gay FSOs: The government deliberately created a no-win situation allegedly worrying that being in the closet left someone open to blackmail, but also that being out gave leverage that foreign powers could exploit.

Organizing is one way our communities can fight discrimination. In 1992, a few brave FSOs created Gays and Lesbians in Foreign Affairs Agencies (glifaa*). Several founders were dismissed when they came out, but the organization persisted. One of our greatest successes came in June 2009, when Secretary of State Hillary Clinton introduced a policy on same-sex domestic partners, under which partners of gay and lesbian FSOs were granted spousal benefits. And in 2017, Secretary of State John Kerry issued a formal apology for the decades of discrimination. Our gay and lesbian siblings fought their fear by coming together and pushing back.

But trans? Fuggedaboutit. Indeed, the status of a trans person anywhere in the U.S. federal government was tenuous at best, and I mean *at best*, until Diane Schroer filed suit against the Library of Congress in 2005 because it had revoked a job offer when she told them that she would be presenting as female after applying as male. With much struggle and aid from the American Civil Liberties Union (ACLU), she won and on September 19, 2008, the United States District Court ruled that discrimination around gender identity or presentation equals sex discrimination under Title VII of the Civil Rights Act of 1964. About the same time, Dr. Chloe Schwenke, a senior staffer at a contractor to USAID, announced she was transitioning and was immediately fired. Chloe went to glifaa. Together they lobbied to have gender identity added to the employee nondiscrimination policies, and Secretary Clinton signed it into Department policy in the summer of 2010. Soon after, President Obama appointed Chloe to USAID directly. Together

---

*   Gays and Lesbians in Foreign Affairs Agencies has become "glifaa, lgbt+ pride in foreign affairs agencies" in lower case to emphasize that it covers inclusion of the full LGBTQIA+ spectrum.

with Amanda Simpson and Dylan Orr, Chloe became one of the first high-level trans appointees in the U.S. government.[4] We started to find our own voice.

But where was I? Deeply in the closet.

Eisenhower was in his first administration when I was born. The first word I heard to describe what I felt was "transsexual" and I did, ultimately, go for surgeries. I have trouble with the term "transgender" because gender is the one aspect of my life that has never changed: I have identified as something closer to female since I was young. What changed was my body and how society viewed me.

I was so desensitized to my internalized transphobia that I really thought I was insane. How could anyone be transsexual? That was the stuff of tabloid headlines, something to run from even as I wondered when my breasts would develop. I played with the other girls at recess until teachers forced me to go to the sports field where I wasn't wanted; instead, I would sit alone with a book. I was desperate to keep my secret private. What would people think if they knew what was going on in my head?

Only in college when I read Jan Morris's *Conundrum* did I understand I wasn't alone, and I hope that you, reading this book, realize this as well. We exist; we have always existed. Maybe you are living a double life as I was. I appeared male to friends and professors but female for a night job. It helped a little.

But mostly my survival was avoidance. In graduate school I ran from the label, from the incessant white noise of feelings that could be drowned out but never driven away. I found socially acceptable drugs in academia and career to mute the conflict, and so I overworked by doing a double major in college, getting two Master's degrees, and beginning an intense career in space flight dynamics. I also threw myself into Russian and Soviet history, getting research grants, working in archives, and publishing in academic journals. Along the way I married a friend.

My resolve ran out in 1990, when I was part of the launch and early support team for the Hubble Space Telescope and also had a publication deadline for a major history paper. Not to mention that I was now in on-the-job training as a parent with a one-year-old son.

I spoke the "T" word to my spouse. I had been at the University of Illinois with a writing grant but was unable to work. It wasn't writer's block. I knew. My career was successful and I was so joyful at being a parent, but the contradictions inside me were yelling, "Enough! This can't go on!"

* * *

Then came some of my first direct experiences with social and medical transphobia. The next day I found myself in a psychiatric ward and my spouse had thrown me out of the house. Those first consequences of speaking up were as bad as I feared, even worse. Like so many other transgender people contemplating suicide, I stood at the edge of a subway platform and wondered if it might not be best to end it. Maybe you are considering that too, but *please don't*. Facing my fear, and the transphobia associated with it in my personal life, my career, and the world at large, was how I found happiness, not by running from it.

My own sister took me to the hospital and my earliest encounter with psychiatry was definitely not a pleasant one. I recounted my history of gender-confused feelings back to earliest childhood to some anonymous psychiatrist. We met daily and he sat stony faced, never commenting, until the last session when he pronounced his verdict: "What you are is overworked and depressed." He was convinced there was no such thing as gender dysphoria, so prescribed an antidepressant and then released me to the care of my spouse, assuring her I would be fine.

Discussions with her made it clear that I had to choose. Transition or psychiatric medication, and they were stark options. The former meant divorce and no access to our son, so feeling a deep responsibility, I stayed married and a parent. I ignored my own needs, took the antidepressants, and soldiered on for the good of all. I went back to work after a week gone, and no one said a word. Transphobia won.

Our son grew and I made a radical career change to the U.S. Department of State, yet in my denial, I made my situation worse. I lied through omission at work, fearing my secret would be revealed. But when? In 2000, a NASA scan of its computers determined that someone had been visiting "pornographic" websites. A warning went out. No one was named, but I knew it was me. The notice identified a URL for a website about gender transition. What would the State Department do if it found out about my gender-conflicted life? And I still felt deep shame and the pressure of culture, so I continued to hide.

In my second year, State sent me to Moscow. I did visa interviews, cringing that I held lives in my hands. Then someone realized that a rocket engineer who had worked on Hubble could be put to better use, so I covered Russian nuclear energy.

I found peace from both internal and external transphobia on a bicycle. Weekends I would ride on a track built for the 1980 Olympics. I often bike-packed, camping in the woods where I hoped no one could see. It was my bicycle that kept me sane, providing space where I didn't have to interact with anyone, and the physical exertion calmed my emotional distress.

In 2008, I moved on to Tashkent, Uzbekistan, where the State Department in its wisdom had assigned me to cover economic and business issues. When I objected that I knew nothing about either, they replied, "Neither do the Uzbeks. You are well matched."

But my fears were realized in 2010. In 2007, with our son in college, my spouse and I began divorce, and it was *messy*. My trans history, including the 1990 psychiatric sojourn, was laid bare in the discovery materials, and it became a factor in the settlement agreement where I gave up, essentially, everything.

From there word spread and my dread increased. I was summoned for an interview with Diplomatic Security, more accurately an interrogation with Diplomatic Security, thinking the institutional, governmental transphobia would seal my fate to a life that no longer included public service. I found myself on leave without pay and expecting the worst, but I knew nothing about Chloe Schwenke or the others. Although I was stripped of a posting back to Moscow, I was startled when I was allowed to take what the Foreign Service calls a "down-stretch" position below my grade in Bucharest, Romania, as an information management specialist (i.e., data tech) instead of as a political officer. I felt somewhat better, but it was hardly ideal. I pondered one afternoon as I watched the foliage change colors in fall 2010, and it dawned on me that my biggest issue was that I had a *secret* and that secrets make someone vulnerable, just as State had suggested in the 1950s. What if I came out?

Experience as a bicyclist taught me about visibility. Early on I hugged the curb, trying to stay out of everyone's way, which resulted in mishaps and injuries when motorists pushed me off the road. As I gained experience, I learned that safety means taking one's rightful place in the traffic lane and being seen; it is far less risky to position oneself as a vehicle, occupying as much space as needed. Drivers might not like seeing me there, but they had to accept me as something that could not be ignored.

Could this lesson be applied to my life as a trans person? In college I ventured into public as myself only in the darkness. In my trans life I stayed aside to be out of everyone's way. Now I began to apply the same, hard-learned rule of riding: Be visible, be assertive, and join the traffic. I had as much right to walk down the street as anyone, I realized, as do you, the reader. "Yes, I am trans, and I don't care who knows or what anyone thinks." Just as you can hold deep inside that you too are trans, no matter how risky your situation, regardless of what others may believe.

That's how it happened. On November 10, 2011, I became the first FSO to transition gender while posted overseas. But that wasn't enough for our community; we needed more, so I refused to sit still.

One senior official wanted me out on (false) psychiatric grounds, and Washington fretted about how the Romanian government would react. The Department insisted on press guidance that both the Embassy and the Department crafted on the eve of the announcement. But Washington's concerns evaporated when there was barely a ripple, and they quickly came to see me as an asset with access to the underground Romanian LGBTQIA+ community. I penned numerous cables, including *Roma and Gay: A Triple Stigma; Transgender Community*

*Comes Out of the Shadows but Remains a Fractured Minority; Moldova Makes Progress on Transgender Rights;* and *Anti-LGBT Protesters Win a Battle, Lose a War?* In 2012 and 2013, I organized the Embassy's participation in the annual Bucharest Pride march.

Meanwhile, my apartment often hosted the local community, notably once after the release of activists arrested for protesting at the Russian Embassy and again when Olympia, a young trans woman beaten by her transphobic father, lived in my guestroom. In aiding others, I also improved my own self-esteem.

In 2013, I returned to Washington on assignment at the Nuclear Risk Reduction Center that oversees our nuclear and conventional arms control treaties. But the real work was at glifaa, which had elected me president, alongside an entirely new board. We became activists, transforming our fear into advocacy.

Stay with me; this may be acronym heavy. We chose three top priorities:

- Post-Defense of Marriage Act strategy and the fate of the Same-Sex Domestic Partner program

- privileges and immunities for same-sex spouses and domestic partners

- removal of the transgender exclusion from federal employee health and retirement plans.

We wrote and lobbied, meeting repeatedly with officials on "Mahogany Row," where the senior administrators have their office suites. We approached Secretary Kerry's counselor and chief of staff. We met with the undersecretary for management and the acting director general. These were the people with power to make change.

I'm very glad to say we did better than expected. The first two were addressed in policy enacted by Secretary Clinton in 2009, continuing through and after the 2012 Supreme Court ruling in *United States v. Windsor*, which codified that same-sex couples could not be denied rights afforded to opposite-sex couples. No position against equality could be maintained.

The third I personally added to the agenda. A clause from the 1970's still denied trans health coverage to federal employees. The Office of Personnel Management (OPM) administers insurance plans, but how could we influence an agency entirely outside the Department?

We used what we had. Officials at State and USAID sent letters advocating for removal of the transgender exclusion, and OPM replied that it was under study but offered no deadline. We needed this for our trans community at State and elsewhere so we backchanneled, sending copies of the letters to the Foreign Service union, asking that it request elimination of the exclusion. We weren't alone; we worked alongside the National Center for Transgender Equality (NCTE) and the Human Rights Campaign.

Our greatest opportunity came when I was to introduce Secretary John Kerry as our guest of honor at a Pride commemoration. I leaked that, without progress, I would denounce this discrimination before the Secretary and the press. It worked! Only days before Pride, the NCTE revealed privately that the Office of Personnel Management had relented, allowing benefit plans to drop the exclusions on the condition of discretion. The director said glifaa's advocacy had made the difference and I beamed with pride, knowing we were helping so many. So instead of denouncing the organizations maintaining the restrictions, I thanked them for their unfailing support of the Foreign Service family. We survived the transphobia by advocating for the changes we needed.

My overseas career ended in Kazakhstan as the regional representative for environment, science, technology, and health (ESTH). I, a trans woman, now ran my own section with my own budget and travel that took me to all five post-Soviet "stans," covering issues as diverse as climate change, water management, and global health security.

I had earned a position of authority, and I was determined to use it. As in Romania, my apartment became a gathering place, and I added LGBT-related meetings when I traveled regionally. Covert interest groups existed in Almaty (Kazakhstan), and Bishkek (Kyrgyzstan) was home to Labrys, the leading organization in Central Asia. I met with community members in Dushanbe (Tajikistan). In Tashkent (Uzbekistan) I spoke with a transgender artist and actor who shared how trans people managed in his authoritarian country. Turkmenistan was more difficult, but I did connect with an activist in Ashgabat, the two of us on an evening stroll until she detected we were being followed. We separated quickly. Two women walking together in Turkmenistan were suspect by definition. These meetings happened in the evenings, on the margins of my official responsibilities.

My duties as the ESTH officer included health, so here was overlap. I incorporated HIV/AIDS into my reporting, meeting with state-financed treatment centers when I traveled.* I next collaborated with the Embassy Astana's human rights officer, and together we got funding for a roundtable on trans rights that included representatives from the Ministry of Health and the Republican Psychiatric Institute. Jamison Green, then president of the World Professional Association for Transgender Health (WPATH), came as our U.S. expert.** That roundtable began a dialog that still continues.

Some of my work was individual. In Kazakhstan I became involved in the life of Sultana Kali, but this story illustrates the gulf between the hopes and realities of a mid-level FSO's ability to improve the life of an individual. We met at a dinner I hosted. She participated in the trans roundtable with poise and dignity, relating how she had been expelled from high school after coming out, just a year from graduation. Surely there must be one school in Kazakhstan that would accept a trans student? No. I found all doors politely but firmly slammed shut. I moved Sultana into my apartment along with her mother, Natasha, who kept us fed as we completed U.S. community college applications. Ultimately, Lane Community College in Oregon accepted Sultana and offered a small scholarship for her essay, "I Just Want to Live an Ordinary Life—and Create a Revolution."

---

\* The HIV crisis in Kazakhstan stems mainly from intravenous drug use, but the percentage from sexual contact is growing. At the treatment center in Karaganda, I asked the deputy director about the LGBTQIA+ community. He acknowledged that the problem is heightened by stigma, but said they were making inroads. When I asked about transgender people, he replied that there were none. When pressed he took umbrage, stating that of course he would know a transgender person if he saw one.

\*\* You can read Jamison's story in his own chapter, earlier in this book.

With a college acceptance and sufficient funds, the visa interview should have gone smoothly. But after three minutes, the consular section chief denied her, saying Sultana didn't have enough money for four years of college. I wrote an attestation of support committing to cover all expenses, and Sultana applied a second time. Refused again. The vice consul didn't even glance at the additional documentation. The third try, three U.S. senators made inquiries on her behalf. No once more. Was she rejected as a trans woman? Did they suspect she would remain in the U.S. illegally?

I could make noise and not permit this to pass quietly, so I published five pieces in *The Huffington Post* accusing consular officers of bias. Kazakhstani *Esquire* picked up and published a deliberately inflammatory interview I had given, forcing the Embassy to respond that privacy concerns prevented it from commenting. I wrote an internal "dissent cable" that earned me a meeting with the deputy assistant secretary in the Bureau of Consular Affairs. Nothing changed. I'd tried desperately to help another trans woman who was subject to governmental transphobia, almost a younger me, but I'd failed.

The positive side was that she landed well. Officially she has only an 11th grade education, but she is better in English than most Americans. Today she is part of an LGBTQIA+ project administered by Columbia University and has traveled to Estonia as a Kazakhstani representative to a regional conference. She also became one of the first Kazakhstanis to succeed in changing her passport's gender marker, a success stemming from our initial trans roundtable.[5]

I am retired now. After seeing more of the former Soviet Union than I had of the U.S., I finally have the time to discover my own troubled country. I celebrated retirement by bike-packing from DC to my home in Maine. Later I rode across the U.S. on a route known as the Northern Tier. The bicycle has been my instrument of inner peace from childhood, and riding it allowed me to survive decades closeted, then transition, and throughout my life as a diplomat.

\* \* \*

That's my story, the highs and lows of being trans at the Department of State. I leave it to the reader to write the continuation. I joined the Foreign Service late in my career. A young trans or gender nonconforming person taking the entrance exam today could become an ambassador, and I hope that I will still shake his, her, or their hand. Several trans Americans have already followed in my footsteps, living their truths while pursuing diplomatic careers. Maybe you will be next.

# Reverend Louis J. Mitchell

## Dancing with a Limp

**Reverend Louis J. Mitchell** (he/him) is a Black trans man and the co-founder of Transfaith, "a multi-tradition, multi-racial, multi-gender, multi-generational organization working to support transgender spiritual/cultural workers and their leadership...[believing] that the experiences, spiritual vitality, and leadership of people of transgender experience make our communities  stronger and more vibrant." He was ordained as a minister of the United Church of Christ in 2018.

An activist for over three decades, his focus is the fight for health, self-determination, and respect, focusing on recovery and disability access. He has been featured in the documentaries *Still Black: A Portrait of Black Transmen*,[1] *Gender Journeys: More than a Pronoun*,[2] and *More than T*.[3] He was the recipient of the 2015 Claire Skiffington Vanguard Award from the Transgender Law Center for his long-time advocacy, the 2011 Haystack Award from the Massachusetts Conference of the UCC for work in Social Justice and Social Ministry, and was honored by the Black Trans Advocacy Conference with a Foundation Award in 2013.

I very intentionally placed this chapter last. The notion of "dancing with a limp" captures what every contributor here has suggested, another "both/and" as described by Colt St. Amand: Trans lives are difficult. And we can find joy. Both are true. He is a compassionate, devoted individual; we began our connection through this book. www.transfaith.info

I was raised in a church environment that celebrated emotive and embodied praise.

I grew up loving the energy and pageantry of Black Baptist worship!

Girls in frilly dresses, lacy roll-down socks, and shiny, black patent leather shoes.

Boys in little suits with clip-on ties. Men and women (there were only two choices) dressed in their finery with vivid colors, matching hats, gloves, and ties. So different from the weekday clothes. This space was special, sacred, and important.

I spent most of the worship dreaming of wearing the crisp, colorful suits and the alligator shoes of the deacons. I'm certain that this dream made church more bearable. Maybe you got through church by dreaming of being someone else, too.

Church was important to me. It was family and community. It was generations of love and service. I looked forward to being there with my mom and my beloved grandma. The colors, the music, the scents of colognes and the peppermints in pockets to keep us kids quiet, the rise and fall of the voices of musicians and preachers were beautiful and magical. Even my discomfort in the costume I was forced to wear couldn't dim my joy of being there.

I eventually learned that the hugs and support were conditional.

I learned that I needed to hide parts of me that weren't deemed holy.

I learned that there was much about my life that was outside of that tiny box.

I couldn't figure out how we partied together and had sex on Saturday, but I was the only one who was queer on Sunday morning when they turned straight and eagerly rode the gay-hate bandwagon in public.

I was nearly an adult when I finally left church...for good, I thought.

\* \* \*

From my earliest awareness, I felt forced into a world of whiteness. Nearly everything I saw on television, in the printed news, in literature, featured heroic white people. If Black or other folks of color were present at all, they were subservient and/or criminal. Church was an exception; it was there that I saw the pride and abilities of my people. I didn't want to lose that place—but it was clear that I couldn't stay and be honest.

My "work around" was Keith, my pastor's nephew. He was gay. We "dated." We went to West Hollywood together, sometimes partied together, and sometimes split up only to meet again before heading back home. Even that was framed by its relationship to whiteness, because being a nerdy suburban kid, I wasn't "cool" and I had no idea where the Black gay folks hung out. When we went out to party, there were other Black folks, Latino folks, and Asian folks, yet all our numbers together were only a small percentage compared to the sea of white faces in every institution and bar.

I remember those days in Hollywood and West Hollywood—trying to fit in at Gino's, The Odyssey, Circus. It was post-Stonewall and pre-AIDS, and the scene was magical. The music was thundering, the walls dripped with sweat, the people were so very beautiful, free, and sure of themselves. I learned to act just like them, but it was only an act. Inside I was an oddball. I learned how to compartmentalize—to be one person at school, someone else at church, someone entirely different in the scene, and a whole other person in my head and heart.

Friend, have you ever felt like wherever you were, you were the "other"? Times when it seemed like there was absolutely no place, other than in your head, that you felt completely safe and seen? This was my constant reality.

Fast forward. I graduated from high school, my cherished maternal grandmother died, and I dropped out of my local junior college with a plan to hitchhike to Texas. I had family there and the drinking age was 18, so it seemed like the perfect idea.

But there was an incident.

My mother and her church friends put my "boyfriend" and I through a Baptist exorcism. My experience happened at home;

I learned about Keith's experience later. They prayed. They extolled God to fix me. They anointed me with holy oil to drive the gay spirit away. Even in this traumatic experience, I felt their love and their fear, knowing they were afraid for my immortal soul. I did my best imitation of Linda Blair in *The Exorcist* and the next morning fled to Texas as I'd intended.

I didn't even know what trans was. I didn't have that language. I just knew I was different. I called myself a lesbian because that's what someone was called when they were in a body like mine and were attracted to women, but that never felt quite right. I would ask my partners if they'd still love me if I was a boy. They thought the question was weird and didn't usually answer. Eventually I stopped asking.

I hated my body. I hated the attention it got from straight men. I also knew that one of the things I was running away from was having to pretend that I liked boys/men. I wanted to *be* them, not to be *with* them.

When I escaped, it felt like I moved from the sunlight to the shadows. I was on the run from God and church, and I went as hedonistic as I knew how. If I was going to sin, I wanted to sin TO THE EXTREME. Can you understand?

There were moments when the pain felt inescapable and insurmountable. Nights when I couldn't get drunk enough or high enough to avoid my feelings. I tried to take my life more than once and wept when I was unsuccessful. I put myself in situations hoping that someone else would kill me, over and over and over again.

I didn't come from difficult circumstances in the ways that you might imagine. I was the spoiled middle-class child of working-class parents. I had no external "excuse" for my behavior; my trauma was inside of me. My self-loathing was self-generated and sustained by society.

I am an alcoholic and an addict. I have done sex work. I have been a thief. I've lied and connived. I have done whatever I needed to do to survive. If you've ever made choices that were from both survival and a complete lack of concern about the consequences, you'll understand what that was like. I felt courageous and I felt like shit.

Take a moment, friend, and think about feelings of frantic desperation and immutable grief—the feeling that who you are is wrong, that you're the only one who has ever felt this way, that no one can ever love you. I truly didn't want to live further into adulthood. I saw no point.

I was in Corpus Christi, Texas. No one knew what an awkward and insecure nerd I had been, so I created a new life based on lies. I walked a fine line of trying to live and wanting to die. I hung out with other sex workers, pimps, and thieves. Once, I went to attempt a theft with someone who I barely knew and got robbed and raped as payment for my troubles. I was broken, and again I was the agent of my own hardships.

I wanted so much to be a guy, to be one of the guys. I hooked up with a group of trans women who were sex workers and drag queens. I became their "man." We dreamed aloud of having sex changes and getting married and being a "normal" couple. What we really did was sell sex, rob johns, and get drunk and high to avoid reality.

I tried to believe that I could love, but the closest I came were the fantasies I'd had with the drag queens I dated, drunken visions that amounted to nothing. After a brief stint in jail for not paying a shoplifting fine, I went back home to Los Angeles to see if I could put my life on a different track.

* * *

I was lonely, desperate, confused, and still wasn't convinced that I wanted to live. All the advantages of my upbringing and my innate intelligence were going to waste, but I didn't care. I didn't see how anything would help. I couldn't assemble my life in a way that made sense.

After returning to southern California and after years of being in the situations that an addiction to freebasing can put you in, I managed to find my way into the 12-step rooms. I wasn't sure that I wanted to get sober, or that I could. I wasn't sure that the folks in those rooms weren't pulling my leg. I knew I felt miserable, and something had to give. My self-medication wasn't working, but if 12-step didn't work, I planned to kill myself, again.

I had long turned away from the God of my earliest years—the God that I'd been told couldn't and wouldn't love me, the God I'd been taught to fear and hide from—and now recovery told me to find a God of my understanding, a higher power. I was resistant and afraid, but I really wanted to stay sober. That's how I returned to praying.

We were taught, in sobriety, that honesty and integrity were important, but I didn't dare risk it, even with my sponsor and recovery friends. I'd finally found a place of acceptance and I was terrified to lose it! I didn't know how to stop wanting what seemed impossible, and I didn't know how to dissociate from my body when sober.

I finally had something to lose. I had a community that I cared about and that cared about me. The only way that I managed to get through this period was by living as a butch lesbian and trying to make that be enough.

After managing to stay sober for about five years, I decided to go back to school. I'd dreamed of studying with Barbara Jordan at UT Austin or Angela Davis at San Francisco State. They were both great icons to me—strong, brilliant Black women! I went on a game show (*Scrabble* with Chuck Woolery) and won enough money to move to the Bay Area to study.

Several things happened there that changed my life.

At a community meeting, I met Yvette Flunder. She was self-possessed and exuded a calm even in the tenseness of the meeting. I was captivated by her power and poise and wanted to know more about her. She said she was a pastor. I hadn't expected that!

I finally made my way to her church. I don't remember much about that worship service, but what made me return the next week was a woman named Doris Robinson. She was a tall, beautiful trans woman who greeted me and others at the door as an usher. I thought that if this person was intentionally the first person folks met upon entering, maybe I, too, could belong. I kept returning.

Then I finally met another trans man. I was overjoyed and terrified! Thrilled because I wasn't the only one, frightened because I now had decisions to make.

Fantasies are frustrating but safe, and I wasn't sure I had the courage to take that next step. I'd gotten comfortable in the lesbian community and knew that deciding to transition meant I'd lose some of my women friends. I understood their upset that I'd chosen to wear the face and body of their oppressors.

Unfortunately, the first Black trans man I met was a total ass. He was sexist and arrogant, regularly saying awful things about women. In hindsight, I suspect he was overcompensating, but I didn't know that then. I also knew that I did not want to be "that guy," the misogynist I'd seen in the person I'd met. How do you choose between affirming your deepest truth and becoming your most awful nightmare? But I couldn't stay sober and live a lie now that I had a chance to make it right, so I talked to other trans men who reassured me that testosterone couldn't make me someone I wasn't. Maybe you've been in a similar position, wrestling with the fear of the dangers of living trans and terrified by the grim notion of staying stuck?

I'd relearned to pray in recovery, so I prayed. I'd joined that church, City of Refuge, and the council of Pastor Flunder meant so much to me. She gave me the support to tell my mother.

I was so afraid that my mother would abandon me, disown me, tell me that she couldn't love me, as her theological position is far more conservative than mine. Her response was clear: She might never accept my choices, but she respected my right to make them and would always love me. That was all that I hoped for.

For the first few years, she messed up my pronouns. She referred to me by my initials or as her first born. She stretched and asked questions. I didn't rush her; I was just grateful that she didn't throw me away.

I get how challenging and painful it can be when we are misgendered by family or friends. The anger and frustration can be almost uncontrollable. But if you can, give them a little time—even if they say they will never change. Maybe they won't, but it's possible they will. They are "transitioning" too. I'm not saying to put yourself in harm's way; you don't have to endure pain while they figure it out. Take space if you can and need to. I also understand that some people don't have the liberty of leaving tough family situations. Please take care of yourself as best you can.

The final amazing thing that happened in the Bay Area is that I met, fell in love with, and married an amazing woman, K, who I'd met in recovery. Someone wanted me! I'd felt certain that no one would be interested in a man like me.

She knew I was trans-identified and that I was planning to physically transition, then gave me my first shot of testosterone on my 39th birthday. We talked about whether she'd still be attracted to me as my body changed. She'd never been with a man and was only attracted to masculine women, so we talked about her loss of visibility as a femme lesbian, erased by appearing straight with a man. I'm forever grateful for the tools we learned in recovery that gave us the courage and integrity to navigate through the hard stuff.

We moved to New England and bought a house. We were living the dream, but grew apart and eventually broke up, mostly because I was so shut down due to my HIV/AIDS-related grief and I was unable to be fully present. My heart was full of loss and fear of loss. I needed to heal before I could fully offer love to someone else.

In the middle of all of that, I found myself entering the seminary and starting a job as an assistant minister. I fell in love with the work and I was good at it! My experiences in recovery taught me how to care and how to be of service to others. My run from God somehow led me right back to organized religion.

While my wife and I were separated, she got pregnant. We'd spent years trying to get pregnant and couldn't. I was so happy for her; she had always wanted to be a mother. She said that she'd only been able to imagine a family with me as the dad. I had the gift of being with her during the birth, cutting the umbilical cord and being legally a father. A dream that came true!

We couldn't make our marriage work, but we still love each other deeply, as kin and co-parents. We are family for life and we both love our amazing kid. K has been partnered for a few years now with a good guy and he loves her very much. I'm still looking. Our child knows that we love them and are here to support them as they find their way through life. They also know both our histories and our journey to each other, and the joy we have of being a family. We are open and communicative with our kid, something neither of us had or knew in our own childhoods.

A few years ago, my mom asked me to move west to be closer to her. Our relationship is solid and full of love. She came to see how much happier I am and how much more comfortably I move in the world.

And more recently, I got diagnosed with multiple sclerosis and have had to adjust to the ebbs and flows of my symptoms. Learning to navigate life with a disability has taught me how much I'd taken for granted.

* * *

Which leads me to why I titled this *Dancing with a Limp*.

In this journey—long, arduous, funny, dangerous, sad, thrilling, and mundane—I have landed in a place of unexpected wholeness and gratitude.

I learned about resilience and community. I learned that some folks in my beloved Black community may never find it in their hearts to love me. They don't understand me and they don't want to, but these are far fewer than most people think. I've heard over and over how communities of color are especially homophobic and transphobic. I haven't found that to be true.

I can't think about overcoming transphobia without thinking about becoming a Black man in the United States. My experience of queerness and transness is literally colored by living in white supremacist society.

I've learned that racism, anti-Blackness, and white supremacy are alive and well in LGBTQIA+ communities. Perhaps I was naïve or too eager to belong, but I was surprised. Look at the leadership of most organizations. Even the places that claim great diversity do not have it in decision-making positions.

One of the hardest things about surviving transphobia for me has been surviving the "isms" in community—the racism, the homophobia, the ableism, the classism, the fatphobia, and the lookism. It means that the "community" isn't safe for everyone, and it hasn't always been for me.

I still believe that if we bring open minds and hearts, we can all be better for the journey. I know I have much to learn and might have a bit of wisdom to offer.

I face the same threats to my safety that every other Black man faces. My heart breaks knowing that in our society I'm both invisible and hypervisible.*

As an ordained pastor, I also must acknowledge the truth about the harm that Christianity has done. I won't run from that history because it is part of my job to own it and to make amends in whatever ways I can. I'm also accountable for the ways that I move in the situational privilege I'm afforded as a man who is able to blend in as cis/het, as an elder, and as Christian clergy in a society that elevates those positions over others.

I fear that there are people who might try to harm me, my congregation, or my loved ones for being who I am, but I've fought long and hard to love myself and I stand on the shoulders of others who fought with their entire lives to be free. If my fear of being me couldn't kill me, I won't let my fear of what others might do stop me either.

People who don't believe what I believe know that they can talk to me without being proselytized or patronized. I don't know everything about life or divinity. Many of my friends have different faith journeys than mine or claim no faith at all. I value them, their gifts and wisdom.

Dear reader, I believe that every one of us has something to give. I invite you to take time to find your superpower! We need you! We've been waiting for you, your singular, unique, beautiful, and amazing self. While we may or may not have similar stories, we are each distinct and bring our own value to life and this shared community.

I want to read your story. I want to know what's challenged you and what has brought you joy. And hope. I want to hear about your losses and how you've managed to get through to today. I hope that my story is an encouragement to you. I'm certain yours would be for me.

And still, I dance! Despite and because of all that I've experienced.

---

\* If that doesn't make any sense to you, read *Invisible Man*, a novel by Ralph Ellison, published by Random House in 1952. It still rings true.

I celebrate every moment and every day because life is so precious.

I've lost too many loved ones to take even my worst days for granted.

My step isn't as steady as it once was, but I'm still on the move.

The things I was so sure of when I was younger, I question now.

I'm absolute about very little.

I'm more eager to learn than to teach.

I'm thankful for the ways that life has humbled me.

I've learned the difference between humility and humiliation.

I'm in awe of the ways that people have moved the community forward since I transitioned 25 years ago.

I hold gratitude for the ancestors: those who blazed trails, held space, created family, tended to the most broken of us.

We may never know their names, but their seeds are still blooming.

And I'm invested in watering those gardens.

My swagger is less pronounced; I move more slowly and deliberately. My feet are tired from the march to wholeness.

But still I dance in joy and hope for the generations to come, their creativity and power to change the world.

Someday, perhaps not all that long from now, I will return to Source—to earth, to Spirit.

But every day between now and then, sure-footed or limping, *I will dance.*

The journey from that little kid to this grown man took twists and turns, and the road was full of challenge and celebration.

As Miss Major says, "I'm still fucking here!" I'm an out Black queer trans man in recovery, in love and awe with the Divine Source, can you believe it?

This is an invitation to dance with me!

# Endnotes

## Preface

1  Nagourney, A. & Peters, J.W. (April 16, 2023.) How a Campaign Against Transgender Rights Mobilized Conservatives. *The New York Times*. Retrieved from: https://www.nytimes.com/2023/04/16/us/politics/transgender-conservative-campaign.html

## Introduction

1  Gonzales, G. & McKay, T. (2017.) What an Emerging Trump Administration Means for Lesbian, Gay, Bisexual, and Transgender Health. *Health Equity* 1(1), 83–36. Retrieved from: www.liebertpub.com/doi/full/10.1089/heq.2017.0002

2  Gonzales, G., Ramirez, J.L., & Galupo, M.P. (2018.) Increase in GLBTQ Minority Stress Following the 2016 U.S. Presidential Election. *Journal of GLBT Family Studies* 14(1–2), 130–151.

3  Gessen, M. (October 22, 2018.) The Trauma of the Trump Administration's Attacks on Transgender People. *The New Yorker*. Retrieved from: www.newyorker.com/news/our-columnists/the-trauma-of-the-trump-administrations-attacks-on-transgender-people

4  Michaelson, J. (March 26, 2019.) Why Chick-fil-A Still Hurts: Queer Trauma in the Age of Trump. *The Daily Beast*. Retrieved from: www.thedailybeast.com/why-chick-fil-a-still-hurts-queer-trauma-in-the-age-of-trump

5  Beemyn, G. (2014.) "Transgender History in the United States." In Erickson-Schroth, L. (Ed.), *Trans Bodies, Trans Selves*. Oxford University Press. Retrieved from: www.umass.edu/stonewall/sites/default/files/Infoforandabout/transpeople/genny_beemyn_transgender_history_in_the_united_states.pdf

6  National Center for Transgender Equality. (n.d.) The Discrimination Administration: Trump's Record of Action Against Transgender People. *National Center for Transgender Equality*. Retrieved from: https://transequality.org/the-discrimination-administration

7  Johnson, C. (September 25, 2019.) HRC President: Trump Responsible for Anti-Trans Violence. *Washington Blade*. Retrieved from: www.washingtonblade.com/2019/09/25/hrc-president-trump-responsible-for-anti-trans-violence

8  Green, E.L., Brenner, K., & Pear, R. (October 21, 2018.) "Transgender" Could be Defined Out of Existence Under Trump Administration. *The New York Times*.

Retrieved from: www.nytimes.com/2018/10/21/us/politics/transgender-trump-administration-sex-definition.html

9   Woodstock, T. (October 29, 2018.) The Trump Administration Says It Wants to Define Sex "On a Biological Basis." It Gets the Science Wrong. *The Washington Post*. Retrieved from: www.washingtonpost.com/outlook/2018/10/29/trump-administration-says-it-wants-define-sex-biological-basis-it-gets-science-wrong

10  Burns, K. (July 17, 2020.) The Trump Administration's Proposed Homeless Shelter Rule Spells Out How to Spot a Trans Woman. *Vox*. Retrieved from: www.vox.com/identities/2020/7/17/21328708/proposed-anti-trans-rule-homeless-shelters-judge-women

11  Levin, D. (June 15, 2020.) A Clash Across America Over Transgender Rights. *The New York Times*. Retrieved from: www.nytimes.com/2020/03/12/us/transgender-youth-legislation.html

12  Freedom for All Americans. (2020.) 2020 Legislature Tracker: Anti Transgender Legislation. *Freedom for All Americans*. Retrieved from: www.freedomforallamericans.org/2020-legislative-tracker/2020-anti-transgender-legislation

13  Burns, K. (January 29, 2020.) Why Republicans are Suddenly in a Rush to Regulate Every Trans Kid's Puberty. *Vox*. Retrieved from: www.vox.com/identities/2020/1/29/21083505/transgender-kids-legislation-puberty-blockers

14  American Psychological Association. (2021.) Transgender Exclusion in Sports: Suggestion Discussion Points with Resources to Oppose Transgender Exclusion Bills. *American Psychological Association*. Retrieved from: www.apa.org/topics/lgbtq/transgender-exclusion-sports

15  The American Civil Liberties Union. (April 30, 2020.) Four Myths About Trans Athletes, Debunked. *The American Civil Liberties Union*. Retrieved from: www.aclu.org/news/lgbtq-rights/four-myths-about-trans-athletes-debunked

16  Ladd, S. (December 9, 2019.) Bill Would Keep Transgender Students from Using Restrooms that Align with Their Identities. *Courier Journal*. Retrieved from: www.courier-journal.com/story/news/local/2019/12/09/kentucky-legislation-would-set-bathroom-rules-transgender-kids/2632897001

17  Serano, J. (June, 7, 2021.) Transgender People, Bathrooms, and Sexual Predators: What the Data Say. *Medium*. Retrieved from: https://juliaserano.medium.com/transgender-people-bathrooms-and-sexual-predators-what-the-data-say-2f31ae2a7c06

18  National Center of Transgender Equality. (July 10, 2016.) Transgender People and Bathroom Access. *National Center of Transgender Equality*. Retrieved from: https://transequality.org/issues/resources/transgender-people-and-bathroom-access

19  Wicks, A. (March 29, 2016.) More Republican Legislators Arrested for Bathroom Misconduct than Trans People. *Complex*. Retrieved from: www.complex.com/life/2016/03/republican-legislators-arrested-for-bathroom-misconduct

20  Avery, D. (December 30, 2016.) 20 Republican Politicians Brought Down by Big Gay Sex Scandals. *LogoTV.com*. Retrieved from: https://www.logotv.com/news/lpa6sk/19-republican-politicians-gay-sex

21 Lang, N. (February 19, 2021.) A Hate Group Is Reportedly Behind 2021's Dangerous Wave of Anti-Trans Bills. *Them.* Retrieved from: www.them.us/ story/hate-group-reportedly-behind-2021-anti-trans-bills

22 Human Rights Campaign. (October 15, 2014.) 10 Shocking Facts About the Alliance Defending Freedom. *Human Rights Campaign.* Retrieved from: www.hrc. org/press-releases/10-shocking-facts-about-the-alliance-defending-freedom

23 Ashley, F. (December 4, 2018.) There is No Evidence that Rapid-Onset Gender Dysphoria Exists. *Psych Central.* Retrieved from: https://psychcentral.com/lib/ there-is-no-evidence-that-rapid-onset-gender-dysphoria-exists#1

24 Restar, A.J. (2019.) Methodological Critique of Littman's (2018) Parental-Respondents Accounts of "Rapid Onset Gender Dysphoria." *Archives of Sexual Behavior* (49), 61–66. Retrieved from: https://link.springer.com/ article/10.1007/s10508-019-1453-2

25 Newhook, J.T., et al. (2018.) A Critical Commentary on Follow-Up "Desistance" Theories About Transgender and Gender Nonconforming Children. *International Journal of Transgenderism* 19(2), 212–224. Retrieved from: www. researchgate.net/publication/324808865_A_Critical_Commentary_on_ Follow-Up_Studies_and_Desistance_Theories_about_Transgender_and_ Gender-Nonconforming_Children

26 Ehrensaft, D. (2017.) Gender Nonconforming Youth: Current Perspectives. *Adolescent Health, Medicine and Therapeutics* 8, 57–67. Retrieved from: www. ncbi.nlm.nih.gov/pmc/articles/PMC5448699

27 Conley, G. (July 8, 2020.) J.K. Rowling's Bigotry Is Painful and Maddening. *CNN.* Retrieved from: www.cnn.com/2020/07/07/opinions/jk-rowling-conversion-therapy-transphobia-conley/index.html

28 Pfafflin, F., MD (1993.) Regrets After Sex Reassignment Surgery. *Journal of Psychology & Human Sexuality* 5(4), 69–85. DOI: 10.1300/J056v05n04_05. Retrieved from: www.tandfonline.com/doi/abs/10.1300/J056v05n04_05

29 Wiepjes, C.M., et al. (2018.) The Amsterdam Cohort of Gender Dysphoria Study (1972–2015): Trends in Prevalence, Treatment, and Regrets. *Journal of Sexual Medicine* 15(4), 582–590. Retrieved from: https://pubmed.ncbi.nlm.nih. gov/29463477

30 Hidalgo, M.A., et al. (October 2013.) The Gender Affirmative Model: What We Know and What We Aim to Learn. *Karger* 56(5). Retrieved from: www. karger.com/Article/Fulltext/355235

31 Turban, J.L., et al. (2021.) Factors Leading to "Detransition" Among Transgender and Gender Diverse People in the United States: A Mixed-Methods Analysis. *LGBT Health* 8(4), 273–280. Retrieved from: www.ncbi.nlm.nih.gov/ pmc/articles/PMC8213007/?fbclid=IwAR0qza2f7WP2k1zRH8GpVr39sm-wwuRIITOK2Wgm-8UfElrB6aTyWbJds9p8

32 Stolberg, S.G. (June 24, 2022.) Thomas's Concurring Opinion Raises Questions About What Rights Might Be Next. *The New York Times.* Retrieved from: www.nytimes.com/2022/06/24/us/clarence-thomas-roe-griswold-lawrence-obergefell.html?searchResultPosition=3

33  Yogyakarta Principles. (2017.) Jurisprudential Annotations to the Yogyakarta Principles. *Yogyakarta Principles.* Retrieved from: http://yogyakartaprinciples. org/wp-content/uploads/2017/11/Jurisprudential-Annotations.pdf

34  Pfafflin, F., MD (1993.) Regrets After Sex Reassignment Surgery. *Journal of Psychology & Human Sexuality* 5(4), 69–85. DOI: 10.1300/J056v05n04_05. Retrieved from: www.tandfonline.com/doi/abs/10.1300/J056v05n04_05

35  St. Amand, C., MA, et al. (2011.) The Effects of Hormonal Gender Affirmation Treatment on Mental Health in Female-to-Male Transsexuals. *Journal of Gay & Lesbian Mental Health* 15(3), 281–299. DOI: 10.1080/19359705.2011.581195. Retrieved from: www.tandfonline.com/doi/abs/10.1080/19359705.2011.5811 95

36  Riley, E.A., et al. (2011.) The Needs of Gender-Variant Children and Their Parents: A Parent Survey. *International Journal of Sexual Health* 23, 181–195. Retrieved from: www.hawaii.edu/PCSS/biblio/articles/2010to2014/2011-gender-variant-children.html

37  Gómez-Gil, E., et al. (May 2012.) Hormone-Treated Transsexuals Report Less Social Distress, Anxiety, and Depression. *Psychoneuroendocrinology* 37(5), 662–670. Retrieved from: www.sciencedirect.com/science/article/abs/pii/S0306453011002629?via%3Dihub

38  Riley, E.A., Sitharthan, G., Clemson, L.M., & Diamond, M. (2011.) The Needs of Gender-Variant Children and Their Parents According to Health Professionals. *International Journal of Transgenderism* 13, 54–63. Retrieved from: www.semanticscholar.org/paper/Surviving-a-gender-variant-childhood%3A-the-views-of-Riley-Clemson/20d1168cecafe4aa6c633e4691b60e88ed 31c901

39  Hidalgo, M.A., et al. (2013.) The Gender Affirmative Model: What We Know and What We Aim to Learn. *Karger* 56(5). Retrieved from: www.karger.com/Article/Fulltext/355235

40  Annelou, L.C. de Vries, MD, PhD, et al. (2014.) Young Adult Psychological Outcome After Puberty Suppression and Gender Reassignment. *Pediatrics* 134(4), 696–704. DOI: 10.1542/peds.2013-2958. Retrieved from: www.acthe. fr/upload/1474383760-696.full.pdf

41  Bariola, E., BA, et al. (2015.) Demographic and Psychological Factors Associated with Psychological Distress and Resilience Among Transgender Individuals. *American Journal of Public Health* 105(10), 2108–2116. DOI: 10.2105/AJPH.2015.302763. Retrieved from: www.ncbi.nlm.nih.gov/pmc/articles/PMC4566567

42  Olson, K.R., PhD, Durwood, L., BA, DuMeules, M., BA, & McLaughlin, K.A., PhD (2016.) Mental Health of Transgender Children Who Are Supported in Their Identities. *Pediatrics* 137(3). DOI: https://doi.org/10.1542/peds.2015-3223. Retrieved from: http://pediatrics.aappublications.org/content/early/2016/02/24/peds.2015-3223

43  Durwood, L., BA, McLaughlin, K.A., PhD, & Olson, K.R., PhD (2017.) Mental Health and Self-Worth in Socially Transitioned Transgender Youth. *Journal of the American Academy of Child & Adolescent Psychiatry* 56(2), 116–123. DOI:

https://doi.org/10.1016/j.jaac.2016.10.016. Retrieved from: www.ncbi.nlm.nih.gov/pmc/articles/PMC5302003

44 Rafferty, J., MD, et al. (2018.) Ensuring Comprehensive Care and Support for Transgender and Gender-Diverse Children and Adolescents. *Pediatrics* 142(4). DOI: https://doi.org/10.1542/peds.2018-2162. Retrieved from: https://publications.aap.org/pediatrics/article/142/4/e20182162/37381/Ensuring-Comprehensive-Care-and-Support-for

45 What We Know Project. (2018.) What Does the Scholarly Research Say about the Effect of Gender Transition on Transgender Well-Being? *Cornell University*. Retrieved from: https://whatweknow.inequality.cornell.edu/about/selection-methodology

46 Gülgöz, S., et al. (2019.) Similarity in Transgender and Cisgender Children's Gender Development. *PNAS 116*(49), 24480–24485. DOI: https://doi.org/10.1073/pnas.1909367116. Retrieved from: www.pnas.org/content/early/2019/11/12/1909367116

47 Leibowitz, S., et al. (2020.) Statement in Response to Calls for Banning Evidence-Based Supportive Health Interventions for Transgender and Gender Diverse Youth. *International Journal of Transgender Health* 21(1), 111–112. DOI: 10.1080/15532739.2020.1703652

48 Call, D.C., Challa, M., & Telingator, C.J. (2021.) Providing Affirmative Care to Transgender and Gender Diverse Youth: Disparities, Interventions, and Outcomes. *Current Psychiatry Reports 23*, 33. DOI: https://doi.org/10.1007/s11920-021-01245-9. Retrieved from: https://link.springer.com/article/10.1007/s11920-021-01245-9

49 Olson, K.R., et al. (2022.) Gender Identity 5 Years After Social Transition. *Pediatrics*. DOI: https://doi.org/10.1542/peds.2021-056082. Retrieved from: https://publications.aap.org/pediatrics/article/doi/10.1542/peds.2021-056082/186992/Gender-Identity-5-Years-After-Social-Transition

50 Turban, J.L., et al. (2022.) Access to Gender-Affirming Hormones During Adolescence and Mental Health Outcomes Among Transgender Adults. *Plos One*. DOI: https://doi.org/10.1371/journal.pone.0261039. Retrieved from: https://journals.plos.org/plosone/article?id=10.1371/journal.pone.0261039

51 Greenberg, D., et al. (June 11, 2019.) America's Growing Support for Transgender Rights. *PRRI*. Retrieved from: www.prri.org/research/americas-growing-support-for-transgender-rights/?fbclid=IwAR2PQz6kfGkAKGW1wGBKsIMIj1I3o_vRJ33I7xgacwyvAgaS8upryA9zkiU

52 American Academy of Child & Adolescent Psychiatry Council. (2009.) Sexual Orientation, Gender Identity, and Civil Rights. *American Academy of Child & Adolescent Psychiatry*. Retrieved from: www.aacap.org/aacap/Policy_Statements/2009/Sexual_Orientation_Gender_Identity_and_Civil_Rights.aspx

53 Mashek, L.D., et al. (2012.) 2012 Agenda for the Reference Committee on Advocacy. *American Academy of Family Physicians*. Retrieved from: www.aafp.org/dam/AAFP/documents/about_us/special_constituencies/2012RCAR_Advocacy.pdf

54  Rafferty, J., MD, et al. (2018.) Ensuring Comprehensive Care and Support for Transgender and Gender-Diverse Children and Adolescents. *Pediatrics* 142(4). DOI: https://doi.org/10.1542/peds.2018-2162. Retrieved from: https://publications.aap.org/pediatrics/article/142/4/e20182162/37381/ Ensuring-Comprehensive-Care-and-Support-for

55  The American College of Nurse-Midwives. (June 15, 2020.) Position Statement on Transgender/Transsexual/Gender Variant Health Care. *Transgender Legal Defense & Education Fund.* Retrieved from: https://transhealthproject.org/resources/medical-organization-statements/ american-college-nurse-midwives-statements

56  Daniel, H., BS, & Butkus, R., BA (July 21, 2015.) Lesbian, Gay, Bisexual, and Transgender Health Disparities: Executive Summary of a Policy Position Paper from The American College of Physicians. *Annals of Internal Medicine.* DOI: https://doi.org/10.7326/M14-2482. Retrieved from: www.acpjournals. org/doi/10.7326/M14-2482

57  American Counseling Association. (n.d.) Nondiscrimination: Position Statement. Retrieved from: www.counseling.org/about-us/social-justice/ nondiscrimination

58  Harrington, R. (August 13, 2019.) RE: Docket No. HHS-ORC-2019-0007 (RIN 0945-AA11), Proposed Rule on Nondiscrimination in Health and Health Education Programs or Activities. *American Heart Association.* Retrieved from: www.regulations.gov/document/HHS-OCR-2019-0007-147945

59  Henry, A.T. (December 31, 2019.) American Medical Association: Exclusionary Bathroom Policies Harm Transgender Students' Health. *American Medical Association.* Retrieved from: www.ama-assn.org/delivering-care/population-care/ exclusionary-bathroom-policies-harm-transgender-students-health

60  Madara, J.L., MD (April 26, 2021.) AMA to States: Stop Interfering in Health Care of Transgender Children. *The American Medical Association.* Retrieved from: www.ama-assn.org/press-center/press-releases/ ama-states-stop-interfering-health-care-transgender-children

61  Meyerhoeffer, W. (July 10, 2014.) AMHCA Statement on Reparative or Conversation Therapy. *American Mental Health Counselors Association.* Retrieved from: www.amhca.org/viewdocument/amhca-statement-on-reparative-or-co

62  ANA Center for Ethics and Human Rights. (2018.) ANA Position Statement: Nursing Advocacy for LGBTQ+ Populations. *The Online Journal of Issues in Nursing* 24(1). DOI: 10.3912/OJIN.Vol24No01PoSCol02. Retrieved from: https://ojin.nursingworld.org/MainMenuCategories/ANAMarketplace/ ANAPeriodicals/OJIN/TableofContents/Vol-24-2019/No1-Jan-2019/ANA-Position-Statement-Advocacy-for-LGBTQ.html

63  American Osteopathic Association. (2015.) American Osteopathic Association Policy Compendium H445-A/15 Gender Identity Non-Discrimination. *Transgender Legal Defense & Education Fund.* Retrieved from: https:// transhealthproject.org/resources/medical-organization-statements/american-osteopathic-association-statements/?fbclid=IwAR1sjXTIq5HDNIjoAWzos XbE-4TLzw7NW2rTuV2XK1xnFMWRNTJcdbEsWNw

64 Drescher, J., MD, Haller, E., MD, & APA Caucus of Lesbian, Gay, and Bisexual Psychiatrists. (July 2018.) Position Statement on Access to Care for Transgender and Gender Diverse Individuals. *American Psychiatric Association.* Retrieved from: https://psychiatry.org/getattachment/d3ef4763-8a0e-4da3-ab01-efe932ca9478/Position-2018-Access-to-Care-for-Transgender-and-Gender-Diverse-Individuals.pdf

65 American Psychological Association. (2015.) Guidelines for Psychological Practice with Transgender and Gender Nonconforming People. *American Psychologist 70*(9), 832–864. DOI: http://dx.doi.org/10.1037/a0039906. Retrieved from: www.apa.org/practice/guidelines/transgender.pdf

66 American Public Health Association. (November 1, 2016.) Promoting Transgender and Gender Minority Health through Inclusive Policies and Practices. *American Public Health Association.* Retrieved from: https://apha.org/policies-and-advocacy/public-health-policy-statements/policy-database/2017/01/26/promoting-transgender-and-gender-minority-health-through-inclusive-policies-and-practices

67 Endocrine Society. (December 15, 2020.) Transgender Health: An Endocrine Society Position Statement. *Endocrine Society.* Retrieved from: www.endocrine.org/advocacy/position-statements/transgender-health

68 National Association of Social Workers. (2006.) Transgender and Gender Identity Issues. *Social Work Speaks,* 366–370. Retrieved from: www.socialworkers.org/assets/secured/documents/da/da2008/reffered/Transgender.pdf

69 American Academy of Pediatrics and Pediatric Endocrine Society. (2018.) Introduction to Health for Transgender Youth. *Pediatric Endocrine Society.* Retrieved from: https://pedsendo.org/patient-resource/transgender-care

70 Yasuda, K.E., FAAP, & Trent, M., MD, MPH, FSAHM (August 13, 2019.) RE: HHS-OCR-2019-0007: Nondiscrimination in Health and Health Education Programs or Activities. *American Academy of Pediatrics.* Retrieved from: www.regulations.gov/document/HHS-OCR-2019-0007-139520

71 Leibowitz, S., et al. (2020.) Statement in Response to Calls for Banning Evidence-Based Supportive Health Interventions for Transgender and Gender Diverse Youth. *International Journal of Transgender Health 21*(1), 111–112. DOI: 10.1080/15532739.2020.1703652. Retrieved from: www.tandfonline.com/doi/pdf/10.1080/15532739.2020.1703652

72 Herrera, A. (March 4, 2022.) Texas Students Heckle Anti-Trans GOP Candidate with "F**k These Fascists" Change After He Comes to Their School. *Comic Sands.* Retrieved from: www.comicsands.com/texas-students-anti-trans-gop-2656844387.html?fbclid=IwAR2RxjLXvQM38gyUNLeL3bxAEZ-votQMAdqdvNP5MdFw390JOQcr55JYrXRQ

## Jamison Green

1 Raymond, J. (1977.) "Transsexualism: The Ultimate Homage to Sex-Role Power" in *Chrysalis, a Magazine of Women's Culture,* No. 3, pp.11–22; p.22.

2 Ibid, p.15.

3 Ibid, p.15.

4    Raymond, J.G. (1979.) *The Transsexual Empire*. Boston: Beacon Press.

## Dana Delgardo

1    United States Department of Defense. (2016.) Transgender Service in the U.S.
     Military: An Implementation Handbook. Retrieved from: https://dod.defense.
     gov/Portals/1/features/2016/0616_policy/DoDTGHandbook_093016.pdf
2    Department of the Air Force. (2018.) Memorandum on In-Service Transition
     of Airmen Identifying as Transgender. Retrieved from: https://health.mil/
     Reference-Center/Policies/2018/11/01/Air-Force-In-Service-Transition-of-
     Airmen-Identifying-as-Transgender
3    Edelman, A. (July 26, 2017.) Trump Bans Transgender People Serving in the Mil-
     itary. *NBC News*. Retrieved from: www.nbcnews.com/politics/donald-trump/
     trump-announces-ban-transgender-people-serving-military-n786621
4    Ibid.
5    Braverman, B. (July 26, 2017.) How Much Do Transgender Soldiers Really
     Cost the U.S. Military? *The Fiscal Times*. Retrieved from: www.thefiscaltimes.
     com/2017/07/26/How-Much-Do-Transgender-Soldiers-Really-Cost-U.S.-
     Military
6    Bowden, J. (July 28, 2017.) Mattis Appalled by Trump Tweets Announcing
     Transgender Ban: Report. *The Hill*. Retrieved from: https://thehill.com/policy/
     defense/344290-mattis-appalled-by-trump-tweets-announcing-transgender-
     military-ban-report
7    Ibid.
8    Mattis, J. (February 22, 2018.) Memorandum for the President, Subject:
     Military Service by Transgender Individuals. *Office of the Secretary of Defense*.
     Retrieved from: https://media.defense.gov/2018/Mar/23/2001894037/-1/-
     1/0/MILITARY-SERVICE-BY-TRANSGENDER-INDIVIDUALS.PDF
9    Lederman, M. (April 1, 2019.) The Mattis Transgender Policy Will Go into
     Effect Next Friday. *Just Security*. www.justsecurity.org/63467/the-mattis-
     transgender-policy-will-go-into-effect-next-friday

## Pooya Mohseni

1    Allen, N. (April 1, 2022.) See You Then. *RogerEbert.com*. www.rogerebert.com/
     reviews/see-you-then-movie-review-2022

## Dee Dee Watters

1    Roberts, M. (June 3, 2014.) Another Tuesday, Another HERO Fight. *TransGriot*.
     Retrieved from: https://transgriot.blogspot.com/2014/06/another-tuesday-
     another-hero-fight.html?m=1
2    Department of Justice. (n.d.) Learn About Hate Crimes. *Department of Justice*.
     Retrieved from: www.justice.gov/hatecrimes/learn-about-hate-crimes/chart

3   Roberts, M. (May 19, 2019.) Number 3. Rest in Power and Peace Muhlaysia Booker. *TransGriot*. Retrieved from: https://transgriot.blogspot.com/2019/05/number-3-rest-in-power-and-peace.html?m=1

## Chris Mosier

1   National Women's Law Center. (December 9, 2016.) Transgender People are Facing Incredibly High Rates of Poverty. *The National Women's Law Center Blog*. Retrieved from: https://nwlc.org/income-security-is-elusive-for-many-transgender-people-according-to-u-s-transgender-survey
2   Human Rights Foundation. (October 2021.) Dismantling a Culture of Violence. *Human Rights Campaign Foundation*. Retrieved from: https://reports.hrc.org/dismantling-a-culture-of-violence?_ga=2.66182446.1491024088.1662579788-1346206488.1659542842
3   Allen, J. (June 10, 2022.) New Study Estimates 1.6 Million in U.S. Identify as Transgender. *Reuters*. Retrieved from: www.reuters.com/world/us/new-study-estimates-16-million-us-identify-transgender-2022-06-10
4   Lambda Legal. (n.d.) Fighting Anti-Trans Violence. *Lambda Legal*. Retrieved from: www.lambdalegal.org/know-your-rights/article/trans-violence
5   Natividad, I. (June 25, 2021.) Why Is Anti-Trans Violence on the Rise in America? *Berkeley News*. Retrieved from: https://news.berkeley.edu/2021/06/25/why-is-anti-trans-violence-on-the-rise-in-america
6   Movement Advancement Project. (n.d.) Equality Maps: Housing Nondiscrimination Laws. *Movement Advancement Project*. Retrieved from: www.lgbtmap.org/equality-maps/non_discrimination_laws
7   Mosier, C. (n.d.) Take Action! *TransAthlete.com*. Retrieved from: www.transathlete.com/take-action
8   Lang, N. (April 14, 2022.) Kentucky Banned Trans Kids from Sports to Keep This 12-Year-Old Girl from Playing Hockey. *Xtra*. Retrieved from: https://xtramagazine.com/power/politics/kentucky-trans-kids-sports-ban-221391
9   Balingit, M. (August 25, 2022.) Kentucky's Lone Transgender Athlete Can't Play on the Team She Helped Start. *The Washington Post*. Retrieved from: www.washingtonpost.com/education/2022/08/25/fischer-wells-trans-athlete-kentucky
10  Savage, R. (March 31, 2020.) Idaho Becomes First U.S. State to Ban Trans Athletes. *Reuters*. Retrieved from: www.reuters.com/article/idUSKBN21I2AF
11  Rezal, A. (December 1, 2021.) States Restricting How Transgender Students Play Sports. *U.S. News & World Report*. Retrieved from: www.usnews.com/news/best-states/articles/2021-12-01/these-states-restrict-how-transgender-students-participate-in-school-sports
12  Crary, D. & Whitehurst, L. (March 3, 2021.) Lawmakers Can't Cite Local Examples of Trans Girls in Sports. *AP News*. Retrieved from: https://apnews.com/article/lawmakers-unable-to-cite-local-trans-girls-sports-914a982545e943ecc1e265e8c41042e7
13  Factora, J. (September 1, 2022.) There are More Laws Banning Trans Girls in K-12 Sports Than There Are Out Trans Girls in K-12 Sports. *Them*. Retrieved

from: www.them.us/story/there-are-more-laws-banning-trans-girls-in-k-12-sports-than-there-are-trans-girls-in-k-12-sports

14  Luneau, D. (March 24, 2022.) BREAKING: Arizona House Passes Anti-Transgender Sports and Medical Care Bans. *Human Rights Campaign Foundation.* Retrieved from: www.hrc.org/press-releases/breaking-arizona-house-passes-anti-transgender-sports-and-medical-care-bans

## Laura A. Jacobs

1  Bennett, H. (Producer). (1974–1978.) *The Six Million Dollar Man* [Television series]. Los Angeles: Harve Bennett Productions.

2  Callen-Lorde. (March 3, 2022.) About Us. *Callen-Lorde.* Retrieved from: https://callen-lorde.org/about

## Finn Gratton

1  Walsh, R.J. & Jackson-Perry, D. (2021.) "Autistic Cognition and Gender Identity." In Kourti, M. (Ed.), *Working with Autistic Transgender and Non-Binary People, Research, Practice and Experience.* London: Jessica Kingsley Publishers.

2  Weig, D. (Host) (March 4, 2019.) Erin Manning and Brian Massumi on Critical Somatic Individualisation and Why We Need More Movement in University Education and Architecture [Audio podcast episode]. In *Remember Your Body.*

## Jack Thompson

1  Leather culture. (n.d.) *Leatherpedia.* Retrieved from: www.leatherpedia.org/leather-culture

2  Sexplanations. (February 13, 2020.) *Sexual Negotiation Featuring Midori* [Video]. YouTube. www.youtube.com/watch?v=g9s0VVjIi38

3  Blinder, A. & Pérez-peña, R. (September 1, 2015.) Kentucky Clerk Denies Same-Sex Marriage Licenses, Defying Court. *The New York Times.* Retrieved from: www.nytimes.com/2015/09/02/us/same-sex-marriage-kentucky-kim-davis.html?smid=pl-share

## M. Dru Levasseur

1  The United States Department of Justice. (2016.) *Attorney General Loretta E. Lynch Delivers Remarks at Press Conference Announcing Complaint Against the State of North Carolina to Stop Discrimination Against Transgender Individuals.* Retrieved from: www.justice.gov/opa/speech/attorney-general-loretta-e-lynch-delivers-remarks-press-conference-announcing-complaint

2  Funders for LGBTQ Issues. (2018.) *GUTC Infographic: Foundation Funding for U.S. Trans Communities.* Retrieved from: https://lgbtfunders.org/research-item/gutc-infographic-foundation-funding-for-us-trans-communities

3    Global Philanthropy Project. (2020.) *Meet the Moment: A Call for Progressive Philanthropic Response to the Anti-Gender Movement.* Retrieved from: https://globalphilanthropyproject.org/wp-content/uploads/2021/02/Meet-the-Moment-2020-English.pdf

4    Rojas, R. & Swales, V. (2019.) 18 Transgender Killings This Year Raise Fears of an "Epidemic." *The New York Times.* Retrieved from: www.nytimes.com/2019/09/27/us/transgender-women-deaths.html

5    The American Medical Association House of Delegates, Minority Affairs Section. (n.d.) *Preventing Anti-Transgender Violence.* Retrieved from: www.ama-assn.org/system/files/2019-05/a19-008_0.pdf

6    National Center for Transgender Equality. (n.d.) *The Discrimination Administration: Trump's Record of Action Against Transgender People.* Retrieved from: https://transequality.org/the-discrimination-administration

## Colt St. Amand

1    St. Amand, C., Sharp, C., Michonski, J., Babcock, J., & Fitzgerald, K. (2013.) Romantic Relationships of Female-to-Male Trans Men: A Descriptive Study. *International Journal of Transgenderism 14,* 75–85.

2    Veale, J.F., Deutsch, M.B., Devor, A.H., Kuper, L.E., Motmans, J., Radix, A.E., & Amand, C.S. (2022.) Setting a Research Agenda in Trans Health: An Expert Assessment of Priorities and Issues by Trans and Nonbinary Researchers. *International Journal of Transgender Health,* 1–17.

3    St. Amand, C., Herman, L.I., Reisner, S.L., Pardo, S.T., Sharp, C., & Babcock, J.C. (2015.) Testosterone Treatment and MMPI-2 Improvement in Transgender Men: A Prospective Controlled Study. *Journal of Consulting and Clinical Psychology, 83*(1), 143.

## Lexie Bean

1    Chappell, B. (October 28, 2021.) A Texas Lawmaker Is Targeting 850 Books that He Says Could Make Students Feel Uneasy. *NPR.* Retrieved from: www.npr.org/2021/10/28/1050013664/exas-lawmaker-matt-krause-launches-inquiry-into-850-books

2    Murney, M. (March 2, 2022.) ACLU Sues Texas Over Gov. Greg Abbott's Directive to Investigate Trans Kids' Families. *Dallas Observer.* Retrieved from: www.dallasobserver.com/news/aclu-sues-texas-over-greg-abbotts-order-to-investigate-families-f-trans-youth-13515213

3    Arnold, A. (July 22, 2020.) A Guide to the "Walking While Trans" Ban. *The Cut.* Retrieved from: www.thecut.com/2020/07/walking-while-trans-law-in-new-york-explained.html

4    Seelman, K.L. (2015.) Unequal Treatment of Transgender Individuals in Domestic Violence and Rape Crisis Programs. *SW Publications,* 59. Retrieved from: https://scholarworks.gsu.edu/cgi/viewcontent.cgi?article=1060&context=ssw_facpub

5    Puckett, J. (April 26, 2021.) Trans Youth Are Coming Out and Inning in Their Gender Much Earlier than Older Generations. *The Conversation.* Retrieved from: https://theconversation.com/trans-youth-are-coming-out-and-living-in-their-gender-much-earlier-than-older-generations-156829

6    Lesley University. (n.d.) The Cost of Coming Out: LGBT Youth Homelessness. *Lesley University.* Retrieved from: https://lesley.edu/article/the-cost-of-coming-out-lgbt-youth-homelessness

## Asa Radix

1    Hughto, J.M. & Reisner, S.L. (2016.) A Systematic Review of the Effects of Hormone Therapy on Psychological Functioning and Quality of Life in Transgender Individuals. *Transgender Health* 1(1), 21–31.

2    Glynn, T.R., Gamarel, K.E., Kahler, C.W., Iwamoto, M., Operario, D., & Nemoto, T. (2016.) The Role of Gender Affirmation in Psychological Well-Being Among Transgender Women. *Psychology of Sexual Orientation and Gender Diversity* 3(3), 336.

3    Das, L.T. (September 1, 2020.) We Need More Transgender and Gender Nonbinary Doctors. *Association of American Medical Colleges.* Retrieved from: www.aamc.org/news-insights/we-need-more-transgender-and-gender-nonbinary-doctors

4    Dimant, O.E., Cook, T.E., Greene, R.E., & Radix, A.E. (2019.) Experiences of Transgender and Gender Nonbinary Medical Students and Physicians. *Transgender Health* 4(1). DOI: https://doi.org/10.1089/trgh.2019.0021. Retrieved from: www.liebertpub.com/doi/epub/10.1089/trgh.2019.0021

5    Kvach, E.J., MD, MA, Weinand, J., MD, & O'Connell, R., MS (2021.) Experiences of Transgender and Nonbinary Physicians During Medical Residency Program Application. *Journal of Graduate Medical Education* 13(2), 201–205. DOI: 10.4300/JGME-D-20-00384.1. Retrieved from: www.ncbi.nlm.nih.gov/pmc/articles/PMC8054580

6    Southern Poverty Law Center. (2020.) American College of Pediatricians. *Southern Poverty Law Center.* Retrieved from: www.splcenter.org/fighting-hate/extremist-files/group/american-college-pediatricians

7    Suen, B. (2017.) Tucker Carlson Teams with Hate Group to Spread Junk Science About Transgender Kids. *Media Matters for America.* Retrieved from: www.mediamatters.org/tucker-carlson/tucker-carlson-teams-hate-group-spread-junk-science-about-transgender-kids

8    GLAAD. (n.d.) American College of Pediatricians. *GLAAD Accountability Project Groups.* Retrieved from: www.glaad.org/gap/organization/american-college-pediatricians

9    Psychology Today. (2017.) The American College of Pediatricians is an Anti-LGBT Group. *Psychology Today.* Retrieved from: www.psychologytoday.com/us/blog/political-minds/201705/the-american-college-pediatricians-is-anti-lgbt-group

10   January, B. (2018.) Anti-LGBTQ Media and Groups Have Been Crying "Censorship" as Flawed Research on Trans Teens is Reevaluated. *Media Matters for America.* Retrieved from: www.mediamatters.org/tucker-carlson/

anti-lgbtq-media-and-groups-have-been-crying-censorship-flawed-research-trans-teens

11 Veritas. (2015.) "P" for Pedophile. *American College of Pediatricians.* Retrieved from: https://archive.acpeds.org/p-for-pedophile

12 Potok, M. (2016.) Quacks: "Conversion Therapists," the Anti-LGBT Right, and the Demonization of Homosexuality. *Southern Poverty Law Center.* Retrieved from: www.splcenter.org/20160525/quacks-conversion-therapists-anti-lgbt-right-and-demonization-homosexuality

13 American College of Pediatricians. (2014.) Legislators Are Not Psychotherapists! *American College of Pediatricians.* Retrieved from: https://acpeds.org/press/legislators-are-not-psychotherapists

14 Gogarty, K. (2019.) Extreme Anti-LGBTQ Groups Family Research Council and American College of Pediatricians Were on Capitol Hill Fighting the Equality Act. *Media Matters for America.* Retrieved from: www.mediamatters.org/family-research-council/extreme-anti-lgbtq-groups-family-research-council-and-american-college

15 Cretella, M., MD, & Trumbull, D. (2004.) Homosexual Parenting: A Scientific Analysis. *American College of Pediatricians.* Retrieved from: https://acpeds.org/position-statements/homosexual-parenting-a-scientific-analysis

16 American College of Pediatricians. (2013.) Traditional Marriage Still the Best for Children. *American College of Pediatricians.* Retrieved from: https://acpeds.org/press/traditional-marriage-still-the-best-for-children

17 American College of Pediatricians. (2013.) DOMA Is Best for Children. *American College of Pediatricians.* Retrieved from: https://acpeds.org/press/doma-is-best-for-children

18 Wilson, L. (2021.) Adoption. *American College of Pediatricians.* Retrieved from: https://acpeds.org/position-statements/statement-on-adoption

19 Zanga, J. (2018.) Elect Candidates Who Support the Best for Children. *American College of Pediatricians.* Retrieved from: https://acpeds.org/position-statements/elect-candidates-who-support-the-best-for-children

20 Cretellan, M., Van Meter, Q., & McHugh, P. (2016.) Gender Ideology Harms Children. *American College of Pediatricians.* Retrieved from: https://archive.acpeds.org/the-college-speaks/position-statements/gender-ideology-harms-children

21 American College of Pediatricians. (n.d.) Deconstructing Transgender Pediatrics. *American College of Pediatricians.* Retrieved from: https://acpeds.org/topics/sexuality-issues-of-youth/gender-confusion-and-transgender-identity/deconstructing-transgender-pediatrics

22 Cretella, M. (2018.) Gender Dysphoria in Children. *American College of Pediatricians.* Retrieved from: https://acpeds.org/position-statements/gender-dysphoria-in-children

23 Olson, K.R., Durwood, L., DeMeules, M. & McLaughlin, K.A. (2016.) Mental Health of Transgender Children Who Are Supported in Their Identities. *Pediatrics* 137(3): e20153223.

24 Rafferty, J., MD, American Academy of Pediatrics Committee on Psychological Aspects of Child and Family Health, Committee on Adolescence,

Section on Lesbian, Gay, Bisexual, and Transgender Health and Wellness, et al. (2018.) Ensuring Comprehensive Care and Support for Transgender and Gender-Diverse Children and Adolescents. *Pediatrics 142*(4). DOI: https://doi.org/10.1542/peds.2018-2162. Retrieved from: https://publications.aap.org/pediatrics/article/142/4/e20182162/37381/Ensuring-Comprehensive-Care-and-Support-for

25   The Associated Press. (May 14, 2022.) A Judge Blocks Part of an Alabama Law that Criminalizes Gender-Affirming Medication. *NPR*. Retrieved from: www.npr.org/2022/05/14/1098947193/a-judge-blocks-part-of-an-alabama-law-that-criminalizes-gender-affirming-medicat

26   Yurcaba, J. (April 18, 2021.) Nearly Half of Trans People Have Been Mistreated by Medical Providers, Report Finds. *NBC News*. Retrieved from: www.nbcnews.com/nbc-out/out-health-and-wellness/nearly-half-trans-people-mistreated-medical-providers-report-finds-rcna1695

27   Adams, N., et al. (2017.) Guidance and Ethical Considerations for Undertaking Transgender Health Research and Institutional Review Boards Adjudicating this Research. *Transgender Health 2*(1), 165–175. DOI: 10.1089/trgh.2017.0012. Retrieved from: www.ncbi.nlm.nih.gov/pmc/articles/PMC5665092

## Robyn Alice McCutcheon

1   Kralev, N. (2015.) *America's Other Army: The U.S. Foreign Service and 21st-Century Diplomacy*. CreateSpace Independent Publishing Platform.

2   Burns, W.J. (2019.) The Lost Art of American Diplomacy. *Foreign Affairs*. Retrieved from: www.foreignaffairs.com/united-states/lost-art-american-diplomacy. And Burns, W.J. (2019) *The Back Channel: A Memoir of American Diplomacy and the Case for Its Renewal*. New York: Random House.

3   Association for Diplomatic Studies and Training. (2015.) *The "Lavender Scare": Homosexuals at the State Department*. Retrieved from: https://adst.org/2015/09/the-lavender-scare-homosexuals-at-the-state-department

4   Schwenke, C. (2018.) *SELF-ish: A Transgender Awakening*. Pasadena, CA: Red Hen Press.

5   Kali, S. (November 30, 2018.) Цена за право быть собой (Price for the Right to Be Yourself) [Video]. YouTube. www.youtube.com/watch?v=e2XT2uCb2qI

## Reverend Louis J. Mitchell

1   Ziegler, K.R. (2008.) *Still Black: A Portrait of Black Transmen* [Film].

2   Kunik, T. (2016.) *Gender Journeys: More than a Pronoun* [Film].

3   Howard, S. (2017.) *More Than T* [Film].

### Hope Hospital S...

*The joy of saving liv...*

Welcome to Hope ... ...aff
are kind, carin... ...rs!

As former foster kids, ... ...ckson took their
ambition to be the bes... ...ould be and turned
it into reality. Now as Hope Hospital's leading
trauma surgeon and nurse anesthetist, they're fully
equipped to prevent some of the heartbreak
they once witnessed.

What they're not equipped to deal with is returning
trauma surgeon Miranda, Knox's fiercest med school
rival, and new orthopedic surgeon Ryann, Jackson's
unforgettable vacation fling. One thing's for sure—
these women are set to turn the lives of these
brooding bachelors upside down!

Enjoy Juliette Hyland's fabulous
Harlequin Medical Romance duet

*Dating His Irresistible Rival*
*Her Secret Baby Confession*

Available now!

Dear Reader,

I know you aren't supposed to have favorites, but if I did, my favorite hero would be nurse Jackson Peters. He is a cinnamon roll hero, wrapped in gooeyness, light and love. Giving him the happily-ever-after he deserved made my day each time I opened the story.

Dr. Ryann Oliver had an unconventional upbringing. Her daughter might have been conceived on a vacation fling, but she is determined to give her the stability Ryann never had. But when she reconnects with Jackson, can she ignore the heat between them to give her daughter the security she deserves...and what if gambling her heart isn't the risk she fears it is?

Jackson never expected a family of his own. When Ryann introduces him to their daughter, Ayla, it's love at first sight. Convincing Ryann he is in his daughter's life forever isn't quite as easy. But Jackson isn't going anywhere, and he's the partner Ryann truly needs.

*Juliette Hyland*

# Her Secret Baby Confession

---

## JULIETTE HYLAND

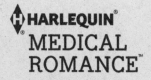

# HARLEQUIN®
## MEDICAL
## ROMANCE™

Recycling programs
for this product may
not exist in your area.

ISBN-13: 978-1-335-59541-6

Her Secret Baby Confession

Harlequin Enterprises ULC
22 Adelaide St. West, 41st Floor
Toronto, Ontario M5H 4E3, Canada
www.Harlequin.com

**Printed in U.S.A.**

**Juliette Hyland** began crafting heroes and heroines in high school. She lives in Ohio with her Prince Charming, who has patiently listened to many rants regarding characters failing to follow the outline. When not working on fun and flirty happily-ever-afters, Juliette can be found spending time with her beautiful daughters, giant dogs or sewing uneven stitches with her sewing machine.

### Books by Juliette Hyland

### Harlequin Medical Romance

### *Boston Christmas Miracles*

*A Puppy on the 34th Ward*

### *Hope Hospital Surgeons*

*Dating His Irresistible Rival*

### *Neonatal Nurses*

*A Nurse to Claim His Heart*

*The Prince's One-Night Baby*
*Rules of Their Fake Florida Fling*
*Redeeming Her Hot-Shot Vet*
*Tempted by Her Royal Best Friend*

### Harlequin Romance

### *Royals in the Headlines*

*How to Win a Prince*

Visit the Author Profile page
at Harlequin.com for more titles.

For my furry coauthor, Abby, on our last
book together. Run fast sweet girl, catch all the balls,
see you on the other side.

# PROLOGUE

TWELVE HOURS. That was all the time Jackson Peters had left to spend with Ryann with two *n*s and no last name.

They'd agreed when they'd met on the plane to Hawaii, both catching a layover in LA, that this week was fun and nothing more. No strings, no attachments, just bliss.

And bliss it had been.

They'd shared nothing too personal. He knew she was a surgeon and lived on the West Coast. She knew he was a nurse living in the southwest. That was as deep as they'd gotten conversation wise.

He did know that she smelled like summer rain, tasted like morning dew and made his body hum with the lightest touch of her fingers.

She knew every inch of his body and nothing about his past. It was ecstasy.

Jackson's story wasn't a happy one. It wasn't one he wanted to dwell on, particularly on vacation. This was supposed to be his time away.

The "honeymoon" he hadn't gotten because Marie had decided she'd prefer to marry someone without so much childhood baggage. A week to forget the pains of the past and loneliness dwelling in his condo.

Part of him—the part that still hoped someone might not look at him as though he was somehow broken—wanted to share with her, wanted to believe that maybe Ryann wouldn't care about his past, wouldn't treat him differently because of it. But once someone knew, it was like they couldn't help but pity him.

And the last thing he wanted was to watch the pity dart into Ryann's eyes when she broached questions he didn't want to answer.

"Hmmm." Ryann ran a hand over Jackson's thigh as she sat up in the bed they'd shared for the last week.

The sheet dropped from her perfect breasts, and his hand automatically went to her brown, already perky nipple. *Beautiful* did not come close to describing the breathtaking creature before him. "Do we bother going to get dinner or just spend the night doing this?"

Her hand cupped him, and his body sprang to life. This was heaven. A temporary heaven that his soul was soaking up.

Jackson continued to twirl a finger around her nipple as her hand stroked him. Both of them so familiar with what made the other purr that they were drawing pleasure close but not making it impossible to think of nothing else.

"We could always do room service." Jackson lifted his head, running his tongue over the places where his finger had just traced, enjoying the tiny hitch in Ryann's breath. "Unless you want to spend the final night walking on the beach."

As much as he wanted to spend tonight crystalizing the memories of every single part of Ryann's body, this was the first vacation she'd had in a decade. One of the lone pieces of personal information the beauty had parted with. If she wanted to spend tonight walking the sandy beaches and running through the tide, he'd make that memory, too.

Her fingers curled around his manhood as she pressed her lips to his. "We could always enjoy each other, then walk on the beach, grab some fish tacos and come back for a final round."

Had her breath hitched on the words *final round*?

Did it matter if it did?

Not really.

No strings attached. Pleasure. Vacation memories. Stolen time away from the real world. That was all this was.

"Sound like the perfect way to say goodbye." Then he captured her mouth, devouring her before she could say anything else. He wasn't wasting a single minute.

# CHAPTER ONE

DR. RYANN OLIVER covered a yawn as she walked toward the elevator bay at Hope Hospital. It was her first day on rotation at the hospital since accepting a private-practice gig earlier this month.

The Arizona desert was as far removed from the green of Washington State as possible. Moss had grown on her home there, the sun not daring to peek its head out of the clouds most days. The greenery was like walking in a forest paved with roads—at least according to Ryann's mother, Lydia.

The woman prided herself on never settling for the "normal" way of life. She'd seen a different side of everything.

Sometimes it was nice…but when *different* meant running off to find herself or chase some new soul calling…it was Ryann who suffered.

Chaos never benefited anyone.

At thirty-nine Ryann might not have known exactly what normal was, but she knew it was more than just doing whatever you wanted when you wanted to, with whomever you wanted. That lifestyle might've been fine if you didn't have a child to care for.

When Ryann had been a child, Lydia—the only name her mother would answer to—had disappeared for weeks at a time. Ryann had been left in the care of the multitude of stepparents who had entered her life for months to a year or so at a time. If her mother had been between partners, Ryann had stayed with "friends" or acquaintances.

Lydia had always seemed to return just before social services had gotten really involved. The overworked system had let Ryann slip through the cracks again and again.

There'd been some good moments—night trips for ice cream, road trips where they'd stopped at the "biggest spoon this side of the Mississippi" or alligator farms or haunted farms. Ryann still got giddy whenever a roadside attraction popped up.

But stability, the knowledge that she was safe, that the lights or water wouldn't be cut off because Lydia had forgotten to pay the bills… Ryann had not known that until she'd created it for herself.

She yawned again. Her reason for taking the private-practice gig and moving to Arizona had kept her awake most of the night with what had turned out to be a gassy belly.

Around three this morning she'd let out a toot so loud it should have come from a grown man rather than Ryann's not-so-tiny-anymore six-month-old daughter. Ayla had let out a sigh, then yawned and fallen asleep. Ryann had slept in the rocker in Ayla's room, ready to react to the smallest sound, but her daughter had slept until the alarm sounded at six thirty.

Then she'd fallen asleep as Ryann had been driving to the babysitter's, comfortable in the knowledge that she was safe and loved. Ayla might have been unexpected, but she would never doubt that she was cared for.

Ryann's job was to protect her daughter. To control the world's chaos as much as possible. Ayla would never fear the way she had. Never know rotating caregivers or worry her mother might forget to pick her up from school.

Private practice paid well, and the hours were considerably better than staff hospital work. She was in the office two days a week, in surgery for two days and on rotation at the hospital for a day. After spending so much time at her old hospital, a regular schedule with two days guaranteed off was close to heaven.

The world of orthopedic surgery was competitive. There were more women in the field now, but they still made up less than ten percent of all practicing surgeons.

When Hope Hospital had hired Dr. Patrick O'Sullivan as the new head of surgery over her, it turned out to be a blessing. After all, he was at the hospital at all hours, and she kept close to a nine-to-five.

Her phone buzzed twice—the sign of a personal email.

Ryann's stomach dropped. It had been five months since she'd first contacted her daughter's father through a DNA-matching website. Five months of radio silence. Yet on the first of every month, she sent the same email through the online portal she was supposed to reach out on and stupidly hoped that this might be the one he'd respond to.

She and Jackson, if that had been his name, had shared a blissful week in Hawaii. The first vacation Ryann had taken since completing her residency. It had been a fling, the most unstructured thing Ryann had done since leaving her mother's side.

*Pure chaos with the hottest man I've ever seen.*

It had felt good. So very good. There were nights when she still woke from dreams of his dark lips trailing along her body. She'd never regret that week; it had given her Ayla.

And as she saw the latest email—from her mother, with an image of her on a sandy beach with a new partner—she was reminded why she didn't plan to repeat the wild-and-free days she'd spent with Jackson.

Not that she'd get the option. Ryann took a deep breath as tears coated her eyes. She was not going to cry over this. Months of silence from the man who'd fathered Ayla was nothing new. She was just tired and already craving foods she'd decided to give up to help with Ayla's gassy belly. That was why the frustration was bubbling too close to the surface.

It wasn't like she even needed him to co-parent. She'd been very clear in her notes that he didn't need to be involved if he didn't want to be. But she wanted a family health history for Ayla—and for him to know that he had a daughter.

Had part of her hoped that he might want more? Maybe. But she'd buried that feeling months ago. Not that it mattered.

Because five months and six days after the first note had been emailed there was still nothing from Jackson.

"Good morning." A white woman with curly brown hair smiled as she offered her hand. "I'm Miranda Paulson, one of the general surgeons at Hope."

"Ryann Oliver, orthopedic surgeon with the Lowery Group." Ryann pushed the elevator button again, wondering how long it took the parking-garage elevator to arrive.

"The button is funny." Miranda moved a little closer, pressed it twice, then held it until it lit up. "The hospital keeps telling us they will have maintenance look at it." Miranda shrugged as she stepped beside Ryann. "But since only staff park in this lot…"

She let the words run out, but Ryann knew what had been unstated. Since only staff used this entrance, it was not a priority. Technically it functioned. Profit over everything else.

"Thanks. I guess I look pretty dense standing here waiting for something that won't arrive." Ryann was tired enough that she'd have stood here for several more minutes before finally searching out a stairwell.

"No." Miranda shook her head, offering a bright smile. "You look new. I was the newbie not that long ago."

"The elevator hasn't worked for months?"

"This only started two weeks ago. My issue was with the pagers. They did finally fix that— though since you are private practice you won't get paged as often."

The elevator arrived, and they stepped in. Miranda lifted her mug, and the sweet scent of coffee nearly made Ryann weep. She hadn't had a drop of caffeine since learning she was pregnant. And since she was breastfeeding and Ayla was prone to tummy issues, she was still avoiding it.

She could hold off until her daughter was weaned, make it to at least a year of breastfeeding…more if Ayla was willing.

Just a few more months. *Few*…six or seven… ten…who was counting?

"You okay?" Miranda raised a brow, and Ryann knew the image she saw.

An exhausted mom…one craving the liquid that was in her cup.

One that had come darn close to beating the new head of surgery…if the rumors floating around the practice were right. Ryann needed to be on her game today. And she could do that without coffee—after all, she'd done without for so long now.

She plastered on the smile she wore whenever exhaustion was on her doorstep—so most days. "My daughter was awake well past her bedtime with a gassy tummy. She's fine, but I'm operating on less sleep than usual and your coffee smells delicious."

"It is. My boyfriend likes to joke that I prefer a little coffee with my sugar and syrup."

Ryann laughed. She did not enjoy sugar in her coffee—at least she didn't think so. Her first cup had been from the creaky machine in the library at her local college. A machine that should have retired to appliance heaven a decade before her arrival at the college but was probably still there.

It had functioned, but the coffee had been less than stellar. At least according to the others who'd partaken with her. It had tasted fine—ish—and woken her up. That was all Ryann had wanted. The coffee she'd drunk was the cheapest, with the highest caffeine count possible.

The elevator doors opened, and Miranda stepped out. "The locker room is this way," she said.

Ryann heard the words. They registered, vaguely, as she forced her feet to move in step with Miranda's. Her feet obeyed the commands of her brain, but her eyes stayed rooted to the black man standing behind the nurses' station, his head bent over a tablet.

The distance between the staff elevator and nurses' station was probably over five hundred feet, but even from this distance she recognized the shoulders, the stance, the black-rimmed glasses that he had to push up his nose.

It couldn't be. It wasn't possible.

Blood pounded in her ears. Heat coated her cheeks, and her mind was torn. Part of her was already plotting to run back to Ayla. Scoop her up and find another new start. Jackson hadn't returned her emails, and yes, she'd craved that just a few minutes ago, but seeing him now?

Her fight-or-flight instinct had definitely picked flight!

Ryann's mother had taken that route with her second stepfather. Lydia hadn't been prepared for that move. Even her fly-by-the-seat-of-her-pants mother, who figured everything would work out fine, had felt the hardship of starting over with basically nothing.

Ryann wasn't prepared for a move. It would be

disruptive for Ayla. This was just panic, her nervous system overreacting.

She had a good job and a mountain of med-school debts. Protecting Ayla meant staying here. At least for now.

That was the main thought running through her mind. The other, the thought that made her chest burn and embarrassment wrap around her spine, was the impulse to run to Jackson and hope his silence was just some misunderstanding.

Her mother would do that. Pretend the silence was the universe's way of giving her a big moment. Gush that karma had led her back to her soulmate and rush to him. Which was why Ryann wouldn't give in to that notion, either.

Control. That was what was needed here.

"That's Jackson Peters," Miranda said. "He's a nurse anesthetist, so you'll be working with him regularly. He's a good guy." Her voice was silky smooth, clearly misreading the reasons for Ryann's interest.

Ryann bit back all the words that threatened to tumble forward. She'd met Miranda less than ten minutes ago. It was better for the other woman to think she was ogling the hot nurse than to spill the truth.

She'd spent a week memorizing his body and come home with a baby surprise, followed by months of silence since their daughter's birth.

Not exactly knowledge you laid at a new colleague's feet.

"Is he the hospital's only nurse anesthetist?" A certified registered nurse anesthetist, or CRNA, provided anesthesia during operations just like an anesthesiologist. Instead of holding a doctor of medicine, they held a doctorate in nursing and passed different exam boards.

Many rural hospitals employed only CRNAs, but Hope wasn't rural. Not huge, but far from rural.

"Yes. He got the degree about two years ago. Jackson worked his way from certified nursing assistant to APRN. I joke with him that he's running out of degree advancements."

That was impressive. Ryann had met many nursing assistants, or CNAs, that went on to become registered nurses. But an advanced practice registered nurse, or APRN, took years of schooling and exams on top of the requirements be a registered nurse.

The time, *and cost*, meant many qualified and passionate professionals stopped at the RN stage.

"So you know him well?" She hadn't meant to ask the question, but there was no good way to shift the conversation as they stepped into the women's locker room. It didn't matter if Miranda knew Jackson, didn't matter if he was great at his job.

He hadn't responded to her contact on the DNA-matching site. The entire reason for being in that database was to find family. To reach people. To make connections.

Their daughter deserved a response.

"He's my boyfriend's best friend. Knox is one of the other general surgeons here. Jackson and Knox grew up together—basically brothers. They used to joke the universe gave them the same last name to make sure they found each other. Always together." Miranda chuckled as she closed her locker.

Information to file away. Jackson had a friend close enough to consider him family. And he was close friends with at least two of the surgeons here. How was he going to react to seeing Ryann in person?

She was the outsider. The one who would need to move on, if necessary.

"Ready to meet the rest of the crew?" Miranda's smile was bright—hopefully she'd dismiss any hint of uncertainty on Ryann's part as first day jitters.

"I met a few people when I did the hospital orientation last week. Not a lot, and I didn't have to do the full thing."

"The joys of private practice," Miranda said as she clapped.

"You ever consider it?" Ryann hadn't until the offer had come through from Lowery. She'd worked for hospitals her entire career; the switch was nice. She had her own office, a better schedule and a paycheck that was quite nice. Overall, the pros far outweighed any cons.

"Not really." Miranda opened the door of the locker room and gestured for Ryann to leave first. "I like the fast pace of the trauma-surgery suite. I know how that sounds, but it gets me going."

Spoken like a true trauma surgeon. That was the one specialty Ryann had never sought out. The wins in that field were brilliant—the losses… earth shattering.

That specialty dealt with everything. You had no control over the type of cases landing on your surgical table.

Ryann took a deep breath. She was about to see Jackson, about to make contact with the man who'd made it clear by ignoring the outreach she'd made that he wanted nothing to do with her.

And because the universe was the way it was, she was at work. Which meant she had to have no reaction, tamp down on all the emotions raging through her.

"Knox!" Miranda waved to a man walking down the hall. "Meet the new orthopedic surgeon."

The white man smiled at Ryann and offered a hand. "Dr. Knox Peters. Nice to meet you."

"Dr. Ryann Oliver." Ryann hoped she looked professional, that the interest she was giving to the periphery of her vision wasn't clear. And that no one was noticing her heart attempting to jump out of her chest.

"I'm off shift. I'll have dinner ready when you're home, sweetheart." Knox leaned forward, placing a quick platonic kiss on Miranda's cheek.

So, this was Jackson's friend. What would he think when he learned that Ryann wasn't just the new ortho surgeon but the mother of his best friend's vacation baby?

A worry for another time.

Knox moved through the locker room door, and Miranda watched him until he was completely out of sight.

"Right, then, let's go find Dr. O'Sullivan. Patrick should be the one to introduce you to staff you didn't meet during orientation."

Ryann nodded, not sure she could trust her voice. They rounded the corner, but Jackson wasn't by the nurses' station. That was good.

So why was disappointment coating her soul?

"Meet the new ortho?" Knox, Jackson's best friend in the whole world and the closest thing he had to family, asked, already wearing his street clothes.

"Not yet. But shouldn't you be heading to your new home? You know, the fancy one." Jackson threw a hand over his heart. He wasn't really upset that Knox had moved in with Miranda last month.

Though the new neighbors, a young couple that probably shouldn't have been living together, had upset the quiet ambiance he'd cultivated living next to Knox. Their fights were epic. Last night it had been over the lack of broom use. At least that was what he thought they'd been screaming about.

The walls weren't that thin, but he'd listened to make sure there were no sounds to indicate the argument had turned physical. Jackson hadn't wanted to involve the authorities for a noise complaint. But for intimate partner abuse? That was something he wouldn't ignore.

After an hour, whatever cleaning decision they'd been angry about had been overcome, or set aside for another time, and make-up noises had rumbled on the other side of the wall.

"It is weird not being right next door. But Icy was already comfortable at Miranda's place." Knox hit Jackson on the shoulder. "Want to come over for dinner tonight? I promised Miranda I'd make something."

Jackson made a face. Bad enough that Knox was using his girlfriend's cat as an excuse, though he understood not wanting to upset the feline princess. But he was not eating anything his brother cooked.

Not now. Not ever.

"I'm warming up one of the premade dinners that Miranda orders in bulk." Those services were what Knox had lived off of after he'd moved out of Jackson's place. It was a little funny that the woman he'd fallen for also refused to use the kitchen for more than reheating leftovers. They were perfect for each other.

"Oh, then yeah, I'll stop by," Jackson said.

He looked over Knox's shoulder and blinked twice. A woman with curly black hair and olive skin was walking next to Dr. O'Sullivan. They passed down the hallway, out of sight before Jackson could register more about the new doctor.

The new doctor.

Dr. Ryann Oliver.

The woman he'd refused to look up online after learning about their new hire, not wanting the disappointment of knowing it wasn't *his* Ryann when he found her picture.

She'd only been his for a week. A blissful, beautiful week almost two years ago didn't matter. *Ryann* wasn't a common female name, but it wasn't uncommon.

Now, from a distance, it felt like she was here.

It couldn't be. What were the odds? Such things happened to other people.

Others got miracles. Others got stories that sounded like the plots for television stories. Others got happily-ever-afters.

Not Jackson Peters. All life ever delivered Jackson was disappointment wrapped in hurt and coated with trauma. Hoping for anything had only ever left him wanting.

It wasn't his Ryann. Wherever she was, it wasn't

Hope Hospital, but he sent a thought into the universe wishing her happiness.

"We'll see you after the shift, then," Knox said. He raised a hand and headed down the hall.

Jackson looked to where Dr. O'Sullivan and Dr. Oliver had gone. Better to get the introductions out of the way, let the dim light of hope playing in his brain snuff out.

Besides, he'd be working with the new surgeon at least a few times a week. The Lowery Group contracted with the hospital to use their anesthesiology staff so the practice didn't have to pay for a few of their own.

He turned the corner, hoping to get a glimpse of the doctor before he arrived at the nurses' station, but Miranda and Patrick were blocking his view. Of course.

Stepping up to the group, he tapped Patrick on the shoulder, and the doctor moved aside to let him in.

People always talked of the world standing still in these kinds of moments. But as he met Ryann's eyes for the first time in more than a year and a half, the axis holding the world in place seemed to rush forward.

"Good morning. I'm Dr. Ryann Oliver, the new orthopedic surgeon with the Lowery Group." Ryann held out her hand, the words as sterile as an operating room.

Was she really going to pretend they hadn't

spent the week together? That he hadn't held her every night, kissed every inch of her skin? For that week they'd breathed the same breaths, their hearts thumping with a single beat.

The memory meant the world to him. The fact that he hadn't asked to break the pact they'd made and give each other their contact information was the biggest regret in his life.

And the handshake and greeting seemed like her way of saying *We're not talking about this.*

His chest moved as his lungs preformed their function, but it felt like the weight of the entire hospital was sitting on him. And he had to act normal. Unbothered.

*Damn.*

"Jackson Peters, CRNA."

He saw Miranda move her head, but if he looked at his best friend's girlfriend, his friend, his tongue might unleash all the thoughts running through his brain.

"I need to see to a pain patient." Jackson nodded to Miranda and Patrick, then turned his focus to Ryann. "It's really good to see you."

*Meet you. I should have said "meet you."*

He cleared his throat, "Welcome to Hope."

Then he made himself walk away. He didn't turn to look at the woman behind him, at the person who'd made him feel whole.

He was forty years old. Disappointment had been the only constant in his life. At least he knew the routine. Push down the emotions. Ignore the pain. Move on.

"Is your patient room 242?" Ryann's words hit his back, and she was walking beside him less than a second later, her cheeks tinted with just a bit of color.

From catching up with him or shock that they were in the same place? No way to ask in the hospital, and he wasn't sure he wanted the answer.

"Yes. She had hand surgery—"

"Left hand, Dupuytren's disease affecting the fourth finger. Finger curling toward the middle of the hand. Dr. Jenks performed a fasciectomy—not fully successful."

"Yes." Jackson shouldn't have been stunned by Ryann's systematic recitation of the facts. He'd heard dozens of doctors give the same type of statement—a factual outline with limited thought to the patient attached to the symptoms and outcomes. He hadn't thought Ryann was that way.

However, he'd only known her on vacation—for a week—more than a year ago. The disappointment he felt was his own fault. People were different on vacation, particularly with people they never expected to interact with again.

The part of him that had hoped for more was his own fault. By now he should've known better.

"Tina," he said.

Jackson always used his patients' names. Growing up in the system, he'd too often been referred to by his case number. Even to his face. Everyone was a person, and that meant they deserved to be called by the name they wanted.

"Tina is aware that the surgery didn't have the outcome Dr. Jenks wanted," he explained. "She's hoping that there might be another option for her." The fasciectomy had released a decent amount to the tension in her ring finger, but she still couldn't straighten the digit all the way.

And twenty-four hours after the procedure, she should see more movement—at least from what Jackson had heard the doctors saying yesterday.

And then there was the pain. Jackson had tried to reassure Tina that pain post-surgery was common, that the swelling in her finger was normal, and given a few days it would subside some.

*Some.* He'd been very clear on that word. *Some*, not *all*. Dr. Jenks believed she'd likely have pain in her hand for the rest of her life.

How debilitating? That was still to be determined. And pain was felt by the patient. What one could live with, another couldn't.

"She isn't going to like that Dr. Jenks isn't here," he said. "I know you're on rotation today." Maybe their first interaction was sterile, but Ryann deserved to know what she was walking into. "Tina isn't happy."

"And she feels like Dr. Jenks is avoiding her. He warned me…via text." Ryann let out a sigh. "She isn't wrong. I told him she deserved more follow-up from him, even if it isn't pleasant. He disagrees."

The words were said in the same formal tone she'd used for everything else. But there was a hint under it. A not-so-subtle disappointment.

That made him happier than it should've. Dr. Jenks was a competent doctor, and when his procedures went well—which they most often did— he was excellent at bedside manner.

That was the easy part of the job. The part Jackson would argue didn't matter as much. Everyone enjoyed good news. Everyone liked a success.

It was the bad outcomes, the less than successful, the ones that came with—sometimes a lifetime of—disappointment that mattered most. The doctors who stood there and took the anger, the tears, the frustration—those were the ones Jackson respected the most.

"How is her pain level?" Ryann paused just before Tina's room. Another good choice—asking the question before and not in front of the patient.

"She says it's a five on the scale of one to ten."

"But she was in pain for years. As a black woman, her pain was dismissed regularly until her finger was so bent there were no other choices. So, a five for her is likely a seven or eight for others."

Probably more. But it certainly wasn't a "typical" five.

Jackson was relieved Ryann understood his concern regarding Tina's 'level five'. Women's pain was often dismissed; women of color experienced it even more often.

"Pain is difficult," he said. "Only the person living in the body really knows, but yes, I suspect she has pain not consistent with twenty-four hours post-op."

Ryann nodded and made a few notes on her tablet. "Right. Let's go."

Jackson led the way. Ryann was here for rounds; he was here for pain management. People often thought anesthesiologists and CRNAs only put people to sleep for surgeries. That was a major part of the job, but the positions were really focused on pain management.

No pain or feeling during surgery, as little pain as possible during recovery.

"Good morning, Tina." Jackson put on a big smile. The notes in her chart indicated that last night had been rough. The night nurse had written that she was rotating between barking orders and tears. The doctor on shift had told her she couldn't have more pain pills and had indicated in the chart that he thought she was drug seeking.

That note had infuriated Jackson. Drug-seeking notes could follow a patient for years. What she needed was compassion, not judgment, from her care team.

Tina's eyes welled with tears. She looked exhausted, and her face was pale. This was not level five pain. Period. "I hurt. My hand—it feels like it's on fire."

Jackson looked at Ryann. "I can give her something for the pain, but…"

"No." Ryann shook her head and stepped to the bed.

Tina glared at her, but if Ryann noticed or cared, she didn't respond. "Ms. Priat, I'm Dr. Oliver, an orthopedic surgeon."

"Right, because Dr. Jenks is avoiding me. The man swore my hand would be better. If this is better…" Tina choked and put her head back against the pillow. "I don't know if I can do this."

Her word's flashed a bright red warning signal in his brain. First address the pain, then the mental health concern.

"Jackson, I need her entire palm numb—as fast as you can do it."

"What?" Tina's voice broke; her eyes met his, scared and confused.

Jackson grabbed the phone on the wall that went directly to the nurses' station. "I need a nurse in room 242 with lidocaine and a scalpel tray."

"Ms. Priat, I know your hand hurts. It hurts a lot. I need to relieve the pressure with a fasciectomy."

"That's the procedure I just had." Tina looked to Jackson. "Please don't leave. You're the only one who's listened to me."

"I'm right here." Jackson had no plans to leave.

He knew Tina from the local community that had provided him a safe place to study and learn when he'd been at the group home. They'd all learned to take care of each other because no one else would.

"You have every right to be upset with your care. That is your right as a patient," Ryann said, her words soft. "But the pressure from the wound dressing is what is causing the pain. I need to open the wound to release the pressure."

Ryann looked to Jackson, and his breath caught. The look in her eyes was the one he'd seen so often during the week they'd spent together—like they were of two minds. "Can Jackson please numb your hand, Ms. Priat, so I can help you?"

Giving the patient a choice. That was good, though there really wasn't a choice here.

"What if I say no? What happens to my finger if I try to wait it out?"

Ryann sat on the edge of the bed, put her hands in her lap and looked Tina directly in the eye. "The pain will get worse. You're describing it as a five, but I suspect if a man were laying in this bed, they'd be screaming and saying it was an eleven out of ten."

Jackson agreed. As a pain-management specialist, women had higher levels of tolerance than men, on average. By a lot.

"Then the pressure will cut off blood supply. We're within hours, if not an hour, of that happening. Then your finger tissue will die, and it will require amputation to keep the rest of your body from going septic."

Tina blew out a breath. "Thank you for explaining that to me."

"Of course." Ryann's voice was soft but firm. The perfect bedside manner for this moment. "Can Jackson numb your hand for me?"

"He can."

Ryann looked over her shoulder at him.

"I'm going to get washed up and gloved," she said. "I can do the procedure here. It will be fast, once I start, and you'll feel immediate pain relief."

Tina nodded and watched Ryann walk out of the room. "I like her."

*Me, too*, Jackson thought.

# CHAPTER TWO

RYANN KISSED AYLA'S HEAD, smiling as her daughter's hand tapped her cheek. At six months old, Ayla was moving past the newborn stage and starting to show off her personality. Ryann had always loved children.

When she'd been eight her mother had joined a group living in a commune for almost a year. They'd followed some man there. Ryann had had five "stepfathers" and two "stepmothers" during her childhood. Each one swore her mother's choices were hers, that it didn't mean they didn't love her. But they'd eventually floated out of Ryann's life, forgetting all about her.

Ryann had spent her time in the commune helping with the younger children. Playing with the young ones, even though she'd hardly been an "older" child, had given her some peace and structure during that unusual time.

"You and me, sweetie. You and me…" The chorus she sang her daughter every morning caught in the back of her throat. "You and me. You and—"

Tears coated her eyes as she looked at her daughter's smiling face. She had Ryann's curly brown hair, her dark eyes. But the heart-shaped lips, the tilt of her nose—all of that was Jackson.

He was here. Yesterday he'd been so attentive with Tina. The only one who'd recognized the woman wasn't drug seeking, wasn't acting. It was a sad state of affairs that women's pain was often overlooked.

She'd seen a woman in her office with a degenerative bone disease that had sent waves of needles through her feet when she'd walked. Several doctors had told her she'd needed anxiety medication, that it was all in her head.

Old-fashioned ideas that were far too prevalent in modern medicine.

Jackson, though, he listened. He'd comforted Tina while he'd been numbing her hand. In the patient's room he'd seemed every bit like the man Ryann had spent a nearly perfect week with.

Reconciling that with the man who hadn't responded to her outreach on the website, who'd seemingly ignored her requests for information that might help their daughter…it didn't make sense.

She looked at Ayla, pulling her daughter's smile deep into the pool of her soul. Jackson deserved to meet his daughter. Or at least have the option of meeting her.

He got one more shot. One more.

The next time she was at the hospital and saw him—which in theory could be weeks, if they weren't scheduled together—she'd ask him for dinner, make it very clear that it wasn't a date. And then introduce him to Ayla.

Mentally it all sounded so easy. Realistically there were a whole lot of things that might go wrong.

If he wasn't interested in them…in Ayla…then she'd start looking for a new position somewhere else. Her daughter would be protected.

Nothing else mattered.

"All right, sweet girl." Ryann snuggled her close for one more moment. "Time for work."

Ryann looked at her watch. She'd called the Lowery Group to let them know she was stopping in to look after Tina. It wasn't her day on rotation, but the woman hadn't had the best outcomes to date and Ryann wanted to alleviate as much of the unease as possible.

Jackson had been on yesterday and wasn't scheduled for the day. Twelve hours and she was already keeping tracking of him. She hadn't needed to ask after his schedule yesterday, but she had.

So she knew there was no reason to look for him, no reason for her head to swivel as she walked toward the elevator bank. At least today she knew the trick to getting the elevator to drop.

She pressed the "code" on the elevator's call button, taking a little too much pleasure when it dinged and opened on the first try. Sometimes life really was about the little things.

Stepping onto the floor, she waved a greeting to Nicola, a nurse she'd met yesterday. She wasn't technically here, but she grabbed a tablet chart from the charging station and quickly pulled up Tina's chart. The patient had slept through the night and had not requested additional pain medication. There wasn't a better outcome.

Ryann walked to Tina's door and knocked before walking in. She took two steps in and opened her mouth to say good morning, only to stall out completely when she saw Jackson sitting in the visitor's chair next to the empty bed.

"She's getting an X-ray." He yawned and looked at his watch. "Should be back any second."

The man looked like he'd been here for hours. "Did you sleep here?" she asked.

Jackson rubbed his eyes and rolled his shoulders. "*Sleep* is a relative word in the hospital."

"Jackson." Ryann took a step toward him, then stopped herself. Why was she so drawn to this man?

"Tina never married. She has no children, and her only sister passed away about two years ago."

Information not available in her charts. Knowledge he could only have learned from Tina. How much time had he spent with her?

Ryann had met many patients who were alone in the world. It was far more common than people wanted to discuss. Many liked to imagine they'd grow old together on a front stoop with the one they loved next to them and a bevy of grandchildren around them. Reality looked different for many.

"So, she's alone?"

"I'm here." Jackson winked. "And no, she's not alone. She's part of Patty's Community."

"What is that?"

"A community started by a woman I know named Patty for those that need a place. It started in her home, then moved to the community center. It's about a hundred people strong now," he said, rolling his shoulders again. "I started…volunteering there when I was a teen."

She heard the pause. The heaviness in the milliseconds between *started* and *volunteering*. Why? Many teens wouldn't bother with volunteering, and they certainly wouldn't have continued once they were well into adulthood.

Jackson rubbed the back of his neck, the color of his cheeks shifting a little. "I stopped by after dinner last night. I was worried about the notes put in her file about drug seeking."

So he had slept here. "That was kind of you," she said.

"It sure was. But now he has a crick in his neck and needs to go home." Tina was all smiles as she waved at Ryann. She looked like a completely different woman.

Amazing what not being in pain could do for you.

"I see you're feeling better." Patient smiles were a great way to start her workday.

Tina held up her hand. The bandage covered the entire palm, but it was clear from her attitude that the second bedside emergency surgery had been a success. "You should do all the hand surgeries."

"Funny you should say that," she said. "My specialty is hand surgery. Though I do more than just that." Most orthopedic surgeons had a specialty. Some were fortunate enough to only do that sort of surgery, and maybe one day Ryann would be, too.

"It shows." Tina winked.

Ryann felt the heat flood her cheeks. Praise, even from a stranger, always gave her a tingly feeling. "I'm glad you're doing better." She didn't want to look at her watch, but she knew she needed to get moving before her first appointment at the Lowery Group.

Still, she'd made a promise to herself this morning. If she put it off once it would be easier to put off again and again. Excuses were easy. Lydia put everything off...and it had never solved one of her problems.

Now or never. Ryann took a deep breath. "Jackson, can I speak with you? Tina, if you need anything please have one of the nurses call me and if you would prefer to see me for your follow ups just let the office know."

Ryann put her card on the bedside table. "That has my direct office line—use it if you need anything."

"Don't suppose I'll need anything. You did a great job." Tina tapped the card. "But thank you."

Jackson stood, and she could see hints of something in his eyes. Hope, exhaustion, worry—she didn't know. And it didn't matter.

There was one person who mattered, and that was Ayla.

"Walk me out? I assume you aren't on today?" She knew that, but she didn't want him to know that she knew that. Besides, he'd have never slept in Tina's room if he were, no matter his concern for the patient. The staff break room had uncomfortable cots, but they were better than the chairs the hospital swore pulled out into a bed.

No, they did not.

"I'm not back on until Tuesday." Jackson followed her to the elevator bank. "So, you want to talk?"

"No." Ryann cleared her throat. He had a right to meet his daughter. One chance. She needed to focus on that.

"What I mean is no, I don't want to, but we should. Damn, that sounded worse. I… I would like for you to come to my place for dinner."

"Your place." Jackson raised a brow. "We could do dinner out if you wanted. Your place seems a little intimate."

Ryann let out a chuckle. "I think we're past that." She started to lean toward him and pulled herself back quickly. "It needs to be my place. I'll explain. Tonight. Six thirty. Um…" She pulled a pad from her purse and quickly wrote out her address. "Park in the driveway. The woman who lives across the street goes ballistic if there's a car in the street. She claims it's in the HOA, but…"

She was rambling. Ryann never rambled. She was cool. She was collected. She was in control even when the world was spinning out of control. That was how she worked. Period.

"Ryann—"

His voice was soft. It called to the places that hadn't been able to resist him all those months ago. Her skin vibrated, and her heart yearned for things it didn't need.

"This isn't a date." The words came out harsher than she'd meant. Maybe she should have put this off. "I mean…" Her brain froze. Ryann's pager buzzed and relief flowed through her—saved by the buzzer. "And now I have to go."

"The elevator isn't here." Jackson pointed to the door that still hadn't opened despite them putting in the right "code."

"Well, I have appointments I need to get to. Six thirty." She pointed to the paper, then turned and walked down the end of the hall. She wasn't exactly sure where the stairwell was, but it couldn't be that far. Besides, that was knowledge she needed anyway.

Stairwell locations were a safety issue. What if they had to evacuate patients? Granted as private practice she would almost certainly never be in that position.

The excuse didn't even sound good in her head. She was running away, pure and simple. But there was no dodging him tonight.


Jackson stood outside the address Ryann had texted him after the most awkward exchange of phone numbers he'd ever been a part of. Honestly, he was not quite sure what he was doing here. He wondered for the umpteenth time if he should walk back and put the flowers in the car. She'd stated…before racing away from him…that this was not a date. But she'd asked him to meet at her place.

Demanded it.

What other reason might there be?

Only one way to find out. Jackson looked at the pink lilies in his hand. They weren't exactly like the plumeria Ryann had worn in her hair the night they'd danced under the moon, just before leaving the island. But it was as close as the local florist could get.

Jackson squeezed his eyes shut, taking a deep

breath. When he opened them, he walked deliberately toward her door. The flowers were nice, even if this wasn't a date.

He raised his hand and knocked, his chest tightening with the passing moments waiting for Ryann. Except she didn't answer. Now what?

Most of his younger life had been spent waiting for those who'd never showed up. He'd promised himself that he'd never leave someone waiting for him, that when he was an adult people could count on him. It was a principle he maintained—and the only thing keeping him from walking away when she didn't open the door.

He'd promised to be here at six thirty. So he was here. He'd wait as long as necessary.

Raising his hand, he knocked again. A few seconds later his phone dinged.

Busy. Door open. Be in the living room in a second. No. Seriously. How...?

The last few words read like she was dictating the note and the phone had caught the last of the conversation.

Jackson read it again, then reached for the handle. The door swung open, and the sweet scent of Ryann flooded his system...mixed with a hint of baby powder? That was unexpected though not unpleasant.

Everything was orderly. The entranceway had

a place for a coat and shoes. Jackson slid his off, setting them next to Ryann's. The sight gave him too much pleasure. They hadn't seen each other in more than a year. Yes, they'd had a great week, but the ache in his chest...

He'd wanted a family more than anything growing up. There were even a few times he'd thought he'd gotten it. A foster family who'd sworn they'd adopt him, only to choose a baby when given the opportunity and dump him back into care. The fiancée who'd sworn she'd loved him and wanted to create the life he hadn't had, only to leave him three months before their wedding for a businessman who could offer her a better life. A life free of baggage—according to her.

Even his biological family didn't want him. His father and mother, both of whom he'd located through a DNA database...and had sent similar expletive-filled rants telling him not to get back in touch.

A family might've been what he craved, but it was always out of reach. Women always seemed to run when they found out about his unstable youth. One had even asked how he could be stable after all the trauma. And that was with only sharing a tiny bit of what his childhood had looked like.

*What other choice do I have?*

Even Marie, his ex-fiancée, had changed after begging him to tell her everything—something he couldn't do. She'd wanted someone who shared their past. But what was he to share? All the hurt? No one needed that.

No, his partners were better off not knowing the demons floating through his past.

"Ayla!" Ryann's frustrated call made him look up the stairs.

Jackson left the flowers on the entry table and started toward the sound. He wasn't sure who Ayla was, but it was clear Ryann was upset. Rounding the corner he heard the cries—Ryann's and an infant's.

"What…?" He stepped into the room that was clearly a nursery and stopped as giant watery brown eyes met his—eyes he saw staring back at him every morning in the mirror.

"She's blown out three diapers in the last hour and has a horrid rash that burns. I must have eaten something that upsets her, but I can't figure out what." Ryann pressed her head to Ayla's, tears mixing on their cheeks.

The child let out gas designed to clear the room, then immediately started screeching.

"Oh, Ayla." Ryann looked at her own shirt, then at him. "I've already changed her three time today. She's just so miserable."

Jackson reached for the little girl he knew was his daughter. "Let me. Go change, or take a shower or just fifteen minutes of rest."

Ryann looked at Ayla, then at Jackson. "She needs another diaper change."

"I grew up in foster care, Ryann. In many houses I was basically help for the little ones. I can change her diaper." He ached to hold the little girl. This was the reason he was here.

Her insistence that this was not a date clicked into place. His daughter.

*His.*

They'd used protection all week, but that was hardly one hundred percent effective, as he'd explained to more than one person when he'd been an ER nurse.

Ryann looked at her daughter, then handed her to him. She hovered by the door.

"Promise, Ryann. I got this." Jackson looked at Ayla, his heart swelling. "Hi, cutie."

She didn't smell baby fresh, but his daughter was gorgeous, even red in the face with tear streaks.

He lifted the onesie off her and dropped it into the laundry hamper right by the changing table. Organized. He took the diaper off and knew why she was so uncomfortable.

He cleaned her as quickly as possible, but she screamed when the wipe touched her raw skin. The best thing for her would be a baking-soda bath. Not so easy with a little one who still couldn't sit up on her own without support.

"Want to play in the kitchen sink?" Jackson booped her nose, knowing she didn't understand the words yet.

He took off his own shirt. Unlike Ryann, he did not have an endless stock here. If the baby got sick between here and the kitchen sink, he could just take off his white undershirt.

Then he lifted his daughter and took her down the stairs, talking nonsense in a fun voice. He might've been her father, but to Ayla he was a stranger.

Filling the sink with barely warm water, Jackson started opening cabinets. He found the baking soda and dumped a healthy amount into the water. In just a few minutes the little bath was ready.

"Here we go!" Jackson made silly sounds as he helped Ayla sit in the sink.

She let out a surprised sound, then sighed.

"Feels good, huh!" Jackson dipped his hand into the water and dribbled a little over her face.

Ayla giggled.

"That was a nice sound." Ryann's voice was tired as she crossed her arms and looked at her daughter.

"Baking soda. Works wonders," Jackson said. He winked before putting a little more water on Ayla's head.

"Was that a trick you learned taking care of foster kids?"

"Yep." And he didn't want to discuss his past, particularly when his future looked so bright. "You have a toy she can play with in here? Ideally she should soak for ten minutes. That will help neutralize the acids."

Ryann nodded and wandered to another room before coming back with a little rubber ducky.

Setting the toy in front of Ayla in the bath, she leaned against the counter. "Not exactly the way I planned to introduce you to your daughter."

Jackson looked at the little girl and couldn't stop his grin.

*Your daughter.*

There were so many things to figure out. A world of changes this news brought, but those two little words were as close to perfection as he'd ever gotten.

"Nice to meet you, Ayla," Jackson said. Then he looked at Ryann. She was clearly exhausted. Parenting was difficult—parenting alone, even more so. But she had help now.

"She's beautiful. Just like her mother." Turning his attention back to Ayla, he cooed as the little one pushed the duck around the sink. "Sorry I missed so much, Ayla, but we'll get caught up."

"If you'd have responded to *any* of my messages, you wouldn't have!" Ryann's sharp tone echoed in the kitchen.

*Messages?* What messages?

"Ryann—" His brain refused to supply any additional words. It was overloaded with happiness and trying to process the anger he saw steaming from her face.

She wiped a tear from her cheek and bit her lip so hard he feared she was tasting blood.

"Ryann…" he started again, but no words materialized this time, either.

"I need to get a towel to dry her off. Then I'll feed her and put her to bed. After that…" She blew out a breath. "After that we can talk." Each word was choked with sobs she refused to fully let out.

Jackson was holding up their daughter in the sink, but he ached to pull Ryann in, to hold her tight as she let out whatever she needed to.

But he also wanted to know why she thought he would have ignored any messages from her. He'd have moved heaven and earth to find her if he'd had more than a first name. Hell, he hadn't even had a city until her CV had arrived at the hospital. Seattle…and he only knew that from hospital gossip.

Learning about Ayla would have meant uprooting himself from Phoenix. Leaving his condo—the one place that was his, only his. The place no one could take from him.

And he'd have done it as soon as physically possible to support her.

Ryann came back in holding a baby-blue towel that looked softer than anything that had ever touched his skin. He lifted their daughter and let her mother wrap her in the towel. She kissed Ayla's head and went back up the stairs. Jackson didn't follow.

* * *

She dressed her daughter in just a diaper and took a few deep breaths while Ayla cooed on the changing table. The baking-soda bath had been a great idea—one Jackson had thought of within five minutes of learning he was a father.

There was no handbook for introducing your child to their vacation-hookup father.

And no handbook for the butterflies that danced through Ryann's stomach when she'd walked in on Jackson in his white undershirt taking care of their daughter. She'd done this alone every second. She'd been prepared to see Jackson walk away.

Hell, her father, and every stepparent, had walked away because dealing with her mother had been too hard. She knew how to act for that, the armor to don to protect her daughter.

But if Jackson was here, was ready to step up…

*I've seen him handle one situation!*

How many of her stepparents had handled a few situations, even a few years of situations before walking out on her mother?

*And me.*

They'd all walked away from Ryann, too. Even the ones who'd sworn that it wasn't her fault and they'd keep in touch. A birthday card, a couple of phone calls, maybe a holiday gift and then silence.

It had happened so often that she'd recognized the pattern each time it had started. Knowing that hadn't stopped her from hoping, at least a little, each time. Never mattered, though. If they didn't love her mother, they couldn't stay in her life.

Picking up Ayla, she kissed her cheek. The way she protected Ayla was making sure Jackson only saw his daughter. There'd be no relationship with Ryann for him to walk away from. No disagreements with his daughter's mother.

They'd shared a wonderful week and gotten the most precious gift from it. That was enough. It had to be.

"Ready, sweet girl?"

Ayla moved her mouth and reached for Ryann's chest. "Yep. Snack time, then sleep."

After breastfeeding, Ayla would be down for a few hours. Up for another feeding, then down again...if her stomach issues calmed down. No guarantees.

When Ryann reached the living room, Jackson was sitting on the couch, his right leg crossed over his left, his arms resting on the back of the couch. He'd put his shirt back on, but if someone snapped a photo they'd could title it *Smoking-Hot Man at Relaxation.*

"She needs to eat," Ryann said as she walked to the rocking chair Ayla liked, lifted her shirt and put Ayla to her breast. Her daughter latched, and the room settled into silence.

Jackson looked at her, a look crossing his face that she didn't know how to read.

"Does my breastfeeding bother you?" It was a

normal human requirement. Still, she'd been told by more than one person to cover up. Feeding her baby was not a sexual act, and she refused to feel any shame over it—particularly in her own home.

"No." Jackson smiled as he looked at them. "You and Ayla. You're so beautiful, and this moment…" He closed his eyes and took the deepest breath, his muscular arms moving up and down in a way that was damn near hypnotic in its own way. "I never knew happiness felt so good."

"Jackson…" She looked at Ayla, whose eyes were heavy. Ryann would pump the other breast and put it in storage. "Why didn't you answer my messages?"

She'd done this alone, and she could have continued. Women had done so for centuries, but the fact that he could sit there looking like he'd won the lottery was so at odds with the silence.

"What messages?" Jackson asked, shaking his head. "I never got anything. I swear to you if I had, I'd have been on the plane to you."

He seemed so sincere. But she'd sent one a month. Five total. All unread.

"I sent them through the DNA site," she said. "I was looking for her health history. I told you that I needed to know. I reached out the month after she was born and on the first of every month ever since."

"Oh." Jackson pulled a hand over his face.

"Oh." Ryann was glad Ayla was asleep. It meant

there was no way she was going to raise her voice. After months of silence, all she got was *Oh*. "That is really all you have to say—oh. Our daughter is six months old, and you can't tell me you didn't get the results. I get notifications from them weekly. It seems everyone and their mother is taking the tests and registering. Hell, they're even solving murders with these databases."

Ryann sucked in a deep breath. She was usually so good at controlling herself.

*Not with him.*

In Hawaii, she'd been free, had felt deeply for the first time in her memory.

She wasn't on vacation now. And there were real consequences to her week of no rules.

"Everyone is on those systems these days." Jackson pulled at his face again. "I…uh… I… sent all the notifications to a hidden folder about a decade ago."

A decade. "What?" she asked. "You expect me to believe you've been in the system that long? That would make you one of the first."

"Yes. I've been a member since I was eighteen, but even then, there were several," he said. "DNA tests and databases have been around since the late nineties. I was one of the first to apply to them all."

"All of them? That's…"

"Not as many companies now actually. Most have been acquired. They don't give you back your money when they combine databases." He chuckled.

"Not sure I see the humor."

"There isn't any." He shifted, darkness crossing his features. "I joined to find my parents. They abandoned me in foster care when I was seven. Or at least that's when they stopped trying to earn their parental rights. I was in care most of my life."

His body seemed to shrink, and it made her heart shudder. For a moment, he was far away from them, in another life.

"You didn't find them." That would hurt.

"I did." Jackson shook himself, the self-assured man returning. "Not directly and not for several years, but through a hodgepodge of cousins, half siblings I've never met and a nephew I didn't know existed."

Jackson looked at his hands, lost to her and the world as a whole.

"And they didn't want to be found?" She whispered the words more to herself than anything else.

"They did not appreciate my attempts at reconnection, no." He cleared his throat and blinked quickly. "So that's why I set up any emails to come from there into a hidden folder. I didn't want to see the results anymore but couldn't make myself unsubscribe. It…well… I didn't see you reach out. I apologize."

Ryann looked away for a moment, not sure what

to say. She'd been so angry. Furious. The silence had felt personal. And it was, but not toward her. She believed him. The man who'd taken his angry baby and gotten her a sink bath would not have ignored her.

"No apology needed. A misunderstanding, and one that is cleared up now."

"I am sorry I missed the first few months. And your pregnancy, but I want to be involved now." He smiled at the curly haired little girl in her arms.

"I want you involved with Ayla."

"And us?" Jackson tilted his head.

She looked at the flowers down the hall. He'd brought them and dropped them onto the table by the door. Ryann had seen them when she'd come downstairs. From her position here, she could make out the bright pink collection, though not the individual flowers.

Plumeria? The flower she'd worn all week with him in Hawaii.

"There is no us." Her throat burned as she said the words. If they'd met some other way, if she was sure he'd stick by her forever...

But you could never be sure of that. They'd had lust and passion, but that didn't mean they'd have made it more than that week if it had been an option.

Declaring you were in love had seemed to be the kiss of death for her mother's relationships.

"I want to be in Ayla's life," Jackson said.

"And I want you in Ayla's life." Ryann meant that. She wanted her daughter to have the parental figures she'd lacked, wanted it more than anything.

Which was why it was better if Ryann and Jackson were co-parents. That limited the drama. He'd never hate seeing his daughter because he was upset with her mother.

"Ryann, we had something special."

His words called to her soul. Part of her—a larger part than she wanted to admit—wanted to throw caution to the wind. They could put Ayla to bed together, and she could kiss Jackson, maybe even invite him to stay the night. Not for intimacy, but because she hadn't slept so well since the day she'd left his arms.

Life was short—her mother had said that so often when she'd been giving in to a whim. It was Ryann who'd paid the price each time. Ayla would never feel that. "We had passion," she said. "And we got something special from it."

She looked at Ayla. That was true. Their daughter was a blend of the two of them. Hopefully the best blend. The safe blend. The blend that would never worry about if she was loved.

The protected one.

"If that's what you want."

Ryann nodded. It wasn't. But it was what was best for Ayla.

She yawned and looked at the clock.

"Will she be awake soon?"

"No." The change in topic was welcome. "Or at least she hasn't been until lately. I think something I'm eating is upsetting her. I started an elimination diet, but she's still up at all hours. I have a surgery tomorrow, so hopefully tonight isn't one of those."

Jackson nodded, then gestured to Ayla. "Why don't you let me take the night shift tonight? I don't have work tomorrow."

That sounded absolutely delightful. "I couldn't ask that."

"You didn't ask. I offered to take care of my daughter tonight so her mother can get some rest," he said. "She must take a bottle while you're at the hospital. Point me to the supply, then go get some rest."

Ryann opened her mouth to decline. This wasn't what she'd asked him over for. And him spending the night here while she slept felt oddly more intimate than anything they'd done before.

"Ryann—let me take care of *my* daughter."

It was the emphasis on the word *my* that made her smile.

"All right." She stood. "Let's put her down, and I'll show you around."

# CHAPTER THREE

JACKSON YAWNED AS he unlocked the door to his condo. Ayla had been up almost every hour. Between the diaper rash and the gas, she'd had trouble getting comfortable. Finally, he'd gotten her off to sleep on his chest in the recliner in the living room.

His back ached. His head throbbed. He felt like he could drop into bed and sleep for hours.

And Jackson had never been happier.

Ryann had gotten a full night's sleep. She'd looked refreshed, and there'd been a gleam in her eye when she'd gently tapped his shoulder before lifting Ayla off him.

She'd gotten Ayla ready for the babysitter, and Jackson had fixed Ryann some oatmeal using the coconut milk in the fridge. Day four of Ryann's elimination diet.

Before sleeping, he'd spend a little time researching what foods she could eat. He hadn't been there for her during pregnancy and Ayla's newborn stage, but he could be there now.

A supportive co-parent. That was the role Ryann wanted him to play, so that was what he'd be. Maybe he wanted more—craved more—but you dealt with what life gave you.

Back at his own condo, he started the coffee and booted up his laptop. The ancient device took forever. Knox kept telling him to upgrade, and he should, but it still worked...mostly. Maybe he should chuck it, but Jackson had made a conscious decision not to throw out useful things for better options.

If people had treated him the same way growing up, maybe his life would look different. Though he'd done pretty well for himself.

Grabbing a cup of coffee, he slid into his kitchen chair and stared at the screen. First the hard task. Taking a deep sip, he pulled up his email, clicking into the hidden folder he hadn't checked in so long.

Jackson could have unsubscribed from the DNA-matching websites, but part of him hoped maybe his mother or father would reach out. The rational part of him knew that was never going to happen, so he hadn't checked the folder since setting it up.

There were now over a thousand unread emails. He sorted them quickly. The majority, around nine hundred, were notifications that people had been added, of price changes and policy adjustments for the automatic renewal he just couldn't make himself cut off.

About a hundred were direct notifications about people related to him. Second and third cousins. A half brother who'd sent one message asking if Jackson knew where their father was.

That one was from two years ago. Jackson knew where their father had been five years ago and knew that the man wanted nothing to do with any children he'd fathered.

*If I'd wanted anything to do with ya, I'd have kept up with ya.*

Words engraved on Jackson's heart. The wound might not bleed now, but it would never fully heal. If his half brother had found their father in the last two years, he'd know the man wanted nothing to do with them. If he hadn't…well, Jackson didn't think anyone deserved to know how much their parents resented them.

But that wasn't his choice to make for another. He sent a short note with an apology for the extremely tardy response. The rest of the message was as gentle as he could make it—a warning that their father wasn't pleasant and had no use for the children, so to reach out with caution if he chose to. His half brother would need to decide for himself what do with the information.

A note that Jackson's daughter was in the system was flagged as important from the company. They were right. If he'd seen it, he'd have contacted Ryann immediately. He'd have known about Ayla from month one.

Been there from almost the start. Not half a year in.

The last four messages were from Ryann. All said the same thing and were dated on the first of the month.

Jackson,

We have a daughter. Her name is Ayla, and she is the most precious gift in the world. You do not have to be involved, but I need to know any medical conditions that might run in the family.

For her sake, I hope you reach out.

Followed by her contact information.

He'd missed the first months of Ayla's life because he hadn't wanted to read the emails in this file, unintentionally letting down the mother of his daughter and his own flesh and blood.

If Ryann hadn't happened to land a job here, he might never have known about Ayla. His past wasn't rosy, but running from it had kept him from his daughter.

*And her mother.*

He clicked a few buttons and confirmed he wanted the messages to come to his inbox from now on.

The front door opened, and Knox walked in holding a pickleball racket. He'd gotten into the sport a few weeks ago. His partner, Miranda, had no interest in the game, but Jackson had had fun with it a few times.

At least it was something other than darts, though Jackson figured his brother would go back to that game in short order. Outside of the surgical suite and Miranda, darts were Knox's passion.

Jackson had agreed to play a few rounds on the court at the condo complex today, a fact he was remembering only because Knox was here and ready for competition.

"You aren't even dressed." He crossed his arms, the short paddle sticking up out of his elbow.

"I forgot—sorry. Long night."

"Did you and Ryann have fun?" Knox slid into the chair across from him, a smile gleaming on his cheeks, the insinuation palpitating across the table.

"I was up most of the night with my daughter," Jackson said. "She's got some stomach issues. Ryann is trying an elimination diet, but it's only been a few days since she eliminated dairy. It can take up to four to have any lasting effect."

At least that was what Ryann had told him. Jackson had never worked in peds. Kids were great, and he'd always wanted them. But working in peds meant dealing with domestic violence and child abuse. Not often, but not never, either.

And he'd seen enough abuse to last a lifetime.

"I'm currently looking up some recipes that

might work for her. Particularly since she's pulling out eggs and soy, too," he said.

"I know you didn't just give me data on breastfeeding and elimination diets while telling me you have a daughter." Knox leaned back in his chair. "A daughter. You hear what you're saying? A kid." He let out a laugh and then a muttered "Wow."

Knox had never felt called to fatherhood. He'd stated more than once that taking care of himself was more than enough. Jackson understood, but he'd always felt different.

Though now that the moment was here, a tiny voice whispered he'd let everyone in his life down. So much so that they'd walked away from him.

But that was not happening with Ayla. He'd never let his daughter down.

"Yes. Daughter. Six months old. A Hawaiian souvenir."

"You're very calm about this."

"I've had a few hours. Want to see a picture?" He'd snapped a photo of her around three this morning.

"Of course." Knox looked at the image on his phone and smiled. "She's cute."

"No." Jackson ran a finger over the picture he'd immediately made his phone's background. Ayla sleeping on his chest, her body relaxed, her mother's curly hair, Jackson's broad nose and lips that had cooed the sweetest sounds—when she wasn't screaming. "She's gorgeous."

He ran a hand over the tiny bundle on the screen. *How is she today?* he wondered. *Any better?*

Probably not. Elimination diets took time, and Ryann still needed to build up her stockpile of elimination breastmilk.

Something that had clicked in his head early this morning when Ayla had been so upset.

"Gorgeous. Just like her mother?"

*Yes.*

"Ryann and I are co-parenting. The details are still to be worked out. But that is all." The final words were rough as they exited his mouth. His brain was forcing them, but his tongue didn't want to repeat them.

Knox's head shifted, the recognition clear in his eyes. "I'm sorry, man."

"She doesn't want a relationship. A baby doesn't make happily-ever-after." Jackson didn't understand Ryann's intense statements on them only co-parenting. They'd had something special in Hawaii.

At least he'd thought so. But it was only special if two people thought so. If they didn't, well, unrequited feelings were unfortunate, but they wouldn't keep him from caring for their daughter.

"Maybe she'll come around." Knox shrugged.

"She doesn't need to come around." Jackson looked at his phone one more time, his daughter's soft face on the screen. "She gets to decide her life."

He'd spent a lifetime with disappointment. He could handle this, too. If Ryann didn't want anything more than co-parenting, then he'd honor it. Wants and decisions were something he wasn't granted as a child, and as an adult he wouldn't try to take those from another. He'd just adjust himself.

"Want to take out some frustrations on the pickleball court?" Knox held up the racket.

"I don't have any frustrations, Knox."

What was the point of them? They'd never solved anything. He was a pro at letting the emotions go, not rocking any boats or causing others to worry over him.

Jackson yawned and pushed back from them table. "Let me change. Give me ten minutes."

"You can just take a nap," Knox said.

It was a kind option. A good one. But even with exhaustion coursing through him, Jackson didn't think he'd manage to sleep. Maybe after a few games it would be easier for his mind to let go of the last twenty-four hours of material and let him rest.

Ryann looked over the chart in the office of the Lowery Group. Her mind refused to focus on the words on the paper chart. Dr. Lowery, a man who hadn't held a scalpel in more than a decade, didn't like the look of computer charts in front of patients. He thought it made the patients feel like the computer was their doctor, something Ryann couldn't always dispute. But her entire career had been on computer, and the younger patients had a tendency to think the paper was old-fashioned.

Which it was.

It was also not the main system for the office. Each note was copied into the computer system by an assistant whose sole job was to collect the file as soon as the appointment was over.

If Dr. Lowery ever fully stepped away from the practice that would likely be the first thing to change.

And contemplating paper versus electronic was not going to help her focus any better. Jackson would be here in five minutes and their patient in ten.

The sixty-year-old carpenter had done every trick in the book for his basal arthritis. All conservative treatments had failed. So his daughter was bringing him in for a surgical consult.

Forcing him in, if the note from the receptionist was accurate.

It was why Jackson was attending this meeting—trying to give him some reassurance that he wouldn't be in pain during the surgery.

Jackson...

The man had looked downright delicious sleeping with their daughter the other morning. She'd come down to find him sitting up in the chair, his and Ayla's snores synced.

She'd snapped a quick picture and let her heart yearn for what it couldn't have for a few minutes—a dream that would never be hers. Not if she wanted Ayla to continue to have the relationship Jackson was developing with their daughter. That was too precious, too easily lost if her parents couldn't stand to be in the same room if something went wrong between them.

"You ready for this?" Jackson was smiling as he entered her office. He let out a whistle. "This is fancy, Ryann!"

It was. Her "office" at her hospital in Washington had been a shared space with a framed stock image the hospital had probably purchased two presidential administrations ago. She'd used it for charting and not much else.

"It is nice. How have you never been in one of the office suites here?" she asked. "They all look pretty much the same."

"Never invited." Jackson shrugged. "Just the CRNA, remember." He tapped his nose.

The underlying statement cut at her heart. CRNAs did everything that anesthesiologists did. They held doctorates, too. But there was still a preference in some circles.

And given the little he'd told her about his background, she suspected he'd had many judge him.

"That's not fair, Jackson. I can speak to the partners," she said. She wasn't sure it would do any good but maybe.

"Eh, doesn't matter." Jackson pointed to a picture of Ayla on Ryann's desk. "Besides, this is the only office with a picture of the prettiest baby in the world in it."

"That was snapped by the hospital photographer that offers sky-high picture packages. I think I was taken for a ride, but she was so cute." It was the only professional photo she had. Ryann ran a hand over Ayla's cheek in the image.

"Beautiful, just like her mother," Jackson said, then cleared his throat.

Now was a good time to get to the topic at hand. *No mental pun intended.*

"Mr. Nigili will be here shortly," she said. "Basal arthritis in the thumb. Going on nearly three years of failed conservative treatment. He cannot grip anything anymore."

"And it's painful—at least according to the daughter," Jackson added while looking at a tablet.

The small tech in his hands sent jealousy rippling through her. "Where did you get that?"

"Snuck it from Dr. Kelson," he said. "The man has a suite of them on chargers in the storage room next to his office. He and Lowery have been having a go of it over tech revolutions versus necessity versus the role of physicians. Once you're well-established in the practice, I suspect they'll ask you to choose sides."

That would be a simple choice. "I might just steal one."

"Wait at least a year. You're technically still a probationary partner. In a year, Lowery can't vote against your full partnership and you can side with modernity all you want." Jackson winked. "But you can borrow this one while we're in here."

Ryann took the machine, her fingers brushing his for less than a nanosecond. Yet heat and need floated through her.

It was like that moment when he'd first sat down on the plane beside her. Her whole body had hummed. She'd never experienced full-body lust before. Then he'd said hello, his deep, rich voice singing straight to her soul. Ryann had been lost.

It would be so easy to let herself fall into that again. But lust burned bright…for a while. How many partners had her mother claimed were her soulmate, only to hate them six months later?

"Pain is his concern." Ryann's tongue was thick, and her brain had fogged for just a minute. But it was Mr. Nigili they needed to focus on.

She ran her thumb across the tablet chart and watched the images of Mr. Nigili's thumb pop up. She'd seen these several times, but Ryann always looked back over notes before seeing a patient.

"There's no cartilage left in the base of the thumb," she said. "The fact that he's dealt with bone rubbing on bone for at least a year, more likely all three years he was trying conservative treatment, means his pain tolerance is extreme." Ryann shook her head.

"And at its breaking point," Jackson added.

The thumb was used for every movement of the hand. It was the reason humans could do so much compared to other mammals.

A knock echoed on the door, and an older man, his daughter and the office nurse stepped into the room.

*Sour-faced* was the description Ryann's mother would have used for Mr. Nigili. He was already glaring at her and Jackson.

"Come on, Dad." The woman offered a smile to Ryann and Jackson, but there was more than a hint of resignation in her shoulders.

"It's nice to meet you, Mr. Nigili." Ryann held out her hand, but he didn't take it.

"I don't shake hands," he said. His shoulders were stiff, and he didn't meet her eyes.

It would be easy to find the offense. Hell, as a woman in surgery, a female orthopedic surgeon, she'd faced more acts of misogyny than she could count. Add in that she was a mixed-race woman...

But she didn't think that was the issue here.

"Because you don't like to shake hands, or because it hurts to grip someone's hand?"

Ryann saw Jackson nod out of the corner of her eye. He was picking up on the same energy she was. This was an embarrassment issue.

Mr. Nigili looked at his daughter and shrugged. "A man's grip is important. I ain't got none now."

"Which is why we're here, Dad," his daughter said, patting his shoulder.

"I don't want anyone cutting me." The man looked at his daughter and then at Ryann. "Nothing personal, but I'm only here because Ella will not let it go."

Ella rolled her eyes. "Because you're in pain."

"And surgery is painful." Mr. Nigili shrugged his shoulders.

Jackson shifted, taking a commanding presence beside Ryann. "That's the reason that Dr. Oliver asked me to sit in on this conversation. I'm Jackson Peters, the certified nurse anesthesiologist. Think of me as the pain-management specialist."

"The one who knocks me out."

Jackson nodded, saying, "Yes, but it's more than that. It's about pain management before and after surgery."

"The surgery cannot be worse that the pain you are in constantly now," Ella said. "I hear the moans when you don't think I do. The curses. I see the looks you give your old woodworking tools, the ones with so much dust on them now. I know you miss it." She looked like she was about to cry. This was clearly an argument they'd had more than once.

"Surgery killed your mother." He crossed his arms, not quite covering his flinch as his thumb wrapped around his arm.

That was a problem not listed in his file. They'd

not prepped to make an argument about survival rates. Ryann couldn't guarantee anything, but this was about as safe a surgery as possible.

"Mr. Nigili, I monitor your vital signals during the surgery," Jackson said. He moved to the desk, leaning against it—the picture of a man in control of himself, laser-focused on their patient. "This is about as simple a procedure as possible, with limited time under anesthesia. But I understand your concern."

It was like Jackson was reading her mind. Why did he have to be so perfect? It would be easy to keep her distance if he had glaring flaws.

"Tell me what happened with your wife." Jackson's words were soft but commanding. It wasn't a question or request.

Which was good—if they were going to have any hope of helping him, they needed to know the real reason he didn't want to be on Ryann's surgical table. And it looked like this was the first time he was being fully honest with anyone about these hesitations.

Mr. Nigili looked at his daughter, then at Ryann, before focusing on Jackson. "Doctor said she needed surgery for a herniated disk. A routine surgery. Except she coded on the table. Not sure why, but they never got her back." He sniffed and looked at his shoes before looking back up.

His eyes were cloudy, but the tears didn't fall.

"I am so sorry for your loss," Jackson said as he

tilted his head. "As Dr. Oliver will tell you, there are never guarantees with surgery, but it is rare for a complication—"

"Rare, until it happens to you. My wife left me a single father at the age of forty-two. My children are grown, but I'm the only parent they have left. My thumb hurts, but leaving them..." He choked back a sob, then cleared his throat. "It is not an option."

"My daughter is almost six months old." Ryann turned the picture on her desk around. "I understand being scared. I can't tell you that there is no chance of complications—there are always risks. What I can tell you is that it is very minimal and significantly less than spinal surgery."

Ryann moved around the desk beside Jackson. "It is admirable that you want to be around for your children."

"And grandchild." Mr. Nigili huffed. "Six months old, just like yours."

"All the more reason to get the surgery," Jackson interjected. "The thumb will get worse—the pain must be excruciating now."

"I make do." Mr. Nigili barely covered the flinch as he made a fist with his hand and immediately released it.

Ryann could almost hear the bones rubbing together. The man was in excruciating pain. And it would only get worse.

"*Making do* and *living* are not the same," Jackson said. "Think of all the things you'll miss with your grandchild—picking them up, swinging them in your arms, throwing a ball with them." He ticked off the items on his fingers as he listed them.

"Teaching them carpentry." Ella rubbed her father's knee. "Some of my fondest memories are of us in your woodworking shop. The smell of sawdust. You showing me how to make something, guiding me." She let out a choked noise. "I want that for Gretchen and any cousins she may have in the future. I want her to tell her grandchildren one day when we're all long gone that the table she's showing them how to build is just like the one her grandfather showed her how to make."

The older man looked at his daughter, and Ryann could see him remembering Ella as a little girl. You always needed a parent, even if that parent wasn't there for you. Ella'd had that—she was lucky. Ryann also saw the moment he tilted his head and the look she hoped was acceptance crossed his eyes.

Maybe, maybe he was going to agree.

"You can do the surgery?" Mr. Nigili raised his chin as he looked at her, more defiance in the posture than anything. "*If* I decide to let you cut me."

Progress. Not much, but she'd take anything she could get.

"If you decide, yes, I can do the surgery," she said. "It takes about an hour and half in total, but

I'm only operating on your hand for about twenty minutes. The rest is Jackson making sure you're out and then bringing you into recovery."

Overall, the surgery would be quick, but she understood the fear. He'd heard "routine" with his wife. That was a word Ryann personally didn't like associated with anything related to the spine. There were too many what-ifs, too many factors that could go wrong, even if you'd performed the surgery hundreds of times before.

But this surgery was about as close to no-risk as possible. And it would provide him relief.

"I'll think about it." He stood, the conversation clearly at an end.

"You can call the office anytime, and they'll get you on my surgical schedule."

Ryann kept the smile on her face until they were gone. "Think he'll make an appointment?" she asked.

Somehow this meeting felt like a failure. He'd agreed to consider it. But thinking on it, away from the office, meant there was a decent chance he'd change his mind. She'd seen it happen again and again with patients.

If they didn't make an appointment when they left her office, the odds of them making one ever went down exponentially.

The words *I'll think about it* were some of the worst for a surgeon to hear.

"I don't know," Jackson said. "He has strong reasons to say no."

"The surgeries are completely different." Ryann crossed her arms. She knew it wasn't personal. The man wasn't doubting her, but that made it worse. He was in pain, and she could fix that. If he'd just let her.

Jackson put his arm around her shoulder and squeezed it. She let herself lean into him for just a second before pulling away.

"I know he lost his wife…" Ryann didn't understand that pain, but she could see that even after decades he still missed her. What was that kind of love like?

"It's not about that," Jackson said. He stood, pushing his hands into his pockets. "It's about the kids. Grown or not, he's the only parent they have. And he can't imagine them losing him. Pain—" His eyes moved to Ayla's picture. "Pain is a price he's willing to pay to make sure he's still in their life. I kinda get that."

Jackson rocked back on his heels. "I hope his kids realize how lucky they are." He waited a moment, then reached for the tablet. "I have a few patients at the hospital today. I'll see you later."

"Come by for dinner tonight?"

*Say yes*, she begged him in her mind. *For our daughter*.

Jackson smiled. "Of course."

"Not sure you want to smile too much," she

said. "I'm making a rice pilaf without flavoring other than pepper and salt. Maybe this weekend I'll have time to research some recipes." It was rough eating from such a limited range of food, but Ayla had been better the last two days.

So it was worth it.

"I don't mind if you want to bring your own food."

"I happen to love rice pilaf." He raised a hand as he walked out of the office.

# CHAPTER FOUR

JACKSON GRABBED THE warming bags from the back seat of his car. He had sweet potatoes and wild salmon to go with the rice pilaf Ryann was making. She might not have had time to do the research, but he'd found several recipes online that were quick and easy.

Pulling the bags out of the car, he tried to shake the mental unease that had settled there since the meeting with Mr. Nigili this morning.

"Mental unease. Pfft! It's jealousy plain and simple." He was not in the habit of talking to himself, but Jackson hoped by naming the emotion he'd find a way to release it. That was what his therapist would suggest.

He was jealous of children and a grandchild he'd never met. It wasn't their fault they had a parent who cared for them. And it wasn't Jackson's fault that his parents hadn't cared for him—at least that was what his therapist had told him… repeatedly.

Rationally he knew that was true. But part of

him would always wonder why he hadn't gotten what other kids had, why the universe had picked him for the hardships, for the loneliness.

Life wasn't fair. It was a phrase people said all the time. But why the hell wasn't it? He hadn't chosen his parents, hadn't chosen the difficulties.

But those were feelings to handle in his own place, feelings to write in his journal or let explode on his therapist's couch.

They were not emotions to burden Ryann and Ayla with. The front door opened before he could knock. Ayla was on Ryann's hip, her hands wrapped in her mother's hair, and they were both grinning. He mentally snapped a photo.

Maybe his early life had been hard, but this was exactly where he wanted to be. And his past was not going to taint his present. He would not allow it.

He ached to lean over and kiss both of them. But Ryann had been specific about their relationship, and he wanted to honor that boundary.

"That smells divine!" Ryann took a deep sniff of the food bags. "Probably a good thing you brought your own dinner—the rice pilaf looks a little sad. I'm definitely finding time to research recipes this week."

"This is for us, to go with the rice pilaf." Jackson smiled and leaned forward to kiss Ayla's cheek. His daughter squealed. There was no better sound in the world.

"What?" Ryann said as she backed up, letting him through the door.

"Salmon and sweet potatoes." Jackson looked over his shoulder as he headed toward the kitchen. He knew she liked salmon—she'd told him in Hawaii that she'd never met a fish she didn't enjoy eating. "I used a garlic-herb blend for seasoning instead of lemon. No citrus in the elimination diet, but this should be good."

"And sweet potatoes." Ryann's sigh was a good sign.

That one he'd guessed on. White potatoes were not part of the diet, but people seemed to have very distinct opinions about sweet potatoes. Love or hate—there was little in between.

"I had some time, so I looked up a few recipes. I'm no culinary master, but I can manage an easy dinner."

"Thank you, Jackson." Ryann pursed her lips, burying her head in their daughter's curly hair for a moment. "This was a really sweet gesture."

"Any time." He meant the words more than she understood. She'd given him the best gift. He'd take care of her, too. After all, Ryann was the mother of his child.

They were a family. Platonic co-parents still equaled family. And he'd do anything for his girls.

"Want to hold her while I get the plates ready?"

He didn't answer, just held his hands out for Ayla to come. The little one looked at her mom, then came to him. She wasn't scared of him, but Jackson was still a stranger. Not for long, though. *Hopefully.*

"So, now that we're several hours from it, any new thoughts on Mr. Nigili?" Ryann asked. "I keep running through reasons I might give him to get him on the table. I have his daughter's contact number, and I can reach out from the office tomorrow. Assuming I have something new." She clicked her tongue as she grabbed the rice pilaf from the stove and put it on the plates. "Right now, I feel like everything I've come up with are simple twists on what I said today."

Work talk. That was safe, at least usually. It wasn't Ryann's fault that Mr. Nigili was the last patient Jackson wanted to discuss. He was overreacting—he knew that.

Yet his brain refused to cut off the jealous feelings. It shouldn't matter, particularly when he was holding his daughter. Life was pretty amazing for Jackson Peters these days.

"Jackson?"

"Sorry." More time must have passed than he'd realized. "No ideas." Mr. Nigili would schedule the surgery, or he wouldn't. The only ones who might be able to change his mind were his kids.

Kids who had a father who loved them so much he was willing to live in pain—constant pain—rather than risk them losing him. Hopefully they knew what a gift that was, that people would change places with them in an instant…if given the chance.

"Why the frown?"

He looked at her, raising a brow.

"Don't play me like that," she said. "Your frown was so deep I was a little worried your handsome features might stay frozen that way."

"Handsome." Jackson made a fun face for Ayla. "Did you hear that, baby girl? Mommy thinks I'm handsome."

"Don't change the topic." Ryann wagged a finger at him as she plated the salmon, rice and sweet potatoes. "And clearly I find you handsome— that's why she's here." She laughed, then her features took a serious look. "Why the frown?"

"It's dumb." Jackson kissed the top of Ayla's head and moved toward the table where Ryann had set up a high chair a few days ago.

Almost six months old and starting solids before too long. But tonight, the plan was just to let her play with some toys while they ate, let her get used to sitting in the high chair and with them at the table. The next season of Ayla's life was already here. So much happened in the first year. He'd missed her newborn stage; he wasn't missing any more.

Whether the toys entertained her at all, let alone long enough for them to finish dinner, they'd soon find out.

"So it's dumb. So what? Why the frown?"

Ryann said. "Did you see something in Mr. Ni-gili's records I should know about?" She set his plate in the space next to hers before sliding into her chair.

Sitting between Ayla and Ryann…it made the jealousy seem so pointless. He was happy in this moment. Getting upset about what he hadn't gotten wouldn't do him any good.

"There was nothing in the records," he said. "If there was, I'd say something. Some physicians might not trust their nurses, but I always speak up for the patient." He'd run into more than a handful of physicians who'd thought their degrees made them masters of the universe.

Never mind that he had a doctorate, too. He was never quite enough.

"Anyone who doesn't trust their nurses shouldn't be in the field. You speaking up for the patients is the least surprising thing I've ever heard." She smiled, then motioned with her hand. "So why the frown? I'm not letting this go."

"Your mother is very stubborn," Jackson said to Ayla. He took a bite of his salmon. Then he took a sip of water and finally a deep breath. "I'm jealous of his kids."

"The ones who forced him to come in?" Ryann chuckled. "I suspect he's quite cranky with them."

"Probably." Jackson took another drink of water. Cranky, but not furious. Not 'drop them off and forget about them' furious. Not 'refuse to acknowledge any connection, even when they were adults and didn't need anything from you' furious.

"My mother was never cranky with me," Ryann said. "She was flighty and forgetful. Neglectful. But I can't remember her ever getting mad."

That was fortunate. Though neglect manifested trauma, too.

"What about your parents?" she asked.

This was not a topic he discussed. He'd already told her the reasons he hadn't seen her emails. That was more than enough of a burden for Ryann to know about.

He cleared his throat. The past was the past. He'd beaten the system. He'd put himself through college working as a nursing assistant and massage therapist. He'd gotten his nursing license and eventually a doctorate in nursing.

It didn't matter that his fiancée had left or that the mother of his child didn't want a relationship with him. There was a wall between his past and now. And he wasn't letting any breach occur.

"They were absent." He looked at Ayla. "Do you like the blue ball or rattle better?"

"We know the answer to that." Ryann chuckled as Ayla shook the rattle right in Jackson's face.

"I can't imagine a parent loving their child so much they would take the pain rather than a simple surgery with almost no risk," he said.

"You can't?" Ryann leaned forward and looked

from him to Ayla and back again. "Wouldn't you risk anything for her?"

Jackson smiled at their daughter. Ayla blew bubbles with her lips, soaking up the attention. "I know the answer I am supposed to say is that I wouldn't risk anything for her. But that isn't the case."

Ryann's eyes widened. "Wha...?"

"I would risk everything for her." Jackson ruffled Ayla's curls. She'd get to have everything he had learned early not to even ask for.

Gymnastics lessons—sure. Learn to play guitar—give it a go. Drama class—he'd be in the front row of every performance and bring roses at the end of the play no matter the size of her part.

Ayla would get a world of experiences.

"I would have the surgery without even thinking about it too hard. For me it would the easiest choice," he said. "I would want to throw balls and pick her up and swing her. Those things I ticked off, they were my wants. And I would want the pain-free experience I know you can give him, so I can show her the whole world."

Ryann tilted her head, a host of questions floating through her eyes, but she didn't ask them. "You accept risks." Her voice was soft, a lilt to it he couldn't quite place.

He didn't see it as risks, more as experiences. After a childhood devoid of fun experiences, how could he want anything else? He wasn't risky by nature, but if something fun was available or an exciting opportunity dropped in his lap, hell yeah, he took it.

"I want a world of experiences. Remember hang gliding over the ocean?" He reached for her hand but pulled back before they connected. She'd asked for this to be platonic. If it changed it would be on Ryann's terms.

Which was why it was good that he caught the comment about the bright pink two-piece she'd worn that day being one of his favorite memories before it dropped off his tongue. Most of his favorite memories revolved around Ryann and Ayla.

Ryann looked at Ayla and shuddered. "I cannot imagine her hang gliding. The guy who hooked us up to that contraption was clearly just some random guy doing it as a side job. We got basically no instruction. The fact that we didn't crash into the ocean or the side of a volcano is a minor miracle."

It wasn't that bad, though she was right, they should have gotten more instruction! "It was fun." Jackson pointed his fork at her. "Fun—and I dare you to say otherwise."

"It was fun. But also dangerous." She held up her fork, pointing it at him just like he was doing to her. "Admit it was dangerous."

Ayla giggled at the display in front of her.

"Are Mommy and Daddy silly?" Ryann asked, then she held the fork up a little higher, shaking it at him. There was a gleam in her eye that made everything a little better.

Jackson laughed enjoying the sound of his chuckles mixing with the wonderful sounds of Ayla and then her mother joining in. Goose bumps rose on his arms as he drank in the happiness.

Pressing the call button for the elevator, Ryann frowned when the pattern Miranda had shown her didn't deliver the elevator. She looked at her watch. There were stairs…at the other end of the garage. But it was hot and she didn't want to be all sweaty for rounds.

"The metal box giving you trouble?" Jackson's deep voice made her insides jump. Not from surprise, either.

The other night she'd nearly leaned over and kissed him when he'd brought her dinner—something he'd repeated every night for the last week. It was such a simple declaration of care, but no one had looked after Ryann in so long.

It would be easy to start craving it, start expecting it…

But they were maintaining a platonic parenting partnership. That was best for Ayla.

At least their daughter was sleeping better now. Ayla was only up once a night since her belly no longer gurgled all evening. Yet Ryann's nighttime routine still wasn't restful.

Instead of infant cries of pain, the tossing and

turning in her bed was caused by dreams—all focused on the hunk standing next to her. The urge to lean against him, invite him to come over tonight for dinner, then ask him to stay was clinging to her chest.

Taking a deep breath didn't help. His scent wrapped through her—hints of maple, wood and male that was just Jackson made her mouth water. Memories rushed at her.

Running her hands down his hard body had been the highlight of her vacation. No, kissing him—that was the highlight. The sweet touches that had escalated to heady need…

"Ryann?" Jackson leaned closer, the scent of coffee and him pulling her from the indecent thoughts.

"Sorry."

"It's still early." Jackson winked and held up a travel mug of coffee. "Brain not quite functioning."

Her brain was functioning fine. It just wasn't focused on work appropriate topics. "Mmm…coffee," she said.

"Actually," Jackson said, lowering his backpack from his shoulders, "it's tea."

"Not unless my sniffer is off!" Ryann tapped her nose. Just because she hadn't drunk the stuff in months didn't mean she couldn't identify it.

He pulled out a second travel mug and handed it to her before putting his backpack back on. "It's herbal coffee—caffeine-free," he said. "Miranda mentioned you looking longingly at hers. I thought you might like this. Chocolate-mint flavored."

"You really are too good to be true." She took a sip just as the elevator arrived. "Finally."

They stepped on together as they waved good-bye to two night-shift nurses who looked like they wanted to dart to their cars.

"This is good," Ryann said. She took another sip as Jackson pushed the button for the surgical floor. It wasn't quite coffee, but it satisfied most of the craving.

"Right?" He held up his own mug. "I admit that I wasn't sure when I bought it. I was worried it might taste like roots or dirt or worse, but figured it was worth a try."

"What's worse than dirt?" Ryann giggled, then took another sip.

"Not sure. But I bet it's one of those things that you know it when you taste it. And then you think, *I bet eating dirt would be better.*" Jackson winked and leaned a little closer to her.

Her skin buzzed. Surely he wasn't trying this just for her? "When did you get this?"

The skin of his cheeks darkened.

"Jackson?"

Before he could answer the elevator shuddered, then dropped a floor. "Jackson!"

He was by her side, his arm wrapping around her waist just as the lights went off.

The elevator shuddered again, then stopped moving. What the hell?

"Ryann?" His arm tightened on her waist. "You all right?"

"Yes." The word was chirpy, but it was true. Physically she was fine. Mentally, her brain was already spinning. Both Ayla's parents were trapped in this tin can. What if the worst happened?

Jackson's refusal to discuss his parents the other night had made it clear they were not an option if something happened to him and Ryann. And her own mother wasn't much better. She was somewhere on the East Coast with a new partner, wholly uninterested in her granddaughter.

At least she had been two weeks ago. By now she could be in Europe, India or headed to Arizona for an unannounced visit. She was not a good option in case anything happened to them.

"Take a deep breath," Jackson said. He held her tightly as they slid down the wall.

"I'm fine."

"Your teeth are chattering." Jackson pressed his lips to her temple. "You're not alone. We're going to be fine."

"You don't know that." Now was not the time to argue. She didn't want to, but it was easier than letting the worry consume her.

"Stay here," he said.

*Where exactly am I going to go?*

She bit back the retort as Jackson slid across the floor, used the flashlight attached to his phone and pressed the emergency button.

"Compton Elevator Security line, what is your emergency?"

"Never realized that the red button called an elevator security line." Ryann leaned her head against the wall, tapping it gently in a rhythm. The motion wasn't likely to wake her from a dream, but just in case…

Jackson didn't respond to her comment—the right move. He gave the information to the operator and then slid back over to her.

"Hopefully it won't be too long for them to send someone out," Jackson said as he sat beside her. His body heat called to her, and she leaned her head against his shoulder.

He turned off the flashlight on his phone, the elevator blinking back into darkness. "It will drain the battery."

"Right." The flashlight app wasn't meant to actually replace flashlights, which was a nicer thing to worry over than if the elevator was supposed to have emergency lights. And what it meant if they didn't kick on.

"Think this will make the hospital fix the elevator?" Ryann laughed, though she could hear the hint of hysteria in the sound. If you couldn't be hysterical in pitch black after falling a floor in an elevator, when could you be?

Jackson chuckled. His laugh did not sound like he was fighting back panic. "I think so, but honestly, who knows. The corporation that took over last year seems hell bent on cutting costs."

"Capitalism in medicine. Fun!" Ryann rolled her eyes, even though she knew he couldn't see her.

Jackson wrapped his arm around her shoulder and leaned his head against hers. If they weren't in this tiny box, it would be very sweet.

Of course if they weren't in this tiny box she wouldn't let him hold her. She liked it too much.

"You never answered my question," Ryann said, placing her hand on his leg. She needed him to talk, needed something to distract her from imagining the elevator plummeting to the basement.

"I fear I have forgotten the question." Jackson squeezed her arm, then started to pull away. "A lot has happened in three minutes, after all."

"Hold me." The two words slipped out, but he didn't say anything, just put his arm back in place.

"All right." He took a deep breath and moved his feet, probably trying to find a comfortable position, but he didn't let go of her. "What was the question, Ryann?"

She held up the travel mug, knowing he couldn't see it in the pitch darkness. Somehow she'd held onto it during the drop—reflexes were weird. "When did you start drinking this?"

*And was it for me?*

"Yesterday." He whispered the words.

"So you'd have an option for coffee if you took this on with me too?" He was eating the same food as she was. At least around her.

It was sweet, given the limited options she'd have until she figured out exactly what was causing Ayla's issues. Many partners didn't take that on, and Jackson wasn't her partner.

*Because I told him I didn't want that*, she thought.

Jackson's leg moved like he was tapping his leg in the dark. The silence hung between them. "I wanted to give you an option," he said. "You've done everything by yourself for over a year. Cooking, finding a coffee alternative, staying up with Ayla when she isn't feeling well…it's not too much to do for you."

"You are perfect, aren't you?"

She covered her mouth. *Like that could force the words back in!*

"I fall pretty far short of that. But I try." His head leaned against hers. "Is that why you want to keep everything platonic between us? Because I'm so close to perfection?"

His tone had a jokey vibe to it. Would he have asked it if they weren't sitting in the dark, trapped in a metal box waiting for rescue?

"Yes." Ryann took a sip of the herbal coffee.

Jackson moved, and she could tell he was looking at her face.

"Yes," she said again, "the reason I want us to

remain co-parents is because you are nearly perfect. Ayla deserves to have you in her life forever."

"Ayla *is* in my life forever." He turned the flashlight app back on.

"I thought we needed to save the battery life," Ryann said, looking away from his dark eyes.

"I want you to see my face for this." Jackson didn't say anything else until she met his gaze. "I am Ayla's father. I am in her life."

She wanted to believe him. In this moment, he probably even meant it. But she'd had stepparents say the same thing. They'd meant it.

Until they hadn't.

"Ayla deserves two parents who can be in the same room with each other." That felt like the middle of a speech, but it was the most important part.

"I see," Jackson said. He pulled at the back of his neck with his free hand. "Did your father stop talking to you because of your mother?"

"Yes. And so did my stepfather and my stepmother and a host of other partners that swore they were in my life forever no matter what." When she was little, she'd waited patiently for pickups and opened the mailbox for days waiting for letters.

And each time the dream had fallen away, another little piece of her had died.

That was not a life she wanted for Ayla.

"All right." Jackson shrugged.

"All right?" Could it be that easy? And why did her heart feel like it was breaking from getting what she wanted, what was best for Ayla?

He leaned his head back, inches from hers. If he turned, his lips would rest against her head. "Do you want me to fight this?"

"No." Two little letters. One little word. And a world of pain. Better to wonder *what if?* than to take the risk and find out.

"Then I won't." Jackson smiled, but there was no happiness in the gesture. "Ayla is what's most important. That will always be the case. But if you don't trust us to be civil for her sake no matter what, then—"

His words cut off as banging echoed in the elevator. "I think the rescue team is here."

Flashlights peered through the top of the elevator.

"Good morning." A firefighter waved as he lowered a rope ladder. "You guys are between levels, and the doors are stuck. Your hospital admin swears they had this thing inspected earlier this year. Chief doubts it."

"So do I." Jackson grabbed the end of the rope ladder and held his hand out to Ryann. "Ladies first."

She put her hand in his, looking at the ladder. "This doesn't seem super sturdy," she said.

"Don't worry. I got you." His words were deep,

the pressure of his hand holding hers sturdy. "I got you."

The repeated words infused her with calm— Jackson had her.

# CHAPTER FIVE

"I THINK AYLA'S teeth are bothering her." Jackson yawned as he drove them to the hospital. A week after the elevator incident, one the hospital CEO had apologized for profusely—before asking them to sign something releasing the hospital from damages—and Jackson's car and townhome were now fully "Ayla'd."

At least that was the term Ryann had come up with for the car seat he'd installed, the babyproofing he'd done at his condo, the bottles he'd bought and the crib in his guest room. Not that Ayla was spending much time there.

*He isn't, either*, Ryann thought.

She yawned. "You aren't the one she bites while feeding. Her teeth are definitely hurting her." Ryann rolled her shoulders. She needed new pillows on her bed.

*Or Jackson sleeping next to me instead of in the guest bedroom.*

He'd moved in. Sort of. He still spent at least one night at his condo. A way to maintain the platonic relationship she'd demanded? Ryann didn't know. And there was no way she was asking.

"Your neck still bothering you?" Jackson asked. His hand moved on the steering wheel, and for a moment she thought he might take her hand. Instead, he started tapping his thumb against the wheel.

She swallowed the pain brought on from being near him and not acting on the desires bubbling within her. It was funny—before reuniting with him she'd have sworn what they'd had was instant chemistry.

Hot. Steamy. Perfect for a vacation because then she wouldn't have to watch the fire of passion burn out. Now, though...

What if soulmates were real? The fanciful idea that her mother was always seeking. The thing that seemed too "out there" to be real. What if she was wrong? What if what she and Jackson had...

Ryann cleared her throat. If only it was as easy to clear her mind. When his hand laid on her knee, she moved her head to look at it and winced.

"So I'll take that wince as a yes." He pulled his hand back.

He'd been trying to get her attention while she was lost in fantasy thoughts about him.

Ryann placed her left hand on her shoulder and pushed two fingers into the tight ball of knots she could feel under the skin. It didn't give her much relief, but it was better than nothing.

Jackson pulled into the parking space, turned off the car and looked at her. "Put your shoulders against the back of the seat."

"Wha...?"

"Just do it," he said, gently pushing her shoulders back. "Take a deep breath."

She did as he instructed, not quite sure what he was doing as his hand rested on the top of her head. Then he gently pulled her head forward and to the left. The tight muscle burned but in such a nice way.

"Another deep breath."

This time she didn't hesitate. As she blew out, he pulled her a little further forward.

"Ooh," she moaned as the pressure released. "That feels delicious."

"It's temporary." Jackson let go. "You need an actual massage to release what I suspect are knots upon knots upon knots in your back."

Ryann laughed. "Sure. I'll just add that into my very open calendar." She leaned over and kissed his cheek, then pulled back so fast her neck let her know that even with the stretches it wasn't happy.

"I... I..." What was she supposed to say? The kiss had been unintentional. It had simply felt right, and she'd given into the impulse, something Ryann only seemed to do with him.

"Releasing muscular tension often makes you react differently." He winked, then grabbed the handle of the door and exited the car.

Grabbing her backpack, she followed him. "Is that true?" she asked. They were heading to the stairwell. The elevator where they'd been trapped had been fixed, but she wasn't ready to get back in, and so when they arrived together, she and Jackson went up the stairs.

"Yes," Jackson said as he opened the stairwell door. "Not sure why, but some people hold their emotions in tension. Releasing it brings the emotions out. I had more than one person cry on my massage table. They rarely knew why and all swore they weren't physically in pain. It was just the release."

His phone dinged, and he answered it. "Jackson." His dark eyes met hers. "She's right next to me."

Ryann could see the news in them. She picked up her speed, taking the stairs two at a time. Jackson didn't stop her, confirming her suspicions.

"Be there in ten, scrubbed in in twenty. Who's on the gas?"

She was already huffing, but Jackson was carrying on a conversation while rushing up the stairs. The man was as close to an Adonis as possible.

"Yeah, I can do it—I'm on call. Give me the details." He made a few noncommittal statements, and from the questions she heard it was clearly a crush incident.

The worst kind of accident for bones. Broken

bones she could fix. Bone dust…well, that required amputation or massive reconstruction.

Jackson hung up just before they hit the sixth-floor entrance. Two more floors.

"Thirty-two-year-old female. Crushed left hand. Hang-gliding accident."

"Hang gliding?" How did you crush your hand doing that? When they'd done it in Hawaii they'd listened to a safety briefing, been warned that if they had to choose between crashing into the beach and landing in the surf they needed to crash on the beach. Though their pilots had been the ones driving the machine. A crushed leg made some sense, but a hand?

"All that really matters is that she's getting prepped now." Jackson's voice was tight, his face devoid of emotion. "We can ask after the details after surgery."

It was a surgery face. Prepping for entering the OR. Putting emotions away and focusing on what you could control—which was less than what most people thought their doctors controlled.

A cold hard truth: sometimes fate controlled things.

"Breathing is normal. She's under." Jackson rolled his shoulders behind the paper curtain separating him from the rest of the surgical staff. He used to joke that he'd become a CNA because he got to sit during surgeries.

"Scalpel." Ryann's voice was tense. He'd seen the patient's hand, knew the bone saw for amputation was already ready to go.

And he knew that Ryann wouldn't amputate unless it was absolutely necessary.

"All right," she said. "The thumb is mostly intact. Middle and distal phalanges on all four fingers crushed. The rest of the hand is also mostly intact, though I will need pins."

"Amputating the fingers?"

A sigh followed.

The question came from Dr. Ian Prots and the sigh from Ryann. It was surprising how much one could pick up from behind the curtain.

"We're not getting that bone saw out, Dr. Prots." Ryann asked for another tool, and the room took on an uneasy silence.

The bone saw was not something anyone should want to use. It was a necessary tool, but many residents were a little too eager to see it the first time. After that…well, reality set in quick.

"Ry—Dr. Oliver." Jackson looked at the monitors, then over the curtain to watch a few breaths. They were shallower than he liked.

"Yes?"

"Her breathing is shallow. Still in the normal range, but…" He had a weird feeling, an uncomfortable pull in his chest. One learned not to ignore those.

"I need at least another two hours to pin and reconstruct. Am I going to get it?"

"I don't know." There was nothing on the system that showed extreme distress. The patient was healthy. The arm was an extremity. No surgery was without risk, but this was minor compared to open-heart surgery.

"All right, we go as long as we can," Ryann said. "Jackson will tell us the moment she needs to be brought out."

He smiled behind the curtain. He wasn't surprised that she was trusting his suspicions, but it was always nice when surgeons accepted the feelings he had.

But he'd put hundreds of patients under. He had a sixth sense about these things by now. One he did not take lightly.

The God-complex stereotype was a stereotype for a reason after all.

"This is a hand surgery. I mean, come on. What is the actual problem, Jackson?" Dr. Prots proving that stereotype as a surgical resident didn't bode well for his future patients.

"I need a pin for the distal four." He heard the sound of Ryann's breathing over the hum of the surgery. It was like he was keyed into her, like they were one.

It had been that way from the beginning. A draw. A need. And he knew how stressed she was right now.

"Dr. Prots."

Jackson knew Ryann was looking at the hand, but her tone felt like it was daggers. At least it wasn't focused on him.

"If you question the CRNA or any of the team again you will exit my OR," she said. "Pin for distal five."

The sputtering was too easy to hear. "So, I'm not allowed to ask questions? This is a teaching hospital."

"It is. But I'm in private practice. Residents don't have to be in here. And ask any question you like about the surgery, about what we're doing, about why Jackson might have a bad feeling. But do so the right way." There was a clink as Ryann dropped something onto the hospital tray.

Jackson smiled behind his mask, but the feeling was short lived. "Ryann!"

The seizing started at the same time as his call.

The next few minutes were a blur as they attempted to stabilize the patient. It took less than three minutes and felt like three lifetimes.

"Two more pins, then we close," she said. "It will take me ten minutes, Jackson."

"All right." His eyes didn't leave the monitors. The patient would need additional surgeries, but that was likely even without the seizure. Some days the fates had more control of the OR than the surgeons.

\* \* \*

Ryann slipped into the post-surgery recovery suite, her eyes meeting Jackson's in the semi-darkened room. "How is she?"

"Lauren is sleeping," he said. "She woke about an hour ago. Groggy, unsure of what happened. Not surprising. She was calling for her fiancé." Jackson watched the monitors. It was standard protocol for Anesthesiology to sit with any patient who'd seized on the table.

He'd be here anyway, but the few minutes she'd been awake had been heartbreaking.

"Is her fiancé here?" Ryann asked.

"No." Jackson didn't know the full situation, but based on Lauren's few wakening moments it sounded like what he'd experienced with Marie.

"Has anyone called him?"

"No," he said again, then sucked in a deep breath. "Her fiancé called off the wedding two weeks ago. No reason—just called it off. At least that's what I gathered. She wasn't really coherent."

"Oh." Ryann crossed her arms. "She was groggy. Maybe she'll remember why when she's fully awake. There had to be a reason."

"No, there doesn't." Jackson shook his head. This wasn't the place to talk about Marie. But Ryann was cautious. She wanted order, and she was putting her wants aside for the benefit of their daughter.

He understood. Jackson also knew that you

couldn't control much in this world. Sometimes there were no answers. Maybe the woman's fiancé had had a reason. Maybe he hadn't—either way it didn't matter; the end result was the same.

Heartbreak.

"Jackson…" Ryann said. There was a hint of pity in her eyes. That was the last thing he wanted from her, the last thing he needed.

"It's fine, Ryann. But sometimes there aren't answers," he said. "One of the nurses was able to reach her mom. She's on a plane right now. Hopefully the next time Lauren wakes, she'll be here." He looked at his watch. The anesthesia had cleared her system. The patient was stable, and he needed a walk.

"I need to see to a few things. Is there anything else, Ryann?"

He could see the questions floating in her eyes. The wonder. She knew there were things he wasn't saying, but she didn't press. "No. See you tonight?"

"Of course."

Ryann kissed Ayla's cheek as she sat her in the swing. It was her daughter's new favorite spot. Ayla would spend all day on the motorized contraption if they let her.

"I see she's in her happy space." Jackson was smiling, no hint of the unhappiness she'd wit-

nessed in Lauren's room. And he was carrying…
Ryann wasn't sure what.

"What is that?"

"Massage table." Jackson hit the side of the
large contraption on his left side. "This is a mo-
bile one I used to use for house visits."

"Do you need a place to store it?"

"No," he said. Jackson made a face at Ayla, and
she giggled. "Mommy is so silly."

The conversation in the car snapped back into
Ryann's memory. How could that have only been
twelve hours before? It seemed like days ago.

"My shoulder is better," she said. She wanted
to talk to him tonight. To find out what had happened today to drive such sadness into his eyes.
And why he'd seemed so sure there was sometimes no reason for a relationship to end.

There were always reasons for things. Sometimes you just didn't want the answer. That was
her mother's issue. The end of her relationships
was always one hundred percent her partner's
fault…at least in her version.

Jackson set the table down and walked over to
her, looking at her shoulder. "Can I?"

"Sure." Her shoulder really did feel better. Her
neck was still sore, but it was always sore. That
was just life now.

Two fingers pressed against her shoulder, and
she nearly fell into his arms as pain radiated down
her back.

"That sure seems like you're fine."

"If you don't push on it, then *it is fine*," she said. Ignoring the shoulder ache or popping a few pain pills before bed would help. It wouldn't fix it, but it would help.

"Let me help you." Jackson turned and started setting up the table.

No argument came to mind to stop this. "Jackson—"

"I'm going to go to the bathroom. Get undressed, lay on the table and cover with the blanket."

"Undressed?" His hands running over her body with thin cotton between them was going to be torture enough. But skin to skin?

Her throat burned, and her body tingled with just the memories of his touch.

"Yes. We need to get those muscles loosened, which won't happen nearly as fast with clothes on."

"Ayla—"

"Is yawning and almost down. And is also the reason that this shouldn't feel weird," he said. "She's proof that I've seen a lot more than I'll see tonight. I promised we'd keep this platonic. I meant it."

*What if that isn't what I want?*

"Let me take care of you," Jackson said, tapping the bed. "If you don't feel better after the massage, you can berate me all night."

"I would never."

He nodded, then disappeared down the hall to the bathroom.

Ryann stood there for a second, looked at Ayla, then at the bed. She rolled her neck, then pulled off her pants and shirt. Her bra fell to the ground, but she left her panties on. It wasn't much, but it was something.

She shimmied under the blanket and took a quick look at Ayla. She had nodded off.

"Ready?" Jackson asked.

*No.*

"Yes."

His steps were quiet, and when she put her head in the table's face hole she could see his bare feet. So she was getting a real massage from the only man who'd ever made her body sing.

"Take a deep breath for me."

She followed his command as he oiled his hands. The moment he laid them on her back she let out a whimper. The next hour was going to be the most blissful form of torture.

Ryann waited for him to ask if the pressure was too hard and didn't know how she was supposed to respond when he'd barely touched her. But thankfully Jackson started working on her upper trapezius.

When she let out the next moan, it was due to the tenderness of her flesh, not from desire.

"That spot is tight, honey."

*Honey.* He'd called her that in Hawaii, had said it was because she tasted like honey.

"All right, I need to move these knots, so take a deep breath and let me know if this pressure is too much." His elbow lay between her shoulder blades, and he pushed his elbow along the edge of blade.

It hurt, but in the best way. What an odd feeling to crave the pain knowing how much better she'd feel tomorrow.

Then when his thumb trailed the same path, the pressure was different. Lighter. Little circles tracing lines across her tight tendons. It felt delicious, and her body liked it in a much different way.

"How did you learn to do this?" she asked. She needed conversation, anything to keep her focus off the hot hunk rubbing oil down her body as much possible.

"I went to school." He pressed his elbow into her other shoulder, following the same path. "It took about nine months. I worked as a home health aide in the morning, went to night school for my RN and worked as a massage therapist on the weekends. I was willing to work Sundays, so I made bank."

She laughed but still felt her mouth fall open. "So, you took no breaks ever?"

"I was young and figured I could get all the work done early in life then so I could relax later."

"And then you became a nurse anesthesiologist.

Not exactly relaxing." She sighed as his fingers worked their way down her spine. He was really good at this.

"I got into the CRNA program when my fiancée walked out on me. I had free time and needed something to focus on." He said the words automatically, like they didn't really matter. But was that because he'd pushed aside the feelings or because it no longer caused pain?

"Why did the relationship end?" And why was there a bead of happiness in her belly that he'd never wed? What kind of person was happy that the man who'd fathered their child had been dumped?

"Because she didn't want to marry me."

Jackson rolled a knot in her shoulder with his thumbs, and when it released, Ryann let out a massive moan.

"That one felt good," she said. He leaned closer, and for a moment she thought he was going to kiss her head.

But he pulled back, and she barely bit back her whimper.

"I bet it did."

She sucked in a deep breath as he gripped the blanket. "All right, time to roll over."

"Roll over?" Her eyes met his dark gaze. He was holding the blanket up—head turned away— to give her modesty.

"Yes. Come on."

She did, sliding down the table as he adjusted a pillow under her knees. He was exceptional at this—like everything else he did.

"What was the actual reason she left?" Ryann should drop it. She knew that. But she craved information about him. The good and the bad. The past and the present. She knew about his job, knew his love for Ayla, but he seemed far too good at shifting topics away from his past.

"I wasn't what she wanted." Jackson let out a sigh as his thumb worked its magic on her back. "There is no sensational story, Ryann. A few years ago, she married a neurosurgeon, an upgrade."

"An upgrade." Ryann nearly shot off the table. "That isn't possible."

"It was years ago, honey. Water under the bridge," he said. "Take a deep breath—your neck is really tight."

She followed the directions, giving in to the care he was providing. Her body felt so much looser. The pinch of a headache that seemed her constant companion was gone.

He was taking care of her, taking care of Ayla... but who took care of him?

# CHAPTER SIX

JACKSON ROLLED HIS SHOULDER, trying to push away the sleepiness and touch of sadness that had been with him since Ryann and Ayla had reentered his life. The sleepiness likely wasn't ending until Ayla was a little older.

The sadness? He worried that might be with him for the rest of his days. Ryann didn't want him—not in the way he wanted her. She thought it best for Ayla.

That was a nice sentiment, but it also meant that she thought they were temporary. A bright flame that warmed the heart but didn't ignite the soul. Meaning she didn't want to keep him, either.

He cleared his throat as he finished charting. It was fine. It was. This was nothing he hadn't dealt with before. He was Ayla's father and Ryann's friend. That was more than he'd had a month ago.

More than he ever thought he'd get.

Maybe it was selfish to want more.

"Good afternoon, Jackson," Miranda stated as she walked up with Ryann.

"Hi." Ryann waved, a hint of color in her cheeks.

"I didn't think you were working today, honey." Jackson looked at Miranda and grinned. "And I know Miranda is on the schedule…because when are you not?"

"Ha-ha." Miranda wagged a finger. "I'll have you know that Knox and I never work overtime these days. Well, almost never."

"*Almost never* means they went from working all the eligible hours they could to only picking up one or two extra shifts a week." Jackson wagged his finger back to Miranda. "But I thought you were at the office this morning, Ryann." He'd called her honey a few seconds ago, just like he'd done last week during the massage—an hour he'd spent working out the knots of her body while fighting every feeling racing through his.

He was still waking from dreams where he'd spent the night worshipping her body after the massage. An alternate universe he'd give nearly anything to live in.

"I came in to see Lauren," Ryann said.

"I thought she was discharged." Jackson turned back to his computer. Lauren's seizure had been small, and after multiple neurological tests they'd released her with orders for physical therapy.

And Jackson had gone over the notes he'd placed in her chart with her and explained what to tell any future anesthesiologist or CRNA. Seizing on the table once didn't mean it would happen again, however she needed to be treated as a potential seizure risk from this point forward.

"Did something happen?" he asked.

The hand injury was tough. It would need months of physical therapy and at least one follow-on surgery. However, it wasn't an injury you generally worried about sending you back to the hospital after discharge.

"Only profit in the health-care system." Ryann rolled her eyes and sighed. "If I see her here, the cost to her out-of-pocket is about a hundred dollars. At the office, it's three hundred. So I agreed to meet her here. I'm going to see to a few patients and make rounds."

Her pager beeped, and she bit her lip as she read the message. "I guess word is out that I'm in the hospital."

"What is it?" Miranda looked at her own hip as the pager on it started buzzing.

"Handsaw accident," Ryann said. "We're needed in OR three. When he sliced his hand, he stumbled. So, we're tag-teaming this one." Her eyes met his, and she looked at her watch. "I'll have someone call Lauren—looks like we're going to be in surgery for hours."

"Good luck," he said. Time in the OR passed in a weird way, flying by and slowing down all at once. When your day shifted from a routine check-in to the OR with multiple surgeons, you could use all the luck possible.

"Thanks. If I can't get out by pickup time, can you grab Ayla?"

"Of course." He'd never met the babysitter, but Ryann had asked to place him on the backup list last week, something Jackson had immediately agreed to.

"You sure?" she asked.

He understood why she might ask the question. Jackson had been in Ayla's life for less than a sixth of his daughter's life. But it still stung.

He was her father—that meant everything. "I'm not on call. I won't get held up here. This is one worry you don't need to have."

"Thank you!" She waved a hand over her shoulder as she and Miranda took off running.

She didn't need to thank him. No one thanked mothers for doing what needed to be done for their children. Picking his daughter up from the babysitter, handling the evening routine was not a thank-you moment. It was a parenting moment. No matter who was doing it.

About an hour later, the final chart was clear when his cell rang. He didn't recognize the number and nearly sent it to voicemail, but something pulled at him.

"Hello?"

"Is this Jackson? Ayla's dad?"

Jackson's face turned to the clock, seeing it was eleven thirty. No reason for a call except trouble. His stomach dropped, and years of working in trauma sent a flood of horror through his mind. "Is she all right?"

"Yes, but I have been trying to reach Ryann for an hour."

"She's in surgery. I'm the backup."

*And if I'd been given your number, then I'd have answered immediately.*

That was a frustration he'd keep inside and bring up to Ryann.

"We've had a power outage. We aren't legally allowed to keep the kids here once it goes past the hour mark," the babysitter explained. "Almost everyone else has been picked up."

"I'm on my way." Jackson hit a few buttons and sent an email to the floor supervisor, Kelly. He was only on for another half hour; still, he'd take a half day if they wanted him to.

Though he suspected Kelly would just tell him not to worry over the thirty minutes.

"Thank you." The woman hung up the phone without waiting for another comment, her attention clearly jumping back to one of the other kids who hadn't been picked up yet.

Ryann had three panicked messages from the sitter. Luckily Jackson had texted her a picture of him and Ayla in the swing at the park by her place. He really was the perfect father.

"That was a rough shift" Miranda said as she

pulled her scrub shirt off and threw it into the laundry bin.

"And I wasn't even supposed to be here." The Lowery Group had rearranged her schedule for the patient today. The fact that it was a local politician who'd needed the surgery was probably why they'd been so willing to shift her day to the hospital.

The hand surgery had been successful—at least as successful as possible with a reattachment. He'd have some nerve damage and his hand wouldn't work the same as before.

But the hand was a minor injury compared to what Miranda had dealt with.

"Falling forward on the saw was beyond unlucky." Miranda bit her lip. The initial call had claimed he'd dropped the saw when the hand injury had occurred, but with his injuries it had likely been intentional.

The mental health staff had been alerted, and his public relations team was already spinning the story. Which was interesting when he was in the ICU, critical, and might not make it through the night.

"Unlucky." Ryann muttered. "Mind if I shift topics?"

"Please!" Miranda threw a blue shirt over her head and pulled her dark curls into a ponytail. "The sillier the topic the better!"

"Not sure this is silly," she said, "but what

can I do for Jackson as a thank-you or to make him smile because he's so helpful, you know, because of Ayla. Or…" She'd almost said because she wanted to see him smile.

Not that she didn't see him smile all the time. The man was always beaming when he looked at their daughter. But ever since she'd kissed his cheek—

Ryann shut down that line of thought. She was trying to do something nice for Jackson. He did a world of nice things for her. There was nothing more in-depth to it than that.

"Or…" Miranda raised her hands and smiled.

"I want to do something nice for him." Ryann's cheeks were hot, and Miranda was looking at her with a knowing smile.

She looked at her watch and then pulled out her phone. "I need to check with Knox—I don't keep the schedule on this as well as he and Jackson."

Ryann had no idea what schedule she could possibly be talking about. But if it was something Jackson tracked, then it was important and she wanted to know.

When Knox answered on the other end, Miranda asked, "Is it tots night?"

*Tots night? What does that mean?* Ryann wondered. *Toddlers?*

"No, I'm sure that Jackson is not headed to Mulligan's tonight. But I am sure they can make them to go." Miranda made a face that Ryann couldn't decipher.

*That was a bar name.*

"They don't taste that good at the bar, but he loves them." Miranda winked at her as she said, "Yes, Ryann is asking."

It was weird to hear the conversation from one side. She wasn't sure what Mulligan's was or tots night, but the conversation was one Miranda was enjoying. After the day they'd had that wasn't nothing.

"Love you, too. See you soon. No, I am not bringing tots home, Knox."

"Did he want tots, too?" Ryann asked as Miranda pushed her phone into her back pocket.

"No." She grabbed her backpack, clearly ready to put this day behind them. "Jackson loves tots. We don't understand it, but we roll with it. Like Knox needing to compete at darts or lately pickleball." She rolled her eyes.

"All right, so Jackson loves them," Ryann said. "We are talking about the little potato things right?"

"Yep. The bar food." Miranda pulled notebook from her backpack and made a quick note, ripped it out and passed it to her. "Tonight is tots night at the bar. It's five dollars for all-you-can-eat. I'm sure that you can ask the bartender for a to-go box. It might not be what they usually do, but if they give you any trouble, mention that it's for Jackson."

"Does he spend a lot of time at the bar?" Her mother's second husband had basically lived in one. But Jackson didn't seem the type.

"*A lot* is relative," Miranda said. "He and Knox used to go once or twice a week, mostly to play darts and for the tots. They each nursed a beer. When I pointed out that you can eat tots any-where…well, I will let Jackson explain why they taste better at Mulligan's."

"I see." Ryann put the address into her phone. Grabbing some tots on the way home was now priority one.

"They're in a new season of life." Miranda opened the stairwell and waited for Ryann to head through. "Knox and I were residents to-gether. Jackson was in his first year as an RN then, working in the ER. We were so young, and yet now, with years of experience behind us, there are days I still feel like that twenty-five-year-old resident. The more I learn, the less I know."

"A new season." Ryann liked that phrase. "It is weird. I'm a mom, and I remember thinking adults must have the answers." Not her mother, but other adults. Those were the people she'd wanted to be when she grew up.

The ones who knew what they were doing. Who had the answers. Who didn't worry because they'd figured everything out. Adults with their lives together, who knew what they were doing was right. At least she'd thought so.

"And now you realize they were all just doing their best and winging it at just about every step." Miranda laughed.

"Some kind of universal joke, right!" Yet she understood it. Particularly with Ayla at home. She wanted so badly to do her best for her. No matter the sacrifices for herself.

Opening the door to her condo she almost wanted to call out, *Honey, I'm home*. It felt nice and weird and somewhat unfulfilling to know Jackson was here with their daughter and they were just friends.

Who was she trying to fool? She and Jackson were more than friends. Less than what her body craved.

"Hi." Jackson rounded the corner with Ayla on his hip. Their daughter was squirming, trying to get back to whatever game she'd been playing just a moment before.

"Nice to know she doesn't care that I'm home," Ryann said. She kissed her daughter's cheek, then let out a gasp as she stepped into the kitchen area. The pots were on the floor along with her wooden spoon and the chair they let Ayla sit in.

"It's one way to keep her busy while making dinner!" Jackson said, chuckling as he put her back into the chair.

Their daughter immediately grabbed the spoon and started banging on the pots.

"It does add to the number of dishes I have to clean, though. Good thing you're worth it, little miss." He booped her nose, then turned his full attention to Ryann.

"I'd ask how your day was, but I already heard from Knox." He opened his arms.

She hesitated only a minute before putting the tots and her bags on the counter and stepping into them.

Her body seemed to exhale the tension in her life as his strong arms wrapped around her. Nothing seemed like it could get to her, like when she was standing in his arms she was protected. Really protected.

Her heart yearned to lift her face. Kiss him. Lose herself in the longings only Jackson had ever brought out in her.

"I have something for you," she said. She needed to move, or she'd give in to all those urges.

"For me?"

The tone of surprise cut. He never expected anyone to treat him. That was changing. He was caring for her, and she was going to do the same for him. Friends and co-parents could do that.

*Couldn't they?*

"Yes, for you." She pulled away and headed for the bag. "I'm not sure they'll be any good. Bill wasn't sure, either. But hopefully…"

She handed him the to-go box. She was not sure how tater tots were going to make his day, but she was trusting Miranda and Knox.

"Are these…?" Jackson shook his head and popped one into his mouth.

"They probably need to be warmed," she said. She enjoyed tater tots occasionally. But only hot. They were not great otherwise.

"Nah, they're always a little chilly at the bar," he said. "Since food isn't really their thing."

That seemed like a reason not to get them, even for the low price of five dollars for all you could eat. "Miranda mentioned you only like them from Mulligan's."

"Yeah," he said. "Silly, I know, but they're greasy and a little cold, just like my mom used to make them. Well, *make* is relative—she'd pop them in the microwave and then set them on the counter and forget." He sighed as he chewed. "Weird how this is the thing that I miss."

Ryann understood that sentiment. Children, even those with parents who didn't care enough about them, found things they missed. It was random ice cream nights for her.

"Were there any other things she made often?" Anything else Ryann could do for him. Any insight into his past.

"Nope. Tots though…" He popped another into his mouth. "Thank you." Jackson leaned forward, like he was about to kiss her cheek, then pulled back.

How she wished he'd close the distance. She'd give in to the impulse. But the man across from her would always respect the boundaries she'd placed. As he should.

Grabbing another one, he said, "I hate that you can't share one."

For the first time she was more than a little happy that she was on the elimination diet. She was glad he enjoyed the tater tots and glad she had a reason not to share.

"Those are all yours!"

# CHAPTER SEVEN

"THINK SHE NEEDS her diaper changed?" Jackson did his best to keep the smile on his face while their daughter screamed from the back seat. She'd started about ten minutes into their hour-and-a-half drive to the outlet store Ryann wanted to visit.

"She didn't when we checked ten minutes ago, or five minutes after that. So far we've stopped twice in forty minutes, and as soon as we get her out of the car seat she's fine. Maybe car sickness?" Ryann leaned over the seat and made some cooing noises to their daughter.

Ayla either didn't hear her over the screams or didn't care. With the car seat rear-facing it was difficult to know which it was. Weren't car rides supposed to calm babies?

Their daughter sounded nearly desperate, and it broke Jackson's heart.

"How about we stop off here?" he said. "There's a roadside attraction. They'll have bathrooms, and you can maybe see if she's hungry." The signs for the largest fork in Arizona and spoon museum were plastered all around the area. Jackson had never been, but desperate times…

"And if she just wants out of her car seat?" Ryann looked at him, her eyes stating that she was fairly certain that was the main issue here.

He agreed, but what other choice did they have besides letting her scream for an hour?

"If that is the case, I can drive us back to your place. She and I can hang out there, and you can enjoy a solo trip to the outlet." That way Ayla didn't lose her voice from screaming, Jackson and Ryann didn't lose their hearing, and Ryann still got to enjoy part of her day off.

Pulling into the attraction, Jackson couldn't stop the laugh. A giant four-story fork stood next to a small building with the words *Spoon Museum* written in bland script. Somehow he'd expected more.

"Oh! This is fantastic. How did I not know this was so close?" Ryann clapped and made an oohing sound that was very at odds with the sight before them.

"Why do they have a large fork and a spoon museum? Shouldn't it be the largest spoon?" Jackson turned off the car, and Ayla's screams turned to sniffles.

"Oh, it's a marketing strategy so that you say exactly that." Ryann hopped out of the car and went back to Ayla. She lifted their daughter from the seat and rubbed her nose against Ayla's, eliciting a laugh.

"So it is the car seat," Jackson said. He wasn't sure what they were going to do about that. Until she was old enough to tell them what the problem was, there was no good way to know why she was intent on only spending a few minutes in the seat.

"Looks that way." Ryann rubbed Ayla's belly as their daughter babbled. "So, plans change."

They did. Jackson was hoping to spend the day with Ryann and Ayla. Shopping wasn't his first choice of entertainment, but spending time with them was. "So, I'll run the two of us home."

His throat tightened on the word *home*. He'd meant to say *I'll run the two of us to your place*.

Ryann's condo was not home, something he shouldn't have to remind himself of. Yes, he was staying there most nights—in the guest room. But that was to help Ryann, not because it was his place.

"Today is a family day. Shopping isn't super necessary. I can order the shoes I was looking at online. I mostly wanted out of the house." Ryann pointed to the fork. "You have to take our picture!"

*Family day.*

His soul vibrated with the two words. The thing he'd wanted most—family.

Maybe this family didn't look like the one he'd wanted, but Knox was his brother even though they shared no DNA. Family didn't have to be some standard picture-book definition.

"Smile!" Ryann beamed as she looked into his phone, and he snapped a picture. "Ayla isn't looking. Look at Daddy."

"Da—" Ayla started.

Jackson held his breath.

"Can you say *Dada*? Dada? Dada?" Ryann looked at him. "I hope you're rolling the video."

*Only the one in my mind.*

He didn't want to move an inch, look away for even a second to change to video in case he missed it.

"Dada?" Ryann parroted, but Ayla just giggled.

She was babbling. A happy baby who didn't know exactly what the sounds meant…yet. It wouldn't be long before the word *Dada* turned to *Daddy*.

Time would pass so fast. She was already bigger than when he'd met her three weeks ago. Soon she'd be seven months old and, in the blink of an eye, seventeen. He didn't want to miss a minute.

He pushed the button on the phone, grabbing several pictures of the happy scene in front of him. "I've snapped several pictures. You want me to keep going?"

"Was she ever looking at you?" Ryann asked.

He wasn't sure he'd gotten one of them looking at him together, but several were perfection of mother and daughter giggling at each other.

"I don't think that ever synced, but look at this one." He pulled up his favorite. Their heads were both tilted the same way, the wind picking up their curls, smiles as wide as possible.

It should simply be titled *Happiness*.

Ryann leaned her head against his shoulder. The motion felt so right. He wanted to lean in, wrap his arms around them both. Kiss their heads and just be.

Instead, Jackson forced himself to step away. "So, are we going to try diaper changes or feeding or just walk around out here?"

"The spoon museum." Ryann pointed. "I assumed we'd do that instead. You know—family day."

"You want to go to the spoon museum? It probably isn't great," he said.

The sign needed to be repainted. The windows could use a dusting. The place had certainly seen better days.

Ryann slipped her hand into his and pulled him toward the back of the car. She opened the trunk, got out the wrap she carried Ayla in, put it on and fastened their now very happy child in.

"I'm counting on this place being a little bad," she said. "That's part of what makes it so fun. Anyone can go to a fancy museum—only a few actually stop at roadside attractions. That's what makes them so special."

She clapped her hands and kissed Ayla's cheek.

"Baby's first roadside attraction." She snapped a photo with her phone.

"Wow." Jackson chuckled. "I would never have guessed you liked these."

"Love them. My mom used to stop at all of them. I saw more baby alligator farms, thimble collections and even the second-largest taxidermy collection in the US."

"Second largest?"

"Right." Ryann was practically bouncing. "I have no idea where the largest is or how you even measure that. But their sign clearly marketed them as the second largest. Mom thought it was fun. Even with everything else, I still love these. Kind of like your tater tots, but with four-story forks."

"Four-story forks." Jackson laughed. "There is a phrase I never thought I'd say."

"Then this is going to be quite the experience for you, Jackson Peters. Ready?" She slid her hand back into his.

He looked down at it. It would be so easy to pretend that they were the perfect little family today. And rather than pull away, Jackson was going to give in to it.

Just for the afternoon.


"You have to admit that was something." Ryann was swinging Jackson's hand in hers, very aware that she'd held it the entire time they'd been in the museum. She should have released it, should have put a little distance between them.

Yet Ryann felt incapable of letting him go. Today had felt different.

No. Her life had felt different from the moment the man beside her had stepped back into her life—into their daughter's life.

If she leaned over to kiss him, what would happen? Their passion had burned so bright in Hawaii. But what if the spark stayed alive? What if she could have this little family? Forever...

"*Something* feels like an apt description," Jackson said. His laugh seemed to touch the center of her body as he leaned forward.

*He's going to kiss me.*

Instead, he beamed at their daughter, then pulled back and released her hand. Disappointment flared and heat burned her cheeks as she fought every fiber in her body screaming for her to take it back.

He was focused on Ayla. That was what was most important.

"I mean, it isn't every day you see a spoon that was used by a president." Ryann started to laugh, trying to get back to the happiness she'd had all afternoon before covering her giggle with her hand. Ayla had fallen asleep halfway through the museum—which was the loosest description of that word as possible. Besides the gift shop, the place had three rooms, none of which was larger than her living room.

"I'm not sure we have seen a spoon used by a president," Jackson said. He opened the back door and got the buckles ready so they could transfer Ayla as quickly as possible. Hopefully she'd sleep all the way home.

"The artifacts did seem to have a bit of a dubious origin," she said. Most of the signage looked like it had been printed on regular computer paper with an ink cartridge in desperate need of a change.

"Artifacts, Ryann, honey." Jackson chuckled before sliding into the front seat and starting the car. "Those were junk-store finds put behind glass— in need of dusting—and given a new 'history.'"

He was right. That was part of the fun she always had at places like this. It was random and weird and usually someone's passion that they hoped sparked passion in others. Roadside attractions were leftovers of the days of cross-country road trips. Most were either out of business or closed.

The few that remained relied on major gimmicks. Like the largest fork next to a spoon museum. Ryann would still stop at them, though, gimmicks and all.

"The admission price was perfect!" She clicked Ayla's seat belts into place, letting out a little sigh as her daughter kept sleeping. Hopefully the car ride home would be less eventful.

For all three of them it had cost five dollars to walk around the museum for forty-five minutes. Ayla, like all children under twelve, had gotten in for free.

"Yes, they're clearly hoping you'll spend your coin in the gift shop." Jackson pulled out of the parking space as she was clicking her own seat belt closed.

"If the frame hadn't been broken, I would have bought the 'my first visit to the fork' picture frame." Ryann had one picture of herself and her mother that had survived countless moves, life on communes and couch surfing. It was of them at a building in Ohio shaped like a giant basket. Faded and the corners creased, it represented one of the few happy times in her childhood.

A time that had passed so quickly. She always knew her mother's focus would vanish the second her mother found a new partner or "path of life."

It was that happiness she was giving Ayla. Without the worry.

"So, what's for dinner?" Ryann asked. She had a few things in the fridge they could make, or Jackson had done some research on which take-out places had options for her.

"Oh." Jackson looked in the rearview mirror and cleared his throat. "I'm…um… I was going to go back to my place tonight. I haven't stopped by in a few days."

"Need to water plants?" It was a weak joke, but she didn't want him to see the pain the statement brought.

"No." Jackson looked at her briefly before turning back to the road. "I just a need a night away. A night to put myself back in the place I need to be for you."

"Oh." Ryann understood, and she appreciated his honesty. After all, it was she who had held his hand. She who had called this a family day. She who was setting the boundaries he was honoring. She who should've been happy right now.

Or at least content.

"I'll bring the tea first thing tomorrow, help with morning shift before sitter drop-offs," he said. The staccato words punctuated the quiet car.

"Sure." Ryann looked back at Ayla, then turned her attention to the road. Forty minutes in a silent car with Jackson…it was going to feel like an eternity.


"Such a good girl," Jackson cooed at Ayla as he finished up her bath. Ryann was fixing them dinner, and after today's trip it would be so easy to let himself keep pretending that they were the happy family that did day trips, came home for dinner, then went to sleep without one parent in the guest room. The whole white-picket-fence-without-the-fence idea.

It was what he wanted more than anything. But that wasn't the relationship he and Ryann had. He needed a little distance, to spend tonight in his condo. *His space*. Force his brain and heart back into check.

That was why he'd panicked when she'd asked him about dinner. He'd seen her eyes widen when he'd said he wasn't staying, watched hurt race across the dark hues of her eyes and seen her cover it so quickly, too. That wasn't fair. It was a simple question, one they'd asked nearly every day. A blasé phrase that resulted in him hurting her feelings.

Grabbing the ducky bath towel, he lifted Ayla from the bath. She laid her head on his shoulder, and his heart melted. "You had a busy day, huh, sweet girl?"

Most of that busyness was due to screaming on both sides of the trip. Her eyes had popped open just as they'd hit the highway. The screams had started moments later.

She yawned and put her thumb in her mouth as he got her ready for bed.

"Think she'll eat any of the oatmeal I made for her?"

Jackson lifted Ayla, passing her to Ryann. "No idea. She's a very sleepy girl." He used a singsong voice that he swore he'd never had before finding out he was a father. It was like the knowledge had unlocked some gene that forced silly voices. "If you nurse her, she'll probably go down, and then you can have a nice low-key night," he said.

The words should've been right, but he saw the same look of hurt pass through Ryann's eyes. The urge to pull them both into his arms, hold them until the world righted itself and they were the family he'd always dreamed of wrapped through his soul.

A host of words were trapped in his mind. But none of them were the right ones. Remaining platonic co-parents was one of the hardest things he'd ever done.

"Stay."

Had she truly whispered the word, or was his brain pushing the fantasy he was desperate to seize?

"Ryann, if you want me to feed her and get her to bed for you—"

"No." The curls bounced as she shook her head. "No."

"What do you want, Ryann?" he asked.

She bit her lip, her eyes focusing on Ayla. "I don't know. But I don't want you to go yet."

What was he supposed to say?

They stood there looking at each other, a mountain of unsaid words standing between them.

"Okay. I'll stay," he said.

Tomorrow, though, for his own sanity, he was going to spend time at his place.

# CHAPTER EIGHT

"GOOD MORNING." At least Ryann's voice was bright as she welcomed her first appointment into her office, and that was what her patient needed. The rest of her…the rest of her was exhausted and torn and dealing with emotions she'd never expected—or wanted.

Today was the first time in almost two weeks that Jackson hadn't stayed at her place. She'd gotten Ayla ready without him, actions that she'd done for months alone. Ryann could do it; it was just better with him.

In fact, everything was better with Jackson Peters around. The whole condo felt less homey without him.

Her day felt off, and it wasn't yet nine.

"Morning, Doc." Her patient seemed to have no issue smiling. Or perhaps she was faking it just like Ryann.

"You're here because your fingers are hurting, Ms. Laird?" she asked. She'd read through the chart a few times, but the family doctor who'd recommended Ms. Laird see an orthopedic surgeon had put precious little in the notes.

"Peggy, please. I'm here because my niece is worried about my arthritis and hands cramping."

"Your niece, Peggy?" Now Ryann was more confused.

"Yep. The rascal is also my family doc," she said. "Super proud of her, but she's very straitlaced and a bit of a worry wart. I know why my hands hurt, and I'm all right with it."

"All right?" Ryann leaned against her desk. "Why do your fingers hurt?"

"Arthritis." She smiled and held up hands. Her knuckles were noticeably swollen but far from the worst Ryann had seen.

"Is it getting worse?" Arthritis was common. If you were lucky enough to see your seventies, the odds you'd get the diagnosis were more than seventy percent.

Peggy chuckled.

Ryann wasn't sure what was so funny, but patient reactions could swing wildly on the emotional spectrum.

Her patient smiled as she looked at her hands. "I'm seventy-two." Peggy's eyes filled with tears, but Ryann didn't think it was physical pain. "I'm painting every morning now and every night and sometimes for almost eight hours at a time."

"That amount of painting would hurt anyone's hands. I'm surprised your wrists aren't burning."

"Oh, they are." Peggy laughed again. "I made the mistake of asking my niece if the pain pill recommendation on the bottle was serious or if I could double it without issue." She pointed at Ryann. "That face. That face is the one my niece made. Guess it's a doctor face."

Ryann closed her mouth and took a deep breath, hoping that her face looked more normal now. "Have you considered painting less?"

"I've spent the last thirty years not painting, thirty years behind a desk doing a job I hated." Peggy blew out a breath.

"So you started painting again when you retired?" Ryann asked. That was actually good. Many people lost themselves in the early days of retirement. But keeping a work schedule for a hobby wasn't necessarily healthy, either.

"No." She pulled her phone and held up a picture. It was of a young Peggy and another woman dressed in paint clothes. "This is Molly. We ran a small artist's shop in San Francisco in the nineteen eighties." Peggy looked at the image, then put it away. "Molly wanted to have a commitment ceremony and spend our lives together, but I... I didn't want to disappoint my family."

It was a tragic story. And one that was all too familiar for so many people.

"She died about a year ago." Peggy closed her eyes for just a second. "Left a note for me with her partner, a lovely woman named June. Anyway, she wrote that she hoped I got what I wanted."

*And I didn't.*

Ryann didn't need to hear the words to know what they were.

"I retired the next month, bought my weight in oil paints and just started. And my hands ache. There are days that my wrist burns, but my soul is at peace for the first time in my memory."

She wiped a tear away, and Ryann handed her a tissue. "I don't want surgery, and I'm only here so I keep my cool Aunt Peg cred with my niece. Which I think she knows, but…"

"Have you tried sleeping with a carpal tunnel brace?" It would keep her wrist in a neutral position, help the carpal tunnel in the wrist and maybe even alleviate some of the finger pain.

"No. Which one do you recommend?"

Ryann smiled—at least there was something she could do for Peggy to give her a little relief.

They spent the rest of the appointment going over options, all of which Peggy turned down on the side of not wasting any more time. But between the brace and anti-inflammatory meds, she was going to get at least some relief.

"All right, Ayla is down." Jackson rolled his shoulders as he stepped into the living room. He needed to use a racquetball on his sore shoulders. Unfortunately, that was at his place.

He'd make do though because Ryann wanted to watch some home-decorating show tonight. The woman loved them, even though he really thought the rooms all looked the same after it was done.

"Glad she's down because *Small Homes, Big Future* is starting," Ryann said. "Not that we couldn't stream it later, but somehow live it feels different."

"Sure." He didn't care what they watched. He was just looking forward to the evening. Jackson slid onto the couch beside her, wincing as his shoulders complained at their first position.

"You okay?" Ryann's curls shifted as she stared at him.

Her dark gaze called to him, and his soul ached for him to reach over and run a hand along her cheek, then ask to kiss her.

Instead, he smiled and carefully shook his head, making sure not to aggravate the muscles any further.

"I'm fine. What kind of name is *Small Homes, Big Future*?" he asked. He'd spent two nights at his place and probably should've gone back tonight. But he didn't want to.

He wanted to be here, having a random night with her.

"They all have names like that." Ryann threw him a look as the program started. Then she hit Pause.

"Thought you wanted to watch this live? It's

better that way, remember." Jackson shifted, and his neck and shoulders reminded him that he'd chosen poorly.

"It's only a little delay—we can skip the first couple of commercials," she said. "Don't change the subject. Your neck is sore."

"Happens. I sit still in weird positions during long surgeries. You get lower back pain, and I get neck pain. Which you also get." He winked. This wasn't a big deal. Just a factor in his life.

"Move up." Ryann moved before he could process more than her soft scent wrapping through him. She slid behind him, wrapping her legs around his waist as she pushed on the base of his neck.

"Oh." Her fingers found the exact right pressure point.

"I might not have massage background, but I know where each muscle connects to the bones."

"A built-in bonus." Jackson sighed as her thumb followed the trapezius muscle pushing hard enough to hit the smaller muscles under it.

"All right, I can do this while we watch the show." She reached around him.

Her hands brushing his shoulder lit up his skin. He hadn't reacted to a woman like this since high school.

He'd felt this way every second with her in Hawaii, like he'd never be able to get enough of Ryann. He'd chalked it up as vacation fun, but what if it wasn't? What if they could be so much more?

Not that that mattered, since it wasn't what she wanted.

"What color of gray will they paint the bedroom?" Jackson chuckled as the camera panned the currently dark red bedroom, trying to focus on anything other than the woman wrapped around him rubbing his shoulders and neck.

"They have other colors!" Ryann's hand hit his chest, resting on it for a moment before she pulled it back and started rubbing his shoulder again. "And you have to admit that red is horrid." Her soft words were breathed against his ear.

"No one can argue that," Jackson said. He preferred brightly colored rooms. Probably because he'd never been allowed to paint any room a color of his choice until he'd become an adult.

He was decent at interior decorating…provided you were going for something with personality. His kitchen was a nice shade of light green. His bedroom was a dark blue—for the relaxation and to keep as much light out as possible when he worked nights. His bathroom was pink with flamingos because it made him smile every morning,

And the extra room that was now Ayla's was light yellow with clouds on the wall. The light yellow had been there before. The white clouds were wall clings he'd found the day after discovering he had a daughter.

Not that Ayla had ever slept there. One day he hoped she'd like it. But if she wanted a different color, he'd do it immediately.

And thinking about interior decorating was doing nothing to stop his growing desire for the mother of his child as she ran her hands over his sore muscles.

"I bet they paint it any other color than gray." Ryann pointed to the screen, then pushed her elbow into his shoulder.

"Oh." That felt like heaven. Torture, but heaven.

"The homeowners don't look like they want gray." She kept rotating her elbow, thankfully unaware of the turmoil cascading through him.

"Fine. If it is gray, what do I win?" he asked. Focus on a bet. That would be something to draw his attention—maybe.

Ryann looked around the living room, then made a face. "Umm, there isn't a lot here to bet. Oh…how about a question. You win you get to ask me any question and I have to answer. And if you lose, you have to answer mine."

His stomach flipped, and he thought of just playing it off, then shrugged. How bad could one question be? And he was going to win.

Because they were painting this house gray. Now he had thirty minutes to come up with the perfect question while she loosened the muscles in his shoulder. Not a bad way to spend a night.

"I told you!" Ryann squealed as they picked out

the purple paint that the designer was begging the couple to consider as just an accent wall. "Sorry— that was way too close to your ear."

It was, and he didn't care. "Not a problem. Why have these two agreed to be on a show with designers they had no intention of listening to?"

"Money, ratings, as a dare," she said. "Who knows, but it did make for a far more interesting show. Most importantly..." Her lips were right his ear. "I was right—they're not gray-loving people."

She was. And he was a man of his word. "So, what is your question?" They'd gotten closer over the last few weeks—so much, but there was still a wall between them. A distance they seemed to be trying to keep in order to maintain the balance they had.

She leaned her head on his shoulder and took a deep breath. "What would you do if I kissed you?" Ryann's cheeks darkened, but she didn't look away.

That wasn't a question he'd been expecting. She shifted, the soft scent of her soap hitting his nose as he tried to see if any of the synapses in his brain would fire.

"Ryann..." He wanted to kiss her. Wanted so badly to hold her, to see if the magic they'd had in Hawaii, the magic that had created Ayla, was still there.

It was. He was nearly certain of it. But he didn't

want one night, didn't want to release the pressure because for him, it would still be there tomorrow.

"If you kiss me," he said, "I would kiss you back and then push you away. I don't want a night, Ryann. I want you. I want to give this a real go. I know you don't…"

"What if I did?"

Ryann's fingers twitched. From rubbing his shoulders, or because she wanted to do something else with her hands?

"What if…" Ryann paused. The quiet seconds stretching on forever between them. "What if I did want to see what happens with us? But you can't leave Ayla if we—"

He put his finger over her lips. "Ayla is my daughter. I will be in her life for the rest of my life. I swear it."

Then her lips were on his. The universe sang as she slid into his lap. His arms wrapped around her waist, anchoring her to him.

This was heaven, pure and simple. "Ryann…"

"I love when you say my name between kisses." She trailed her lips down his throat as he lifted the shirt over her head.

Her tan skin was perfection, but he saw her hesitate.

"Ryann…" Jackson put his hands on her hips. If she'd changed her mind, they'd stop.

"My body is different," she said. She grabbed

his hand, tracing it along one of the dark stretch marks on her belly. "Pregnancy and…umm."

"You're the most beautiful woman in the world." He traced his hands along the dark stretch marks. They'd probably lighten with time. But even if they didn't, they did nothing but add to her beauty.

"My breasts aren't sensitive like they were." Ryann bit her lips. "From feeding…"

"Then I get to rediscover what turns you on." That was a chore he was very much looking forward to completing.

"Jackson…" Ryann's mouth captured his. "You're so perfect."

No one was perfect. And he knew that he was devastatingly far from it. After all, if he'd been perfect his life would look so much different. People would have stayed.

Her fingers traced his chest before she lifted his shirt off. "If I remember correctly…" Her lips skimmed the hollow between his neck and shoulder, her tongue flicking just the right place.

She moved her hips, rubbing against his already painfully hard erection. "You are very hard."

He was. His body wanted nothing more than to rip the tiny white shorts from her body, slide into her and feel her crest into oblivion. But Jackson wasn't rushing a single moment of this.

"I haven't been with you in almost two years, sweetheart." He wrapped his hands through her hair, pulling her mouth to hers.

"I haven't been with anyone since you." She purred, "I feel like I might burst with need."

*Burst with need.*

There were no sexier words.

"I haven't been with anyone, either." Despite Knox's attempts to set him up with someone, no one had compared to the woman in his arms now.

Her tongue met his, and she wrapped her legs around his waist. When Jackson moved his hands to her bra strap, she grabbed his hand.

"I leak." She bit her lip, color that he knew had nothing to do with passion erupting across her features.

"Do you want to keep your bra on?" he asked. This evening was about pleasure. For both of them. He wanted Ryann to enjoy every minute.

"Yes."

"All right." He grinned and moved his hands to her shorts, the elastic band allowing him easy access to her bottom. "You are so gorgeous," he said.

Ryann let out a giggle before kissing him again. "I certainly feel that way with you."

"Good." He gripped her hips, sliding her off him and onto the couch. Jackson needed to taste her. He pulled the shorts off, and then the plain white panties dropped to the floor.

Lifting her legs, he ran his finger across her folds, enjoying the flickers of desire running through her dark gaze.

She lifted her hips, moaning as his thumb found her clit. "Jackson…"

His manhood screamed as she called out his name. Dipping his head, he ran his tongue along her folds before suckling her. Ryann bucked against him, panting out his name.

"I need you, Jackson!" She sat up, grabbing for his pants, unbuttoning them and releasing his manhood.

He was so close to losing himself just from her touch.

"Jackson…" She pulled him close, then paused. "I don't have condoms."

He took a deep breath. He hadn't carried a spare condom in his wallet in years. "Then tonight is just about you."

He bent his head again, capturing her mouth. He wanted her, but waiting wouldn't kill him.

"Jackson." His name echoed in the room as she came again. Then she sat up, kissing him the whole time.

"It's about you, too." Her mouth trailed down his neck, down his chest, his stomach. She pulled his jeans and boxers off in one touch.

Then her mouth was on him. "Ryann…" Jackson took a deep breath as she ran her fingers over his shaft, moving with her mouth in a way that was as close to divine as possible.

"Sweetheart." He gripped the couch as his orgasm overtook him.

# CHAPTER NINE

JACKSON ROLLED OVER, his hand reaching for Ryann, only to find an empty pillow. He blinked, then stretched. His back and neck were sore, but it was like the feeling the day after a good deep-tissue massage. Ryann certainly knew what she was doing with her fingers…and her mouth.

They'd spent the night pleasuring each other. It had been a lovely experience. One he planned to repeat, once he had condoms. Now, though, he needed to find Ryann.

If Ayla had gotten up last night, he'd not heard her. Pulling on his boxers, he went in search of Ryann and Ayla. The baby's nursery was empty and so was the living room. They were probably just running an errand.

Jackson went back to the bedroom to look at his phone. No message. All right, look in the kitchen.

No message there, either. His skin prickled as his brain reminded him of all the times he'd woken up alone. Not alone in his place, where it was expected, but alone at a foster home or on the few occasions when his mother had had custody.

It had never been a good sign. He'd had two families who'd taken their biological kids out to breakfast without telling him. When his case worker had showed up, he'd been told to pack his bags.

The case worker had been sweet each time, but the message had been clear: *you're not enough—get your stuff.* It was weird how he hadn't considered that for years and now it was all his brain could remember.

His chest tightened. He was an adult, forty years old with a doctorate in nursing. This was a morning errand. Nothing more. Breathe.

*Breathe!*

The front door opened. "Jackson?"

Oxygen filled his lungs as Ryann rounded the corner with Ayla in her car seat in one hand and a bag of groceries in the other. "I thought you might still be asleep. Knox said you like to sleep in."

"Knox?" He wiped his face, trying to clear the cobwebs of panic from his brain.

"Yeah. Are you okay?"

"Fine." Jackson took a deep breath. Damn, he hadn't had a panic attack in years. And he wasn't having one now—not when everything was going so well.

"Not sure I believe that," Ryann said. "But yes,

I texted Knox this morning to find out your favorite doughnut."

"Doughnut?" He'd never been a huge breakfast person. He usually grabbed coffee, or tea now, and a granola bar. Mostly because he usually slept until it was time to leave for work.

Or he had before Ryann had walked back into his life with a cute bundle of joy on her hip.

"Yep. I didn't just want to buy contraception." Ryann laughed and raised both her brows in a funny motion. "I'm turning forty this year. I have a six-month-old, and there is almost no one there, but somehow walking in to grab only condoms made me feel like someone was looking over my shoulder the whole time."

"Like your mother was watching?" Jackson lifted Ayla from her car seat, kissing her cheek. He'd never had a parent who cared about what he did, but he'd heard friends at school joke about it.

*Or complain.*

Never realizing how lucky they'd been to have parents who worried, who were frustrated when they made bad choice, who wanted the absolute best for them. It was a gift you only really understood when you were outside looking in.

"No. My mother would never judge contraception," Ryann said as she chuckled. She pulled a chocolate cake doughnut from the container, then lifted a pastry that was marked as dairy and wheat free. "Figured you wouldn't eat it if I didn't have a treat, too."

He might not have. So far, he'd stuck to her diet exclusively, except for the tots she'd brought home. Ayla was doing so much better, too. So now it was time to start adding back in a food a week to see if they could identify the item, or items, that upset her.

"So your mother wouldn't have judged you for buying contraception?" Jackson was always fascinated by parental reactions.

"My mother gave me the talk, as it was, at twelve," Ryann said. She bit into her pastry and gave a sigh. "Not sure this is that good or if I'm just missing doughnuts!"

Twelve wasn't that young, and it was good for parents to have an open communication line. But there was something about the phrasing that made him shudder.

Ayla giggled and reached for the pastry in Ryann's hand.

"No, sweet girl, you're not big enough for this, and it might hurt your belly." She tapped their daughter's nose. "My mother would say it was no big deal and give her a little piece, damn the consequences." Ryann shuddered. "At twelve, she gave me six boxes of condoms."

"Six!" Jackson shook his head. "Did she not realize they expire?"

"Oh, she knew. But Mom is a free spirit," she

said. "At least that's what she calls herself. I call her wildly irresponsible. The woman let me do whatever I wanted."

"I guess you plan to be super strict with Ayla?" Jackson asked. He wasn't opposed to rules. Boundaries were helpful, but you could overcompensate, too.

"Not super strict. But I do want to know what she is doing. And protect her."

*Protect her.*

"Your mom didn't protect you?" He'd seen some of the worst the world had to offer—both in foster care and in medical work. Jackson would do everything possible to keep their daughter safe.

But experiences were important, too. And hurt happened. No life was lived without it. Ensuring his daughter always had a safe place to land was his priority.

"My mom wanted to be my friend. And she wanted to laugh and do whatever she wanted. And she rarely wanted to pay bills or keep house or pay attention to schoolwork."

"And yet you're a surgeon. An orthopedic surgeon," he said. That was impressive as hell.

"Yep. I succeeded, but I struggled. And I never felt safe," she said. "Ayla will never feel that way. She is never going to be hurt."

That wasn't possible. Ryann had to know that. But pressing the point now wouldn't do any good. Instead, he held out his hand to her, pulling her close. His little family. "Thank you for the dough-nut."

"It's almost the best way to start the day." She winked at him, then playfully covered Ayla's ears. "Tomorrow we'll do the best way."

His body heated as her lips brushed his.

"You look happy." Miranda closed her locker door and leaned against the locker bank. "In fact, you're glowing."

"Don't say that." Ryann tossed a surgical cap at her. "The last time someone said I was glow-ing I got an eight-pound baby girl."

"Oh!" Miranda shook her head and made a waving sound with her hands toward Ryann. "I release any of that energy. I release any of that en-ergy." She shrugged as Ryann raised a brow. "My sister swears by energies. No idea, but no wishing babies around here."

"So there won't be a little Miranda or Knox dressed as a surgeon on Halloween in a few years?"

"Nope. And Knox would shudder as hard as me. Jackson is the one that always wanted a fam-ily, and now he has one."

*He does.*

"I wanted a family, too." The words felt funny as she let them out. But it was true. When she was alone and wondering where her mother was, she'd dreamed of having her own family, one that loved her.

In the brief times she'd gotten that dream, she'd clung to it tightly hoping this time it would last forever. Except it never did.

"Well, Knox and I are family. Us and Icy—my cat, who kind of likes Knox. He would argue that she puts up with him. I would say that Icy putting up with you is her liking you."

"Drama-queen cat?"

"Yes." Miranda's vigorous nods were silly.

The light moment was one Ryann hadn't shared with another woman in so long.

"But I can never tell Icy that." Miranda giggled. "Do you have any pets?"

"No." She'd had a lizard once. Sort of. She'd begged for a turtle. Ryann wasn't sure why now. The whims of a child.

Her mother had said maybe, then she'd come home with a bug-catching kit. Not exactly the same. Or even in the same ballpark.

"Maybe one day. But right now, a six-month-old is plenty of excitement."

"Ryann?" Jackson's voice on the other side of the locker room door nearly made her jump. She and Miranda instinctively looked at their pagers as they both raced to the door.

"What?"

"Mr. Nigili's having the surgery." He was beaming so bright.

"Jackson, I thought something was terribly wrong," Ryann said. "We both did!"

His smile made her desire to lightly push him disappear. This was good news.

"Not sure I'd say *terribly*, but you should know better, Jackson." Miranda pulled her left arm in front of her, stretching it, then doing the other. "Time to start rounds!"

"Ryann, this is good news."

"It is like you're reading my mind." She winked. She was a little stunned. The man had seemed more determined to avoid surgery than just about any patient she'd ever seen.

"Sometimes the unexpected is good news." Jackson put an arm around her shoulder and squeezed tightly before releasing her.

"Sometimes," she said. Unfortunately, it was often an emergency or tragedy. If one were to rate the likelihood that an excited call in the hospital was good news versus bad the metrics would look tragic.

Looking at her phone, she frowned. "Wait, I don't have a message from the office. Is he not on my schedule?"

"He will be. As soon as the scheduler gets it on there." Jackson put his hands in front of him and mimicked taking a deep breath. "Think positive thoughts."

"Why do you know before his surgeon?" That

didn't make sense, even if she was only focusing on positive things.

"Because he had questions about the anesthesia. The office called me and patched him through. I answered everything. He thanked me and told me to make sure it goes exactly like I told him."

"And you told him you would?" Ryann was stunned. Doctors rarely spoke in absolutes. Routine procedures became emergencies. Things that looked unsurvivable sometimes beat the odds. You could never count the fates out.

"I told him I would do my best." Jackson bopped her nose. "That's all I can do. Ryann—"

"Right. Of course that's what you did. You're perfect." She blew out a breath. Jackson was so close to it.

"No, not perfect," he said. "But I do a pretty good job. After we were done, the scheduler picked him back up. I suspect you will see him on your books shortly."

"Thanks." Ryann hit his hip with hers. "And you are pretty perfect." She liked telling him that. No one had. She knew that.

Rationally she knew no one met the actual definition of the word *perfection*, but Jackson was pretty damn close.

He gave a her a playful salute. "Happy to be of service." Jackson looked at his watch, then said, "Time to prep a little one for tonsil removal."

Jackson headed down the hallway. Watching

him walk away was not difficult. His backside was delicious.

Still, her belly twisted. What if he walked away…

It was an intrusive thought. A small one. Easy enough to ignore. Mostly. Clearing her throat, she moved her fingers, doing anything to change her brain's patterns and trick it into focusing on something else.

"Dr. Oliver." Dr. Jenks raised his hand as he started toward her. "I just got paged. They need two orthos in the ER. Now."

"I didn't get paged." She looked down. She was on call here today.

"Nope." Dr. Jenks motioned for her to follow him as he started for the stairwell. "They tried reaching Lewis Anderson first—he's hospital staff. However, he's somewhere else, so you're with me."

"Any idea what we're walking into?" she asked.

"The ER didn't specify, just called it an emergency. Always a good sign." The words were dripping with a sarcasm she understood. The ER was the most overworked place in the hospital. When they said it was an emergency, they had a whole different meaning of that word.

"Dr. Jenks, Dr. Oliver. Here." Mandy Plar, an ER resident, flagged them down. "I have a little boy, age three, in bed six with a broken left tibia. Was playing with his brother and fell off the porch. Can you follow me into the consult room?"

"All right." Dr. Jenks looked at Ryann, and she just shrugged as they followed Mandy. That sounded like a terrible day for the little boy and his family, but broken bones were not uncommon in children. "Is the break that bad?"

A fall from the porch could break a leg, but it often didn't need more than a plaster cast.

"I don't know what I'm looking at, but I'm pretty sure it isn't cancer. Which is why I called the bone guys...and gals." Mandy pulled the X-ray up on a tablet, then pushed it to the consult room's big screen.

Technology!

Ryann blinked as she stared at the image. "How old did you say the patient is?"

"Elijah is three—just had a birthday. Despite the pain, he'll tell you he had balloons at his party." Mandy smiled. "Kids are fun."

"CPT is rare. Extremely rare. And it almost always presents before three." Dr. Jenks ran his finger over the bow in the leg. "I've never seen this."

"Me either."

"Great—something you know but haven't seen." Mandy clapped. "Now clue in the ER doc?"

"It's congenital pseudarthrosis of the tibia, or CPT." Ryann pointed to the bow in the tibia. "It's a rare presentation, and it means Elijah will need multiple surgeries to lengthen his leg."

"Or amputation." Dr. Jenks shook his head. "Only three."

"Amputation is typically reserved for failed reconstructions." Ryann wanted to shake Dr. Jenks. Amputations happened. They were things that orthopedic surgeons were trained to perform early on. They were also the last resort. They hadn't even met Elijah or his parents.

"Amputations happen with this diagnosis," Dr. Jenks said. "Not unrarely, either."

*Unrarely isn't a word.*

That wasn't a line that needed to be stated so Ryann kept it to herself.

Dr. Jenks wasn't wrong. However, the parents had come in today thinking their little boy was going to get a cast and were probably wondering how they were going to keep a toddler calm and off the foot for six weeks or so. Now they were finding out their life was changing.

There were worse diagnoses to receive, but that didn't change the fact that this was a difficult day.

The fact that the first fracture hadn't occurred until he was closer to three might mean his bone would heal easier. It could also mean that this first break would be so bad grafting the bone back would be difficult. It was far too early to tell.

"Right now, the important thing is to let them know what we see. Because this treatment isn't happening in the ER." Ryann looked at Mandy. "You need to refer them to an ortho. Splint the broken bone. There's nothing else that can be done today."

"Come with me to talk to the parents?" Mandy asked, looking at the X-ray.

"You don't need both of us." Dr. Jenks lifted a hand and headed off.

He was right. This wasn't an emergency consult, but Mandy was young and this was a condition she might never see again. Even as an orthopedic surgeon, this was likely the only time Ryann would see it.

If the boy came to the Lowery Group, one of the surgeons specializing in legs would be recommended. This wasn't a condition Ryann was ever likely to treat, but she could answer some questions now. And assure the parents that while this was a tricky diagnosis their son was going to live a close to normal life.

It might not be overly comforting today, but she'd do her best.

"So, what food are we thinking of introducing first?" Jackson laughed as Ayla reached for his spoon. The cereal they'd given her over the last week was working well. It was rice-based instead of grain, but she was tolerating it.

"Maybe bananas? Or sweet potatoes?" Those were safe foods because Ryann had eaten them and Ayla hadn't had a reaction.

He bopped Ayla's nose, then turned to Ryann.

She was looking at her phone, focusing on it intently. "Ryann?"

"Did you know that an allergy to bananas can mean you're allergic to latex?"

"No." He'd spent time in many specialties but never dealt with allergists. It was an important, vital area of medicine but held little attraction for him.

"Did you have a patient with a latex allergy today that was discovered through bananas?" he asked. He really wasn't sure where the train of thought was coming from, but some days were hard at the hospital.

And it didn't take a tragedy for the day to be heavy.

"No. I saw CPT today—a first." Ryann bit her lip as she looked up at him.

"CPT? Honey?" Jackson was certain she didn't mean chest physiotherapy, which helped cystic fibrosis patients break up the excess mucus in their lungs. What one specialty meant with acronyms did not always transfer.

"Congenital pseudarthrosis of the tibia." She moved her fingers like he'd seen her do several times—twitching the first few fingers, then pulling at them. He wasn't even sure she was aware of the motion.

"All right. I have doctorate, but that is not a diagnosis I know. Rare?"

"Very. I'll probably never see it again in my

life," Ryann said. "The little boy broke his leg jumping off a deck. And it probably won't heal. Not without pins and grafts, and he's in for multiple surgeries until he stops growing just to keep his left leg close to the same length as his right."

"Did the parents miss any signs?" he asked. It sounded like a rough diagnosis, but he wasn't sure what it had to do with bananas and latex.

"No, there were no signs. Nothing they could have done. They did exactly what they should have done—brought him to the ER with a broken leg." Ryann put her hands on her hips and blew out a breath. "Sorry. This doesn't have a point. I just… I don't know. You asked about food and said bananas, and my brain just leapt." She tapped the side of her head and rolled her eyes. "Nothing like thoughts running wild, right?"

Maybe that was all it was, but maybe not. "Nothing wrong with a wild thought every once in a while."

Ryann rubbed her arms. "But…"

"But maybe its anxiety." It was a common enough condition, and Ryann saw things the general public didn't every day.

"It isn't."

The certainty in her voice surprised him.

"It isn't a problem if you have anxiety. Lots of people do." Jackson stepped a little closer. "In fact, more than sixty percent of people report—"

"I know the stats, Jackson. You don't have to

play nurse with me." Ryann reached for Ayla. "It was a rough day, that's all."

She kissed his cheek. "Now, how about we get this one down and we spend a fun night watching the home and garden channel? I've got a few episodes of *Tiny Home, Big Dreams* saved. I know how much you enjoy it."

"I enjoy spending time with you." Jackson kissed her cheek.

It was only when the show ended that he realized they'd never gotten back to the conversation about which food to start Ayla on.

# CHAPTER TEN

RYANN RAN HER hand along Jackson's solid thigh. He let out a soft sigh in his sleep. She couldn't take her eyes from the stunning man. In the light of the early morning, everything seemed relaxed and easy.

The worry that was her constant companion hovered in the very back of the mind as she traced patterns on his dark skin. She wasn't necessarily trying to wake the hot man in her bed, though as his manhood sprang to attention her mind turned to all the delicious ways her body sang when he touched her.

"Jackson Peters." She whispered his name, loving the sound of his name on her tongue. He was such a beautiful man.

"Good morning," he said. His eyes weren't open, and his tone still held all the vestiges of sleep.

"Morning." She dropped a kiss onto his nose. "Did I wake you?" Ryann gripped his manhood, stroking the hard skin. "I didn't mean to."

"I think you got exactly what you want." Jackson grinned as he shifted to his side. His fingers found her folds and stroked her, each pass mimicking the motion she made on him.

When his thumb found her most sensitive spot, she couldn't control the gasp. "I want you." She shuddered as he matched every rhythm on her body.

"Mmm-hmm." Jackson nuzzled against her shoulder, molding his lips to the spot by her throat that sent tingles from the tip of her head to the bottom of her feet. "I want to savor you."

She pushed on his shoulder, rolling him to his back. "We have a six-month-old who is sleeping but might wake any moment," she said. "Savoring is something we get to do in a few years."

*A few years...*

The phrase was out and she held her breath, but Jackson didn't seem bothered by it. They hadn't talked long-term plans. They were in each other's lives for forever because of Ayla. But this...just like in Hawaii...they'd slipped into it.

Because it felt so natural.

"Ryann..." Jackson ran a hand along the outside of her breast.

She whimpered as his spellbinding touch held her in rapture.

Grabbing a condom, she slid it down his length, then she slipped down his erection, slowly taking him deep within.

His large hands wrapped around her waist, guiding her but not forcing her motions. Jackson looked at her like she was the definition of beauty, his eyes holding hers as she took him.

Ryann let out a breath when they were fully joined. She hadn't misspoken—Ayla could wake any moment. But right now, in this moment, she agreed with Jackson.

Savor…

Her body molded to his. She was a siren, a goddess, a mythical female united in harmony with him.

Jackson's thumb found her clitoris again. He filled her, and she arched, enjoying every bead of pleasure.

"Ryann." His voice was gruff.

He was on the edge of orgasm; she was on the edge, too, but now she wanted this to last forever.

Their daughter had other plans.

Her screech echoed just as Ryann tipped over pleasure's edge. Jackson came seconds later.

"Guess you were right," he said. His lips brushed hers as she slid from him. "You think it's five years or ten before we can safely savor?" Jackson chuckled as he rolled over and waited for her to clean up before following.

*Five or ten years.*

Tears coated her eyes. Could this be her life… forever?

She wanted to hope so.
*Please.*

Ryann looked at the jars of baby food Jackson had pulled out last night. Pureed bananas, sweet potatoes, peas and carrots were all in tiny jars with cute cartoon baby faces. Ayla was able to swallow the rice cereal they'd had her on for a few weeks, so this was the next step. Today was a big deal, but not as big a deal as Ryann's brain was screeching.

"Are we trying something for breakfast?" Jackson walked in with Ayla on his hip.

She was wearing a little yellow dress with flowers, and he'd put a headband in her curly hair. She was happy and content, and the image of her in Jackson's arms was a memory Ryann wanted to hold on to for forever.

"I thought maybe." The jars were right there. It was pureed food, and Ayla would have to try something new eventually. Today was as good a day as any. And if there was any reaction, she and Jackson would watch her. Not like her own mom had.

But what if Ayla's tongue itched? That was the feeling Ryann got with peaches. The allergy made her itch, and if she ate them in high enough doses, she got hives.

It wasn't life-threatening, only uncomfortable. But her mother had told her it was in her head, that the itchy feeling was in her brain—when she'd listened to Ryann at all. Often, she'd waved away the concern.

"Ryann, why is this making you anxious?" Jackson asked.

"She can't tell us if something is wrong," Ryann whispered.

The odds of any of these fruits causing a reaction was slim. But rare outcomes happened. Look at Elijah—his parents had thought he'd broken a bone, only to find out he had a chronic illness that would impact the rest of his life.

"Yes, she can." Jackson's hand rubbed Ryann's lower back, reminding her that she wasn't alone in this.

"Not with words. Not with statements that let us know when she's uncomfortable. Look at the diet I've been on. Her stomach must have ached when I breastfed her with dairy in my system. It must have." And she'd been too tired to catch it until the diaper rash and screams had become unmistakable.

If she'd noticed sooner, her daughter wouldn't have been in such pain.

"Ryann—"

"My tongue itches if I eat peaches." She needed him to understand that this wasn't just an anxiety reaction. She knew what she was talking about, knew the uncomfortable feeling it left her with, even if it didn't send her into an anaphylaxis reaction.

"Oh." Jackson kissed the top of her head. "Well, peach allergies aren't uncommon in those with Mediterranean heritage. Do you know if your mother or father had an allergy?"

Ryann couldn't contain the sad laugh. "Jackson, my mom never discussed anything that might be helpful or that didn't have to do with her. She still doesn't. She told me until I was eleven that that peach allergy was all in my head."

"In your head." Jackson lifted up Ayla, made a funny face for her, then walked her over to her swing.

After strapping her in and getting the swing going, he moved back to Ryann and pulled her close. "I know she can't say *Mommy, my tongue is itchy*, but there are other ways that she'll let us know."

"Like pushing away a spoon or spitting it out," she said. "Babies do that for things they love when they're testing boundaries. It isn't that simple." There were a million ways for parents to miss things, even when they looked and monitored all the time.

"Yes, and those boundaries are important whether they are because she doesn't like the food, because she isn't hungry, because she is hungry but doesn't want that right now, or because her tongue itches," he said. "We should try the same food with her eight times—that's what the parenting books recommend. That way if it is a new texture or something she might change her mind. But we don't like every food, and neither will she."

"You read a parenting book?" Ryann pursed her lips as her eyes coated with tears for the second time today. This man really got to her. In all the right ways.

"No." Jackson winked. "So far I've read *four* parenting books—well, read two the traditional way and listened to two with audiobook credits."

"Perfection, thy name is Jackson." She'd been with Ayla since the first twist in her belly. The first breath. First diapers, baths, breastfeeding. And yet she wasn't nearly as confident as the man standing beside her.

"Not perfect," he said, the tone shifting, but the darkening of his cheeks was unmistakable.

He liked being called perfect, and for her, he'd certainly been.

"So..." Jackson gestured to the jars. "What's the first pick?"

Ryann looked at them, then over at her daughter. "What if we let Ayla pick? All of these are good starts, so we can make a game of it."

"That's a perfect plan."

The pea puree hit Jackson square in the eye, and if his glasses hadn't protected him Ayla would have scored a direct hit to his eyeball.

"I did tell you not to try the peas again. I know

the baby book suggests introducing the food to them several times, but she hates peas."

Ryann didn't even attempt to cover the grin on her face as she poured their tea into travel mugs. She'd been sprayed with peas last night and swore it was still in her hair after her shower. It hadn't been—Jackson had made sure of that for her before going to bed.

"Ah. Ah." Ayla pointed to the cupboard where the banana puree she adored was hidden out of sight. The kid liked carrots, would tolerate the sweet potatoes, but the peas…those were simply weapons in her tiny fingers.

Ryann wandered to the cabinet and pulled out the carrots. "I know that at six and half months she can't technically be a tiny dictator."

"Oh, I think she certainly can. She just isn't trying to be." Jackson took the washcloth and the carrots from Ryann, opening the can as soon as his glasses were clear —again.

He started feeding Ayla as Ryann whispered the day's plan to herself.

"The surgery is going to go fine. Tell Mama that she's going to do great." Jackson spooned the carrots slipping down Ayla's chin back into her mouth.

"I know it will be fine."

He wasn't sure she heard her heavy sigh at the end of her sentence. "It's standard."

"I know," she said.

"The patient is healthy." Jackson could list a million reasons why Mr. Nigili's hand surgery would turn out fine. Unfortunately, there were a dozen reasons it might not.

A dozen reasons compared to a million didn't sound like much—unless you were the patient or the one holding the scalpel.

"I know." Ryann looked at her watch and tapped her foot. They weren't due at the hospital for another hour. And he was technically due first, as he needed to get the sedation prep done.

But she was already antsy.

"It's standard. Minor in the grand scheme of things, but he's terrified." Ryann pulled her curly hair out of the ponytail and then put it back up again. "I mean, he's heard *standard* before."

His wife's surgery had been back surgery. Even routine back surgery was not routine. The same argument they'd made that day in her office to Mr. Nigili hung in the back of Jackson's throat. It hadn't done any good that day, and he doubted it would help here.

"Sometimes I just wish life had a fast-forward button." Ryann playfully picked up the TV remote and pointed it at herself. "Nope. Fast-forward doesn't work on me." Her dark gaze found his. "Want me to try it on you?"

"Don't you dare." Jackson tossed the rag with peas at her, deliberately aiming a foot in front of her feet so it didn't cause any actual damage. "I'm having too much fun in my life. I already missed months—I'm not rushing anything else."

Last night when she'd joked that it would be years before they could trust their intimate times wouldn't be interrupted by a baby's cry had been the third happiest of his life.

Third only to meeting Ryann and then meeting Ayla. Two things that could never be topped.

"Yes, yes, Mr. Perfect wants to live every moment," she said. She grabbed the rag and kissed his cheek on the way to drop it in the sink.

"Not perfect." Jackson grinned at Ayla, enjoying Ryann's favorite description of him a little too much. It wasn't true, and that was something people always seemed to realize about him at some point.

And then they disappeared from his life.

Jackson blinked, forcing the uncomfortable thoughts away. They were both just antsy today. Or maybe Ryann's antsy was rubbing off on him.

"Spall!" The sound his daughter made was the only warning he got before she grabbed the spoon and threw it over the high chair onto the floor.

"I guess breakfast is over, then." Jackson kissed her head, reached for the spoon and handed it back so she could throw it a few more times.

Ryann picked it up on the fourth throw. "Time to go," she said. She bent down and kissed the top of Ayla's head while passing him the wet rag.

"Making me the bad guy that has to clean her

up?" he said. How a tiny human could manage to fight off a wet rag so well while strapped to a chair was an answer only the heavens could give.

"I'm the bad guy putting away the spoon. We each play our roles." Ryann's smile showed that she knew which was the better role…and this morning she'd taken it.

The music floated through the surgical suite as a nurse pressed a cloth to Ryann's forehead. The sweat on her brow was from the surgical lights, nothing more, because this was going routinely.

"I'm going to close." Ryann looked to Jackson and saw him nod as his gaze stayed focused on the patient.

Everything about this had been textbook. There were two surgical residents who'd asked to watch from the gallery, and what they'd seen today was how surgery was supposed to go.

"Closed," Ryann said as she passed the tool to the nurse at her side and stepped back from Mr. Nigili. She'd be able to give his daughter the good news, and when he woke his family would be at his side.

"All right, let's get him to recovery." Jackson's deep voice echoed in the room, and she looked over her shoulder.

The man was hot in anything. But the blue surgical scrubs that looked drab on everybody else made him mouthwatering. Because he was in his element here.

In the surgical suite he was confident, in total control, and it was intoxicating.

She wasted no time giving Mr. Nigili's family the update and letting them know that a nurse would be out to take them to his recovery room shortly.

Today was exactly the kind of day a surgeon wanted.

"Ryann!" The call came from behind her.

Knox was running. Never a good sign.

"ER page—all hands on deck."

*Damn.* When was she going to remember that the good times always were warning signs of the bad to come?

Knox pushed open the ER doors, and the sound of chaos echoed through the halls. To the uneducated eye, the ER always looked a little chaotic, but it was a well-oiled machine that functioned in that kind of chaos.

This kind. The all hands on deck, the waiting for multiple traumas. Trauma situations like this were what television show thrived on and what every doctor feared.

"Crane collapsed downtown. Four inbound with internal injuries. Two head traumas, one amputation and others to be determined!"

The head nurse's call echoed in the hallway

as Miranda ran up next to them, followed by Dr. O'Sullivan and Dr. Jenks.

"Are they all coming here? What about County Hospital?" Knox crossed his arms, them uncrossed them. The wait was the worst. Knowing each moment counted in trauma but unable to start supporting the patients until they arrived and were assessed.

"Every hospital in the city with a trauma bay will be full. And it still might not be enough. It is going to be a long, hard day." Dr. O'Sullivan let out a sigh as the first siren sounded in the distance. "All the elective surgeries are canceled, and I've got every available suite readying to put patients under."

"The crane hit a building, going through a boardroom before crashing to the crowded street. Many were hit while videotaping and the debris field." One of the nurses called as she started passing out details for the cases they knew were headed to Hope.

Dr. O'Sullivan looked at his watch. "The first priorities are the internal injuries. I'll take the first one, Knox number two, then Miranda, then Stephen. Amputations go to Ryann and then Dr. Jenks. After that, we each handle whatever triage sends us next."

The siren sounded in the parking lot. "All right, people. Here we go."

# CHAPTER ELEVEN

*EXHAUSTING* WAS NOT a descriptor for today. *Exhausting* didn't even come close to the feeling deep in Jackson's bones as he stared at what was hopefully the screens of his last patient.

"Everything all right over there?" Ryann's voice was strained. She'd done six surgeries in the last twelve hours. This one was minor—reattachment of ligaments torn when a woman had pushed her daughter out of the way of the crane.

The woman was a hero. The video of the incident had already gone viral—at least according to the nurse, who'd heard it from one of the techs, who'd heard it from someone in triage, who'd heard it from a patient. Or that was the trajectory of the rumor.

"She's fine," Jackson said. She'd waited longer than any of the other patients, which meant she'd been in pain for longer than any of them but also meant that she'd been stable enough to wait.

"The tendon was already inflamed. Her shoulder must have hurt for months." The nurse's mused thoughts were probably designed more to keep her focused following the long day than to produce actual conversation.

"We're almost done, Renee." Ryann asked for a scalpel and then let out an expletive.

"She's still out," Jackson said. He wasn't sure what Ryann was seeing, but his monitors were all showing the patient was stable, which was most important.

"The ulnar nerve is entrapped."

"At her shoulder?" Renee sounded shocked.

"It's less common than wrist or elbow entrapment, but it still happens," Ryann said. "But it means this went from a short tendon repair...to an entrapment repair. How did I miss this on the X-ray?"

"It's been a long day." Jackson could tell from her tone that she was mad at herself. Ryann's perfectionist streak ran deep.

"It's standard," she muttered.

It was. Sort of. If it had been an X-ray of the wrist or elbow it would have been spotted immediately. Still, Ryann felt she should have seen it. But then so should've the ER doctor. She wasn't solely at fault here.

"She'll be okay." Jackson kept his voice level. He was a colleague in this situation, not her...his mind blanked on terms.

They'd never actually discussed what they were. He was practically living at her condo. They were sleeping together, and not just in the intimate way but falling asleep in each other's arms. They were raising their daughter.

Boyfriend...partner...baby daddy? Certainly not that last one. It was technically true, but he wasn't a fan of the term.

"The compression is significant. I'll have to clear a larger area." Ryann sighed. "She must have used all the force she could to push her daughter out of the way."

Nerve compression caused weakness, tingling and eventually muscular wasting.

"That's what moms do." The nurse's voice was bright, and he heard the awkwardness that followed when Ryann didn't say anything.

He was glad the nurse seemed to have had that kind of mom. When she was an adult, Jackson hoped Ayla would have the exact same reaction.

Growing up without such a figure hurt. Children knew when their mom didn't want them or was exasperated by them. Everything reinforced the societal expectations that moms protected their children.

And neither of their mothers had done that. In fact, those women had pretty much taken society's expectations and stuffed them.

"She should feel better once she heals." Ryann cleared her throat. "I need my forehead wiped, please."

She was tired. If today had gone the way they'd

expected, they'd have been back at the condo, eating dinner, getting Ayla ready for her nighttime routine. The babysitter had been alerted to the emergency, though it was apparently all over the news. Ayla would be with her until they were cleared to leave.

"Why didn't I catch this?" Ryann's words were barely audible over the pop music they'd piped into the surgical suit. Every song was above eighty beats per minute, a weird trick to force the brain to stay active.

"Are you close to closing?" He rolled his shoulders. They both needed some sleepy-time tea and decompression.

"Is there a problem?" she asked.

*Not with the patient.*

"No, she's handling anesthesia well." It was Ryann who Jackson was worried about. She blamed herself for things others let slide away.

"All right, I've got about twenty minutes left."

Then they were finishing up the paperwork and going home. They'd both earned the rest, and he was going to spend the evening reminding Ryann that she didn't need to never make mistakes to be the best version of herself.

Jackson flipped on the news and looked at the damage the crane had done in downtown Phoenix. The tallest crane in Arizona...at least until yesterday afternoon. It was a miracle only one person had lost their life, though dozens of lives had changed forever.

The anchor's solemn tone shifted, and he offered a smile. "There are many harrowing videos from the tragedy. However, one video is giving people a sense of awe and showing the world a mother's love."

Jackson reached for the remote; Ryann didn't need to see this.

"No, wait. That's Priscilla." She grabbed the remote before he could. Slowing the screen down to half speed.

"Remember when we had to watch the television in real time?" Jackson leaned toward Ayla. "Once upon a time, you had to watch a show when it was on, and if you missed something…oh, well."

Ryann gave him a look, but she didn't say anything. "Look. Right there." She pointed to the grimace Priscilla made before she pushed her daughter.

A few milliseconds later the shrapnel hit Priscilla and then screen of the camera.

"That video already has over six million views." The anchor's voice started then stopped as Ryann ran the video back.

"The pain in her shoulder was there before."

"Just like you said it would be." Jackson reached for Ayla as she made a face that was nothing more than a warning sign. They had about three minutes to get her fed before she decided to try to bring the walls of the house down with her cries.

He walked into the kitchen and grabbed the bananas. "If you think about it, she's lucky the crane went down in a weird way."

"How?" The horrified look on Ryann's face made it clear what she thought of his statement.

"It's clear she was in pain before the incident, and that pain was picked up by the ER."

"Who misdiagnosed a tendon tear." Ryann crossed her arms. "Then I looked and didn't…"

"Let me finish before you castigate yourself for something that is not your fault." Jackson took a deep breath. That was not what he'd meant to say. "I just mean, let me explain."

Ryann rolled her hand toward him, fire blazing in her eyes.

"She was in pain for a while, maybe years. The crane crash means that her injury gets fixed, and it's likely the crane company, or rather their insurance, will have to pay for it. Those are bright points."

"A crane collapsed!" Ryann looked at the television, then back at him. "The thing fell on twenty people, and it hit five in the boardroom, the shrapnel struck an additional six and then there was the four car accidents caused from rubbernecking."

"I know." Jackson held up the spoon with banana puree enjoying Ayla's smile. This tragedy hadn't touched her but others would. It was unfortunate but no life was lived without pain and loss. "I'm just looking for the silver lining."

"Silver linings are a myth." Ryann sucked in a deep breath, then turned on her heel. "I'm taking a shower."

He stared after her for a second, then looked at Ayla. "Any ideas?"

Ayla made a few gibberish noises.

"Sounds reasonable." Jackson tapped her nose, keeping the smile he didn't really feel on his face for her.

The sun was streaming through the window when Ryann rolled over. Her hand hit Jackson's empty pillow, and she immediately sat up. She'd told him she hadn't wanted to talk about what had upset her yesterday morning.

He'd agreed. Half-heartedly.

She could tell he'd wanted to argue, wanted to have out whatever issue had been standing between them. But the issue wasn't his fault. Nothing about what he'd done or said was wrong.

Hell, the man was perfection. She almost wished he'd forced the argument. Then she might feel better about overreacting to his statement about silver linings.

*Don't get upset; look for the silver lining.*

Her mother's voice echoed in her head as Ryann slid out of bed. She needed to find Jackson, apologize for getting upset and then for spending the day quiet and upset.

"Morning." Jackson handed her a cup of tea as soon as she stepped into the kitchen. Ayla was asleep in her swing.

"She got up about two hours ago," he said. "Wanted a bottle and then went back down."

Jackson smiled at their daughter, answering the unasked question before Ryann's brain had even formed it.

Sometimes it was tough to live up to the flawlessness that was the man in front of her. "Aren't you mad at me?"

She'd spent yesterday brooding and rethinking and just sad. No, mad. She'd been mad at herself, mad at the world and mad at…

"Do you want me to be mad?" Jackson leaned against the counter.

"Maybe." That wasn't rational. "No. Of course I don't." She blew a curl away from her eye. "It's just… Don't you have anything in your past that you just can't stand now? A phrase, a food?"

"I try to keep the past in its place." Jackson shrugged.

Maybe he had put everything from his past in a nice box marked Do Not Open, but she wasn't able to.

"I… I…hate silver linings." She was tapping her fingers against the tea mug. "Not the actual things but the words. I hate that phrase." Ryann shook as she drew in a breath. "There's nothing positive about suffering, about resiliency."

She set the mug of tea down, worried that she might drop it or spill it as her hands shook. "*Resiliency* is a fancy term for surviving. What other choice do you have?"

"Ryann—"

"No. No. I don't want you to *Ryann* me in that sweet voice that tells me everything is going to be fine. I messed up. I didn't see it on the X-ray. I messed up. And…"

"And it happens. The patient, Priscilla, is fine. Better than fine. She is going to make a full recovery and have little to no pain moving forward." Jackson said. "Yes, you should have seen it. So should the ER doctor. So should her primary care physician."

"Her primary care physician wasn't there." Being pedantic wasn't a great look. But her argumentative side didn't seem to want to shut the hell up.

How many times had she just let words like this roll over her?

*Have you considered that your upbringing prepared you for the hectic life a surgeon leads?*

*Maybe everything happens for a reason and it made you the person you were supposed to be.*

*Ever thought that maybe the universe chose you for that life because you could handle it?*

All platitudes to make others feel better. If it

was a grand plan or something that made her stronger, then it was okay that she'd had a rough childhood. It was okay that people had missed the signs, let her fall through the cracks.

That made them feel better, not her.

"I looked at her records after surgery while you were finishing up your paperwork," Jackson said. "She's complained to her primary care physician about the weakness and tingling for almost two years. He told her to lose weight."

Now Ryann really was seeing red. Women's complaints were often overlooked. Add in someone who society labeled *fat* and you got a recipe for pushing aside any issues.

As much as she hated the term *silver lining*, this one actually did have one. For Priscilla.

"You looked at her records for me, didn't you?" Of course he would pick up on her beating herself up in the operating room. The man seemed to miss nothing.

"I looked at her records as her anesthesiologist," Jackson said. "We missed the nerve compression—I wanted to make sure there wasn't anything else."

*He doesn't miss anything.*

"This isn't your fault, Ryann. And she's fine."

"I know." That was the thing. She knew Priscilla was fine. She knew there was nothing she could have done once she'd gotten her open. But her brain kept playing things back, asking what-ifs that had no answers.

It kept looking for a sign she'd missed. Except in this case, it knew exactly what the sign was. The X-ray and what she'd missed in it. So it had a latch. Something to cling to.

"I know she's fine," Ryann said. "And I even know that given the day, there's nothing I could have done differently. I was looking for obstructions and broken bones on that X-ray, not nerve compression. She was the last patient on a day when triage saw the worst. I know all of that."

"But your brain won't shut off."

"Spoken like someone who can shut theirs off." Ryann shook her head. "I'm sorry. I don't know why I'm hyper-focusing on this."

"Maybe because it's the easy case to hyper-focus on, the one that turned out all right." He tilted his head.

Had he ever considered going into one of the therapy career fields? Ryann wondered. He'd be an excellent therapist.

And he was right. The night's other cases had not been nearly as straightforward. The change in those patient's lives less rosy.

She'd saved one hand from amputation…for now. But the odds were not in the gentleman's favor. And she'd had to amputate a teenager's foot. Priscilla's shoulder had been the easiest, the one where the oversight had mattered least.

"You should be a therapist, Mr. Perfect." Ryann took a deep breath, mentally releasing the anxious thoughts. Or trying to.

Jackson chuckled. "I never felt called to the mental health field. I love nursing, love learning. Most of it is listening."

"You're an excellent listener."

"Well, when no one listens to you growing up, you either listen to everyone or no one." Jackson grabbed the cup of tea she'd sat down and put it back into her hands.

"Jackson," she said, laying her hand over his. "I'm sorry no one listened to you."

"I turned out fine." He winked.

"Jackson..." It felt like he was close to giving her more information, to opening himself up to her. Outside of knowing that no one had responded well to his outreach on the DNA-matching sites, she knew next to nothing about his past. It was like he'd erected a solid wall around that part of his life. All of it locked away, never to be visited or discussed. But that didn't mean it didn't impact him.

"So do you think we should take Ayla to the balloon festival tomorrow?" he asked. "I know she's too little to get the full experience, but they are brightly colored."

"You don't have to change the subject." Ryann squeezed his hand.

"I'm not." He kissed her cheek. "There's nothing to discuss."

"I think there is," Ryann said, seeing his jaw twitch. It was the first time she'd seen him frustrated with her. And it was tiny, barely even noticeable.

"There isn't." He let out a heavy sigh. "I was foster-care kid. My parents abandoned me. My fiancée left me for reasons only she fully knows. I love my job, my daughter and…"

*And me?*

She saw words dance through his eyes, but he didn't say anything else.

"And?" Ryann shouldn't push, but she wanted to. She loved him. Maybe she had from the moment he'd sat on the plane next to her. Everything with Jackson came so easily.

Scarily easily. Like it was fate. Her mother would love that analogy.

"My life in general. It's pretty close to perfection." Jackson set his teacup down and pulled her close. "So, Ryann…"

Her heartbeat accelerated. He was going to say he loved her, going to kiss her. Maybe hearing those words, knowing someone like Jackson loved her would drive out the voices that never seemed to quite let her think she was enough.

"Do you think Ayla would like the balloon festival? Or should we find something inside so the heat doesn't get to her?"

"Oh…" Ryann blinked. Of course that was where this conversation was going.

Ayla let out a cry, and Jackson kissed Ryann's head, then went to get their daughter.

"Mommy is trying to figure out what we're going to do on our day off tomorrow." Then he looked at his phone. "Oh…um… Knox needs me."

"Is he okay?" Ryann took Ayla, hating that she was a little happy that he needed to leave. That would give her some time to compose herself, to get the feelings, the urge to tell him she loved him fully under control.

"I think so. He's being secretive, which probably means he's planned something for Miranda. The man's favorite hobby is spoiling the woman he loves."

"Sounds nice." Ryann nuzzled her head into Ayla's curls. "Let's get you changed, sweetie."

# CHAPTER TWELVE

JACKSON DRUMMED HIS fingers on the steering wheel as he drove up to Knox and Miranda's condo. He'd nearly told Ryann that he loved her this morning. He'd wanted to tell her. His entire soul ached with the desire.

But the woman was a flight risk. She hadn't even wanted to date him. She'd given into that urge, but would she worry about his love ending?

Her mother's relationships all seemed to evaporate after she and her partners pledged their undying love.

Jackson would love Ryann for the rest of his days. There wasn't a single doubt in his body. But Ryann's body was riddled with worry. He wouldn't add this to it. The second she told him she loved him he'd make sure she understood the depth of his own devotion.

But until then, he'd keep the feelings—and the worry—to himself.

Pulling up to the condo, Jackson couldn't stop his mouth from falling open. Outside, there were at least three dozen balloons and boxes upon boxes stacked. What had Knox gotten himself into?

He parked on the street, got out and wasn't surprised to see Knox look over a box as he heard the car door slam.

"What is going on?"

"That is a good question." Miranda sighed as she moved a box to the side. "Knox?"

"I won a bar in an online auction. Or rather, I won the bar's contents."

"That clears up nothing." Jackson looked at the boxes.

"I thought I was bidding on a vintage Maitland-Smith dartboard. I mean, that is what I was bidding on. Who clears out a bar for two grand?"

"Two grand?" Miranda's leaned against the box in front of her. "You spent two thousand dollars on a dartboard? Knox! You can get a super nice board—one that doesn't have holes in it—for less than a hundred."

"I know, but I mean, come on, sweetheart. A Maitland-Smith."

Jackson crossed his arms and didn't manage to catch the laugh in the back of his throat. "I don't think that means anything to anyone but you, man."

"It should." Knox looked to Miranda, who just shook her head.

She threw up her hands before walking over and kissing his cheek. "I love you. I'm going on my spa day as planned," she said. "Any chance you and Jackson can get this gone before I'm back? And not in the house," she added. "Other than the very impressive Maitland-Smith dartboard."

"She's perfect." Knox said. He waved as he watched Miranda walk to the car.

When she was gone, Knox looked at Jackson. "What exactly am I supposed to do with this?"

"Bit off more than you could chew, huh?" Jackson laughed. "Your love of darts finally got you."

"Think Ryann needs barstools? You can probably get the cigarette smell out of them."

"You heard yourself, right? The thing I want to ask the woman I love—honey, want some old barstools? Knox thinks they won't always smell of smoke." Jackson laughed. "I'm sure our baby would enjoy pulling them over."

He could see Ryann's exasperated face. Hell, it would look almost identical to Miranda's.

"Love." Knox leaned against a box. "You love her."

"Yes," he said. Knox was the one person in the world who understood the childhood he'd had. Sort of. They'd become brothers as teens. Inseparable. The rock each had needed.

But even Knox didn't know everything. No one but Jackson needed those memories.

"And she loves you?" Knox raised his brows, enjoying this too much.

"Don't know." Jackson opened a box and made a face at him. "This is trash."

"Probably. I think they legit packed everything but the booze and just shipped it." He pointed to a pile by the side of the house. "If nothing is salvageable, it goes in that pile. But don't change the subject. You're too good at that."

"Ryann agrees on that," he said. But it wasn't true. Not really. Or maybe it was, but he'd had to get good at shifting topics. It was survival skill in care—and life.

"So you love her but don't know if she loves you?" Knox opened the box in front of him, made a face and closed it back up.

"Woulda been cheaper to just toss this rather than ship it."

"I paid for shipping. That was one thousand of it."

"And that didn't raise your brow? Really, Knox." Jackson opened another box—this one had glasses in it. He didn't need them and they weren't Ryann's style, but someone would use them. "Where is the donation pile?"

His and Knox's first place had been stocked with odds and ends picked up for free on the side of the road or dirt cheap at garage sales. They knew every place that took donations to help out those needing to start fresh…or just start period.

"Over there," Knox said. "Stop changing the subject."

"No, I don't know if she loves me. And I don't want to tell her that I love her because then she might run. She thinks love doesn't last." Jackson pulled at the back of his neck. "And the worst part is I can't even take that worry away from her. I mean, who do I know that has stayed together more than a few years?" he said.

"My parents rotated through partners, most of the foster homes I was in weren't exactly loving relationships and Marie left with little warning, never telling me exactly what I'd done wrong." She'd wanted him to talk more, to open up to her. When he had, when he'd told her his whole story, she'd looked at him like he was broken. Like she hated that she had the burden of knowledge. Two weeks later she'd told him she didn't think they were a good fit.

When he'd asked why, Marie had just said the words again. Not a good fit. Then she'd left.

"Maybe you didn't do anything wrong. Maybe it was just Marie." The words were quiet, and he was glad Knox's head was buried in a box.

Jackson's stomach was at his feet and tears threatened. It was comforting to think he hadn't done anything wrong. Comforting, but wrong. Everyone left him eventually. So that meant it had to be him.

"And Miranda and I are still in love." Knox held up a hand. "Before you say, *Oh, but it's only been six months.* So? The woman had thirty-two boxes of trash, sixteen barstools and one very nice vintage dartboard delivered to her condo this morning, and she still loves me."

"No small miracle there," Jackson said. He opened a box containing nothing but old rags. Seriously, who packed this?

"Yeah, she really is the best."

"You make good points," he conceded, mostly to end the conversation.

"I know." His brother's smile was bright and happy. "So you are going to tell her that you love her?"

Jackson shrugged. "Sure."

"I don't believe you." Knox sighed. "All right. Let's open each of these, see if there is anything salvageable."

Ryann waved at Jackson as he wandered down the hallway, unable to stop the worry pressing at the back of her mind. He'd been different for a week…since getting an emergency call to help Knox with one of the most off-the-wall scenarios she'd ever heard of.

"Why the long face? Do you also have a 'vintage' dartboard hanging in your living room?"

"Miranda." Ryann bit her lip to keep the laughter in her chest from slipping out. "You are the last person I would have expected to see use air quotes."

"It is fitting." She pulled her phone from her scrub pocket. "Look at this."

The screen showed a picture of a dartboard— an ugly one, though were any dartboards cute? Aesthetics were in the eye of the beholder.

"It's something." Ryann bit her lip, unsure of what else she was meant to say.

"It's ugly as hell," Miranda said as she slid her phone back into her pocket.

"Then why is it in the living room?"

"Because that's the only place in the condo big enough for the man I love to stand regulation distance to throw the darts."

"I see." She didn't.

"He loves darts. And I love him." Miranda chuckled. "Good thing he never misses."

"Never?"

"No, he hustled in bars growing up." She paused. "He and Jackson had a rough upbringing. But you know that."

Ryann knew some of it but really nothing more than the basics she'd learned the day he'd met Ayla. And the fact that he'd had a fiancée who'd "upgraded," as though that was even possible. The man was a pro at shifting the topic.

"Jackson doesn't talk about it." Ryann whispered the words—somehow that felt like a secret, though it wasn't. Not really.

Miranda reached out, rubbing Ryann's shoulder as she said, "Jackson protects people."

"Yes, but I'm not people, I'm…" Ryann lost the words. What was she? The mother of his child. The woman he woke up next to every morning.

The woman who loved him. That was terrifying. Love was an emotion without control. You couldn't stop it, couldn't hold it. There was no way to manage it, only the effects of its loss.

Her mother had managed by falling for another person fast, dancing between loves. Ryann had never felt this way, so certain that Jackson was hers and terrified that one day he might not be. It was as if her body was simultaneously thrilled and terrified.

"You are—" Whatever Miranda might have said was interrupted by both their pagers. "Damn."

They took off toward the ORs. Whatever today might have been was morphing fast into something much worse.

Ryann pulled the surgical cap off her head and leaned against the locker banks.

"I hate days like today." Miranda threw her surgical cap to the ground and wiped a tear off her cheek.

"Me, too," she said. Ryann's patient had a traumatic brain injury. She'd repaired the damage to the leg, putting it in traction, while the neurosurgeon had done everything they could. To say it had been touch-and-go was an understatement.

And even if he survived, his life was going to look different.

One patient was gone, the other fighting for their life.

"I want to go home, hug my cat, eat a pint of ice cream and scream into the shower." Miranda slammed her locker closed. "I don't know what's worse—the days where the trauma feels routine... I mean, hell, this was a car accident. They happen every hour."

"Or days like today?" Ryann wrapped her arms around herself. "When it feels personal."

It was always personal, but to survive in this field you had to be able to put it away. At least somewhat. Or it would drive you from the profession.

"Ice cream. Cat. Hugs from Knox."

"Sounds like a good plan." Ryann grabbed her keys. Jackson wasn't off for another few hours, but she was going to get Ayla. And then lose herself in design shows.

She waved to Miranda as she headed to the stairwell.

"Oh!" Ryann grabbed the door before it could hit the young woman sitting in the stairwell. "Are you okay?"

The answer was no. The tear streaks on her cheeks, the runny nose and the red eyes should have clued in Ryann's brain. But it was a phrase you uttered automatically when you nearly hit someone with door.

"My boyfriend died." The woman choked back a sob. "Boyfriend. We lived together for six years. He asked me to marry him half a dozen times, but I don't—didn't—believe in marriage." She leaned her head against her knees. "But he did. And I…" She lost herself in sobs.

Ryann pulled her phone from her back pocket. She sent a quick text to the head nurse, requesting the assistance of a counselor or chaplain. Then she sat on the step beside the woman.

"He wanted it, and I just… I just never did. I think he thought I'd come around." She hiccupped. "And I would have, too. I would have. I almost said yes last time. He never pushed. Not Kellen. He just said *you let me know when*."

Ryann made some noncommittal noises. There wasn't much to say. There was little she could do to provide comfort right now. The woman was in shock, and Ryann was a stranger, a person she'd never remember—or if she did, her brain probably wouldn't be able to place her.

"I should have said yes. Why didn't I say yes? Life is so short, and I just…"

The stairwell door opened, and the chaplain slipped in. The older white woman motioned to the step where Ryann was sitting. She got up, changing seats with the chaplain without the sobbing woman noticing.

The chaplain squeezed Ryann's hand before she put her hand on the crying woman's shoulder. "I am so sorry for your loss."

Ryann started down the stairs; she made it a flight before her own tears started. Life wasn't fair. She'd known that since she'd been a child.

Today, though, today was a reminder that it was short. Miranda wanted her cat, a pint of ice cream and Knox. Ryann needed Ayla, a pint of ice cream—which she couldn't have—and Jackson.

# CHAPTER THIRTEEN

"WHY DO YOU have a dozen balloons?" Ryann backed out of the doorway as Jackson pulled the balloons through the door.

"It was a rough day. I thought you might like them." Jackson's laugh was full, but there was a look in his eye that sent a bead of worry across her skin, like he was assessing something.

Was this the day he said she was too much?

*Ryann, come on!* she told herself.

Everything was fine. Mostly. Yes, over the last few days she'd caught him watching her, a pensive look in his eyes, like he was waiting for something.

And her brain was intent on filling the questions it developed with the worst-case scenarios, despite there being no evidence that would make anyone else worry.

"I love balloons," Ryann said as she smiled at the pink, purple, blue and black balloons in the bunch.

"I remember." Jackson grinned.

His smile lit a flame in her soul. Today had been rough as he'd said, but there was good in just about every twenty-four hours.

And balloons from the man she loved would always count as good.

She pushed one, unable to contain the laughter as it moved. "This is so silly." She pushed it again. How many times had she asked her mom for a balloon after her first stepfather had left, just because it was something happy he'd brought? Probably hundreds.

And no balloons had ever appeared.

But Jackson remembered a throwaway comment from before they'd ever gotten back together. Something he'd had no reason to lock away in his memory. He'd remembered, for her.

"Of course. You were so jealous of the get-well balloon. Who gets jealous of a get-well balloon?" His strong arms wrapped around her. His head rested on her shoulder, and she leaned into him. "Your text said you were craving ice cream and can't have it for Ayla. I walked through the frozen section. I didn't find anything that would work, then I thought—balloons!"

This was peace. This was perfection.

"I love you, Ryann," he said. "You don't have to say anything. I just need you to know I love you."

Such simple words. Words people had told each other in some form from the beginning of time. Words they believed in the moment.

Her mother had said them to countless partners—repeated them, then screamed them, then
cried over them, then moved on from them. Ryann
wondered if she'd ever had the deep peace of them.

*And if she did, does that mean the words are
still cursed?*

"I love you, too," she said. Turning in his arms,
she wrapped her hands around him, holding him.

It was such a small moment. Yet part of her expected the heavens to start singing, for the world
to hold its rotation for a second. A recognition of
this important step.

But maybe this was what love really was. The
peace of knowing you were with the person you
were meant to be with.

"Where's Ayla?" Jackson's hand slid down her
stomach. Even through the cotton of her shirt her
skin flamed.

"Sleeping. Not sure how long she'll stay down."
Ryann captured his lips. She relished the way their
bodies fitted, the need to be with him, to push
away the day's unhappiness with him.

His arms shifted, and the next thing she knew
she was cradled in his arms. His tongue traced
her lips as he carried her back to their bedroom.

*Their.*

"Ryann…"

Her name on his lips sent her body into pleasure. He laid her on their bed, stripping her clothes
from her piece by piece. When she reached for

his shirt, he grabbed her fingers, kissing the tips of each one.

"I plan on enjoying every single second with you, honey, and I can't do that if you touch me. Because…" He leaned his head into hers, swirling his tongue on the sensitive spot where her neck met her shoulder. "…I'm already on a knife's edge just from your words."

"Jackson…"

"I do love when pleasure makes you slur my name." His fingers danced across her breasts, teasing one nipple and then the other before tracing the curvature. The touch was not enough and too much all at once.

"Ayla?" As much as she loved the idea of spending the evening being worshipped by the man she loved, they might have all night or just a few minutes.

"Will wake when she wakes. If tonight is about your pleasure only, that's fine with me." His fingers skimmed her inner thigh, stroking ever closer to her core. "Let me pleasure you, honey."

Then he dipped his head to her mound, and Ryann lost the ability to track anything but the cascading waves of pleasure falling over her.

The morning sun was basking Jackson in all his glory as she lay on her side looking at him. Ayla had cooperated last night. And she'd only been up once all night. She'd likely make her presence known in a few minutes, but for now, this precious time was Ryann and Jackson's.

She let her fingers trail along his stomach. Not enough to wake him. Not enough to drive pleasure through him. But enough to remind her that he was here. In her bed. A man she loved, who loved her.

The twinge of uncertainty pressed at her core, but with the sun dancing on his features it was easy to ignore.

Just because her mother had terrible luck with men didn't mean Ryann had, too. She bit her lip as the memories of her mother, tears spilling down her cheeks, screaming at a partner, filled her mind. Her mother's life.

*And mine.*

But not in the same way. It wasn't the same. Jackson wasn't the same.

"If you bite your lip any harder, you're going to taste blood." Jackson ran his hand down her back. A morning ritual between comfortable lovers, not a passionate touch. It was weird to like this one as much as the other.

"I wasn't," she said.

His finger reached up, pulling her bottom lip from between her teeth.

"I… I wasn't even aware."

"I believe that." Jackson sat up, grabbed his glasses from the bedside table, then pulled her into his arms. "So, what were you not-thinking about?"

"My mother's failed relationships." Ryann let out a sigh, curling into him. "I know I'm not her and you aren't any of my stepparents, but I only ever saw one kind of relationship growing up."

"The kind that ended." Jackson kissed her forehead. "Yeah, me, too."

"Your mother got through a lot of relationships?" Ryann wrapped her arms around his waist, leaning her head against his shoulder. She felt the deep pull of his breath, heard the start of his statement and then a pause.

"Not sure."

The words were crisp. But there was a hint on the end of them. Like it wasn't the truth. Or at least not the whole truth.

Her tongue felt dry. "Jackson?"

"I'm here for you and Ayla. Forever." Jackson kissed her head.

*Forever.*

That sounded nice. It was exactly what she should want to hear. Her soul craved the idea, but her brain seemed determined to think the word had meant very little in the past.

*Not with Jackson.*

"I can see the wheels spinning," Jackson said. He tapped the side of her head, then kissed the same spot. "It's okay."

"Right." Of course it was. She was letting a

past that wasn't even technically hers cloud to-day's pleasures.

"If you didn't see your mom's relationships—"

Before she could finish the question, Ayla whimpered over the baby monitor. Jackson was out of bed in a flash.

"Give her a second." Ryann ached for him to come back. The noise wasn't a cry. It might be one in a few minutes, but often Ayla let out a few soft noises and then drifted back to sleep for a few minutes.

"I love getting her in the morning," Jackson said. "And if you go in, she'll want to eat imme-diately. This way I can get her changed and ready while you either relax or get ready for the day."

He grinned as he strutted through the door. The look of an incredibly proud father.

It was everything she should want, everything people craved in a partner. Yet part of her couldn't help but question if he'd used it as an excuse to avoid answering her questions.

"Patty, where exactly am I supposed to put all this?" Jackson held up his hands as the woman who'd raised a community pulled a sixth box from the ancient van that he was certain ran more on fear that Patty would scream at it than actual abil-ity.

"Ever think of getting a new ride?" He asked

this every time he saw her. And so, he mouthed along her response with her.

"This one works fine. I get along." She held up a finger, wagging the now crooked digit at him. "Don't sass me. I can still send you to the corner, young man."

"Uh-huh." The corner. He remembered the first time Patty had threatened him with that at the community center that everyone lovingly called Patty's Place, even though the meetings had outgrown her home where she'd started her work years before she'd taken in Knox and Jackson.

When he'd gone to "the corner" in the community center, it had been filled with books, coloring pads, knitting supplies—things to occupy an overstimulated mind without feeling like punishment.

She handed him the box and went back to the trunk.

"If you pull out another one without letting me help…" he warned.

She had unloaded the boxes onto his condo driveway before he'd arrived and sworn there was only one left…three boxes ago. The woman took care of everyone but still did things her own way. Eighty or not, she didn't stand for help when she didn't want it.

"This is the last one." She winked as she rounded the corner of the van with what was the supposed last box.

"Heard that four boxes ago now." He took it

from her, setting it with the others, happy when she didn't rush back to the van.

Tapping her forearms, Patty gave him a grin, "If you don't use these they wither, and I got too much left to do." Her smile broadened, then fell a little as she pushed on her dentures. "Damn things are loose again."

"The story of your life." He gave her a hug. "Tell the community I appreciate the donation, and I'm sure Knox and Miranda will, too, but I think we're good on the supply closet for a while."

The supply closet, Miranda had asked for more space for. Because the little one-cabinet closet Knox and Miranda had set up when she'd first gotten to Hope to give their patients something to do besides watch television was an ever-growing thing. It had a little of everything now.

And following this donation—a lot of everything.

Ryann pulled into the drive, and he saw the look of confusion pass her eyes as she stared at the boxes. He'd mentioned that he'd be over after meeting Patty, that there wasn't a need for her to stop by. Honestly, he hadn't wanted Patty and Ryann to meet.

These parts of his world were separate, a divider that he rarely crossed. Yes, he still volunteered with Patty's Place. Yes, he and Knox both helped the community to navigate the medical world and sat with someone at Hope when they had no one else. But they were pillars of the community to the people there.

To Patty, they would always be the scrawny, hungry boys who'd been chased out of every coffee shop for trying to study without purchasing more than one drink. The library had been a haven, as long as the ancient Mr. Ilona hadn't been there. The man had been convinced every student—particularly every student of color—was a delinquent.

Never mind that they had just wanted to study.

Patty had taken them in. She'd seen and tended to the bruises, physical and mental, that life in state care brought. She'd given them the upstairs room and told everyone to leave them be so they could study. She'd seen them both at their absolute worst and had shepherded them to their best. She knew the trauma—and the things he kept hidden from everyone else.

"This the girlfriend you're hiding."

"I'm not hiding her."

Patty gave him a look that said *You keep telling yourself that*.

"I'm not."

"I didn't say anything." Patty winked. "But your past is your past. It isn't my place to share." She laid a hand on his arm; her skin was so much thinner than he'd remembered. She was old, elderly. All the spirit in the world wouldn't stop

Father Time. "But you've got nothing to be ashamed of."

"I thought you might like some help with the boxes and then you could just ride over to the condo with me." Ryann shook her head. "But, umm, there's more here than I thought there would be."

Patty held out her hand. "I'm Patty. Don't suppose you've heard much about me."

Ryann looked at Jackson and then shook her head before taking Patty's hand. "No. Sorry. I'm Ryann. Have you heard much about me?"

"Nope." Patty hit Jackson's thigh. "He's a good one, though." She waved, then started back toward the van. "Give me a holler when you need more stuff. We got it coming out of the woodwork."

"That was a lie," Jackson whispered. "She holds drives for it."

"And the people were very generous," Ryann said. She privately felt the hospital should fund the supply closet, but given that the it did nothing to up profit, she doubted that would ever happen.

"Yes. Still willing to help me sort it?" Jackson asked. He grabbed the first box and started toward Ryann's car. They had the next two days off and no need for his car, so riding over with her would be nice. Some quiet time before the nighttime routine with Ayla started.

"Of course." She grabbed a box, and they loaded them in silence.

"You okay?" Jackson asked as she slid into the driver's seat. Ryann wasn't the overly chatty type, but her silence as they'd loaded the boxes sent off warning signals.

She looked at him, then started the car and backed out of the driveway.

No immediate answer. Warning signal number two. And not a subtle one!

"Ryann?"

"It's like you have two lives." Her fingers tightened on the steering wheel, her eyes never leaving the road.

"No. I have a past—one that isn't very pleasant. And my present." Jackson touched her knee, grateful that she didn't pull away. "Which I love very much."

"And never the two shall meet, right?" Ryann drummed her thumb on the steering wheel. She rolled her head from side to side, like she was stretching out her neck.

"Do you need another massage?"

"No," she said. "Or yes, but that's not what we're discussing."

"It could be, though. That's far more fun to talk about." Jackson didn't want to talk about the past. His present was lovely—the only thing his past had ever caused was loss. "So, massage tonight?" he asked.

"Jackson."

"Let it go, Ryann." He heard his tone and

wanted to slap himself. "I love you, and I want to focus on the present. On us."

"All right." She offered him a smile, but it didn't quite reach her eyes.

"Did you pack Ayla's extra clothes?" Ryann looked through the diaper bag for the fifth time.

"The clothes are in the bottom, just like—"

She laid her hands on the clothes, touching them, reminding herself they were there. "Just like the other times." Biting her lip, she ran her hands over the clothes one more time and tried to calm her heart. This was silly.

It was just an intrusive thought. A focus that they'd get out on the hike and her daughter would need clean clothes and they wouldn't have them and then.

She stroked the clothes one more time hoping this time it would imprint on her brain that they had extra clothes available and the anxiety bubble would finally pop.

"We can skip hiking." Jackson ran his hand on her shoulder.

"No." Ryann would push through this bout of anxiety. It was only because it was their first outing. "I'm fine."

"It's okay if you're not," Jackson said, then kissed her temple.

The scent of his shampoo wrapped through her, and she tried to focus on that.

"Any idea why the extra clothes bother you so much?" Jackson turned to the fridge, pulling out the water bottles he'd filled last night. They were frozen but would melt along the hike today, giving them cold water all day.

She looked at the clothes, fingering them. "My mom was…is…forgetful. On more than one occasion when we took spontaneous road trips, she'd forget extra clothes." Ryann remembered having to wear the same clothes for almost a week one time. Her mother "washing" them in rest stop sinks and then having to put on damp clothes.

"You are not forgetful," Jackson said. He tapped his head. "You store everything up here." He went over to Ayla's swing and picked her up. "We're going to have a blast today. Aren't we, sweetie?"

Ayla cooed at Jackson, her little hand wrapping around his nose.

Jackson made a honking noise. He'd done it a few nights ago, and Ayla had laughed for almost a minute. Now he did it whenever she touched his nose.

This was perfection. There was no reason to look for worries. Ryann had everything under control.

"Right." She clapped her hands. "We're ready for a fun day. Hiking, here we come."

"Ayla giving you a headache yet?" Ryann laughed as her daughter continued to drum on Jackson's head. This was her first time in the backpack carrier that Jackson had bought. She was strapped in tight, enjoying the sights and the easy access to her daddy's head.

"Nope. And even if she was, I don't think I'd mind."

That wasn't a lie. Jackson probably wouldn't even tell anyone that he was bothered. He'd just let it go—never tell anyone and keep it to himself.

And if he was upset with Ryann, would he ever tell her? Probably not.

"Why don't we stop at the rest point? She's having a blast, but I think a diaper change might be in order." Jackson pointed to the exit then playfully held his nose.

"We can eat lunch, too." Ryann's needed substance and the heaviness in her chest indicated that Ayla needed to breastfeed too. The trail they were on was a short one, designed for families—and luckily within twenty minutes' drive, the exact time before Ayla's lungs opened on car rides, ending anyone's enjoyment.

"Sound good to you, missy?" Jackson tilted his head.

Ayla wasted no time. She grabbed his prescription sunglasses and threw them.

"Not a bad arm," he said. Jackson patted her, then looked in Ryann's direction. "Any chance you saw were those landed? I'm afraid the ground looks like one big blur to me."

Ryann grabbed them, dusting them off before gently putting them back on his face. Pressing her lips against his, she laughed as Ayla's hands wrapped through her hair. "She's enjoying herself."

"The feeling is very mutual." Jackson kissed her forehead. "But I think the diaper change may have become more immediate."

The smell wafted her way, and she backed up. "Let's get moving."

Ryann pulled the sweaty shirt off Ayla and grinned as she pulled out one of the extra outfits. "See, there was a reason I was so focused on these today." Subconsciously her brain must have been tracking the heat. It was a fine day, but babies' bodies didn't control their temperature as well as adults. She stripped the diaper, cleaned Ayla, then reached for the diaper cream.

She reached around the bag, keeping one hand on Ayla on the changing table.

"Give me one moment, sweet girl." Her wiggles were much more vigorous than the newborn stage. And now that Ayla could sit up on her own, lying on her back had lost all its appeal.

Ryann rummaged around the side pouch where she always kept the cream. Nothing. Then her mind flashed with the memory. The cream was on the kitchen counter. Ayla had spilled water and rice cereal all over herself last night. Jackson had stripped her, and Ryann had grabbed the diaper bag supplies because they'd been closest.

She'd repacked new clothes and left the cream. She quickly finished dressing Ayla and went to find Jackson.

"We need to leave."

"Is she sick?" Jackson's eyes went to their daughter, the back of his hand to her forehead.

"She's fine. But I forgot the diaper cream." Ryann couldn't believe it. How could she have not remembered that? She'd looked in this bag more times that she wanted to count this morning. She'd counted the clothes six times. Six times. And never looked for the cream.

"Her rash is back?" Jackson tilted his head, but this time he was focused on Ryann.

Heat crested in her cheeks, but she wasn't sure why. "No." Why wasn't he more concerned? Because this wasn't a big deal. Except with the heat and the lunch, Ayla's rash could come back any time. And it had before. At the height of her allergies, one rash would clear only for another to start without warning. And each one was uncomfortable.

"Then why don't we eat?" he said. "She needs to eat, and you must be uncomfortable."

He said the words as her breasts' ache punched through her foggy mind. She was very full, and Ayla did need to breastfeed.

"Then we hike back down. We'll change her diaper before we leave."

Ryann lifted her shirt, letting Ayla latch. "I can't believe I forgot it."

"It happens, Ryann." Jackson pulled out the sandwich he'd made. It was technically a lettuce wrap with meat and a vegan cheese that Ayla tolerated well. But he always called it a sandwich. He pulled his out and bit into it before taking a swig of water. "It's a small mistake."

"It's my mistake. But Ayla is the one that suffers the consequence. She had no say in it, but that won't matter if she gets a rash." Ryann had paid for all her mother's mistakes, borne the brunt of decisions she'd had no control over.

"Ryann, you cannot protect her from everything."

"Yes, I can." Ryann smiled at him, tears coating her eyes. "No one protected us, but I can and *will* protect her."

"Life won't let that happen," he said. "And if you try, you'll suffocate her." Jackson reached his hand across the table, but she pulled it back. "There has to be a balance, honey." He looked at his hand, sitting on the picnic bench.

Was he hoping she'd reach for it? Should she?

"This is anxiety."

"It's not," Ryann said, shaking her head. "Or if it is, does it matter? If it helps keep Ayla safe."

This time when he reached for her hand, she

let him take it. "Anxiety hurting you doesn't help Ayla. We can talk about this," he said.

"Why? You going to tell me about your past? Are we going to talk about that?" She was upset with herself and lashing out. That wasn't fair. "Sorry. Let's just eat and get going. I'm fine. Really."

"Again, it's okay that you're not." Jackson squeezed her hand.

"I know it *would* be okay if I wasn't, but I *am*. I'll just make sure the diaper bag has two tubes of diaper cream. Problem solved."

Jackson opened his mouth, but he closed it without saying anything. Finally, he said, "All right."

# CHAPTER FOURTEEN

JACKSON WENT OVER his plans again. He'd rehearsed this evening's plan a hundred times. Ryann was only seeing patients at the office. Her schedule was light, and there were no upsetting cases. Miranda and Knox were watching Ayla. They'd stopped by to pick up her things a few minutes ago.

He had reservations at a vegan restaurant that specialized in food allergies. He'd already cleared the elimination-diet issues with the manager. They'd confirmed that Ryann would have multiple options.

They were going out on a date. As a couple. A real couple.

He enjoyed their nights in. Loved them. But he wanted a night for just them.

*A night to recapture—*

No, he was not going to think that. They weren't recapturing anything. They were fine.

He wanted to believe that, wanted to pretend

there hadn't been a disconnect between them lately. Since the hike.

Except that wasn't true. It had started after she'd met Patty.

Ryann wasn't asking after his past. In fact, other than the comment on the hike, she'd intentionally dropped the topic since he'd asked her to let it go. It was what he wanted, what he needed, but part of him hated it, too.

She was already so worried about Ayla, worried that she might not have the perfect life Ryann wanted for her. But no life was perfect.

*Perfect.*

The word only Ryann had ever associated with him. A descriptor she hadn't used since Patty had dropped off supplies.

A descriptor he missed.

"I'm home."

Ryann's call sent flutters through his belly. This was a good idea. But the idea of springing it on her suddenly made him feel like it was a misstep.

"Wow." Ryann's smile was brilliant as she took in his suit and the flowers in his hands. "This is a surprise."

"Glad you like it," Jackson said. He walked over, pulled her into his arms and dipped her back into a kiss.

"It's nice." She pushed a curl behind her head as he straightened. "Kisses and flowers—a nice surprise."

"It's not only kisses and flowers." He took a deep breath, then said, "I have dinner reservations at Ines."

"Ines?" Ryann crossed her arms. "The upscale vegan restaurant that Nicola and the other nurses were talking about last week?"

Her posture made his tongue thick. She was already on the defensive. Why? "Yes," he said. "Though I didn't know the nurses were discussing it. I could have asked them instead of doing research on my ancient laptop."

"You need a new laptop, but we aren't shifting the topic now."

He tilted his head, but before he could work out that statement, Ryann continued. "Not exactly the kind of place to bring a baby."

"Oh. Well, that's part two of the surprise. Knox and Miranda are watching Ayla."

"What!"

Okay, that was way more of a reaction than expected. "Honey, it's just for a few hours. She's at the babysitter's for way longer than that sometimes."

"That's the babysitter, not a strange—"

"Miranda and Knox are not strangers," he said.

"They are to Ayla! They aren't to us, but they are to her. What if she doesn't think we're coming back?" Ryann uncrossed her arms and then crossed them again. "What if she eats something that upsets her? What if—"

"Take a deep breath," he said. This night had morphed and they probably wouldn't get to dinner, but she needed to breathe, acknowledge the anxiety and find a therapist.

"Don't tell me to take a deep breath." The words were rushed, like she wasn't getting enough air. Panic attacks were frightening, and she was on the verge of one, if not in a full spiral.

"Ryann, take the breath with me." He overexaggerated his breath, then started again.

The color was draining from her face.

"This is a panic attack," he said. "I've had them. You are safe. You are fine."

"But is Ayla?"

Jackson pulled out his cell and called Miranda.

"Hey, did Ryann like the surprise?" Miranda's cheery voice was at odds with the situation here. But that wasn't the point now.

"She's panicking because Ayla is there. Is she okay?" Jackson's words were firm; he did not drop eye contact with Ryann.

"Um…"

"Not the time for 'um,' Miranda." God, if something had happened…

"She's fine."

"But!" Ryann's voice echoed in the room.

"She has a small bump on her head," she said. "Icy went past while we were sitting on the floor. Ayla reached for her tail and lost her balance. She cried for a second, then laughed. *Bump* is even too big of a word. It's a little red mark. She and Knox are currently dancing in the kitchen. She's fine."

"I'm on the way." Ryann grabbed her purse and was already moving toward the door.

"She really is fine, Jackson."

He felt the same sense of disappointment that he could hear in his friend's voice. "I know. Thanks, Miranda."

Jackson jogged to catch up Ryann. "I should drive—you're close to hyperventilating."

"I'm going on my own," Ryann said, pushing a tear from her cheek. "I know you meant this as a surprise, but Jackson, she is our daughter. She is hurt."

"She has a small bump from reaching for a cat's tail," he said. "She is a child. This will happen. We can't protect her from everything."

Jackson had seen some of the worst cases in foster care—at one point he'd even been a worst case.

"Ayla is loved and cared for, Ryann, but you can't smother her," he tried again.

"I'm not smothering her. I'm protecting her. We didn't get that. Not everyone can just move past their past trauma and let it mean nothing, let it roll away and be unbothered."

He wasn't unbothered. Was that what she thought? Jackson was trying to protect her! Protect Ayla.

Not burden them with memories they couldn't unlearn.

"I am her mother, I will always protect her,". Ryann said. "If you don't want that, then don't be here when I get back."

And with that she got into the car.

Jackson stood on the driveway long after her gray car had faded away. He looked at his car, then shook his head. He wasn't leaving.

Tonight was a shift, not the one he'd expected but the one he needed. He was right—Ryann needed to find a way to deal with her anxiety. Therapy, medications, a combination of both. He would support her through it.

But she wasn't the only one who needed to stop overprotecting. He'd been so worried that she'd find fault in him, see his past as an anchor, because mentally that was how he still saw it.

His anchor. His burden.

If he and Ryann were to be partners—and he wanted that more than anything—then he needed to share, too.

Jackson walked to the door. He needed to cancel their reservations, make some dinner and put on a pot of tea. Tonight was going to be long.

Ryann swiped at the tears running down her face. Not that it mattered. Her eyes refused to stop doing anything but leak.

The idea had been sweet. A date night out. A

surprise. But it was too soon. They needed to do more planning, make sure their daughter was safe.

Yes, she went to the sitter's house, but Ryann had investigated every available option in the city. And the house kept nanny cams going all day while the kids were there. Anytime she wanted, she could use her code to log in and check on Ayla.

There were no nanny cams at Knox and Miranda's. She couldn't just check in on Ayla.

Ayla was so little, and she didn't know Knox and Miranda. When she'd tipped over, had she been scared? Probably. And Ryann hadn't been there to comfort her.

Ryann pulled up to Miranda and Knox's place. She sat in the car for a minute. She didn't want Ayla to see her crying, though she doubted she'd be able to hide it for long.

Icy was sitting in the front window. The white cat twitched her tail as she looked out. The feline judgment sent an uncomfortable laugh through Ryann.

Her cell rang, and she tried not to flinch when Miranda's name popped up. She answered, and the video started. Ayla was in the kitchen, on Knox's hip.

"Any idea why she keeps hitting his nose?" Miranda didn't comment on Ryann's tears, but she offered a comforting smile.

"Jackson makes a honking noise every time

she presses it." Her daughter's father, the man she loved. She'd told him to leave, given him an out. So many people had walked out on her, but this was the first time she'd told someone they had her permission to do so.

"She really is okay." Ryann laughed as Ayla hit Knox's nose, then squealed when he made the most obnoxious honking noise.

"She's fine," Miranda said. "Though we don't have to live with that honking, warn Jackson that she might expect more of a production when his brother is done here. Knox is nothing if not competitive."

"Over nose honks?" Ryann couldn't imagine that, but she'd never had a sibling.

"Over anything!" Knox called, then made another honking noise. "Yep. Uncle Knox is your favorite, right? I'm your favorite."

The image was lovely but tinged with sadness. She looked at her daughter, happy and fine. She was going to get bruises and scrapes as she started to explore the world. Physical scars and some mental. That was life.

Ayla would never fear that she'd be left. Never fear an eviction notice that meant living in the car for a while. Never worry that the stepparent her mother swore was her soulmate was a little too quick to touch her.

But Ryann couldn't protect her from the world. She shouldn't.

Tonight should have been perfect. Yes, until tonight, Ayla hadn't done more than meet Knox and Miranda. But Jackson and Ryann knew them. Hell, Jackson and Knox were basically brothers.

Knox had started referring to himself as her uncle immediately, and Miranda had taken on the role of aunt. She'd even playfully teased Ryann that she fully planned to embrace the fun-aunt mode and to be prepared for her to side with Ayla on everything when she was older.

Controlling everything—or attempting to control everything—was breaking her. Had broken her. She needed help.

For Ayla.

*And for me.*

"Can you watch her for a little longer?" Ryann needed to see Jackson, needed to put things right tonight.

"For as long as you need. Jackson sent a literal house full of stuff for this playdate with Uncle Knox. I swear we have enough stuff for a week, but come before then." Miranda winked, then showed Ryann Ayla and Knox dancing one more time.

"Thank you."

"Jackson! Jackson!" Her voice felt hoarse as she screamed his name as soon as she'd opened the door to the condo. She'd gone to his place first—no Jackson. His car was here.

"Hi, honey." He'd taken off his suit. Now he wore loose sweatpants, a white T-shirt and no shoes. And it was just as sexy as the suit. "Where's Ayla?"

Ryann wrapped her arms around herself. She wasn't sure the script she was supposed to follow. "I...umm, I got to Knox and Miranda's place, video chatted, and she is fine. Knox learned about the nose boops. His noise is very over the top."

"Of course it is."

"I went to your condo, and you weren't there." Such an obvious statement. He wasn't there because he was here. And if her nose wasn't mistaking, he'd made dinner.

"Why would I leave?" Jackson held out his arms.

She didn't hesitate. She fell into him. She let out all the tears. Years of tears. The first person she'd given permission to leave had refused. The man would always be here. For her and Ayla.

The realization healed a piece of her tattered childhood heart. The scar was still there, would always be, but it didn't feel as close to the surface.

"I'm never leaving, Ryann. Not you or Ayla." He stroked her back.

"You're right," she said. "I am trying too hard to protect her. I want the world to be easy for her. To be fair. To be perfect. And I can't grant any of those wants."

"You can't." Jackson kissed her head. "But it's sweet that you want to try."

"I think I should talk to a doctor. Maybe it's postpartum anxiety or maybe it's childhood trauma triggered by having my own kid, but help might be good." Saying the words was a little scary but also freeing.

"I will help you find one, if you want help," he said.

"Thank you. Sorry I overreacted tonight. I love you." She kissed his cheek.

"I love you, too." His arms tightened around her. "But I have been holding back a part of myself. Protecting you from my past. I didn't want it… I didn't want you to see me differently when you hear."

Her hands went to his face, resting on his cheeks. "You don't have to protect me from your past," she said. "I love you. All of you. And I want to be part of your life, know the stories you want to tell. Though I do want to know Patty. That woman seems fun."

"Very."

She dropped a light kiss onto his lips. "I know others have judged your past—that says more about them than it does about you. You are amazing. You have accomplished so much, but more importantly you are an empathetic and caring human to everyone you meet. You're extraordinary."

"*Extraordinary*. I think I like that descriptor."

She chuckled. "Good. Because it fits you."

"Want some dinner?"

"Yes, I'm famished. I can't believe you cooked all this after our fight," she said. "Actually, that isn't true. I completely believe it."

Ryann fixed their plates while Jackson got the drinks.

They sat at the table. Jackson picked up his water glass, took a deep breath and looked at her. "I was five the first time my mom abandoned me..."

# EPILOGUE

"You're a beautiful bride." Miranda reached up and adjusted the flower in Ryann's hair.

She looked at the mirror over her shoulder and couldn't believe she was seeing herself standing in white. "I never planned to be here," she said.

"Life certainly looks different when you love someone, doesn't it?" Miranda reached for the small bouquet.

"It does." Ryann took the bouquet, and her eyes filled with tears. "No—my makeup." This was not a fancy wedding. In fact, it had exactly ten invited guests, and they were heading to a local restaurant as soon as she and Jackson had said their vows.

"You need to make a run for it?" Miranda asked. She winked as she pulled the veil over Ryann's face. "I can get a getaway car here in seconds."

The jest made her laugh. "Happy tears are such a curse when you don't invest in waterproof mascara."

"Momma!" Ayla waddled in, her curls already

escaping the bows Ryann had placed this morning. She was holding the basket that would hold flowers in just a few minutes upside down.

"Maybe we should have waited for her to turn four before doing this." Ryann leaned down and tapped her daughter's nose. She instantly made a honking noise.

Ayla looked at the veil, then held up the basket. "Flowers."

"Yep. We're putting the flowers in there. Just like you and Daddy practiced." She reached for her daughter's hand. "Daddy has the flowers. Let's go see him."

"There's my girls."

*Dashing* didn't begin to cover the description of her soon-to-be husband in his dark gray suit and the pink tie that Ayla had insisted on to match her sash.

They'd decided to walk down the aisle together—the family they were highlighted—rather than alone.

"Ready?" Ryann slid her hand into the crook of Jackson's arm as Miranda put a handful of rose petals into Ayla's basket, then headed down the aisle to take her place as maid of honor with Knox.

The music began, and Ayla started down the aisle. She dropped a few rose petals, then a few more.

"See, just like we practiced." Jackson kissed the top of Ryann's head.

"Don't mess up my veil," she playfully chided. "And she isn't even halfway down yet."

As if on cue, Ayla looked at the basket, then at them. She dumped the remainder of the petals into the aisle, then raced to Miranda's open arms.

"Still perfect." Jackson beamed as they started down the aisle.

"Yes," Ryann said. "It absolutely is."

\* \* \* \* \*

*If you missed the previous story in the*
*Hope Hospital Surgeons duet, then check out*

Dating His Irresistible Rival

*And if you enjoyed this story, check out*
*these other great reads from Juliette Hyland*

A Puppy on the 34th Ward
Tempted by Her Royal Best Friend
Redeeming Her Hot-Shot Vet

*All available now!*